SHOWDOWN *in the* SHOW-ME STATE

SHOWDOWN *in the* SHOW-ME STATE

The Fight over Conceal-and-Carry
Gun Laws in Missouri

William T. Horner

University of Missouri Press / Columbia and London

Copyright © 2005 by
The Curators of the University of Missouri
University of Missouri Press, Columbia, Missouri 65201
Printed and bound in the United States of America
All rights reserved
5 4 3 2 1   09 08 07 06 05

Library of Congress Cataloging-in-Publication Data

Horner, William T., 1968–
   Showdown in the Show-Me State : the fight over conceal-
and-carry gun laws in Missouri / William T. Horner.
       p.   cm.
   Includes bibliographical references and index.
   ISBN 0-8262-1587-4 (alk. paper)
   1. Firearms—Law and legislation—Missouri.   2. Gun
control—Missouri.   I. Title.
   KFM8179.H67   2005
   344.77805'33—dc22   2005009420

♾ ™ This paper meets the requirements of the
American National Standard for Permanence of Paper
for Printed Library Materials, Z39.48, 1984.

Designer: Kristie Lee
Typesetter: Phoenix Type, Inc.
Printer and binder: The Maple-Vail Book Manufacturing
       Group
Typefaces: Berkeley and Binner Display

For my family, Heather, Tricia, and Ellie,
who make my life so happy.

For my parents, Bob and Judy Horner,
without whom none of this would be possible.

For Mary Lou Carver, who has given me as
much love as my own mother.

For Ron Carver, a great man who would have
enjoyed the book.

Contents

Preface

This book chronicles a complex and fascinating fight over the carrying of concealed weapons in Missouri. It is part public policy analysis, part interest group study, and part history. The concealed weapons issue has been fought in every public political arena—the legislature, the courts, and the ballot box. There are two hot-button issues that repeat themselves time and again in Missouri: gun control and abortion. Over the years, they have appeared in the legislature again and again. They are divisive issues that lead to down-and-dirty political fights which cut across party lines: there are Republicans who support gun control, and there are Democrats who oppose it. The biggest battle in the war over conceal-and-carry, fought in 2003, shone a bright light on obvious fissures within the Democratic party.

The complexity of the guns issue and the controversy surrounding it made the writing of this book very difficult. The chronology of events was a simple enough matter, but finding the details to flesh out the story was considerably more challenging. When asking politicians, interest group representatives, and others to speak to me about the issue, I was met with silence, as Rick Hardy, a very fine political scientist at the University of Missouri, predicted would happen. Nearly every request I made for personal interviews with the key players in this story went nowhere. On the rare occasion when someone said they would speak to me, I found myself worrying that including his or her direct input would unfairly bias the story I was trying to tell since the opposition did not want to speak to me.

Eventually, I decided to rely on secondary sources for the quotations I needed to flesh out the story. Fortunately, Missouri is a state with a rich journalistic tradition and many fine newspapers that make a strong effort to cover the machinations of Jefferson City, even in a time of increased conglomeration of media ownership and decreasing budgets. There are many truly excellent, dedicated reporters to whom I owe a tremendous debt for their fine reporting. I relied heavily on these journalists and their work product. Without these reporters who take joy in covering the capitol, much of what the state government does would be lost to the sands of time.

In writing this book, one of my primary goals was to remain as unbiased as possible. Taking a stand would have been exactly the opposite of what I wanted to do, which was to present as straightforward an analysis as possible. No doubt, there are opponents of conceal-and-carry who will read this book and, at various points, say "Ah hah! He's on our side," or "Darn him, he's with the enemy." Supporters of conceal-and-carry will certainly find themselves doing the same. If that happens, as I hope it will, to players on both sides, then I will have succeeded in presenting as balanced a view as possible of the highs and lows of this protracted fight. Regardless of your position, please don't call me at home—it will disturb my family.

Finally, at the end of this book, the reader may be left with the feeling that I haven't quite finished the story. There is good reason for that. One out-going state legislator suggested to me that guns as an issue would never truly be finished in Missouri, and at the time I completed work on this book it was not. Unresolved was the question of how counties would issue conceal-and-carry permits, and floating out there in the ether was the suggestion that the next step for opponents of the right-to-carry would be a constitutional amendment outlawing it. When taking on an issue like conceal-and-carry, an author must simply pick a stopping point. That is what I have done. This examination of Missouri's long gun fight shows us a bit of the past, and perhaps it may shed light on the future.

Acknowledgments

I owe many people thanks. First and foremost, to my wife, Heather Carver, who encouraged and advised me through the process of writing this book and everything else. Without your love and support, life would be far less worthwhile. Second, thanks to my parents, my in-laws, and my extended family for your unceasing support over the years. Third, I would like to thank my colleagues in the Department of Political Science at the University of Missouri. Thanks especially to departmental chair John Petrocik for your continuing support. Fourth, thanks to the editors at the University of Missouri Press and the outside reviewers who made this book much better than it would have been otherwise. Of course, any errors, flaws, or poor writing that remain herein are entirely my fault.

SHOWDOWN *in the* SHOW-ME STATE

Chapter One

Changing the Rules of Regulating Guns

Guns. There are few topics that inspire as much debate, stir up as much emotion, or present as much risk for politicians in America as guns. Nowhere is this truer than Missouri. Guns have long been the subject of bitter acrimony in Missouri's state capitol because they represent a key cultural divide separating St. Louis and Kansas City from the rest of Missouri. Guns were the subject of a knockdown, drag-out fight in 2003 that pitted the Republican-led General Assembly against the embattled Democratic governor, Bob Holden, but it would be wrong to see it merely as a fight between a cocky new Republican majority and a besieged Democratic governor, as many are tempted to pigeonhole it.

The fight over conceal-and-carry took at least fourteen years, and it offers a unique opportunity to examine the evolution of a divisive issue and the role played in it by interest groups, which operated not just in the back halls of the state capitol but also in the media, at the grassroots level, and in the voting booths. It is a study of high-stakes politics at both the state and national levels. This book offers an examination of guns and gun policy in Missouri. In doing that, the book also provides a glimpse into the hearts and minds of Missourians and, by extension, of mainstream America. There is, it is often argued, no state more typically "American" than Missouri. The state is closely divided along partisan lines, like the nation as a whole, and for the last one hundred–plus years the voters of Missouri have correctly chosen the winner of the presidency in every election but one. This is the story of a fourteen-year war to establish the right to carry concealed weapons in Missouri, but it is also an epic tale of clashing ideologies at both the state and national levels. This is the story of the Showdown in the Show-Me State.

The Showdown—A Preview

In Missouri, guns have bubbled to the surface of public policy debates with the regularity of the swallows returning to San Juan Capistrano. Pro–gun control politicians address the issue at their own peril. It *may* be acceptable to oppose guns if one is from Kansas City or St. Louis, but taking a position in favor of gun control anywhere else is playing with political nitroglycerine. It is an issue that cuts across party lines and has been especially troublesome for Missouri's Democrats. For instance, Democrat Thomas Eagleton, a former U.S. senator and vice presidential candidate from Missouri, suggested in a 1992 interview that guns nearly ran him from office in 1968. He described his campaign against former Republican Representative Thomas B. Curtis and said, "After Robert Kennedy and Dr. Martin Luther King were killed, I made a gun-control speech, and one of my county campaign chairmen quit, and another one severely criticized me . . . (gun control partisans) take a calculated risk. It's going to cost some votes, but it's also going to gain some votes. It's one of those incendiary topics with single-issue voters, like abortion."[1] In a state closely divided along partisan lines, there is a small but critical minority of single-issue voters whose decisions are based solely on guns. Party label is unimportant to such voters—if a candidate has voted against guns and gun ownership, he or she can almost be guaranteed of paying a political price.

On April 6, 1999, Missouri became the first, and only, state to put the issue of conceal-and-carry to a public vote. The measure was defeated by a margin of 48.3 percent to 51.7 percent, with most votes against conceal-and-carry coming from the urban centers of St. Louis and Kansas City. The 1999 campaign was neither the first nor the last attempt to bring the right to carry concealed weapons to the people of Missouri, but it illuminated political fault lines that extend well beyond the relatively simple question of "to carry or not to carry?"

While many gun control activists thought the vote in 1999 was the end, they should have known better. Conceal-and-carry came back almost immediately and, at the same time, a new issue arose when legislators began to propose legislation giving the gun industry protection from product liability lawsuits. The legislation was in direct response to a national campaign conducted by the National Rifle Association that advocated such reform and a lawsuit filed by the city of St. Louis against several gun-related companies.

Both issues came to a head in 2003 when the legislature passed, and the governor vetoed, legislation on both subjects. Both vetoes were overridden in a historic veto session in September 2003, handing the governor an embarrassing defeat. When the legislature overrode the governor's veto and made conceal-and-carry a reality, Missouri became one of the last states to adopt such a law, leaving its neighbors, Illinois and Kansas, as two of just four remaining hold-outs. The fact that it took at least fourteen years of concerted effort by pro-gun advocates to make conceal-and-carry a reality says a great deal about how evenly divided Missourians are on this and other issues. The state is in the center of the nation geographically, but it is also centered ideologically, as this history of gun policy in Missouri shows. Conceal-and-carry became legal in the Show-Me State following a decision by the state supreme court in 2004, but no one can say with certainty the issue is forever settled.

Missourians first addressed the legality of concealed weapons in the state's third constitution, adopted in 1875 after Reconstruction. The issue was addressed again in its fourth, and current, constitution, adopted in 1945. Article I, Section 23 of Missouri's Bill of Rights reads, "That the right of every citizen to keep and bear arms in defense of his home, person and property, or when lawfully summoned in aid of the civil power, shall not be questioned; but this shall not justify the wearing of concealed weapons." This clause is very similar to the wording in the 1875 constitution. The meaning of these words from both 1875 and 1945 is controversial. The debate focuses on the phrase "... shall not justify the wearing of concealed weapons." What may seem like plain language is anything but simple. The motive for inserting the provision in the 1875 constitution is cloudy today. While there is an extensive record of the constitutional convention, edited by Isidor Loeb and Floyd C. Shoemaker, there is very little in that record with regard to the concealed weapons provision.[2] This lack of a record makes it difficult to say with certainty what the authors of Missouri's conceal-and-carry constitutional clause intended. Many, especially the supporters of the right to carry, believe there are at least two reasons the clause doesn't prevent the legislature from establishing conceal-and-carry. First, they argue, the phrase merely means there is no natural right to carry a concealed weapon, but it doesn't mean that the legislature can't allow them. Second, they argue, the authors of the clause had racist and anti-ethnic intent and that the words were included to prevent immigrants and freed slaves from being able to carry guns and protect themselves. Opponents of conceal-and-carry argue that no matter what the reason for the clause's inclusion may have been, it is immaterial now. What is important, they argue, is that the language of the constitution clearly outlaws the carrying of concealed weapons and is not something the legislature has the right to change.

In many ways, the Showdown in the Show-Me State wouldn't have happened without the contributions of active and, often, angry interest groups.

There were many points over the course of the fourteen-year period from 1992 to 2005 when the fight could have come to an end, with one side claiming victory and the other retreating in defeat. This didn't happen, of course, and that is why, year after year, the conceal-and-carry question appeared in Jefferson City, some years with more fireworks than others, but always arising. Throughout the showdown, there were always advocates from Missouri who fought tooth-and-nail on both sides of the conceal-and-carry issue, but it was never a war fought in isolation. National groups were never far away, and they always acted like the stakes were high.

The fight over guns has a long, rich history in Missouri, and it has drawn the fervent attention of out-of-state lobbies. The next chapter first introduces the key interest groups at the national level. Second, while this book offers an examination primarily of the last fourteen years, it is important to first take an extra step back and look at a precursor to the showdown. The early 1980s push for a policy called preemption showed politicians everywhere that the National Rifle Association could be just as active, and effective, at the state level as it is in Washington.

Chapter Two

The Gun Lobby and Round One—Preemption

Guns and the Two Sides of the Gun Lobby— Different Resources, Different Results

There are two sides to every issue, with outspoken advocates on both sides. Sometimes there are clear winners and other times there are not. It took fourteen years, but in the Show-Me Showdown, there was *probably* a winner, though it is impossible to use a word more certain than *probably*, because even after supporters won an incredibly rare veto override and a positive supreme court decision, conceal-and-carry continues to face an uncertain future. The best that can be said, therefore, is that after fourteen years of wrangling there was *probably* a winner, a group that prevailed with a combination of gritty determination, superior resources, and more enthusiastic supporters than its opponents.

Over the past twenty years, the NRA has almost always been better organized and better funded than the groups that opposed it, such as the Brady Campaign to Reduce Gun Violence. The NRA has a long history. It was originally organized in 1871, when it "functioned primarily as a national organization to promote marksmanship training in the militia and reserves of the several states."[1] The organization created its lobbying arm, known today as the Institute for Legislative Action, in 1934 in response to the first attempt by the U.S. Congress to write gun control legislation. The organization added an electioneering arm, the Political Victory Fund, dedicated to supporting political allies in races for elective office, in 1975.

The Brady Campaign traces its origins back to 1974 and the founding of the National Council to Control Handguns by Dr. Mark Borinsky, himself a victim of gun violence. The group was renamed Handgun Control, Incorporated in 1980, then changed a second time, in 2001, to the Brady Campaign in honor of James and Sarah Brady. James Brady, former President Ronald Reagan's press secretary, was seriously wounded by a gunshot to the head during an attempt on Reagan's life in 1981. Sarah Brady, his wife, has been the chair of organization since 1991.

By virtue of the global spread of American pop culture, much of the world views the United States as a wild, lawless country where everyone carries a gun and shootouts take place daily on every street corner. American movies and television shows distributed around the world perpetuate this image, but so too does the uniquely American attitude about guns. While most nations severely restrict citizens' access to firearms, in the United States millions embrace guns as an important symbol of freedom. Many politicians are outspoken supporters of the right to keep and bear arms. Others who might not be as supportive loathe suggesting stronger regulation of guns because there is a price to be paid for such advocacy. Leaders who boldly call for greater restrictions on firearms are almost exclusively from urban centers, where there is little chance of political backlash because concerns about high rates of violent crime outweigh support for gun rights. For leaders at the state level, where more conservative values and rural politicians often dominate, gun control is as much a "third rail" as Medicare and Social Security are for federal politicians, meaning that touching the gun issue can bring the death of one's political career.

Not only are many politicians at the state level reluctant to regulate guns, but many are eager to do just the opposite. Over the last twenty years, restrictions on the owning, carrying, and use of guns have been significantly reduced by many states. Dissatisfied with developments at the federal level, the NRA aimed its considerable resources on state governments after Congress passed the Brady Act in 1993 and the assault weapons ban in 1994. By 2004, the NRA was at least partly responsible for the fact that forty-two states had either passed legislation or reached judicial decisions that preempted city and county governments from passing their own gun laws, reserving that power exclusively for state legislatures. The only states that have no restrictions on local gun laws are California, Iowa, Maryland, Minnesota, New Jersey, and New York.[2] By 2004, the NRA also played a part in shepherding laws through thirty-three states that made it illegal for states, counties, or cities to file nearly any kind of liability lawsuits against manufacturers and distributors of firearms and firearms supplies. The states that do not prohibit such suits by law are California, Connecticut, Delaware, Hawaii, Illinois, Iowa, Massachusetts, Minnesota, Nebraska, New Jersey, New Mexico, New York, Oregon, Rhode Island, Vermont, Washington, and Wisconsin, though court decisions in some of those states have stymied liability lawsuits in recent years.[3] The NRA has also successfully fought for a wide array of gun-friendly laws, including limits on the ability of local governments to enforce noise ordinances and other restrictions against gun ranges. So-called range protection laws are on the books in forty-five states.[4]

Finally, by 2004, forty-six states allowed citizens at least a limited right to carry concealed handguns. Of the forty-six, thirty-seven states have so-called "shall issue" laws, which means that the government must grant a concealed weapons permit to anyone who meets state requirements and wants one. The requirements generally include paying a fee, passing a criminal background check, and taking a firearms training course. Nine other states have "may issue" policies, in which governments have more discretion to decide who may and may not carry concealed weapons. For example, a state, or a county, may require an applicant to demonstrate his or her need for a concealed weapon before granting a permit. Only four states now entirely ban the carrying of concealed weapons by ordinary citizens. These are Illinois, Kansas, Nebraska, and Wisconsin. Wisconsin and Kansas remain non–conceal-and-carry states by only the narrowest of margins. In early 2004, pro–conceal-and-carry forces in the Wisconsin legislature missed overriding the governor's veto of a concealed weapons law by just one vote. Also in 2004, legislators in Kansas were just six votes short of overriding their governor's veto of conceal-and-carry legislation. In Kansas, vetoes of conceal-and-carry have been bipartisan, coming from a Republican governor, Bill Graves, in 1997, and, in 2004, from the current Democratic governor, Kathleen Sebelius.

The NRA's record of success is all the more remarkable considering that the group does not speak for "the people," by and large. Opinion polls usually show the public is opposed, by slight majorities, to conceal-and-carry in most places across the country. Even when poll data are broken down to examine the opinions of gun owners alone, they reflect a desire to keep strong gun control laws in place.[5] Furthermore, the NRA doesn't even speak for a majority, or close to a majority, of America's gun owners. Of an estimated eighty million gun owners in the United States, only four million belong to the NRA, according to the group's own Web site.[6] Despite the statistics against it, however, the NRA has been remarkably successful in effecting change in gun laws in the vast majority of states over the past twenty years.

Some groups are influential because of the sheer number of members they boast, like the AARP, which is often credited with forty million members. For the NRA, success comes from the determination and single-minded focus of the group, and its grassroots supporters can be overwhelming to legislators, prompting many of them to vote for less gun control. The group prefers to work behind the scenes, and often both the NRA and local activists deny the group is trying to influence a state's legislature, as was often the case in

Missouri. They are willing to come out of the back halls and committee meeting rooms of state capitols and activate their base, however, when they sense a little well-placed pressure can make a difference. The longtime Wisconsin state legislator and former Speaker of the House, Tom Loftus, offered an explanation of why the NRA has such power:

> Giving in to a powerful interest group with a narrow agenda is almost a natural instinct of legislators. For many it is just not worth the political pain to fight, or even reason with, a group like the NRA. Furthermore, why invite trouble during your next campaign, or even risk your political career by provoking the NRA?[7]

Loftus clashed often with the NRA, and his frustration shows in his words. He is right in this regard—the NRA's institutional memory is long and it is quite willing to work election after election to see to it that lawmakers who don't support its goals are driven from office. It is so successful not only because it spends millions of dollars but also because it is very effective at mobilizing its remarkably dedicated, passionate grassroots membership.

On the other hand, the opposition to conceal-and-carry, represented at the national level by groups such as the Brady Campaign and the Million Mom March, is well organized but not nearly as well funded, effective, or passionate as the NRA. It is also less successful.

This difference is not difficult to understand. In the study of interest groups, organizations are often classified by the type of "goods" they pursue: private goods or public goods. Something that benefits everyone in society is a public good. Classic examples of public goods include national defense, a clean environment, and a safer society. Private goods, on the other hand, are things that individuals can enjoy without having to share. An example of a private good might be a tax cut for a specific segment of society or the elimination of a regulation for a specific industry.

Groups that advocate private goods are always more successful than groups that advocate public goods. Such groups have an easier time recruiting and keeping members because members see a personal stake in the group's success. Public interest groups always suffer from what the economist Anthony Downs called the "free-rider problem."[8] He argued that people are rational, economic beings who use their resources carefully. According to Downs, a person might support a public interest group's goal of cleaning up the environment but will conclude that if the goal is achieved, she will benefit whether she contributes to the achievement of that goal or not. Being a rational economic creature, the average person won't expend energy pursuing a goal she will be able to enjoy either way. This means that groups pursuing private goods generally inspire more loyal, energetic followers than groups pursuing public goods. In the fight over guns, advocates of gun control pursue an amorphous goal of a "safer society," as opposed to the personal safety the supporters of gun rights seek. The NRA, therefore, has traditionally been much more effective than gun control groups such as the Brady Campaign.

The NRA's leadership argues it is waging an important war against government tyranny. On its Web site, the NRA calls itself the country's oldest civil liberties organization and takes the position that the Second Amendment provides individuals, not just state militias, with the right to keep and bear arms. Gun rights, the NRA's leadership might argue, are public goods—everyone is made safer by the right to keep and bear arms. Such rights protect people from both criminals and despotic government. However, the supporters of gun rights also seek an individual good: the ability to wear a gun on one's hip and feel instantly safer. Even though the NRA represents a relatively small percentage of the population, they have a much larger membership than gun control organizations and they are able to have a strong impact on policy debates because they fight not only for a general right to keep and bear arms but also for what they define as the personal right of members to protect themselves in a dangerous society.

On the other side, proponents of gun control disagree with the interpretation that the Constitution provides individuals with the right to keep and bear arms. Such activists argue that a society free of guns is inherently safer than one in which everyone who wants a gun can have one, so they fight for more restrictive gun laws. What they see is clearly a public good from their perspective, but there is no corresponding individual good to motivate activists to keep up the fight. Opposing guns ensures that they, the activists, don't have guns, but it does nothing to impact who else might be carrying a concealed weapon. In short, they pursue a much more amorphous public good—a safer society—than do the advocates of gun rights. Opponents of guns argue that allowing everyone the privilege to carry concealed weapons increases the chances for gun violence, but there is no genuine personal incentive for most of these activists, and while they may be passionate and outspoken at rallies, it is difficult to keep the gun control grass roots as passionate, active, and, by extension, as successful as gun rights supporters.

1984—An Early Victory for Gun Rights Advocates

Before the NRA became genuinely concerned about conceal-and-carry, or liability protection for the gun industry, or gun range protection, or any other issue at the state level, it focused on preempting the ability of local governments to create their own restrictive gun control ordinances. This was no imagined worst case scenario but a reaction to a real local ordinance.

By 1984 the NRA was engaged in a nationwide campaign to limit the national impact of a federal court decision upholding an ordinance passed in 1981 by the Chicago suburb of Morton Grove. The ordinance made the possession of handguns illegal within city limits, and a court challenge of the law ultimately failed on appeal to the Seventh Circuit of the U.S. Court of Appeals in 1982.[9] The Supreme Court refused to hear the case.

The Supreme Court requires the agreement of four justices for it to issue a Writ of Certiorari and hear a case. The justices don't have to share similar reasons for wanting to review a case, but at least four justices must sense there is some unresolved constitutional dilemma. By not taking the Morton Grove case, the Supreme Court continued a long practice of avoiding Second Amendment cases. The Court's rejection of the appeal was the legal equivalent of agreeing with the Seventh Circuit's decision that the Second Amendment had not been incorporated under the Fourteenth Amendment and, as such, was not a restriction on state and local gun laws.

While a Circuit Court's opinion technically is only precedent for the states within the circuit, the refusal by the Supreme Court to hear the appeal cleared the way for state and local governments to pass restrictive gun laws without running afoul of the Constitution, and the NRA and its allies took immediate notice. If the Supreme Court was unwilling to adopt an individual rights interpretation of the Second Amendment and kill the Morton Grove ordinance, then each local government in America was a potential battleground.

Faced with this legal defeat, the NRA turned to state legislatures and began a campaign urging them to pass preemptive laws that would keep political subdivisions—counties, cities, and towns—from passing restrictive gun laws based on the Morton Grove model. As Tom Loftus wrote, "NRA members were urged to lobby the legislatures of these states to enact measures that would, in effect, repeal all local ordinances governing firearms and take the power to enact other gun laws away from cities, counties, and towns."[10] Local governments are, by law, creatures of state government. State constitutions and state legislatures determine what local governments may or may not do. By focusing on state legislatures, the NRA hoped to limit its number of fights to 50. If it could succeed in getting state legislatures to preempt political subdivisions from passing restrictive gun ordinances, it would have much less fighting to do. In states where such laws weren't adopted, the NRA faced the uncomfortable possibility of fighting gun ordinances in many local governments.

Ultimately, the NRA's opposition to gun control laws is rooted in a desire to defend the Second Amendment, which the group believes confers an individual right to bear arms. While protecting the Second Amendment was clearly the group's motive for opposing the Morton Grove ordinance, their public rhetoric centered on the argument that a proliferation of local gun laws would confuse gun owners. This argument was adopted by supportive state legislators, including many in Missouri. As the group's Web site still reads, "The problem with local firearm ordinances is also one of sheer variety. Where no uniform laws are in place, the result can be a complex patchwork of restrictions that change from one local jurisdiction to the next. But it is unreasonable to require citizens, whether residents of a given state or persons passing through or visiting a state, to memorize a myriad of laws."[11] The NRA has been very successful in urging state legislatures to pass laws making it illegal for political subdivisions to pass their own gun ordinances. By 2004, forty-two states had such laws or constitutional amendments. In addition, several other states— Connecticut, Massachusetts, New Jersey, and New York—effectively ban political subdivisions from making their own gun laws thanks to court decisions. This brings the total number of states that prevent local governments from creating their own gun ordinances to forty-six.

In 1984 the NRA came to Missouri, winning passage of a law that barred any local government from passing gun ordinances that differed from state law. The law became effective on January 1, 1985, and reads, in part, "No county, city, town, village, municipality, or other political subdivision of this state shall adopt any order, ordinance or regulation concerning in any way the sale, purchase, purchase delay, transfer, ownership, use, keeping possession, bearing, transportation, licensing, permit, registration, taxation other than sales and compensating use taxes or other controls on firearms, components, ammunition, and supplies..."[12] This was an important victory for the NRA on two levels. First, by getting state legislatures to pass these preemption laws, it truly does limit the number of battles the NRA has to fight. Second, the atmosphere in most state capitols, where rural interests have traditionally had more influence than sheer population distribution might indicate they should, is much friendlier toward pro-gun policies than that which the NRA might find in big cities. In a state like Missouri, for example, the group certainly stood a much greater chance of being successful at the state level than it did at fighting battles in St. Louis and Kansas City, where support for restrictive gun ordinances has been quite strong.

During the 2000 legislative session, the mayor of St. Louis at that time, Clarence Harmon, tried to get the legislature to repeal this law. He announced his intention to pursue this goal in August 1999, arguing that the city should be able to make gun laws for itself. On the other side, the leaders of the NRA pledged to defend the law. NRA spokesperson Randy Kozuch reiterated the group's opposition to a "complicated patchwork of restrictions that change from one jurisdiction to the next" and added, "It's unreasonable to require citizens or people passing through to memorize a myriad of laws."[13] The mayor's proposal to repeal the law was introduced as a bill in the General Assembly by state representative Bob Hilgemann, D–St. Louis, in February 2000 and was cosponsored by seven other St. Louis representatives. Harmon's proposal, however, was a nonstarter with most legislators and never gained traction in the legislature.

When Harmon made his proposal in the summer of 1999, he had the support of at least one outspoken critic of both the NRA and less restrictive gun laws, the city's major daily newspaper, the *St. Louis Post-Dispatch*. The editorial position of that newspaper has long been to support gun control, and it printed a very negative editorial about the NRA's efforts to restrict local governments' legislative authority. It read, "In 1984, the NRA either bought off or bullied enough Missouri state legislators to prod them to pass a law that bars cities, counties and towns from enacting any gun control legislation that differs from that of the state. In effect, it took away Missouri citizens' rights to decide a life and death issue where it impacts them most, where they live."[14] This editorial is a clear example of the hostile editorial position taken by the *Post-Dispatch* toward the NRA over the years. Later, in an examination of the Proposition B campaign of 1999, there were many more examples of the *Post-Dispatch's* disdain for the NRA. The newspaper's editors clearly view the NRA as a carpetbagging, negative force in Missouri politics.

The editorial also reflects a factually inaccurate, perhaps naive, view of the policymaking process. There is a firmly established, legally sanctioned power relationship between the state and local governments. In every state in the country, it is the state government that holds the power. Local governments—counties, cities, towns, school districts, and special districts—are all creatures of state government. They exist under conditions prescribed by state law and they govern at the pleasure of state governments, which are well within their authority to pass laws preempting local governments. To assert that a "right" was taken away from the residents of St. Louis or any other Missouri city in 1984 is simply inaccurate. What they lost, if anything, was the *privilege* to make their own gun laws, not a right.

Preemption legislation was a significant victory for the NRA, not just in Missouri but across the nation because it made it much less necessary for the NRA to fight legal battles at the local level. With such victories nationwide, the group's goals shifted. In Missouri, activists began to rumble about the right to carry concealed weapons as a means of self-defense and in 1992 the legislature put considerable energy into debating conceal-and-carry.

Chapter Three

1992—The Conceal-and-Carry Fight Begins

In 1992, Missourians were legally permitted to carry guns on their persons, so long as the weapons were visible. The carrying of concealed weapons was illegal. As was true in many states at the time, including neighboring Illinois and Kansas, only certain people were allowed to carry concealed weapons: on-duty law enforcement officials, process servers, notaries public, judges, and members of the military engaged in official duty.

During the 1992 session of the General Assembly, Missourians heard the first real rumblings of a movement to legalize concealed weapons when Representative Joe Driskill, D–Doniphan, the chairman of the House Commerce Committee, sponsored a bill that would have allowed people to carry concealed weapons. A rural Democrat from southeast Missouri, Driskill was a strong advocate for conceal-and-carry.

Driskill, a loyal member of the Democratic party who served the state in many capacities, was emblematic of a Missouri political reality that arises repeatedly in debates about guns: guns are not a partisan issue in the state so much as they are an urban versus rural issue. Throughout the showdown, many of the champions of conceal-and-carry were Democrats. Conceal-and-carry seemed like a Republican issue in 2003 and 2004, but this is misleading. Republicans have run Democrats out of legislative office in many of Missouri's 114 counties. This change is reflective of a party realignment, but it is not evidence of an ideological shift. In many ways, Missouri is culturally conservative. While many state legislative seats were held for decades by politicians who called themselves Democrats, those Democrats were not the sort of political liberals one might now associate with the Democratic party label. Rather, people remained loyal to the Democratic name because of old resentments dating back to the end of the Civil War. With the passage of time, that allegiance to the Democrats, as well as an accompanying dislike of the Republicans, has faded.

Missourians divide along many fault lines, and not just geological ones, like the famed New Madrid. The urban-rural division has long been more relevant in Missouri than political party division, though with the growth of a major conservative urban center in southwest Missouri, Springfield, it might be more appropriate to say that Missourians are split between St. Louis and Kansas City on one side and the rest of the state, or "outstate" Missouri, on the other. At times, the residents of St. Louis and Kansas City feud and the people around the rest of the state take advantage. At other times, Democrats and Republicans create the state's major tensions. In other cases, however, as with the division of limited highway money, the state divides with Kansas City and St. Louis on one side and the rest of the state on the other, with little or no regard for party affiliation. Abortion and the gun issue also separate Kansas City and St. Louis from the rest of the herd.

In the 1990s, few issues illustrated the differences between St. Louis and Kansas City and Driskill's hometown of Doniphan more graphically than abortion and guns. In this context, it made perfect sense for Joe Driskill, a leader of the Democratic caucus, to sponsor conceal-and-carry legislation, regardless of how his fellow Democrats from Kansas City and St. Louis felt. As the history of the showdown demonstrates, Driskill was just the first of many Democrats to lead this fight.

Driskill began his career in politics working on Mel Carnahan's campaign for state treasurer in 1980. After Carnahan's election, he went to work in the treasurer's office. Shortly thereafter, Driskill was elected to the Missouri House at the age of twenty-six, where he quickly rose through the ranks of the Democratic party. After several years as a legislator, he left to serve in the executive branch as the director of the state's Department of Economic Development. He left that position in 2004 after holding it for ten years and is now out of state government for the first time in many years.

In 1992, Driskill justified his conceal-and-carry bill on the grounds that many other states, thirty-five at the time, allowed their residents to carry concealed weapons. The bill was killed in the House Civil and Criminal Laws Committee by the committee's chairman, St. Louis Representative Ronnie White. One of many strands in the complicated web that is the history of conceal-and-carry legislation in Missouri, this was just the first time that Ronnie White would be involved in the fight over concealed weapons. White played a relatively minor procedural role in 1992, but he was a major player in the late 1990s and beyond as a member of the Missouri Supreme Court and a thorn in the side of John Ashcroft, another Missouri politician whose career is intimately intertwined with the right-to-carry debate.

John Ross, from the St. Louis area, was a major advocate for the legalization of conceal-and-carry in 1992. Ross, an investment counselor and part-time gun dealer in 1992, formed Missouri Citizens for Civil Liberties in the aftermath of a mass killing in 1991 at a Luby's Cafeteria in Killeen, Texas, to advocate freer access to concealed firearms. In an op-ed piece for the *St. Louis Post-Dispatch,* Ross argued that restrictive gun laws in Missouri worked to the advantage of criminals and that the state's longstanding ban on concealed weapons was really a vestige of state-sanctioned discrimination. He wrote, "Missouri's current law that prohibits citizens from having the means to defend themselves effectively was passed almost a century ago. Like a poll tax, its purpose was to subjugate blacks, immigrants, and other minorities."[1] Ross's charge that the banning of conceal-and-carry was based in racism was a familiar refrain of both the NRA and gun advocates in other states. In Missouri, however, there is little written record to support this claim. The record of debate on the concealed weapons provision of the 1875 constitution is quite minimal and no such argument seems to have been addressed by the delegates. A lack of evidence neither proves nor disproves the charge. Of course, the argument is disregarded by modern-day opponents of conceal-and-carry, many of whom are African American religious and community leaders.

Drawing attention to incidents such as the massacre in Killeen was a common rhetorical tactic of those favoring the right-to-carry in 1992. The argument was that when incidents like Killeen, or an earlier massacre at a McDonald's in San Diego, took place, the police could only respond after much of the killing had occurred. The killings, it was argued, could have been stopped quickly only by people on the scene who were armed and ready to take action. They were unable to do this, of course, because state law forbade the carrying of concealed weapons. Ross argued, "The thing that really convinced us that we needed to get a good concealed-carry law in Missouri was a virtually identical incident to Killeen that came two months later in Anniston, Alabama. At a Shoney's, three gunmen emptied out the cash registers, got all the valuables and were herding people into a cooler to kill them. One of the patrons had a concealed-carry license and a gun with him. He shot and killed the first bandit, seriously wounded the second, and the third one fled."[2] A concealed weapon in the hands of someone willing to use it was the only thing that prevented a massacre, according to Ross. This argument was often repeated through the fourteen-year fight over conceal-and-carry in Missouri.

John Ross was a highly visible advocate of conceal-and-carry in 1992. He testified at committee hearings at the state legislature and claimed to have helped Driskill write his bill. As they advocated for conceal-and-carry, both

Ross's supporters and the NRA also engaged in a curious effort to show that the group was not behind the effort to bring the right to carry to Missouri. Time and again, despite plenty of evidence to the contrary, Ross and other advocates went to great lengths to demonstrate that conceal-and-carry was a purely homegrown issue. Certainly there were many Missourians who supported conceal-and-carry, but their vigorous denial of NRA influence was not especially convincing.

In a 1992 interview, Ross forcefully denied that Driskill's bill was introduced at the behest of the NRA. He said, "This is not an NRA-created or NRA-sponsored or NRA-initiated bill."[3] Similarly, while the NRA clearly favored any measure leading to less restrictive gun laws, the group also denied that it had anything to do with pushing conceal-and-carry in Missouri. Rather, it credited local groups with driving the legislative agenda. Of course, as the next decade showed, local groups rarely acted without the advice, consent, and, often, the financial support of the NRA.

For example, the organization sent a lobbyist from its Washington office to oversee the conceal-and-carry effort in 1992. The lobbyist, James T. Hayes, tried to downplay his role, but the fact that he was dispatched from Washington speaks volumes about the NRA's real interest in bringing the right-to-carry to Missouri. Hayes said, "I've been working the halls, and our membership has been working the phones. Taking somebody to dinner has no bearing." He added, "Big membership produces the wins in these battles."[4] Hayes's reference to the "big membership" is common for representatives of the NRA, who argue that everything the group does is with the blessing of, if not at the impetus of, its grassroots members. Representatives of the NRA are also always quick to point out that without hard work on the grassroots level nothing would get done, and that is almost certainly true. The NRA has a remarkably loyal, hardworking, and effective corps of members.

While state ethics records reveal Hayes's efforts were truly modest in 1992—he spent less than two thousand dollars lobbying and buying meals for legislators—his mere presence in Jefferson City contradicts the NRA's portrayal of a hands-off approach.[5] What can never be known is what Hayes said in closed-door meetings with legislators, or in comments made at the side of a legislator hurrying through the corridors of the state capitol, and what impact those words might have. When a group has a clear willingness to spend heavily at election time, it isn't necessary to spend a great deal of money buying dinners for legislators. Well-placed comments about the next election may be all it takes to win a friendly vote.

What is most confusing about the denials of NRA involvement by both the NRA and Missouri supporters of conceal-and-carry is why they felt compelled to deny it at all when it was so obvious the NRA was involved. At any given time, the NRA has one hundred thousand or more active members in Missouri. Surely a group with so many members in the state has a right to participate in state politics as a representative of its constituents. Why did the group so often make an effort to deny or disguise its activities? The obvious explanation is that both local activists and the NRA feared the group would be accused of carpetbagging. Alternately, perhaps they feared the NRA's national reputation, which is often controversial, might hurt the cause in Missouri. Further, they may have thought Missourians who were neutral on the issue of conceal-and-carry might be more likely to support it, or that opponents might be less likely to protest, if they believed it was a homegrown issue, but neither seems particularly likely to be true. However, if activists wanted to avoid criticism from gun control advocates and media outlets such as the *St. Louis Post-Dispatch,* they failed miserably. Regardless of the reason, the NRA remained involved but regularly continued to deny its involvement throughout the history of the Showdown in the Show-Me State.

In addition to the efforts of the NRA, there was, in fact, plenty of organized local support for conceal-and-carry in Missouri. In addition to Missouri Citizens for Civil Liberties, other state groups supporting conceal-and-carry were the Second Amendment Coalition, the Missouri Sportshooting Association, the Eastern Missouri Shooters Alliance, and the Western Missouri Shooters Alliance. However, they clearly had help from the NRA. It is difficult to sort out how much of the effort made by these groups, such as letter writing and phone campaigns aimed at state legislators, was made possible with the aid of the NRA's very impressive databases and significant financial resources, but there was clearly out-of-state aid.

There was also, of course, organized opposition to conceal-and-carry. In 1992 much of the law enforcement community was opposed to conceal-and-carry, although this would change in later years. The Law Enforcement Officers of Greater St. Louis, representing fifty-two area law enforcement agencies, lobbied against the omnibus crime bill as amended by Driskill. The St. Louis chief of police at the time, Clarence Harmon, another player who surfaced time and again during the Showdown, said, "Kids will see their relatives and parents armed to the teeth, and a logical extrapolation will be that they will want to arm themselves."[6] An alliance of ten groups called the "Coalition Against Concealed Guns" included the League of Women Voters, the Missouri Police Chiefs Association, the Missouri Council to Control Handguns, and others. Carl Wolf, the chief of the Hazelwood Police Department in suburban St. Louis County, was a member of the coalition who remained a vocal opponent of conceal-and-carry for many years. In late April 1992 Wolf claimed that he and his colleagues spoke for a majority of the state's citizens and cited public opinion data that Missourians opposed conceal-and-carry by a margin of three to one.[7]

One opponent of conceal-and-carry in 1992 was Governor John Ashcroft, who said, "Overall, I don't know that I would be one to want to promote a whole lot of people carrying concealed weapons in this society. Obviously, if it is something to authorize everyone to carry concealed weapons, I'd be concerned about it."[8] Despite this reluctance in 1992, Ashcroft's attitude changed dramatically over the next several years after he left the governor's mansion and became one of Missouri's two U.S. senators. In 1999 Ashcroft was very vocal in his support of the pro–conceal-and-carry ballot referendum known as "Prop B." During the 1999 campaign, Ashcroft spoke vigorously in support of conceal-and-carry. He also taped radio advertisements for the main pro–Prop B group, Missourians Against Crime. When Steve Hilton, an Ashcroft spokesman, was asked about the senator's new view on conceal-and-carry, he characterized the change as an evolution. He said, "States with the provision, and at present this is most of the country, report positive results and no serious problems. Second, there is a growing body of academic research, starting in 1997, showing this has a strong deterrent effect on violent crime. Senator Ashcroft's concerns have been satisfied in these respects."[9] In 1999 Ashcroft was preparing for his reelection campaign and his challenger was his successor as governor, Mel Carnahan. Carnahan had long been outspoken in his opposition to conceal-and-carry, and Ashcroft may have felt no choice but to clearly differentiate himself from his opponent on this issue. Regardless, when his contributions to the conceal-and-carry effort in 1999 are contrasted with his statement in 1992, Ashcroft's shift seems dramatic.

In addition to the local groups that opposed conceal-and-carry, the national organization Handgun Control Inc. (HCI), led by Sarah and James Brady, was also an interested party in the Missouri debate. However, the group did not then, nor does it now, possess the resources of the NRA. This was acknowledged by David Weaver, a lobbyist for HCI, in 1992, when he said his group couldn't afford an NRA-style direct mail campaign or a lobbyist to go to Jefferson City. In addition, he admitted there were only about three thousand HCI members in Missouri, which he said was just 5 percent of what the NRA could claim.[10]

The vote on the amendment was preceded by a strong effort on the part of the NRA, which coordinated a phone campaign by its members from around the state. As it often used to do in the days before the Internet really took off, the group alerted members and urged action through a mass mailing that contained the home phone numbers and addresses of members' legislators. Representative Phil Tate, D–Gallatin, a supporter of the amendment and a member of the NRA, said, "They have an incredible data bank. That is where their strength comes from—their ability to generate public pressure."[11] According to Joe Driskill, "There were hundreds and hundreds of phone calls made this week and hundreds more over the weekend. Obviously people were interested in this amendment."[12] In 1992, as it has time and again, the NRA showed that one of its greatest strengths is its ability to inspire the participation of its rank-and-file members.

Driskill's amendment to the omnibus crime bill gained wide bipartisan support and was adopted by a vote of 124–24 in March of 1992. The amendment would have granted all citizens at least twenty-one years of age the right to apply to their county sheriffs for permits to carry concealed weapons.[13] Predictably, the response from Kansas City and St. Louis was negative. Representatives from these cities were outspoken in their opposition to the measure, and all twenty-four votes against the amendment came from Kansas City, St. Louis, and the notably liberal city of Columbia. The debate prior to the vote was heated, pitting urban representatives against rural representatives and, in some cases, Democrats against Democrats. For instance, Representative Mary Bland, D–Kansas City, said, "An amendment like this does not protect—in fact, it gives a license to kill."[14] This prompted the amendment's sponsor, Joe Driskill, to reply, "It does not increase violence; it does not increase gunplay. We're aiming at the law-abiding, honest people," and he insisted that the intent of the bill was simply to allow people to protect themselves against violent crime.[15] This line of argument remained a constant theme throughout the long fight over conceal-and-carry. At times, the debate degenerated from a civilized discussion of the issue into something more unseemly.

The emotions at work were clearly evident in an exchange between Representatives Chris Kelly, D–Columbia, Paula Carter, D–St. Louis, both opponents of the amendment, and Joe Driskill. The exchange was captured in colorful detail by the *St. Louis Post-Dispatch*'s Virginia Young, who wrote, "While a lobbyist from the NRA in Washington watched, the House debated whether members were kowtowing to the powerful gun lobby. 'We've gotten as close to the back end of the NRA as anyone needs to be,' said Rep. Chris Kelly, D–Columbia. He predicted that sheriffs would 'give the permits to white people and they won't give them to black people. This is simply about being nice to the NRA and being discriminatory to black citizens.' Driskill responded that he opposed racial bias and resented being called the 'buttboy of the NRA.' That prompted a comment from Rep. Paula Carter, D–St. Louis, who said her district had the most murders in the state last year. 'If you come to my district, you won't have to worry about being the buttboy—you won't have one,' said Carter, who opposed the bill."[16] It is worth noting that, once again, this rancorous debate, usually reserved for partisan disputes, was between members of the same Democratic team, graphically illustrating where the true fault lines of Missouri politics lie. The omnibus crime bill to which the conceal-and-carry amendment was attached passed by a vote of 110 to 40 and was forwarded to the state senate.

This victory for the supporters of conceal-and-carry was obviously distressing to its opponents. Following the vote, St. Louis Police Chief Harmon criticized members of the house, saying, "I hope the Senate has a better handle on what the result of gun violence is in this society. Many of us in the law enforcement community think this is not the most well thought-out thing that the House has done in recent years . . ." He added that he hoped Governor Ashcroft would veto the measure if it passed in the senate.[17] Harmon had some reason for optimism, for while the bill passed easily in the house, many state senators were more hesitant about the legislation.

In the state senate, the house's omnibus crime bill was referred to the Criminal Jurisprudence Committee, where the conceal-and-carry provision was rewritten in subcommittee by Senator Steve Danner, D–Hale. Danner was a veteran of state government and the Democratic party, having worked as an aid to both the Speaker of the House, Bob Griffin, and to Mel Carnahan when Carnahan was the lieutenant governor. He also served as a judge and a state representative. None of this, however, made him fearful of promoting conceal-and-carry and in a later campaign he was quite proud to announce his independence from the governor.

Danner's new version of conceal-and-carry included more stringent requirements for permit applicants with the hope that this move would gain more support in the senate. Danner's version made many changes. It raised the minimum age to twenty-five, required an applicant to show proof of liability insurance, required an applicant to obtain signatures from ten people attesting to his or her stability, and required an applicant to obtain a written statement from his or her doctor attesting that the applicant was in good mental and physical health. When Danner offered the proposal to the full Jurisprudence committee, however, no one seconded his motion, effectively killing the proposal. The chairman of the committee, Senator Jeff Schaeperkoetter, D–Owensville, said the bill didn't have the committee's support because "There have been threats to filibuster the bill . . . It just doesn't seem to have much of a chance."[18] The filibuster is a powerful tool in Missouri's senate. There are procedural means to bring a filibuster to an end, but they are used so rarely that in almost every case the only thing limiting a senator's ability to bring the senate to a halt is his or her own stamina. It seemed that if the omnibus crime bill was to pass in the senate, it would do so without any conceal-and-carry provision.

Frustrated by the lack of support in committee, Senator Danner promised to introduce the bill as an amendment to another piece of legislation on the senate floor, much as Driskill had done in the house. Representative Driskill offered his support for Danner's more stringent proposal, saying he would seek to have it introduced in the house. He said, "If people are more comfortable with more safeguards, I'm all for them."[19] Clearly, the supporters of conceal-and-carry were not to be easily discouraged.

One factor that might have done serious damage to Danner's proposal as it was debated in committee was a shooting that took place in the St. Louis County courthouse in Clayton on May 5, while the committee was at work on the jurisprudence bill. The incident involved a man, Kenneth Baumruk, who shot and killed his wife, Mary Louis Baumruk, just after a hearing in their divorce case began. Baumruk wounded five others, including his own attorney, Garry Seltzer, and his wife's attorney, Walter Scott Pollard.[20]

The shooting came at a terrible time for conceal-and-carry, as the press, politicians, and one of the victims turned the shooting into anti–right-to-carry propaganda. One state representative from Clayton, Sue Shear, the sponsor of a major gun control measure in 1992, said, "The more guns you put in people's hands, the more dangerous it's going to be . . . The gunman may have been a law-abiding citizen who went crazy over a divorce. If the concealed weapons amendment passes, instead of just him having the gun, hundreds of people, thousands of people, will have them."[21] An editorial in the *St. Louis Post-Dispatch* read, "The county incident explains why the legislature should pay more attention to gun control than to the bill that would give people permission to carry concealed weapons. That bill is an invitation to more tragic shootings like the one in Clayton."[22] Victim Walter Scott Pollard said, "I was against it before and I'm even more against it now. . . This kind of thing is going to happen more often if they allow that bill to pass. I think this is just the tip of the iceberg."[23] At the very time the shooting took place, a meeting among top-level St. Louis County officials was also being held in the courthouse about how to improve security.[24] Sensing that the incident elevated the opposition to conceal-and-carry, Driskill seized on this fact when he argued that such an incident shouldn't be tied to a legal right to carry concealed handguns. He said, "This terrible act was done by someone illegally carrying a firearm. The passage of a strong law here would not have had any impact on that situation. The bottom line is, we need better security resources to keep this from happening."[25] John Ross took the argument further, asserting a conceal-and-carry law could have prevented the shooting, again making a comparison to Killeen.

He argued that the shooting occurred because the assailant ". . . had a government guarantee that no one in the courtroom could stop him except the bailiff or perhaps the judge, who has a right-to-carry a gun. Everybody else was a sheep ready for the slaughter. That man was prepared to die just like the man in Killeen, Texas."[26] Ross implied that if others in the courtroom had been allowed to carry weapons, they could have quickly acted to stop the shooter. None of this rhetoric, however, was enough to save the legislation. With just days left in the 1992 legislative session, the amendment was withdrawn by Danner. In Missouri, the legislature is part-time, meeting for five months a year, beginning in January and usually concluding business by mid-May. This is typical of many state legislatures, and it means that many proposals fall victim to time. If an issue is something a governor feels strongly about, he may call a special session and bring the legislators back to Jefferson City, but such sessions are relatively rare. Similarly, the leaders of the house and senate can call for a special session, but such a move requires a super-majority vote, which is almost impossible to achieve.

In the House, Joe Driskill promised he would bring the proposal back in 1993 after taking time to work with the law enforcement community and other opponents to craft more acceptable legislation.[27] Despite his guarantee, it was not Driskill who revived conceal-and-carry in 1993, but rather Senator Steve Danner.

With Defeat, a Victory

As the legislators left Jefferson City in the summer of 1992, opponents of conceal-and-carry claimed victory and suggested the citizens of Missouri would never be allowed to carry concealed weapons. In October the Coalition Against Concealed Guns attempted to survey officeholders and candidates for office about their views on conceal-and-carry. The survey suffered from a low response rate of just 17 percent (54 out of 315), which is emblematic of how few Missouri politicians are willing to talk on the record about guns, but of those who responded, the group reported, two-thirds were opposed to conceal-and-carry.[28]

The gun issue has many facets, however, and while gun control forces were able to count the demise of conceal-and-carry in 1992 as a victory, it is worth noting that the right to carry was not the only gun-related issue considered by the legislature in 1992. Lobbying for the defeat of conceal-and-carry was a reactionary gesture by gun control supporters. However, just as gun proponents had a proactive legislative agenda in 1992, so too did gun control advocates. Like the conceal-and-carry agenda, it was controversial and unsuccessful.

Representative Sue Shear, D–Clayton, introduced a bill that would have required owners of guns with children to either use trigger locks or keep their guns under lock and key so their children couldn't gain access to them. The bill also mandated gun-free "safe zones," creating a one-thousand-foot perimeter around schools. The 1992 session represented Shear's second attempt to pass such legislation, and it moved easily through the House Civil and Criminal Justice Committee. Interestingly, Shear had the tacit support of Joe Driskill, who said, "I want to make sure that it does not subject reasonable people to unreasonable burdens. I think most people agree that they have to protect their children and other people's children from the accidental discharge of handguns, and I have no problem with the concept of passing legislation to remind people of that."[29] However, not all gun-rights advocates saw things the same way as Driskill.

The NRA opposed the law and fought hard to defeat it during the session, urging its members around the state to call their representatives. Shear reported that fellow legislators told her of the NRA's action. According to Shear, one such legislator reported having received in excess of three hundred calls from NRA members urging her to vote against the bill. Shear expressed her frustration, saying, "The funny thing is, this isn't a gun control bill. This bill only says that people have to keep guns out of the hands of children."[30] In another interview, she said, "I am not trying to wipe out gun ownership. I am simply trying to save the lives of children."[31] Shear probably should have known better. As is it usually does with any proposals it interprets as restrictions on gun ownership, the NRA opposed Shear's bill on the premise that any law limiting the use of guns, even one that seemed reasonable on the surface, like banning weapons near schools or requiring trigger locks, would open the door to an all-out ban on firearms some day. This may seem to be an extreme position, that the NRA's perspective is to view all gun control measures as the first tottering step down a slippery slope to the elimination of all gun rights. In other words, the leaders of the NRA might borrow a phrase from Barry Goldwater and say, "extremism in the defense of liberty is no vice."[32]

Bud Eyman, a representative of one of the NRA's Missouri affiliates, the Missouri Sportshooting Association, said, "We oppose any unnecessary laws that further encumber honest citizens and interfere with their constitutional right to have guns."[33] A representative from the NRA's lobbying arm, the Institute for Legislative Action, Jim Hayes, commented on the trigger lock and gun safety portion of the bill, saying, "We object to mandating what someone does in the privacy of their home," and added, "Arresting parents after their 4-year-old shoots their 5-year-old doesn't bring the 5-year-old back. It's ridiculous."[34]

After passing easily out of committee, Shear's bill ran into a brick wall, no doubt due, in part, to the efforts of the NRA and its allies. The group was able to claim victory when the Speaker of the House, Bob Griffin, failed to put it on the legislative calendar in time for it to be debated before the end of the session.

Electioneering: Reaching for the Ultimate Goal

While the NRA is always willing to fight for policy, there is a strong belief within the organization that the best way to win in the halls of government is to get the right people elected to office. In addition to its legislative activities, the NRA made its presence felt in Missouri electoral politics in 1992 in several ways. The group endorsed Missouri Attorney General Bill Webster in the gubernatorial race against Lieutenant Governor Mel Carnahan. While Carnahan won the endorsement of traditional Democratic supporters like the AFL-CIO, the NRA supported Webster because it believed he would be more sympathetic to the group's position on gun issues. The group certainly was correct in its assessment of the candidates, though its support for Webster wasn't enough to give him the election. Carnahan won the gubernatorial election, and as the NRA suspected, he proved to be no friend of the gun lobby.

While many observers of politics like to characterize the NRA as an unofficial electioneering arm of the Republican party, this is not always true, certainly not in a state like Missouri. While the organization supported the Republican candidate for governor, it did not limit its support to Republicans in 1992.

In Missouri, Republicans must be just as cautious in taking a pro–gun control stance as any Democrat. There is a price to pay for supporting gun control, as was evidenced by the race in Missouri's Sixth Congressional District. The district, situated in the northwest corner of the state, is a mix of urban and rural areas encompassing the city of St. Joseph, the northern parts of suburban Kansas City, and several rural counties. In 1992 a Democratic state senator, Pat Danner, the mother of state senator Steve Danner, defeated her opponent, Republican incumbent Thomas Coleman, with a significant amount of help from the NRA. As a state senator, Pat Danner was a supporter of gun rights, while Coleman was perceived by the group as being anti-gun.

Chief among the group's complaints about Coleman was his vote for the Brady bill, even though the bill didn't actually pass until 1993. This prompted the NRA to run an independent campaign of television and radio advertisements aimed at driving Coleman out of office. The ads extended beyond guns, providing a more general critique of Coleman's performance as a member of Congress. In fact, the ads attacked his positions on issues such as taxes and legislators' perks more than they focused on guns, perhaps to dissuade voters who were more apt to be sympathetic to Coleman's Brady vote. There certainly would have been voters who agreed with Coleman on Brady in the northern Kansas City suburbs and St. Joseph, both of which would vote against concealed weapons in 1999 when it was a referendum.

Coleman and his campaign staff were stung by the criticism and argued that no matter what the NRA charged in its ads, the attacks were all really about just one thing—Coleman's support for the Brady bill. Coleman's press secretary, Craig Orfield, implied that the NRA's single-minded reason for attacking Coleman would have many negative consequences when he said, "It appears they didn't care about the ideology of the person who followed the incumbent. They just wanted to take revenge on Tom Coleman."[35] In another interview the same spokesman said, "They've gotten very active in going for the jugular," referring to a last-minute phone bank and barrage of advertising.[36]

Federal Election Commission records indicate that the NRA spent a total of eighty-eight thousand dollars in the primary election to make Danner the Democratic nominee and in the general election to defeat Coleman. A spokesman for the NRA, David Gibbons, said the phone bank, which made fourteen thousand calls on Danner's behalf, targeted voters in the district who were NRA members and people who had obtained hunting licenses.[37]

According to Pat Danner, the newly elected U.S. representative, the activity of the NRA was all conducted without any coordination with her campaign, and she said that early in the process she was completely unaware of the group's efforts and that coordination between a group's independent expenditures and a candidate's campaign is of course illegal under federal election law. After the race, Danner said, "I'm proof positive that PAC's don't influence everybody, because I don't pay attention to them."[38] In another interview, she said, "I won that race because I have been working in northwest Missouri for twenty years, I'm not just someone new on the scene that some particular group supported. The people in my district knew the kind of dedication I have to them, and that's what made the difference."[39] Her protests notwithstanding, her election was certainly due at least in part to the fact that the NRA thought she was a good investment, and as she took office, the group reported that she was in the top twenty of their ranking of new legislators, based on the rating they gave her on gun issues. As they do with nearly everyone holding or running for elective office, the NRA rated Danner based on her history as a legislator and on responses to an NRA survey.[40]

The group found quickly it had supported the right candidate in the Sixth District, as Danner voted against the Brady bill in 1993. As the vote approached, Danner reported publicly that she was undecided on the Brady bill, but her decision seemed inevitable as the vote drew near. She said, "I support the Second Amendment. If having stringent laws on the books made for safe streets, then Washington D.C. would be one of the safest places in the entire world. And it certainly is not."[41] While the Brady bill finally passed in 1993 after several years of trying, the NRA certainly narrowed the bill's margin of victory by helping to put Danner in Congress, and they knew they had a loyal friend in Missouri's Sixth District for future gun fights.

The Sixth District was not the only Missouri congressional race where the NRA campaigned against an incumbent, again largely because of the incumbent's support for the Brady bill. Missouri's Second Congressional District is in the St. Louis area, and the incumbent in 1992 was a first-term Democratic congresswoman, Joan Kelly Horn. The NRA spent less money in the Second District than in the Sixth, but they once again contributed to the defeat of an incumbent. While the group was less active in the Second District, the truth is that they didn't need to do more. The Second District is in St. Louis County, which has a strong Republican tradition, and Horn had been elected in 1990 by a very narrow margin. In 1992 Horn ran against Jim Talent, the state house minority leader, a very strong opponent.

This does not mean the NRA's efforts were meaningless, however. According to FEC records, the organization spent around twenty-one thousand dollars in its campaign against Horn, which once again included a last-minute phone bank effort.[42] As NRA Spokesman David Gibbons said, "This was all done in the last four or five days . . . People don't make up their minds until late. Also, when you come in at the last minute, it doesn't give the other person a chance to respond, which is a good strategy."[43] Sneaking up on the opposition, as Gibbons suggested, is always an effective strategy.

In the aftermath of the election, Horn complained about the gun lobby's involvement in the campaign, echoing Coleman's complaints from the Sixth District. She said, "It's very frustrating because you feel totally helpless against it. You don't really know what it is, or where it's coming from."[44] In the two races, Danner defeated Coleman 55.4 percent to 44.6 percent and Talent defeated Horn 50.4 percent to 47.6 percent. Undoubtedly, the NRA contributed to those margins of victory. For Talent, the question of concealed weapons would become very important later in the 1990s. Like Ashcroft, White, and many others, Talent was to be a repeat performer.

In addressing the NRA's involvement in both the Danner and Talent victories, NRA spokesman David Gibbons suggested that the group had very carefully chosen the races, along with five others from around the country, because of the anti-gun incumbents' vulnerability. Horn, for example, had only won by fifty-four votes in 1990, he said, so the NRA felt they could make a very clear difference in that race by getting involved. In addition, in 1992 both Horn and Coleman were running in districts that had been reapportioned after the 1990 census, which added to their political vulnerability.[45] What is odd about Gibbons's words is how proud he seems to be of the NRA's impact on the race because the group went to such lengths to distance itself from the fight in the legislature, but was quite eager to demonstrate its impact at the polls. What was the difference? Clearly, he wanted to demonstrate to politicians throughout the state the consequences of taking a stand against gun rights.

Because of Brady, the NRA was very active in 1992. According to Federal Election Commission records, the organization spent approximately $2.7 million during the 1992 federal election cycle. The vast majority of that spending was in the form of independent expenditures, not direct donations to candidates, which were limited by law to just $10,000 per candidate per election cycle. In a striking comparison, the gun control group, HCI, spent just $53,000 nationally, including approximately $18,724 in Missouri.

Almost all of the money spent by HCI in Missouri paid for newspaper ads on behalf of Geri Rothman-Serot, a St. Louis city councilwoman who was the Democratic opponent of U.S. Senator Kit Bond. While Rothman-Serot gained the endorsement of HCI for her support of the Brady bill, it also made her the enemy of the NRA. During the primary campaign, Rothman-Serot rolled the dice by publicly supporting Brady and staking out a pro–gun control position, while most of her Democratic opponents refused to endorse the bill. She said, "Everybody seems to be running away from it, but I state my opinion. I know there were a lot of state representatives for the concealed-weapons bill, but I don't think more guns is the answer."[46] One opponent, Bill Peacock of Ladue, leaned against Brady when he said in an interview that "As a Marine Corps reserve colonel, I believe in the fundamental right to bear arms. I'm not sure the Brady bill is the solution to the right balance between the right to bear arms and the right to safety of the general public." He added that he thought issues of gun control were more appropriately decided at the state level.[47] The other major Democratic candidate, Dan Dodson of Jefferson City, said he tended to favor the Brady bill, but at the same time he believed that the Missouri General Assembly had the right to pass a conceal-and-carry law.[48]

Rothman-Serot won the party's nomination, but Bond, who voted against Brady, was easily reelected in 1992. He was the NRA's endorsed candidate and, according to FEC records, the group spent approximately forty-two thousand dollars on his campaign. Rothman-Serot lost the election against Bond 52 percent to 46 percent.

The NRA also certainly played a role in the reelection of Missouri's Ninth Congressional District representative, Harold Volkmer, who was very strongly challenged by Republican Rick Hardy of Columbia, a professor of political science at the University of Missouri. Though Hardy and Volkmer shared a similar position on guns, the Democratic incumbent was an old ally of the NRA. Volkmer was an outspoken opponent of gun control and in 1986 had been a major sponsor of the 1986 Firearms Owners Protection Act. The law did not end up being as strong a statement in favor of gun rights as the NRA hoped it would be, but it served to dilute much of the federal government's existing gun regulations, which were created by the 1968 Gun Control Act.

Hardy ran a strong campaign in 1992, attacking Volkmer's ethics and often calling him "PAC Man," in reference to the large number of contributions the congressman received from a variety of political action committees, including several connected to the NRA. To emphasize his point, Hardy refused to take any money from special interest groups and, following the campaign, Hardy's campaign manager, R. E. Burnett, suggested this stance both helped and hurt his candidate. It helped Hardy's attack on special interests, but it hurt because it limited Hardy's ability to pay for advertising.[49] Burnett's assessment may well have been correct, but Hardy's move to reject PAC money was dramatic and popular. Without it, he certainly would have had trouble doing as well as he did against the entrenched incumbent. In addition to Hardy's attack, Volkmer was targeted in 1992 by an organization called the Coalition to Stop Gun Violence, which identified him as one of "a dangerous dozen" congressmen.

Volkmer was at the top of the coalition's list because of his support for the NRA and the contributions he received in return, as well as his sponsorship of the Firearms Owners Protection Act and his opposition to any gun control legislation.[50] A spokesman for the coalition, Michael Beard, called him the NRA's point man in the U.S. House of Representatives. Volkmer responded that he voted with the NRA and took big donations from the group because he agreed with its positions and that there was nothing wrong with such a relationship. He argued that his constituents agreed with his position on guns and that he was not guilty of any impropriety.[51] According to FEC records, throughout his career the congressman regularly received big donations from the NRA. In 1992 Volkmer eked out a victory by just about six thousand votes, beating Hardy 47.7 percent to 45.5 percent. Despite winning, the election left Volkmer looking very vulnerable.

Following the elections of 1992, Missouri's political leaders waited for the new governor's inauguration and the 1993 legislative session to begin. As would happen year after year, the beginning of a new legislative session meant the introduction of new conceal-and-carry legislation.

Chapter Four

1993 to 1994—Conceal-and-Carry Returns

1993 was a relatively quiet year, with only one conceal-and-carry bill, sponsored by Steve Danner, who reintroduced his 1992 proposal in the state senate. Speaking in support of his legislation, Danner argued that his bill was needed because many thousands of otherwise law-abiding citizens were already carrying concealed weapons and this proposed law would simply legalize their actions.[1] St. Louis Police Chief Clarence Harmon disagreed with Danner's contention that his bill was merely an effort to help the citizens of Missouri. Rather, he argued that the effort to pass conceal-and-carry was being driven by the NRA in a state-by-state campaign to create such laws.[2]

While the bill ultimately went nowhere and is now little more than a footnote in the history of the showdown, it is made more interesting because of its sponsor, the son of the newly elected U.S. Representative Pat Danner, who benefited from the NRA's support in her campaign to defeat incumbent Tom Coleman. Steve Danner certainly understood better than most the power the group could wield in support of his own future aspirations.

• • •

While conceal-and-carry left the Missouri General Assembly quietly in 1993, it made a strong comeback in the middle of the 1994 legislative session as part of a debate over anti-crime legislation in the house of representatives. The original anti-crime bill, sponsored by Representative Brian May, D–St. Louis, would have imposed a minimum three-year prison sentence for certain gun-related crimes. During debate on the bill an amendment was proposed by Representative Don Lograsso, R–Blue Springs, that would have given people over the age of twenty-one the right to carry. The amendment was adopted by a vote of 95 to 35, angering May and prompting him to pull his bill from further consideration. Representative May said, "This amendment would do nothing more than put more guns on the street," and suggested that it ran counter to the goals of his bill.[3] When May shelved his bill, conceal-and-carry was again off the legislature's agenda in 1994, but only briefly.

Anti-crime legislation returned in a different form, sponsored by Representative Steven R. Carroll, D–Hannibal, later in the session. The bill contained many provisions to get tough on criminals, including a so-called "three strikes" law. During floor debate, the bill was also amended by Carroll to include a concealed weapons provision. The amendment would have allowed persons at least twenty-one years old to apply to county sheriffs for a permit to carry a concealed weapon. Sheriffs would be given up to seven days to conduct background checks on applicants. The amendment was adopted by a vote of 111 to 40. Following the vote, there were plenty of comments on either side of the issue. Representative Mary Bland, D–Kansas City, called it a "license to kill," while Carroll defended conceal-and-carry by saying it would just legalize what many Missourians were already doing.[4] One constituency that was a key player throughout the years of the showdown was the law enforcement community. Police were often split by the conceal-and-carry question, with police administrators usually opposing it while significant numbers of rank-and-file officers seemed to support it. In 1994, Ron Worsham, the assistant director of the Missouri Department of Public Safety, claimed that 93 percent of the police departments and sheriffs in Missouri opposed the house's conceal-and-carry plan. John Hemeyer, Cole County sheriff and president of the Missouri Sheriffs Association, said the association opposed conceal-and-carry because the house's proposal didn't allow enough time or resources for background checks on applicants.[5]

Another legislator, Wayne Crump, D–Potosi, who was to become a major player in the conceal-and-carry debate throughout the 1990s, added another amendment that would have made it legal for people to conceal guns in the passenger compartments of their vehicles without needing to apply for a concealed weapons permit. During debate on these amendments, Crump said, "It's time that criminals wonder who's carrying a firearm."[6]

Crump's guns-in-cars proposal was interesting because there was considerable opinion in Missouri legal circles that the carrying of concealed weapons in vehicles was already legal, thanks to Jesse James–era provisions in the law meant to protect people traveling through lawless parts of the state. It is for this same reason that carrying an unconcealed handgun on one's person was already legal. Crump argued that his amendment was necessary to clarify the law because, he believed, it was applied unevenly in different jurisdictions across the state. While there was support for Carroll's and Crump's proposals among out-state legislators, it was strongly opposed by most members from the urban centers of Kansas City and St. Louis.

Conceal-and-carry legislation did not survive the 1994 legislative session. While it seemed there was enough support for conceal-and-carry in the house, as had been the case in earlier years, a clear pattern of resistance was developing in the senate. In fact, before the house adopted Carroll's right-to-carry measure, a conceal-and-carry amendment in the senate, sponsored by Harold Caskey, D–Butler, had already failed by a vote of 15 to 18. Caskey, like Crump, was another rural Democrat who would become an outspoken champion of conceal-and-carry throughout the 1990s. In 1994, Caskey proposed an amendment to a juvenile crime bill, sponsored by Joe Moseley, D–Columbia, former Boone County prosecutor. Caskey's amendment would have allowed persons twenty-one and over to carry concealed weapons, providing they received sixteen hours of firearms training, passed a background check, and paid a fifty-dollar permit fee.[7] When Caskey made the proposal, Moseley said if the senate approved the amendment, he would exercise his privilege as the sponsor of the bill and prevent it from proceeding any further.[8] Caskey's argument in support of the amendment was familiar, positioning it as a matter of public safety. He said, "Our citizens are unarmed, and the outlaws know it."[9]

As always, lobby groups on both sides of the issue weighed in on the debate over Caskey's amendment. For instance, Frieda Bernstein, president of Missourians against Handgun Violence and an outspoken opponent of conceal-and-carry throughout the Showdown years, was harsh in her criticism of Caskey's amendment. She said, "This is ridiculous. This is garbage. This is absolutely sick. Once again we are going to have a year in Jefferson City in which anything good will be pitched out at the expense of stopping this obscene concealed weapons bill . . . The minute a concealed-weapons bill is passed, everyone will be carrying one . . . Then, when someone doesn't like the way someone looks at them, they're going to start shooting. Would you feel real safe then?"[10] On the other side, the Second Amendment Coalition, an organization active for many years in the fight for conceal-and-carry, organized a grassroots campaign aimed at getting senators to vote yes for what it called "the public safety law."[11] One senator who voted against the amendment, Bill McKenna, D–Barnhart, described what he called "tons" of postcards he received from Second Amendment Coalition supporters. The cards, he said, read, "I trust you. Do you trust me? If you trust me you'll give me the public safety law."[12]

Following the amendment's defeat, Senator Danner said, "It's obvious there are the numbers to do it," and seemed to suggest it was just a matter of time.[13]

This was bolstered by the fact that there were apparently a number of senators who only voted against the amendment because they were concerned about certain details of the proposal, such as the penalty for carrying a concealed weapon without a permit and whether or not guns would be barred from certain places, not conceal-and-carry itself.[14] This meant that if the flaws were fixed, there might be enough votes to pass the right to carry. One opponent of conceal-and-carry, a columnist for the *Kansas City Star,* Jean Haley, was happy with the amendment's defeat, but seemed pessimistic about the future. Haley wrote, "It would be a relief to think the defeat of the Caskey amendment were the end of the matter, but the proposal was shelved last year, and the year before. And it keeps on reviving."[15] Clearly, even as early as 1994, the proponents and opponents of conceal-and-carry were feeling frustrated that the issue continually remained unresolved.

Related to conceal-and-carry was another issue debated during the 1994 session—an attempt to repeal the 1984 preemption of local gun ordinances and return to St. Louis and Kansas City the authority to regulate everything from the sale of guns to the possession and use of guns. Governor Mel Carnahan championed such legislation, saying, "St. Louis and Kansas City are in a crisis. They are facing an epidemic of violent crime. Young children are killing young children."[16] The governor was joined in his support for such legislation by political leaders in both Kansas City and St. Louis, including state senators such as Senate Majority Leader J. B. "Jet" Banks, D–St. Louis, and Phil Curls, D–Kansas City.

Opposition to conceal-and-carry and support for more local control had many voices in Kansas City and St. Louis. Many officials from those cities, such as Jackson County Prosecutor Claire McCaskill, suggested that the push for conceal-and-carry was driven entirely by the NRA, not by Missourians. Senator Caskey refuted these claims, insisting the organization had nothing to do with his proposal and that he was merely responding to the demands of his constituents.[17] McCaskill argued the 1994 session could have a critical impact on gun laws when she said, "There will be votes on some modest changes in terms of more gun control and there will be votes on 'Let's let everyone strap one on under their jacket.'"[18] While the vote on Caskey's proposal was close, as usual, in the senate, being close isn't enough to pass bills or constitutional amendments. For many years there were enough votes in the senate to prevent conceal-and-carry from becoming a reality.

The NRA's response to the 1994 attempt to alter the 1984 preemption law was predictably negative. NRA state lobbyist George McNeill said Governor Carnahan was trying to scare people and that his proposals did nothing to actually reduce crime.[19] The organization contacted its members with a mailer and informed them that Carnahan wanted every political subdivision in the state to be able to pass its own gun laws. This prompted another grassroots wave of calls and letters to state legislators, chilling the climate for any major changes.[20] Some provisions were proposed during the legislative session that would have allowed St. Louis and Kansas City to pass gun control laws aimed only at people under the age of eighteen or twenty-one. For instance, Senator Steve Danner proposed a bill that would allow Kansas City and St. Louis to pass strong ordinances outlawing handgun possession by people under the age of eighteen. He said, "We're talking about making it a local option in Kansas City and St. Louis," but it wouldn't apply anywhere else.[21] However, even these narrowly tailored bills were easily defeated.

The president pro tem of the senate, Jim Mathewson, D–Sedalia, and Speaker of the House Bob Griffin both strongly opposed the idea of giving more local control to Kansas City and St. Louis. Griffin said, "I can't get anybody in Kansas City or St. Louis to tell me what they are going to do," implying that he was reluctant to give them a blank check.[22] Mathewson was a supporter of gun rights, including conceal-and-carry. In response to this proposal, he argued, as he often would for the next several years, that the law should be consistent for all parts of the state. He said, "I don't think limiting guns in a specific area limits the number of guns out there. What do we gain? Let's do something serious about gun control."[23] He didn't mention, however, what that might be.

A proposal in the senate sponsored by Jet Banks to exempt Kansas City and St. Louis from state gun laws failed overwhelmingly by a vote of 24 to 7. Phil Curls, D–Kansas City, commented, "Not allowing local control is just surprising to me. The size of the vote shows the continuing influence of the NRA."[24] While legislators who opposed the proposal denied the NRA and its members lobbied them to vote against the bill, they all made the same argument opposing it, which was very similar to what the NRA often said about local gun laws. Such legislators claimed that having different laws in different parts of the state would be confusing for their constituents and would inevitably lead some to unwittingly break the law as they traveled from one part of the state to another.[25]

As the legislative session drew to a close in 1994, Governor Carnahan admitted defeat—his attempt to bring more gun law freedom to St. Louis and Kansas City had failed. In an interview with the Associated Press he suggested that the reason special exemptions for Kansas City and St. Louis had failed was because the opposition was directed by the NRA.[26] Although he'd lost on the preemption issue, 1994 wasn't a year of total defeat for the governor. The 1994 session of the General Assembly was the legislative equivalent of a draw. While attempts to strengthen gun control in St. Louis and Kansas City failed, conceal-and-carry failed as well.

The Ballot Box, 1994

If the NRA's record in the 1994 legislative session was mixed, its record in the 1994 election season was very impressive. Nationally, the group certainly contributed to the "Republican Revolution," which gave the GOP majorities in both houses of Congress for the first time in forty years. It was an election in which the NRA's major objective was to punish legislators around the country for supporting the Brady Bill, passed in 1993, and the assault weapons ban, passed in 1994.

In Missouri, the group worked to save its longtime ally in Missouri, Democrat Harold Volkmer, the nine-term representative of the Ninth Congressional District, whose reelection was even closer than in 1992. Volkmer fought a losing battle against the assault weapons ban passed in 1994, but his efforts earned him praise and privilege from the NRA. As one reporter observed, "An NRA official once called Volkmer the 'Cadillac' of gun-backers in Congress. He has bagged hefty campaign contributions and expenses-paid trips from the NRA and, since 1987, he has been a board member of the Firearms Civil Rights Legal Defense Fund, which has worked closely with the NRA to help defend some gun owners."[27] Early in the campaign, Volkmer was again challenged by the populist Republican from the University of Missouri, Rick Hardy. Hardy was forced to drop out of the race due to medical problems, however, and was replaced by a prosecutor from the state attorney general's office, Kenny Hulshof. While Volkmer again managed to hang on in 1994, thanks in part to a nasty negative ad suggesting Hulshof wasn't an effective prosecutor, the end of his political career was obviously near—had the Republican candidate not changed abruptly in the middle of the race, it seems very likely Volkmer would have lost. His victory is almost certainly attributable to the fact that Hulshof had just four months to campaign and was simply not well known outside of his home territory of Columbia and surrounding Boone County.

Two other elections are noteworthy from 1994 because they involved key players in the early skirmishes over conceal-and-carry. First was the race for Missouri's open U.S. Senate seat, which was being vacated by John Danforth. On the Democratic side, there were a number of candidates for the party nomination in the early stages of the campaign. One early strong contender was St. Louis City Councilwoman Geri Rothman-Serot, who had campaigned against Kit Bond for the U.S. Senate in 1992. She dropped out of the 1994 race in late May, however, arguing that raising huge amounts of money had become more important than choosing the best qualified person to serve. This left the Democrats with no St. Louis–based candidates.[28] One of the remaining candidates was Steve Carroll, who had proposed conceal-and-carry in the Missouri House in 1994. Guns were a topic for discussion during the primary campaign season and Carroll, from the out-state community of Hannibal, defended his stance on the issue quite vigorously. During one candidate forum that took place while his legislation was still alive in the Missouri house, Carroll defended conceal-and-carry against attacks from his opponents. He said, "I don't support gun control for law-abiding citizens."[29] Carroll's candidacy was not long-lived, however. In June he announced he was dropping out of the race for the Democratic nomination for U.S. Senate and instead declared his candidacy for the seat of a recently deceased Missouri state senator, Norman Merrell, a Democrat. While Carroll remained in that race until the August primary vote, he lost the nomination to Joe Maxwell, from Mexico, who went on to win the general election in November. When Carroll dropped out of the U.S. Senate race, the Democratic field was dominated by U.S. Representative Alan Wheat and Jackson County Executive Martha Murphy, who had similar positions on gun control.

The race was ultimately a contest between John Ashcroft, the Republican nominee, and Wheat, from Kansas City, the Democratic nominee. Ashcroft, of course, was a former two-term governor, as well as having served as state auditor for two years and state attorney general for eight. Wheat was a former state legislator and had served in Congress since 1982. It was an ugly race, filled with charges and counter-charges the candidates leveled against each other from August to November about unethical behavior, dishonesty, and questionable policies.

While Ashcroft had moved to suburban St. Louis after leaving the governor's mansion in 1992 to practice law, he tailored his campaign to take advantage of his roots in southwest Missouri and appeal to out-state voters. Wheat, on the other hand, was an African American from Kansas City who clearly built his campaign around winning in St. Louis and Kansas City and hoping he could collect some rural votes. Not surprisingly in a campaign with candidates divided along this urban-rural line, guns were a campaign issue. Wheat supported gun control and in 1993 he voted for the Brady bill, which imposed a five-day waiting period on gun purchases, and for a thirty-billion-dollar anti-crime bill in 1994, which included a ban on assault weapons. This drew the financial support of Handgun Control, Inc., the organization led by Sarah and James Brady.[30] In late October 1994, just before the election, the Bradys traveled to Missouri to endorse Wheat, taking the opportunity to criticize John Ashcroft as well.[31]

For his part, John Ashcroft was endorsed and supported financially by the NRA.[32] Throughout the campaign, Ashcroft distinguished himself from Wheat as being strongly against crime involving guns, but protective of the right of law-abiding citizens to own guns. Wheat, he claimed, had often voted against tough anti-crime bills in his career in Congress. For instance, one of the hottest issues decided by Congress in 1994 was an anti-crime bill proposed by President Clinton that included, among other things, a ban on nineteen different assault weapons. Ashcroft criticized Wheat's support for the bill, claiming Wheat had personally contributed to a bill that was much weaker than it could have been. Ashcroft's campaign released a statement that listed several votes Wheat made in the House Rules Committee that Ashcroft claimed weakened the bill. Ashcroft's statement read, in part, "This crime bill is not tough enough on convicted career criminals . . . Every election year Congress slaps together a crime bill in Washington so they can come home and talk tough."[33] In response, Wheat called Ashcroft an ally of the NRA and said, "If John Ashcroft were in the Senate today, he would be joining his do-nothing friends Jesse Helms and Phil Gramm in opposing this bill . . . Missourians want leadership, not partisanship and politics-as-usual on fighting crime."[34] Ashcroft was, perhaps, put in a bit of an awkward spot by the fact that the man he was running to replace, John Danforth, supported the assault weapons ban when Ashcroft did not. Danforth endorsed Ashcroft, but when the assault weapons ban finally made its way through Congress after a protracted fight, many wanted to know what interaction had taken place between Danforth and Ashcroft regarding the legislation. For his part, Danforth admitted that Ashcroft tried to contact him prior to a critical procedural vote in which Danforth and five other Republicans defected and voted with the Democrats, but claimed he had not returned the call.[35] Needless to say, Wheat jumped on the apparent disagreement between the two Republicans and went out of his way to praise Danforth for his action supporting the bill. Wheat's campaign released a statement that read, in part, "One senator exhibiting leadership today was retiring Sen. John Danforth, who stood with Wheat in support of this critical legislation."[36]

Wheat was not well known throughout the state, and the senatorial election was very lopsided, with Ashcroft winning by a margin of 60 percent to 36 percent.

A second race of note was the contest for state auditor, which pitted ten-year incumbent Republican Margaret Kelly against none other than Steve Danner.

Danner was reaching the end of his first term in the state senate, after eight years in the Missouri house. During the campaign, Danner was sure to point out his support for conceal-and-carry as a senator. This was intended, no doubt, to serve two purposes. First, it put him on the record for voters around the state as a supporter of the right to carry. Second, it was meant to show that he was not a person at the beck and call of Governor Carnahan, for whom he had once worked.[37] Ultimately, Danner was not much of a threat to Kelly, and he lost the vote 39 percent to 58 percent, in addition to being forced to give up his seat in the senate, since he had opted not to run again for that job. It was not the end of his campaigning, however.

While the NRA was tremendously successful in influencing the 1994 congressional elections, it was still smarting from its legislative losses in Congress in 1993 and 1994, and it began 1995 eager to gain back some of the ground it had lost. Naturally, the place to do that was at the state level, in capitals like Jefferson City.

Chapter Five

Conceal-and-Carry—1995

In late 1993, the NRA lost its fight against the Brady bill in the U.S. Congress. In May of 1994, the group lost again when Congress passed a ban on certain types of assault weapons. It was then that the organization redoubled its election efforts, far outspending the $2.7 million it spent nationally in the 1992 election and contributing in a real way to the Republican revolution of 1994. This success at the national level buoyed the NRA and in 1995 the group redoubled its efforts to pass conceal-and-carry laws in many states, including Missouri and its neighbor, Kansas. One spokesman for the NRA referred to the effort as "part of a new front" to get states to change their restrictions against the right to carry.[1] Why the new energy at the state level? Because the group felt it could legitimately claim it had real power in elections and that politicians would be persuaded that this was true by the group's record of success in 1994. The NRA predicted that state legislators would not be able to resist the political pressure the group could bring to bear, and when several states adopted conceal-and-carry legislation in 1995, it seemed the organization was right.

In Missouri, there was a strong push for concealed weapons in 1995. However, as much as supporters of conceal-and-carry said 1995 was the year it would pass, Governor Carnahan was just as adamant that it would not and promised to veto any such bill. Despite the clear signals being sent by the NRA about its state agenda, supporters of conceal-and-carry again went out of their way to argue that this was a homegrown issue, not the work of the NRA. Of course, the veracity of this claim was diminished by the fact that, once again, the national organization sent a lobbyist from Washington, John Hosford, to Jefferson City to monitor conceal-and-carry throughout the session.

To foster the image of a homegrown fight, the group that publicly lobbied the hardest for conceal-and-carry in 1995 was the Missouri Legislative Issues

Council, led by the longtime advocate John Ross and a private investigator named Tim Oliver. The group was described by Oliver as an umbrella organization representing thirteen gun groups with up to thirty-five thousand members in Missouri. At the end of the long fight over conceal-and-carry in 1995, one of the main sponsors of the year's conceal-and-carry bill, Harold Caskey, D–Butler, contributed a prickly defense of conceal-and-carry as a homegrown issue when he argued, "The NRA had nothing to do with this piece of legislation. They sent one guy here three days to lobby, and we ran him out of town."[2] This, of course, says nothing about what the NRA could do from long distance.

Though it ultimately failed, the issue came closer to passage in 1995 than it had in the past. Caskey's conceal-and-carry bill passed the state senate, but at a political cost that was too high for some ardent supporters of the right to carry. SB 176 was adopted by a vote of 25 to 7, but not before it was amended to include a referendum on the issue.[3] This meant conceal-and-carry would avoid the governor's veto but would require a vote of the people for final approval. Support for Caskey's bill grew after it was amended because a referendum served several purposes for different senators. First, putting the issue to a public vote was supported by opponents of conceal-and-carry who felt confident it would lose statewide. Second, it gave political cover to members who, while personally opposed to conceal-and-carry, feared the consequences of voting against the issue in a straight up-and-down roll call vote. Third, it was attractive to some supporters of conceal-and-carry as a way to avoid Governor Carnahan's promised veto of any bill creating the right to carry.

The NRA, however, was opposed to a referendum. The group and some other supporters of conceal-and-carry suggested a public vote would entail a costly campaign and urged the house to pass conceal-and-carry without a referendum.[4] While it seemed to some that a referendum was the only chance for success, the most ardent supporters in the legislature felt there were enough votes to override a gubernatorial veto.

When the senate passed its version of conceal-and-carry with a referendum, Representative Wayne Crump, D–Potosi, the sponsor of the conceal-and-carry bill in the house, HB 404, said he felt there was enough public support to pass conceal-and-carry in a statewide vote. But he was sympathetic to those who, like the NRA, did not want it to appear on the ballot. He said a referendum meant "There will have to be a lot of money spent on both sides," and agreed to try and strip the provision from the bill because the NRA was opposed. He said, "I'm not afraid of a referendum. It was my first thought to take it 'as is,'" but, he added "It's their decision. They know they're going to have to pay for the campaign."[5] The "they" he referred to was the NRA, and such an admission, of course, did great damage to claims that the effort to adopt conceal-and-carry was strictly a homegrown issue.

Although Senator Caskey and other supporters of conceal-and-carry continued to claim that the NRA had nothing to do with the bill, the organization clearly had an important influence on the legislature. For the NRA, a referendum was their least-preferred option; therefore, the legislature didn't call for one. In part, the NRA was opposed because it would be a very expensive campaign. Kevin Jamison, a spokesman for the Western Missouri Shooters Alliance and a supporter of the right to carry, said that participation by the NRA would be essential if the legislature insisted on making conceal-and-carry a referendum. Referring to the NRA, he said, "If we're going to raise millions of dollars we'll have to ask them to come into this thing."[6] Certainly, the NRA preferred to avoid such an expense if possible. The NRA wanted to use its money to help elect sympathetic politicians.

The likely expense was also acknowledged by opponents of conceal-and-carry. Tim Jackson, the executive director of the Missouri Police Chiefs' Association, a group opposed to conceal-and-carry, said, "Supporters of concealed weapons have indicated they will raise $4 million—eight to 10 times what we'll raise."[7] The price tag of a referendum didn't scare the opponents of conceal-and-carry away, however; they saw a public vote as the way to eliminate the issue once and for all.

At the national level, HCI supported a referendum in Missouri, believing that concealed weapons would fail in a statewide vote, and there was public opinion data to suggest they were correct. For example, a poll conducted by the *St. Louis Post-Dispatch* found that 60 percent of St. Louis residents opposed conceal-and-carry legislation; statewide it was opposed by 56 percent of poll respondents.[8] While HCI lacked the resources of the NRA, it sent its celebrity spokesperson, James Brady, into the fray. Brady contacted legislators, urging them to support a public referendum. Newly elected Senator Joe Maxwell, D–Mexico, who went on to become the lieutenant governor in 2000, reported receiving a phone call from Brady. Maxwell said, "That did surprise me, but I pay more attention to my constituents."[9] In addition to making phone calls, Brady also visited Missouri. Speaking at a press conference at St. Louis Children's Hospital, Brady said a vote of the people would be the best way "[t]o give this bad idea a proper burial," and added, "The last thing the NRA wants is for voters in Missouri to decide the issue."[10] As Brady lobbied, the legislature continued to consider the issue.

If Crump was successful in redrafting the senate's bill to remove the referendum from the conceal-and-carry bill in the house, senators opposed to concealed weapons promised to prevent a final vote on the bill when it was returned to the senate. No opponent was more outspoken than Jet Banks, who feared conceal-and-carry would put more guns on the street, which would inevitably cause more violent crime in his district. Banks said, "I'd do anything to kill the bill. I'd certainly use whatever power I have."[11] Banks had long demonstrated a willingness to do anything to keep more guns out of his district, and he was in a fighting mood in 1995. Banks was not alone in his opposition to conceal-and-carry, of course. There were several senators, especially those from the St. Louis and Kansas City areas, who stood in the way of conceal-and-carry. One constituency that was opposed to granting citizens the right to carry was the Missouri Police Chiefs' Association, which remained opposed to the idea throughout the Showdown. The group's lobbyist, Tim Jackson, perhaps went too far when, at one point during the 1995 session, he suggested that supporters of conceal-and-carry had an anti-government attitude similar to the Oklahoma City bombers. This inspired an angry response from Caskey, who insisted many police supported conceal-and-carry, ". . . contrary to what that idiot who lobbies for the chiefs said."[12]

Early in the session, as Caskey's bill was being debated by the senate, the senators rejected an amendment proposed by Banks that would have allowed St. Louis, St. Louis County, and Kansas City to write their own concealed weapons laws. It was a repeat of the bill he'd introduced in 1994 and was simply unpalatable to many senators. As they always did, opponents of Banks's proposal argued that any conceal-and-carry law needed to be the same across the state to avoid confusing citizens. As he had in 1994, the president pro tem, Jim Mathewson, argued that it would be too difficult to enforce different gun laws for different counties.[13] Banks fought for his proposal, saying, "I do not want concealed weapons in the city of St. Louis where I live," and adding that if the rest of the state wanted them, they should leave St. Louis out of the plan.[14] Banks's determination to keep conceal-and-carry out of St. Louis didn't end with the defeat of his amendment. As the house began to consider the senate's referendum bill, he made it clear he would do whatever he could to kill any bill that didn't include a referendum.

Senator Banks's promise ensured the debate would be divisive. As the days of the 1995 legislative session drew to an end, the referendum became central in the debate about conceal-and-carry. First, Representative Crump was able to get the conceal-and-carry bill passed in the house without a referendum provision. The bill was then returned to the senate, where it required a new vote approving the change.

Earlier in the session, Senator Caskey added a referendum provision to his bill because he believed it was necessary to ensure its passage. However, he didn't really support a statewide vote and by the time the house returned a version of the bill without a referendum, Caskey was dead set against re-inserting it. This set up a clash between two powerful, immovable senators, Caskey and Jet Banks. The first action taken when the bill returned to the senate was a vote calling for a conference committee to iron out the differences between the house and senate versions of the bill, namely the referendum provision. Opponents of conceal-and-carry could see two positive outcomes of a conference committee. First, with only three days remaining in the session, there was a very good chance the committee would run out of time and the bill would not reemerge. Second, even if the committee acted quickly, opponents of conceal-and-carry believed a referendum would be reinserted as part of a compromise bill because Representative Crump had never been averse to holding a public vote. Either of these outcomes would save the governor the trouble of vetoing a gun bill.

Caskey, of course, was opposed to a conference committee for exactly the same reason. First, he had never really supported a referendum even though he had acceded to one in the senate bill earlier in the session, and second, he felt a conference would mean certain death for the bill because there wasn't enough time in the session for negotiators to work out a compromise and get it back to both houses for a vote.[15] As a result of Caskey's and others' opposition, the senate was split evenly down the middle, 17 to 17, on the motion to call for a conference committee. The tie brought Lieutenant Governor Roger Wilson, whose constitutional duty was to break ties in the senate, into the picture. Wilson, a Democrat and theoretically an ally of the governor, surprised everyone when he voted against a conference committee.

Wilson's decision angered many opponents of conceal-and-carry, including the governor, because they felt that, one way or another, a conference committee bill would kill conceal-and-carry, either by taking up the rest of the session or by resulting in a bill with a referendum that the voters of Missouri would reject. Such a loss at the voting booth, many opponents felt, would put an end to conceal-and-carry once and for all. Explaining his vote, Wilson argued he was simply trying to force the senate to write a tougher, more restrictive bill and that by making himself the key vote that kept it in the senate, he was giving himself extra leverage and promising that the issue wasn't finished.[16] Governor Carnahan expressed his irritation and said he was disappointed in the pivotal vote by his fellow Democrat. When asked whether Wilson was still an ally, Carnahan said, "He is a friend. The consistency of his support is somewhat in question."[17] After this vote, the bill was again open for debate in the senate, and supporters of conceal-and-carry seemed confident they were about to win. For instance, Tim Oliver, from the Missouri Legislative Issues Council, promised that the bill was very close to passage.[18]

With only three days remaining in the session, however, time was short following the failed conference committee vote, and Jet Banks increased the pressure by immediately beginning a filibuster. He took the floor wearing a gun belt and two toy pistols, reciting Bible passages and promising to take up the remaining fifty-one hours of the session rather than let the senate approve conceal-and-carry without a referendum.[19] Banks had worn the pistols on several occasions during the session and he seemed to revel in the chance to bring things to a standstill. Starting a filibuster with so little time remaining was an unusual move for a majority leader, whose main job is to move legislation along, especially in the critical last hours of a session. As majority leader, Banks had procedural tools he could have used to block any further debate on the conceal-and-carry bill, but the flamboyant senator clearly wanted to make a statement. He was dramatic in his denunciation of the bill, saying that if conceal-and-carry were allowed to pass, it would lead to more violence, particularly in his own home city, St. Louis, where crime was already "... rampant as raindrops when it's raining."[20] Banks also promised that if his colleagues passed conceal-and-carry, they wouldn't be safe visiting St. Louis. He said, "I pity you walking in the city of St. Louis if you put more guns on the street. Your life is going to be in danger. I suggest you take out some more insurance."[21]

At one point during Banks's filibuster, President Pro Tem Mathewson grabbed one of Banks's toy guns and reportedly pointed it at his own head in frustration.[22] After three and a half hours in control of the floor, Banks relented and the senate moved on to other business for the rest of the day, but he promised to continue his filibuster if and when the body returned to the bill.

On Thursday, May 12, when the senate reconvened, Banks announced that he had received a death threat from a supporter of conceal-and-carry who was angry about the majority leader's obstruction of Caskey's bill. Outspoken supporters of conceal-and-carry found Banks's claim dubious. John Ross, for instance, characterized Banks's claim as a last-ditch effort to block conceal-and-carry. He said, "It was a desperate act by a desperate man."[23] Tim Oliver was angry when he said, "There was no threat ... That's a damnable lie."[24] Caskey, however, said he believed Banks. He said, "The senator is an honorable person. If he says his life was threatened, his life was threatened."[25] The threat appeared to prompt Caskey to give up his opposition to a conference committee, though it turned out to be a procedural sidestep that added to the weirdness of the final days of the session.

Caskey called for his fellow senators to approve the call for a conference committee as a way to send the message that the senate wouldn't tolerate threats against its members.[26] The vote to send the bill to a conference committee was unanimous, but when Caskey forwarded the request to the house, he deliberately sabotaged it by failing to attach the bill itself to the request, meaning the house received a request for a conference committee about nothing.[27] This was a technicality, but the devil is in the details and without a bill, there was nothing for a conference committee to work on, so the house rejected the request.

Caskey apparently did this because he feared the conference committee would reinsert the referendum. No doubt he knew that although Representative Crump engineered the passage of conceal-and-carry without a referendum in the house, he was willing to accept such a provision if it was the only way to move the bill forward. Crump said he felt Caskey prevented the bill from going to a conference committee because he knew that the house would agree to a statewide vote. He said that Caskey "knew if I ever got my sticky little fingers on it, I had the votes to pass it with the referendum on it," and Crump always felt comfortable that, given the opportunity, voters would adopt conceal-and-carry.[28] Members of the house staged an assault on the senate halfway through the day on Friday, May 13, demanding Caskey relinquish the bill, but this was to no avail.[29]

With no conference committee, the bill was stuck in the senate. With very little time remaining in the session, Caskey tried to push consideration of the bill without the referendum and Senator Banks again moved to filibuster, prompting Caskey to give up, knowing there were many other bills to finish in the remaining hours of the session.[30] As he spoke to the senate, Caskey said he had promised the supporters of conceal-and-carry he wouldn't let it go to a referendum and, for that reason, he was killing his own bill.[31] This put an end to conceal-and-carry for another year, but not before observers of the legislature were treated to one of the most entertaining, strange episodes in years. Of course, not everyone was amused, especially the supporters of conceal-and-carry, who saw Banks as the gun owner's enemy.

John Hosford, the NRA's lobbyist working Missouri at the end of the legislative session, placed the blame for conceal-and-carry's defeat squarely on Jet Banks and praised Harold Caskey, saying, "He went to the wall for the gun owners of Missouri."[32] Rather than admit defeat, supporters of conceal-and-carry put a positive spin on the outcome, taking comfort in the fact that the issue didn't come to a public vote. Tim Oliver said, "Our first goal was to pass a bill this year. Our second goal is to get a good, clean bill next year without a referendum" and suggested that more pressure could be brought to bear on legislators to act during an election year.[33] John Ross echoed Oliver when he suggested the fight would have bigger stakes in 1996. He asserted that the NRA would be much more active the next year and said, "We, in good faith have to let the NRA come in here with their full weight. That is their privilege."[34] In addition, John Hosford promised the bill would be back in 1996 and suggested that it would be a much less restrictive version, with fewer requirements for would-be concealed weapons permit holders.[35] It was as if Hosford was trying to say that opponents of conceal-and-carry would be punished for winning in 1995. Of course, comments like this ran directly against earlier claims that the NRA had no role to play in the Show-Me Showdown.

On the other side, opponents could breathe easier knowing conceal-and-carry was dead for at least a few months. They were, perhaps, disappointed that a referendum failed as a solution to the issue. One longtime, outspoken opponent of conceal-and-carry, Colonel Fred Mills, the superintendent of the Missouri Highway Patrol, criticized Caskey and others who opposed a referendum, saying, "I think they're afraid the citizens will tell us that [conceal-and-carry] isn't the solution."[36] As was true throughout the showdown, many media outlets, especially those in St. Louis and Kansas City, took an editorial position opposed to conceal-and-carry. For instance, at the end of the session, a strongly worded editorial in the *Kansas City Star* assessed the situation in this way: "In tones meant to sound ominous, a supporter of concealed weapons in Missouri direly predicted that the NRA would jump out of the bushes next year to push for a gun law. It was as though the NRA had given local yokels their chance in the recently adjourned state legislature. Now the NRA will move their big guns into Jefferson City."[37] The editorial clearly referred to Ross, and just as clearly rejected claims the NRA had been little more than interested observers during the 1995 session. As the legislators returned home for summer, the 1996 session was already shaping up to be as dramatic as 1995.

Of course, the champions of conceal-and-carry weren't the only ones promising 1996 would be a watershed year. Opponents were also outspoken about the importance of the session to come in 1996. Claire McCaskill, one of the most outspoken opponents of conceal-and-carry in 1995, said, "No one will ever convince me that more guns will mean more safety. Two guns in a situation will only increase the likelihood of bloodshed."[38] Governor Carnahan said, "I believe the concealed-weapons bill is a bad idea. I don't believe the people of Missouri are gong to be safer if that's permitted."[39] For 1995, conceal-and-carry was, once again, dead on arrival, but it rose from its grave in 1996, and as was true with almost every new year during the showdown, it had a little more momentum than the previous year.

Chapter Six

Conceal-and-Carry—1996:
Back for Another Try

In Missouri, supporters of conceal-and-carry began the year with enthusiasm. Once again, bills were introduced in both the houses of the General Assembly. The bills receiving the most attention were SB 679, sponsored by Senator Danny Staples, D–Eminence, and HB 1468, sponsored by conceal-and-carry's regular champion, Wayne Crump, D–Potosi. During the session, Crump dropped his bill in favor of HJR 63, a constitutional amendment. As debate wore on, SB 679 and HJR 63 came to share an important characteristic—both would require a vote by the public before conceal-and-carry became law.

As happened in 1995, opposition to a statewide vote on conceal-and-carry came from outside the state through the NRA and within Missouri from the Second Amendment Coalition and the Legislative Issues Council. Tim Oliver, from the Legislative Issues Council, argued a referendum was a bad way to address the issue. He suggested that government officials opposed to conceal-and-carry, such as Governor Carnahan, would unfairly use the power of their offices to campaign against a referendum. He further argued that organizations opposed to conceal-and-carry, such as the state Police Chiefs' Association, were supported by taxpayers' money, while proponents of concealed weapons would have to raise funds to pay for such a campaign. He said, "It would cost between $4 million and $6 million. We'd rather spend the money electing pro-gun candidates."[1] Opponents of conceal-and-carry, who tended to favor a public vote as a final solution to the problem, said the pro–conceal-and-carry groups opposed a referendum because they knew they'd lose.

Danny Staples's SB 679 would have required the Highway Patrol to issue permits to adults twenty-one and older who passed a criminal background check and took a sixteen-hour handgun safety course. In mid-March he spoke to members of the Second Amendment Coalition and the Legislative Issues Council at a rally and confidently predicted passage of his bill. As March progressed, however, he quickly came to believe his bill was doomed without a referendum. He argued that accepting a referendum vote might be the only way to get the votes needed to approve the proposal: "I'm not going to let the bill die in the senate because of a filibuster or endless debate over an amendment. If I see I don't have the votes to pass the bill without a referendum clause, I'll accept one."[2] In addition to believing that a referendum was necessary to get him enough votes in the senate, Staples also finally accepted a referendum amendment to the bill because, he said, the governor continued to threaten to veto conceal-and-carry bills.[3] A referendum would, of course, circumnavigate the governor's desk, leaving the veto power to the voters of Missouri.

Many opponents of conceal-and-carry believed they could win a public vote. Clarence Harmon, the former St. Louis police chief, had become chairman of the Missouri Coalition Against Concealed Weapons. "The NRA has repeatedly marched in Missouri over the last five years in an attempt to pass this ill-advised legislation," he said. "We have said all along that if put before the voters, this issue will be put down once and for all."[4] Harmon and others believed a public vote was the only way to get rid of conceal-and-carry. Of course, not every opponent of conceal-and-carry believed that a referendum was the solution to their problems. Some worried that conceal-and-carry could win a statewide vote, while others no doubt worried about the costs of a referendum campaign.

Meanwhile, the most influential proponents of conceal-and-carry, the NRA, continued to oppose a referendum, and their opposition turned out to be too much for Staples's bill. In the senate, legislators opposed to a referendum and those opposed to conceal-and-carry combined to defeat the bill by a vote of 17–16 in a preliminary "perfection" vote. "Perfection" is the point at which a bill is judged to be a finished product. If a bill passes its perfection vote, there may be further debate before the final vote on the bill, but perfection is a major step toward ultimate passage.

Time still remained in the legislative session after the perfection vote, and Staples defiantly suggested he would continue to fight for the bill with a referendum.[5] He vowed he would get the votes he needed to ensure passage of the bill. At that point, however, the NRA became even more public in its opposition to a referendum than it had previously.

With his reputation as both a power in the senate and as a stubborn, independent legislator, there was every reason to believe Staples when he vowed to continue the fight. To counteract Staples, the NRA took a direct approach and sent a letter to each of the state's senators, urging them not to support a referendum. Chip Walker, an NRA spokesman, explained the group's action and its opposition to a referendum: "We are no longer supporting the bill in its current form, and we don't want to get it reconsidered . . . We believe the side pushing the referendum is the gun-control side. We have seen this in other states. When they realize they don't have enough votes to kill the bill they start calling for a referendum."[6] The NRA's intent, of course, was to remind senators that in an election year it was never wise to challenge the group's will. The NRA claimed to have one hundred thousand members in Missouri at the time, while the Legislative Issues Council claimed to speak for "up to 35,000 members in Missouri" who could be counted on to get involved in election-year politics.[7] Would they punish politicians who supported a referendum the NRA and its surrogates opposed? The group certainly wanted politicians to believe that was true.

After the NRA's letter was distributed, Staples threw up his hands, pronounced the bill "dead," and said he had no intention of pursuing it further.[8] With several weeks left in the session, Staples could have continued the fight, but he said he was dropping the bill because he believed the NRA's active opposition to a referendum left him permanently short of the votes he needed for passage. In the aftermath of his proposal's defeat, Staples's attitude toward the NRA remained defiant. He said, "I'm not afraid of the NRA. They don't control my life."[9] He also asserted that although he was an outdoorsman and a gun owner, the group had never endorsed him. He wanted to make it clear, in other words, that he was not doing the NRA's bidding by dropping his gun bill; he was merely being a political realist.

Meanwhile, in the house, Wayne Crump put most of his energy into HJR 63, the conceal-and-carry constitutional amendment. Like Staples's bill, a constitutional amendment would have required a statewide vote. The NRA was as busy in the house as it was in the senate, and its behind-the-scenes attempt to get Crump to withdraw his constitutional amendment from consideration became public when Crump announced in April that the organization had been pressuring him. He said the organization asked him to withdraw the amendment because "an expensive campaign would dilute its focus on electing pro-gun legislators."[10] Unmoved by the NRA's concerns, Crump declined to withdraw his amendment, vowing he could get it passed by both the legislature and the people of Missouri, much as he had in 1995.

Crump's prediction of success proved to be too optimistic, however. His proposed constitutional amendment never made it out of the House Judiciary and Ethics Committee. It was defeated in the committee by a vote of 9 to 5 by what was described as "an unusual alliance between concealed-gun supporters and opponents."[11] The chair of the committee, Gary Witt, D–Platte City, said, "This will legitimately kill the resolution for the session."[12] Responding to the committee's action, Crump sounded defeated when he said, "That put an end to my opportunities. I'd say conceal-and-carry is dead—probably for the next four or five years."[13] While Crump was certainly correct that conceal-and-carry was dead for 1996, it certainly didn't go away for the next four or five years.

In 1996, supporters of conceal-and-carry played at least as big a role in killing Crump's and Staples's bills as opponents of conceal-and-carry, because the powerful gun lobby opposed a statewide vote. For yet another year, therefore, conceal-and-carry was a failed issue in the state legislature. Of course, the way it died in 1996 lent more evidence to the conclusion that while there was certainly support for conceal-and-carry within Missouri, it was the NRA that was calling the shots. In both 1995 and 1996 local supporters of conceal-and-carry deferred to the judgment of the NRA because, they asserted, that organization would have to pay the costs of a referendum campaign. It boiled down to the following: it's the NRA's money, so it's the NRA's decision.

The Vote, 1996

The 1996 presidential election year was surprisingly noncompetitive. At the end of 1994, Bill Clinton seemed merely to be marking time until the end of what would be one of the most mediocre one-term presidencies in American history. In November 1996, however, Clinton coasted to an easy reelection victory. He did this by co-opting Republican positions on crime prevention and welfare reform, winning a galactic public relations battle over the fiscal year 1996 budget with Newt Gingrich and the Republicans in Congress, and finding a way to spend Democratic party funds for his own reelection campaign in a way that allowed him to bury Bob Dole in advertising before the Republican senator officially secured his party's nomination. Finally, when Dole did emerge as the Republican nominee, the honored elder statesman was far from an effective candidate. He seemed unsure about his campaign strategy and was unable to overcome doubts about his advanced age.

Seeing the handwriting on the wall, many influential interest groups threw Dole to the wolves and concentrated on what they viewed as a much more important goal: keeping the Congress, especially the House of Representatives, in Republican hands. The 1996 election was viewed as critical by many conservatives because it was the first chance to solidify the Republicans' historic revolution of 1994. If the GOP could hold onto the House in 1996, it was believed they would keep it for many years to come. Acknowledging that

Dole was a weak candidate, many groups opted to focus on the congressional election instead because they saw it as more important for their long-term interests.[14]

For its part, the NRA was, once again, an active participant in election-year politics, both nationally and in Missouri. In 1996, Joan Kelly Horn, who the NRA helped defeat in 1992, attempted a political comeback in Missouri's Second Congressional District. Her opponent was the incumbent Republican, Jim Talent, who defeated her in 1992 and soundly defeated his Democratic challenger in 1994. Regardless, Horn felt Talent was vulnerable because he had only beaten her by nine thousand votes in 1992 and because there were many independent voters in the Second District.[15]

Before she was able to campaign against Talent, however, she had to win the Democratic nomination, and she had some surprising competition within the party. There were six Democratic candidates, including John Ross, the champion of conceal-and-carry. Ross's campaign was unusual for a few reasons, not the least of which was that he didn't even live in the Second District. It wasn't illegal for him to run for the Second District seat under Missouri law, but it was uncommon. To Horn, Ross's candidacy seemed like an obvious attempt to derail her campaign against Talent before it began. She asserted that Ross's real intent was to sabotage her campaign by calling for Republicans to cross party lines and vote against her in the open Democratic primary. She suggested that the NRA was behind Ross's campaign and asked, "Why are they mucking around in the Democratic primary for a guy who's not a Democrat and who doesn't live in the district?"[16] In support of Horn's charges, the NRA was certainly active during the primary campaign, a race that would usually be of little interest to the organization because in that district it would be expected to support the incumbent Talent, a reliable ally.

During the primary campaign, however, the NRA sent a mailing to residents of the Second District, explaining the finer points of primary election law. It informed voters that they could ask for any party's ballot in a primary election and urged Republicans to request a Democratic ballot and vote for Ross. Ross defended the NRA, saying the group was simply telling voters "that there is a Democrat running who respects civil rights."[17] Of course, it is easy to see why such action outraged Horn.

Throughout the campaign, Ross disputed Horn's assertion that he wasn't a real Democrat and he insisted his position on guns didn't disqualify him as a member of the party. Defending himself, Ross said something that is undoubtedly true about Missouri politics: "Anyone who thinks that the gun issue is a Republican-Democratic split is absolutely wrong. The facts show that there are strong supporters and sworn opponents in each party."[18] While Ross's observation certainly rang true, he had a bigger obstacle to overcome as he tried to convince the Democrats of the Second District he was a serious candidate: he had donated money to Talent in the past. This put him in the uncomfortable position of explaining why he now wanted to challenge Talent and contributed to the feeling that he wasn't a real Democrat but, rather, a Republican in donkey's clothing, merely trying to wreak havoc with the primary. Ross explained his decision to oppose Talent by asserting that the incumbent had proved to be too strongly in favor of government power over individual rights.[19]

Ross was a millionaire, and FEC records show he contributed sixty-eight thousand dollars to his own campaign, including fifty thousand the week before the election.[20] Perhaps this was to prove to Democrats he was a serious candidate. Despite this financial commitment, many leaders of the Democratic party in the district came to Horn's defense, calling her the only viable candidate and helping her to win the election. Of course, if Horn was right, the NRA had already succeeded by disrupting the Democrat's campaign and distracting Horn from her real opponent, Jim Talent. Unfortunately for Horn, the general election wasn't even close. Talent defeated her by the comfortable margin of 61.3 percent to 37.1 percent.

In the Sixth Congressional District, Representative Pat Danner faced a challenge in her Democratic primary, though it proved to be a minor bump in the road to reelection for the NRA's ally. Larry Kinnamon of St. Joseph, a former assistant prosecuting attorney and public defender, challenged the incumbent congresswoman for the party's nomination. Kinnamon was a strong gun-control advocate, which put him directly at odds with Danner.[21] The incumbent won her primary handily, however, and was easily reelected in November.

Back in Washington, Danner, along with several other centrist Democrats, enjoyed being a prize wooed by leaders of both the Democratic and Republican parties in the closely divided U.S. House of Representatives. The centrists hung together, forming their own voting coalition that averaged around twenty members, known as "The Coalition" or the Blue Dog Democrats. The Blue Dogs played key roles in bringing to an end the debate over the federal budget that caused the government to shut down in late 1995 and early 1996 and in the passage of the welfare reform legislation that created the Temporary Assistance for Needy Families program, popularly known as "workfare."[22] The Republicans held the House following the 1996 election, but with a slim majority of just thirty representatives, so the Blue Dog Democrats were a key bloc for both parties, as were a group of moderate Republican members, formed in November 1995, known as the Mainstream Conservative Alliance. Interestingly, the Mainstream Conservative Alliance, which was nicknamed the

Blue Dog Republicans, was formed, in part, under the leadership of another Missouri member of Congress, Bill Emerson, from southeast Missouri.[23] The fact that Emerson, an out-state Republican, and Danner, an out-state Democrat, were members of organizations positioning themselves in the same middle ground probably says a great deal about Missouri politics in general—on many issues, Missourians aren't divided by party nearly as much as they are by region.

Speaking of the Blue Dogs, Representative Danner said, "The people in America are in the middle. They're not talking out of one side of their mouth as liberal and one side as conservative. The vast majority are in the middle, and that's where the Blue Dogs have been."[24] Much as the centrist Democrats in the House of Representatives had helped advance President Reagan's agenda in the early 1980s, Republicans hoped the Blue Dogs could do the same for their agenda in the mid 1990s. By being one of the Blue Dogs, Danner made herself an important player, and she continued to be a valuable ally of the NRA.

An old NRA ally lost in 1996: Harold Volkmer. The handwriting had been on the wall for at least the two previous elections. Volkmer was defeated in Missouri's Ninth District by Kenny Hulshof, the prosecuting attorney who had challenged him on short notice in 1994. It is hard to say what impact Volkmer's loss may have had on the NRA. On the one hand, Hulshof proved to be a strong supporter of the organization's goals, so from that perspective, little changed. On the other hand, the group lost a powerful, senior Democrat who was unashamed to put his name out front and sponsor NRA legislation. There were certainly others who did the same for the organization, such as John Dingell, D–Michigan, but in a perfect world, the group would have preferred Volkmer's reelection. His loss was also a black mark on an electioneering record that was almost spotless for the NRA in 1996. The group's chief lobbyist at the time, Tanya Metaska, said that 92 percent of the legislators who opposed the assault weapons ban in 1994 had been reelected, with the help of the NRA. In losing, Volkmer was one of the few exceptions.[25] On the positive side for the NRA, Volkmer's defeat had nothing to do with gun rights, as many Ninth District constituents are rural voters who support gun rights. Volkmer's loss was due more to the fact that the district had largely shifted to the Republican party, following the natural evolution of many Missouri voters as they gave up their decades-long attachment to the Democrats. Perhaps it was also due to the fact that Volkmer was seen as being cozy with too many special interests, a charge Rick Hardy made effectively in 1992 and 1994.

The election in Missouri's Seventh District was also significant in 1996. The district is in Southwest Missouri and includes the cities of Springfield, Joplin, and Branson. The election was not noteworthy because it was especially close or because the NRA lost another friend. In fact, the election was really a passing of the torch from one powerful Republican to another. The incumbent, Mel Hancock, retired from office. Hancock is noteworthy because, as a Springfield businessman, he was largely responsible for the Hancock Amendment, a constitutional amendment that restricts the state government's ability to tax its citizens. Interestingly, the amendment became a major factor in the fate of conceal-and-carry in 2004, but in 1996, Representative Hancock was replaced by a veteran of state politics, Roy Blunt. Blunt served as Missouri's secretary of state before running for Congress and proved to be an immediate success in the U.S. House. In just six years Blunt rose through the ranks of the Republican party in Congress to become the majority whip, the third ranking position in the House. Blunt is also the father of Matt Blunt, who was elected Missouri's secretary of state in 2000 and its governor in 2004.

When the legislature came back in 1997, much of the debate about conceal-and-carry once again settled around the question of whether or not the issue should be settled by state legislators and the governor or by the people of Missouri. While there were many gun rights advocates who opposed such a vote, momentum was clearly building in the direction of a referendum.

Chapter Seven

Conceal-and-Carry—1997 to 1998:
Setting the Stage for Prop B

Guns were hot throughout the Midwest in 1997. Opponents of the right-to-carry in Missouri and its neighbors, Kansas and Illinois, all continued to hang tough against the NRA and its movement for conceal-and-carry. As the Missouri General Assembly began its 1997 session in Jefferson City, Governor Carnahan reiterated his promise to veto any concealed weapons legislation that landed on his desk. Not fazed by the governor's promise, Senator Peter Kinder, R–Cape Girardeau, promptly introduced two conceal-and-carry bills, SB 49 and SB 159, in January. SB 159 would have created the right to carry for anyone twenty-one or older who passed a criminal background check and received firearms training. The bill was reported out of the Senate Civil and Criminal Jurisprudence Committee in April, but it languished in limbo for several weeks, not making it onto the perfection calendar for debate and an initial vote until May 16, the end of the session.

SB 49 was more narrowly tailored and would have allowed only a select group of citizens the right to carry concealed handguns without a permit. The bill included retired judges, active and retired prosecutors, and retired police officers. The judges and prosecutors would have been required to take eight hours of firearms training before becoming eligible for a permit. Kinder explained the need for the bill, saying, "Those people need an immediate right of self-defense."[1] Kinder sincerely believed in the importance of granting this right of armed self-defense to current and former law enforcement officials and promised his fellow senators, especially Jet Banks, that the bill was completely separate from SB 159 and wouldn't be expanded to allow anyone else the right to carry. This bill could have saved a lot of time and energy had it passed into law. As the fight continued into 1998, 1999, and beyond, police officers emerged as major supporters of conceal-and-carry because they wanted retired officers to have the right to carry. Had Kinder's bill passed, it probably would have removed a major source of support from conceal-and-carry in future years.

The Senate Civil and Criminal Jurisprudence Committee combined Kinder's bill with five other bills to create SCS/SBs 49, 213, 130, 32, 235, and 221. The new bill included provisions making it illegal to evade a police officer, illegal to leave the scene of an accidental shooting, illegal to physically harm a police dog, and legal for law enforcement officers to arrest certain persons without a warrant. The bill received strong support in the state senate and was given final approval on April 17. It was then forwarded to the house, where it was rewritten into something entirely different from what Kinder promised his fellow senators.

Wayne Crump was again the champion of conceal-and-carry in the house, though he was true to his words of the year before—he did not sponsor a bill to grant the right-to-carry to all Missourians in 1997. Rather, he was a cosponsor of HB 45, which, like Senator Kinder's bill, would have granted an immediate right to carry to active and retired law enforcement officials. Crump's bill died in committee early in the legislative session, perhaps in anticipation of the arrival of the bill sponsored by Kinder in the senate. Granting the right to carry to all citizens didn't become an issue until the very end of the 1997 session, when the house took up Senator Kinder's bill, under the guidance of Representative Crump. SCS/SBs 49, 213, 130, 32, 235, and 221 was assigned to the House Correctional and State Institutions Committee, which rewrote the bill to give nearly all Missourians the right to apply for a permit to carry concealed firearms, despite Kinder's promise to his fellow senators that the bill would only apply to law enforcement officials. As substituted by the house, the bill would have compelled county sheriffs to grant concealed weapons permits to anyone twenty-one or older who passed a criminal background check, paid a one-hundred-dollar fee, and took a twenty-four-hour firearms safety course. This was, obviously, a much wider right to carry than the senate had approved, and it passed the full house by an overwhelming, veto-proof vote of 116 to 20. To make the bill more palatable to reluctant senators, the house substitute also included a referendum provision, meaning that the more general right to carry would require a vote of the people of Missouri. The referendum was to be held in April 1998.

Defending the bill, Crump said, "Conceal-and-carry is just another crime-fighting tool. The governor has almost sworn in blood that he'd veto it, so if we're serious about having this, a referendum is the way to go."[2] This argument was not terribly compelling in the senate, however, where the bill faced strong opposition for a couple of reasons. First, it broke Senator Kinder's promise to only give the right to carry to a select group of law enforcement personnel, and second, it faced renewed opposition from pro–conceal-and-carry forces who didn't want a referendum.

The NRA renewed its opposition to a statewide vote, once again because of what it expected to be the high cost of such a campaign. Fred Meyers, the NRA's Missouri representative, said, "There'd be no need to go to a referendum if the Legislature would just bite the bullet and make the hard vote. If it goes to a referendum, it will cost our members a lot of money, about $2 million."[3] The NRA's estimate was not pulled out of thin air. In 1997, as Missouri's legislature mulled the possibility of a referendum, the NRA was involved in a statewide campaign against a trigger-lock initiative in the state of Washington. In the Washington election, supporters of trigger locks spent $1.1 million, while the opponents, including the NRA, spent a total of $3.4 million. The NRA spent roughly $2 million, and while the group and its allies won by a margin of two to one, it was an expensive victory.[4] Clearly they hoped to achieve victory in Missouri with a cheaper price tag. The prospect of another election so soon after the Washington victory was unappealing to the NRA.

The house approved its substitute conceal-and-carry bill on May 14, with just three days left in the legislative session. The substitute was forwarded to the senate, where it was quickly rejected. The bill was then sent to a conference committee but there was simply not enough time left in the legislative session to negotiate the major differences between the two versions. Lacking the sort of overwhelming support in the senate that could have pushed the bill through at the last minute, it was doomed. Once again, conceal-and-carry legislation had to wait another year, but 1998 would be a year of significant movement.

• • •

The year 1998 was important for conceal-and-carry legislation. For the first time, both chambers adopted bills calling for a referendum. Political realists who supported conceal-and-carry finally concluded the only chance it had was to put it to a public vote, and they moved forward despite the continued opposition of pro–conceal-and-carry interest groups. At the same time, opponents of conceal-and-carry continued to believe a public vote was the only way to get rid of the issue once and for all. Referendum bills were introduced in both chambers in 1998. In the senate, Senator Caskey sponsored SB 960, which stalled in the Senate Civil and Criminal Jurisprudence Committee in March, just a week after it was introduced.

While Caskey's bill was stranded in committee, Representative Crump's HB 1891, which also called for a referendum, moved forward in the house. In committee hearings on the bill, representatives from many groups, including the St. Louis Police Officers Association, the Western Missouri Shooters Alliance, the Missouri Sport Shooters Association, and the Missouri Legislative Issues Council, all testified in favor of conceal-and-carry, but in opposition to a referendum. House records show the only supporter of conceal-and-carry who testified before the committee in favor of a referendum was Crump.

On the other hand, house records and press reports document that many supporters of the right to carry attended hearings asking the committee to legalize conceal-and-carry without a referendum.[5] Kevin Jamison, a longtime spokesman for the Western Missouri Shooters Alliance, said, "We are unalterably opposed to a referendum," while arguing that he represented grassroots supporters of the bill who merely wanted the chance to defend themselves.[6] As usual, the public objection to a referendum was the cost of a campaign, but as in years past there was also an underlying fear that conceal-and-carry would lose if left to the public. A pro–conceal-and-carry legislator, Representative Charles Ballard, R–Marshfield, expressed both a concern about cost and a fear of failure when he said, "My fear is, with a referendum, we will attract money from all over the United States, all types of bunny-hugging groups will pour money into this state and it will become a very volatile, emotional issue. It's my opinion that both groups are kind of ready for this showdown, and Missouri would be the battleground . . . It's an important issue, an important right—too much to risk in this type of campaign. It's like putting freedom of speech up for referendum."[7] Of course, if the NRA was unable to once again keep conceal-and-carry out of the voting booth, it was certainly expected the organization would campaign vigorously to win the public's votes.

As the end of the 1998 session drew near, Crump's referendum bill moved through the house, first gaining approval from the House Correctional and State Institutions Committee by a vote of 8 to 5. The bill then passed an initial voice vote in the house with just three weeks remaining in the session. Crump admitted publicly that time was against him, but he was determined to beat the clock and worked fast to push the bill through the legislature. As time ran out, he continued to argue that a referendum was the only way to succeed in passing conceal-and-carry, in large measure because the governor had promised to veto it if he had the chance. Crump suggested that while the NRA was opposed to a public referendum, the organization had also promised financial support for a campaign. He further argued that the NRA's own public opinion data showed 59 percent of Missourians favored conceal-and-carry and there was no reason to believe a referendum would fail.[8]

As it began to seem more likely a referendum bill would pass, the NRA tried to establish a position of neutrality on the question of a public vote after years of vocal opposition. On the other side, opponents of conceal-and-carry seemed eager for the voters to decide. Andy Krakowski, a spokesman for HCI, echoed the NRA's concerns about the cost of a referendum campaign in Missouri, but like other opponents, he certainly felt a statewide vote provided the best chance to defeat conceal-and-carry.[9] HCI's symbolic leader, James Brady, expressed a similar view during his visit to Missouri in 1997.

The referendum bill received final approval in the house on April 29 with a vote of 113 to 32. As the bill was forwarded to the senate, the NRA accepted the reality of a public vote on conceal-and-carry and Crump was able to argue, "They are 100 percent for the bill."[10] Of course, in giving up its opposition to a referendum and becoming firmly committed to a campaign, the NRA abandoned any remaining claim that it wasn't deeply involved in Missouri's politics.

Crump's bill was quickly approved by a 5 to 0 vote in the Senate Criminal Jurisprudence Committee and went to consideration by the full senate, where the bill was approved by a final vote of 26 to 8. Pro–concealed weapons legislators decided to accept the referendum idea, concluding it was the only way to avoid a gubernatorial veto, and the anti-gun senate majority leader, Jet Banks, decided to forgo his usual tactic of delay and filibuster because he believed conceal-and-carry would fail if left to the voters. Nearly a year later, however, he appeared to have buyer's remorse, expressing regret in late March 1999 as the vote approached. He seemed to sense the referendum was going to pass and said he wished he had used another filibuster to kill the legislation.[11]

While a majority of legislators were resigned to a public vote, there was still contention about when to hold the referendum. Opponents of conceal-and-carry wanted the vote to coincide with the November election in 1998, while proponents wanted a separate election. Traditionally, turnout in state or local elections that don't coincide with federal elections is quite low, rarely exceeding 30 percent. Even in the United States' highest-profile elections, when citizens elect presidents, turnout has leveled off at roughly 50 percent for the past thirty years.

Representative Crump was determined that the election be low profile. He originally chose an August 1998 date and then agreed to April 1999. Crump freely admitted that he wanted the vote to be held at a time that would lead to low voter turnout, assuming that would work to the advantage of the highly motivated forces in favor of conceal-and-carry. William Lacy Clay, Jr., a state senator from St. Louis at the time, argued that the vote should be held in November 1998, when turnout would be higher. "You'll get a better indication of how Missourians actually feel. In an April election, either side can artificially influence the outcome to make sure their constituents get to the polls."[12] When turnout is very low, it means that concerned interest groups can have a genuine impact on the outcome of an election. One often sees this effect in low-profile elections, and just as interest groups that offer individual gains to members are more successful than public interest groups, voters are more likely to be motivated to turn out when they see the potential for personal gain such as winning the right to carry concealed weapons. Many thought that the goal of denying others that right was much more amorphous and, therefore, less motivating to spur turnout for a low-profile April election. There are many examples of low-turnout elections that have been tilted by dedicated, ideologically driven minorities. During the 1990s, for example, school board elections were heavily influenced by socially conservative interest groups such as the Christian Coalition. Voters who are more motivated than the average citizen truly can make a difference in low-profile elections, and it is a lesson that was well understood by the supporters of conceal-and-carry.

If the conceal-and-carry election were held in April 1999, it would be one of only two statewide issues on the ballot. No statewide officials were being chosen, and there was certainly every reason to believe that highly motivated interest groups such as the NRA would make a difference. Ultimately, Crump prevailed, and the election was scheduled for April 6, 1999, making Missouri the first—and only—state to try to adopt conceal-and-carry through a referendum. It was called Proposition B on the ballot. Prior to the vote, Bekki Cook, the Missouri secretary of state, predicted a voter turnout of just 25 percent, or nine hundred thousand voters, which was exactly the kind of low turnout Representative Crump wanted because he assumed that voters wanting conceal-and-carry would be more motivated to vote than those who opposed it.[13] The great unknown factor, however, was that there would also be local city government and school board elections on ballots throughout the state at the same time. This meant Prop B and isolated, hotly contested local elections in certain parts of the state might interact with each other to influence turnout and the fate of Prop B. What Crump accomplished by getting the date set for April 6 was to pick an election where turnout is generally low and the outcome can be controlled by a core group of passionate voters.

As adopted by the legislature, HB 1891 established the requirements for obtaining a permit, directed government officials to issue permits to all who qualified, and included the wording to be used for the question on the ballot. If passed, HB 1891 would have allowed all citizens over the age of twenty-one to apply to their county sheriff for a permit to carry a concealed weapon. The law would have required that applicants be Missouri residents for at least six months, pay an eighty-dollar fee to their county sheriff, and complete a twelve-hour firearms safety course. The permit holder would have to renew her permit every three years, for a thirty-five-dollar fee. Before issuing a permit, sheriffs would have been required to run background checks and deny a permit to anyone who was 1) habitually intoxicated; 2) a drug abuser; 3) mentally ill or incompetent; 4) dishonorably discharged from the military; 5) a fugitive from the law; 6) convicted of a crime punishable by more than a year's imprisonment; or 7) guilty of exhibiting or threatening violent behavior within the previous five years. Those convicted of misdemeanors punishable by a term of two years or less would have been able to get a permit, provided their crime did not involve the use of a firearm. The bill would have made it illegal to carry concealed weapons into any church, school, polling place, or government office. In addition, any business owner would be allowed to post a "no guns" sign by the entrance, though the penalties for disobeying such signs were light. Finally, the law would have provided the sheriff or a court the right to revoke a permit if the holder a) no longer met its requirements; b) lied during the application process; or c) was later found guilty of stalking, domestic violence, or reckless endangerment with a firearm.[14] All of these provisions, including the wording of the ballot question, became subjects for debate during the Prop B campaign.

Before the Prop B vote in April 1999, however, there was the November 1998 election. The 1998 midterm election season brought one interesting, if not particularly close, campaign. The Second District congressman, Jim Talent, faced off against the gun advocate John Ross, who managed to win the Democratic nomination in 1998 after losing to Joan Kelly Horn in 1996. The fact that Ross won the nomination in 1998 reflected the increasing conservatism in the Second District, the lack of motivation among more mainstream Democrats in the district, or both. However Ross managed to win the nomination, the Democratic party did little to support his campaign. After all, Ross was, as the press described him, "a gun owners' advocate with libertarian views," which was not the picture of a mainstream Democratic candidate.[15] In addition, the Democrats likely understood Talent was a safe Republican who was simply not beatable.

Perhaps confirming the suspicions of those who doubted Ross's ideological bona fides as a Democrat, Ross often suggested during the campaign that Talent was too fiscally liberal and that he was allowing a "continued increase in federal power over our lives."[16] Clearly, these were not words one expected from a Democratic challenger. Ross's criticisms of Talent struck many as odd because throughout Talent's career, most of the congressman's political opponents had charged he was too conservative.[17] On some social issues, Ross was more in line with mainstream Democrats. For example, he believed abortion should remain legal, but overall, his campaign emphasized conservative ideals to such an extent that it was difficult to take him seriously as a Democrat. Throughout the campaign Ross advocated policies that, two years later, would have fit nicely into the campaign playbook of President Bush, such as the privatization of Social Security. He also argued for less government regulation of business and lower taxes.

In his responses to a *St. Louis Post-Dispatch* candidate questionnaire, Ross wrote, "American enterprise is the envy of the world, whole state-run industries in other countries bleed red ink. Our success is due to our freedom. I will fight to preserve that freedom by opposing new restrictions and new taxes on our entrepreneurs and on our citizens as a whole. Industries who must satisfy paying customers in the free market will always make better decisions than government committee."[18] The responses of the Libertarian candidate in the race, Brian K. Lundy, make for an interesting comparison. Lundy wrote that to ensure a strong U.S. economy he would fight to "Repeal all government rules, regulations, restrictions, and mandates that stifle or prevent small businesses from starting or growing. End government subsidies at all levels and let the market work."[19] Comparing the two candidates' words reveals little difference between them. Interestingly, Talent's statement was similar to both, but was more positive about the role of the federal government. He wrote, "Our economy is doing well because of the ingenuity and productivity of the American people. The federal government has helped mostly by moving toward policies that have encouraged economic growth."[20] Whereas Ross and Lundy both derided the federal government, Talent pointed to it as a crucial contributor to a healthy economy. One suspects that no matter which of the three candidates won, voters would have gotten very similar policy positions from their congressional representative.

Incumbency served Talent well, as did the fact that Ross simply failed to energize the members of the Democratic party with his conservative ideology. Talent defeated Ross by a margin of 70 percent to 30 percent. Meanwhile, across the state, Patricia Danner easily won reelection in the Sixth District. She received 71 percent of the vote and seemed destined to hold the seat for as long as she wished.

In Missouri, however, the elections of 1998 were merely prelude to the Prop B campaign of 1999. Advocates on both sides were prepared for an all-out fight, and an all-out fight is what they got, both from within and from outside of the state.

Chapter Eight

The Campaign of 1999—An Introduction

The first four months were filled with loud, sometimes fear-filled, sometimes angry rhetoric. As the *Springfield News-Leader* described it, both sides swamped voters with statistics and reasons to be scared, either about how dangerous it was not to be armed, or how dangerous it would be if everyone was armed.[1] Similarly, the *Kansas City Star* predicted a campaign that would be costly and emotional, designed to play on people's fears. The ongoing debate was described as "hyperbole."[2] One opponent of the bill, Rick Cook, the director of the Kansas City Metropolitan Crime Commission, went so far as to claim that the vote was a battle for the soul of Missouri.[3] Even the names of the organizations created to run the campaigns evoked something beyond a simple question of "to carry or not to carry." On the pro–Prop B side was Missourians Against Crime (MAC), implying that unless conceal-and-carry passed, the residents of the Show-Me State would invite an age of lawlessness. On the anti–Prop B side was the Safe Schools and Workplaces Committee (SSWC), suggesting that if Prop B passed, mass shootings would begin taking place on a daily basis.

As 1999 began, Missourians prepared to do what no state had ever done before: hold a statewide vote on concealed guns. To impartial observers, the energy expended on the Prop B campaign and in the many years of debate leading up to it may seem silly or at least unusual. It wasn't as if Prop B would raise the poor from poverty, or eliminate the state income tax, or something equally dramatic; it was simply a gun law. That didn't mean, however, that Missourians had no interest in the outcome of the election. If people were mystified by the political rancor that accompanied the long fight over concealed weapons it was because they failed to understand Missouri's complex political culture. Missouri has always been a strange mix of Eastern civility and

Western daring, Midwestern Progressivism and Southern states' rights. During the country's adolescence, when many adventurous Americans went west to seek their fortunes, St. Louis was the edge of the civilized world and everything beyond it was the wild unknown. During the Civil War, Missouri was truly a state divided. Many Missourians remained loyal to the Union, and approximately one hundred thousand Missourians fought with the Union Army. At the same time, however, many other Missourians sympathized with the Confederacy, and roughly fifty thousand Missourians fought for the South. It is a state with both a strong rural tradition, where guns are a part of the cultural fabric, and urban environments where guns are viewed as the cause of crime and violence. For many Missourians, therefore, the fight over guns was a fight over the most important things—culture, values, and beliefs.

The NRA clearly felt the stakes were very high, and as promised, the group opened its checkbook, contributing an early seventy-five thousand dollars to MAC in January 1999. MAC's campaign was managed by Fred Meyers, who repeatedly pointed out that the stakes were very high, not just for Missourians but for all Americans. In January Meyers said, "Missouri will be somewhat of a bellwether for a lot of these other states. It's high stakes for everybody involved. Some people have termed it as the last great gun battle of the millennium. The folks who come out on top on this one will have the upper hand going into the future."[4] Meyers reiterated this theme four months later on the day before the vote when he said, "Since this is the first time it's ever been put to a vote, both sides on this issue are going to learn a tremendous amount. This will be a race that political scientists and pundits will mull for years, because it's breaking such new ground."[5] The rhetoric sounded overly dramatic, but given the amount of time, money, and energy that was put into the campaign, many people clearly shared Meyers's sentiment.

For both sides, the debate largely boiled down to a battle of statistics. The pro-gun side claimed that concealed gun permits led to reductions in crime in every state that allowed them. Steve McGhee, president of the pro-gun group Missourians for Personal Safety, argued conceal-and-carry had a chilling effect on criminals and that they could produce data to prove it. He said, "Right-to-carry puts a question mark in their minds. They can't assume their next victim is helpless."[6] On the other side, opponents of conceal-and-carry claimed that allowing ordinary law-abiding citizens to carry concealed guns would lead to more violent crime, in the form of crimes of passion such as road rage and in instances where law-abiding citizens lost their guns in struggles with criminals. Like the pro-gun side, the opponents were able to present convincing statistics to back up their arguments. It was impossible, of course, for either side to convince the other that it was making a mistake. Dedicated advocates of guns and the ardent opponents of guns were immovable, and they both fought to make Missourians in the middle see the light. Once and for all, both sides hoped, the public would decide this question, not the legislature.

A Word about Direct Democracy

While some politicians use initiatives and referenda as convenient ways to avoid tough decision-making, as the legislators in the cash-strapped states of Oregon and Alabama did when they left tough choices about tax increases up to the voters in 2003, many other elected officials are troubled by the increasing use of such tools of direct democracy over the past several decades. Perhaps no voter-sponsored public policy frustrated legislators more than the term limits movement of the 1990s, when twenty-one states adopted term limits for state legislators, with twenty of them doing so through voter initiative. Such term limits are now having an impact in most states, including Missouri, where more than half of the state's legislators were turned out of office in 2002. Missouri has an eight-year term limit for both chambers of the legislature—four two-year terms in the house and two four-year terms in the senate. Every legislative session in recent years has included bills proposing to remove or lengthen term limits in the Show-Me State, but none have succeeded thus far. Though there is a high level of public approval for term limits in Missouri and elsewhere, legislators argue that term limits are reactionary and unproductive for good government. They argue that with term limits, the power of special interests will increase as experienced legislators are put out to pasture and lobbyists are the only ones left who know the rules of the game.

Direct democracy in America is an outgrowth of the Progressive reform movement of the late nineteenth and early twentieth centuries. In an era of machine politics, Progressives wanted to wrest control from what they viewed as corrupt politicians who sought to benefit themselves first, patrons second, and the public third. The motives of Progressive reformers were noble, and referenda and initiatives were seen as an advance for democracy. As with many well-intentioned reforms, however, direct democracy has negative consequences. In the twenty-five states where such citizen-based policy making has become especially common, it can result in reactionary, incoherent, counterproductive policy that elected lawmakers find endlessly frustrating.

Most legislators no doubt believe in the power of *representative* democracy. Representative democracy is the idea that lawmakers were elected to use their better judgment to make policy in the best interests of their constituents. No doubt, most legislators believe they are in a better position to understand their constituents' long-term interests than the average citizen who makes a spur-of-the-moment decision on a ballot initiative. Such legislators find themselves in the company of grand historical figures such as James Madison, who wrote that representative government was the primary cure for the evils of "faction." To Madison, factions were groups of people bound by some common goal that did not serve the best interests of society. The way to defuse the goals of factions, according to Madison, was to filter them through elected representatives.[7] Many scholars and learned observers of politics have come to believe that the growing use of initiatives and referenda is a crisis that threatens to do great harm to our representative form of government. David Broder, one of America's great political journalists, wrote a book about initiatives in 2000 called *Democracy Derailed*. He argued that initiatives, while once designed to eliminate the influence of special interests, have become a preferred method of operation for such groups. He suggests that they have "given the United States something that seems unthinkable—not a government of laws but laws without government."[8] In his book, Broder may be a bit extreme, but clearly initiatives and their cousins, referenda, make the job of governing at the state and local level more complicated, often creating a confusing mess of contradictory laws.

Missouri's initiative and referenda measures were adopted by constitutional amendment in 1908, following a years-long campaign by a Progressive organization called the Direct Action League of Missouri.[9] Use of the initiative has been relatively frequent in Missouri when compared to the other states with direct democracy, though no state can touch California, where several initiatives appear on every ballot. Since the adoption of initiative and referenda in Missouri, the state has averaged close to nine initiatives per decade, with the exception of the 1950s and 1960s when just one initiative appeared on the ballot.[10]

While it is certainly safe to argue that many lawmakers cringe when asked about direct democracy in general, their support for individual initiatives and referenda depends on the circumstances. Direct democracy was seen by Progressives as an excellent way to break the hold corrupt officials had on power in the late nineteenth and early twentieth centuries. In a perfect world, the kind idealized by the Progressives, citizens are informed and engaged in the policy debate when they cast their votes. In reality, however, voters generally know little about the initiatives and referenda on which they vote. For most, the printed question on the ballot is the first they have heard about an issue, which means that policy decisions, some trivial, some quite serious, are made by voters who have no idea what they are doing, or what the consequences of their actions will be. In a complicated world, it is probably not a great way to run a government, democracy or not.

The reality, however, is that many states have initiatives and referenda, and Missouri is one of them. This meant that both sides of the gun control issue, after many years of fighting for the support of elected officials, were ready to fight for the hearts and minds of Missouri voters in 1999. It was time for a campaign, and campaign they did.

Chapter Nine

The Campaign of 1999—The Activists

Celebrities and Elected Officials

James Brady, grievously wounded by John Hinckley in March 1981, was the first of many "celebrities" to visit Missouri in 1999. Brady has been an outspoken advocate of gun control for twenty years. His wife, Sarah Brady, is the current president of the Brady Campaign to End Handgun Violence and was the president of its predecessor, HCI, in 1999. James Brady appeared in St. Louis to welcome Pope John Paul II to America in January 1999 and took the opportunity to speak against Prop B. While in St. Louis, he met with the Anti-Concealed Weapons Coalition and spoke to officers of the St. Louis Police Department's Traffic Division. Despite his assertion that police officers were his allies in fights against concealed weapons in other states, his speech to the St. Louis officers was reportedly flat because many St. Louis officers were, in fact, supporters of Prop B.[1]

HCI was the preeminent national organization in the fight against Proposition B. It contributed money, advice, and moral support, but its efforts paled in comparison to the contributions made to the pro–Prop B campaign by its national patron, the NRA. The state legislative director for HCI, Joe Sudbay, predicted in late March 1999 that the NRA would spend $5 million in its campaign for Prop B, meaning, he asserted, the NRA would outspend HCI by a ratio of 10 to 1.[2]

Brady returned to Missouri in March of 1999 and spoke to a group of child advocates in Kansas City who opposed Prop B. Neither side in this fight was above demagoguery, as was evident in Brady's speech. He said, "The armed society that Proposition B creates is filled with so many loopholes that it literally would allow convicted criminals to carry hidden Uzi pistols into bars, stadiums and onto school property. I don't think that is the kind of society the people of Missouri want or need."[3] His statement was certainly designed to scare voters, and it was also misleading because the kind of Uzi Brady was trying to conjure in people's minds was outlawed by the federal assault weapons ban and would not have been legalized by Prop B. Of course, that didn't matter to his receptive audience.

While James Brady came to Missouri to campaign against Prop B, Charlton Heston, the famous actor and president of the NRA, came to the state on multiple occasions to promote it. In late March Heston appeared in St. Louis and Kansas City along with the group's executive vice president, Wayne LaPierre, and its chief lobbyist, Jim Baker. The men spoke on behalf of the proposition at rallies sponsored by the NRA and MAC. In St. Louis, Heston appeared on stage with Sue Kleeschulte, a rape victim who appeared in a pro–Prop B television commercial paid for by MAC. In addition to praising Kleeschulte's bravery, Heston called conceal-and-carry "safe, sane, sensible reform" and, like Brady, relied on old-fashioned demagoguery. He said, "Its opponents would have you believe the law would turn Missouri into a Wild West shootout. I've got advice for those critics: Leave deception to the Hollywood filmmakers . . . the biggest question is this: When a state passes a right-to-carry law, how many citizens aren't murdered, how many women aren't raped, how many storekeepers aren't robbed, and how many pensioners aren't beaten? Not because they're armed, but because criminals can't tell who is armed and who isn't."[4] Both Brady's and Heston's comments were oft-repeated propaganda, but such stock messages can be powerful when they're delivered by famous, well-liked people. In Kansas City on the same day in late March, Heston again addressed supporters of Prop B. He said, "The best way to deter crime is to allow lawful citizens to carry handguns. Right-to-carry creates a climate of uncertainty. In a world where the wolves can't tell the lions from the sheep, the entire flock is safe."[5]

The demagoguery continued when a group opposed to Prop B, Missourians Against Handgun Violence, issued a response to Heston's appearances in St. Louis and Kansas City: "It is pretty scary. Moses has joined the NRA spouting fear, distrust, and hate with the philosophy that in America to resolve conflicts, everyone should carry a concealed gun. The result, ordinary fistfights become a funeral."[6] A true believer, Heston was undeterred by such criticism and returned to Missouri the day before the election, speaking at a rally in the pro–Prop B stronghold of Springfield.

Missouri's elected officials also staked out positions on Prop B. Missouri's U.S. senators, Kit Bond and John Ashcroft, supported Prop B. Ashcroft became very involved in the campaign, taping radio advertisements for the pro–Prop B side. In so doing, Ashcroft invited criticism, because he had made statements in 1992 that put him firmly on the record as an opponent of conceal-and-carry.

Kenny Hulshof, the congressman from the Ninth District, and Jim Talent, the congressman from the Second District, were also vocal supporters of Prop B. On the other side, opponents included Governor Mel Carnahan, St. Louis Mayor Clarence Harmon, and Kansas City Mayor Emanuel Cleaver. A spokesman for Cleaver said, "This is an important issue to him. It's the kind of issue that will have a long-lasting impact."[7] Cleaver himself said, "While a gun may provide a psychological sense of security, it actually makes people more vulnerable. When you bring out a weapon, it increases the chances that you will be killed by a weapon."[8] Harmon, long outspoken in his support for gun control, said, "Under Proposition B, as it is now written, a known gang member could legally carry his weapon concealed into a stadium, into a saloon, into a bank, into a Wal-Mart."[9] Numerous other elected officials from the two metropolitan areas spoke out against Prop B throughout the campaign.

The Groups

The fight was waged at the local level by a handful of groups with close ties to the NRA and HCI. In favor of Prop B was MAC, which opponents regularly claimed was nothing but a local proxy for the NRA. There was certainly evidence to support such a charge. To reiterate, MAC was led by its campaign manager, Fred Meyers, a Maryland-based lobbyist who, in 1997, led the successful campaign to defeat a ballot initiative in Washington state that would have required the use of trigger locks on firearms. The NRA spent approximately $2 million in the Washington campaign; in Missouri, MAC received roughly 97 percent of the $4 million it spent during the Prop B campaign from the NRA.

Meyers was a veteran of many gun campaigns, and while he was officially tied to MAC, he was clearly sent to Missouri by the NRA. As was widely reported, Meyers had a remarkable record of success: "He has helped handle nine issue campaigns in various states—and has won every one of them. He helped defeat attempts to outlaw bear hunting in Michigan, to prohibit wolf trapping in Alaska and to require trigger locks on guns in Washington state."[10] MAC spent the bulk of its budget on television ads, billboards, radio ads, direct mail, and phone banks. A second group, Missourians for Personal Safety, also campaigned in favor of the proposition, though they raised and spent considerably less money than MAC. Both MAC and Missourians for Personal Safety based much of their operations in Columbia and both were aided in their efforts by other organizations from around Missouri, such as the Western Missouri Shooters Alliance, the Second Amendment Coalition, and the Conservative Federation of Missouri. Columbia is perhaps the most liberal city in the state, so it might seem unusual that it was the base of operations for the pro–

conceal-and-carry campaign. There are many possible reasons for this, including the city's proximity to the state capitol in Jefferson City. Columbia is also home to two of the NRA's strongest supporters, Brenda and Larry Potterfield, the owners of MidwayUSA, located just outside of Columbia. The Potterfields were a driving force behind the conceal-and-carry movement. Brenda Potterfield was MAC's Treasurer and MidwayUSA provided warehouse space for MAC to use as its campaign headquarters.[11]

Many factors influenced the supporters of conceal-and-carry. For some, the fight was purely about ideology and civil liberties. For others, however, there were economic reasons. Many supporters of conceal-and-carry in Missouri stood to gain financially, or at least believed they stood to gain financially, from its implementation. These included gun dealers, firearms educators, and sporting goods companies. The NRA itself has many partnerships with Missouri businesses and sponsors firearms training courses. Sheriffs' deputies who supported the proposition often moonlighted as gun dealers and firearms instructors. Of course, the Potterfields and their company, MidwayUSA, stood to gain financially if conceal-and-carry was legalized. MidwayUSA's Web site and promotional material assert the company is the nation's largest distributor of shooting and reloading equipment.[12] The family also owns a company that manufactures firearms and accessories, especially ammunition.

According to its Web site, MidwayUSA is also one of the nation's largest corporate supporters of the NRA. One MidwayUSA innovation is its "round up" program, which is described on the Web site. Customers placing orders with the company are asked if they want to round their purchase up to the next whole dollar and donate the difference to the NRA. For example, if a sale totaled $27.50, the customer would be asked to round up to $28.00 and donate 50 cents to the NRA. In addition to the round up program, the company also donates the services of its marketing and advertising staff, producing free advertisements for the NRA. Since 1992, the company claims to have donated almost $3 million to the NRA and its political arm, the Institute for Legislative Action. Larry Potterfield claimed on his company's Web site that there weren't any companies in the United States that were more dedicated to the NRA and its goals than MidwayUSA.[13] Why donate so much to the Prop B campaign and to the NRA? Certainly the Potterfields are gun enthusiasts and supporters of a broad interpretation of the Second Amendment, but less stringent gun control could also lead to greater gun ownership. Anything that creates a bigger market for guns and gun supplies is beneficial for a distributor of such products, and Prop B stood to increase the size of the handgun market if it passed.

The opposition to Prop B was largely organized by SSWC. Based in St. Louis, it was led by the daughter of Governor Mel Carnahan, Robin Carnahan, who served as the group's campaign manager. Carnahan was an attorney and a veteran of her father's political campaigns, having managed his successful election as lieutenant governor in 1988 and worked on his ascension to governor 1992. She became involved in the anti–Prop B campaign almost by accident, she claimed, when she saw a Prop B sticker on a car and subsequently found there was no organized opposition. She said, "I got in like most women get involved; they have an issue they believe in, and then they find themselves up to their eyeballs in making it come out right."[14]

Carnahan and SSWC were often critical of what they characterized as the vague language of the proposition and what seemed to be a broad variety of concealable weapons that would be legalized if it passed. "Our theory is you have potentially the wrong people, being able to take the wrong kind of gun into the wrong places," Carnahan said.[15] Again, there was not much evidence to support such claims, but they made effective sound bites. After the Proposition B campaign in 1999, Carnahan was largely out of politics until 2003, when she declared her candidacy for secretary of state, an office she won in the 2004 elections.

Other prominent public figures served on the SSWC's board, including Clarence Harmon, Emanuel Cleaver, former Republican U.S. Senator John Danforth, and the former superintendent of the Missouri Highway Patrol, Fred Mills, who had been involved in campaigning against concealed weapons for years. Governor Carnahan's former chief of staff, Marc Farinella, served for a time as the group's spokesman before joining Carnahan's campaign for the U.S. Senate. The bulk of SSWC's early money came from its national partner, HCI, although the seed money the SSWC received from HCI was less than a tenth of what MAC received from the NRA in the first month of 1999.[16] By the end of January the SSWC had raised $9,000, $7,000 of which came from HCI, while the NRA had given $75,000 to MAC. "We will be outspent big time," Farinella said, striking a theme the anti–Prop B side used many times throughout the campaign.[17] Other groups opposed to Prop B included the Anti-Concealed Weapons Coalition, led by former State Highway Patrol superintendent Fred Mills, and Missourians Against Handgun Violence. It was, for instance, Missourians Against Handgun Violence that issued the statement following Charlton Heston's first visit to Missouri, condemning "Moses" for joining the NRA. Concerns about Prop B were also reflected by those in the higher education community, such as the dean of student life at Southwest Missouri State University, Bob Glenn, who said he feared that people would be allowed to carry concealed weapons on campus and added, "That just scares the heck out of me. I've had plenty of occasions to observe situations that would make me very uncomfortable with people having guns on campus."[18]

Given the lack of rational thought often displayed by college-age young adults, it is not difficult to understand why university officials had concerns about anything that made it easier to carry guns on campus.

Some regional groups from the St. Louis and Kansas City areas also joined the campaign against Prop B. For instance, the St. Louis Area Clergy Coalition, made up largely of leaders of African American congregations, worked to get out the black vote against Prop B. Religious leaders in Kansas City spoke against Prop B, and the Greater Kansas City Chamber of Commerce also opposed conceal-and-carry, with officials arguing that the employees of businesses felt safer knowing it was illegal for their coworkers to carry guns. Late in the campaign, Peter Levi, the president of the Kansas City Chamber of Commerce, complained about the tremendous funding imbalance between the pro– and anti–Prop B campaigns when he said, "Opponents to Prop B are truly outgunned in this effort."[19] For its part, the Chamber of Commerce donated $25,000 to the SSWC.

Despite the fact that there were many groups opposed to Prop B and that some organizations, like the Kansas City Chamber of Commerce, contributed money to the anti–Prop B campaign, the pro–Prop B forces' funding advantage was consistent throughout the campaign. The vast majority of MAC's $4 million budget came from the NRA, while the SSWC raised most of its roughly $800,000 from organizations and businesses within the state, with only $150,000 coming from HCI. The SSWC spent its money on a controversial television ad, phone banks, and a get-out-the-vote drive focused on groups likely to oppose the proposition, including African Americans, women, business leaders, and religious groups.[20]

A Community Divided—Law Enforcement and Prop B

Law enforcement officers were largely divided by rank, with many rank-and-file officers supporting Prop B and the right to carry. For instance, both the Springfield and St. Louis Police Officers Associations campaigned in support of the proposition, as did the Missouri Deputy Sheriffs' Association. The bill's sponsor, Wayne Crump, was himself a former deputy sheriff from Washington County. The president of the St. Louis Police Officers Association, Sergeant John J. Johnson, said, "Other states that have passed right-to-carry laws have not experienced the carnage that opponents predict."[21] Gary Collins of the Springfield Police Officers Association said, "[Opponents] can't offer statistical data for not carrying. Just look at the homicides we've had here, they've been with bricks and strings and knives."[22] It seems unusual that organizations representing rank-and-file police officers would support such a measure, but there were logical reasons for it.

In March 1999, John Johnson explained, "The reason we are for it is because for years we have been trying to get bills passed for retired police officers to carry a weapon. It's never going to happen until Missouri is no longer a non-right-to-carry state. It cannot be passed for one group of private citizens without opening it up to all law-abiding citizens."[23] Later in the campaign he said, "I admit it's a bit self-serving, but our members want to carry legally because most officers do continue to carry after they retire."[24] Roy Bergman, a retired Highway Patrol captain and member of several pro-gun groups, said, "My firearms skills have not diminished . . . In the right hand, with the right training, firearms are critical to protecting people, businesses and our communities from the criminal element."[25] In addition to allowing retired officers to carry concealed guns, the measure also included language that expanded the rights of active police officers to carry concealed guns. The bill would have allowed officers to carry concealed weapons, "whether such officers are within or outside their jurisdictions or on or off duty."[26]

Granting retired and off-duty officers the right to carry wasn't the only reason rank-and-file organizations supported Prop B. For instance, many officers moonlighted as firearms instructors, gun dealers, or both. For such officers, there were clear financial reasons to support the passage of Prop B, since it mandated firearms training for anyone seeking a permit. For at least one rank-and-file organization that supported Prop B, there was yet another reason to cooperate with the NRA.

In return for Prop B support, the NRA acted on behalf of the St. Louis Police Officers' Association by supporting a bill in the state legislature that would have granted collective bargaining rights to public employees, including police officers. Collective bargaining was an important priority for the association, and the two groups clearly sought to help each other. The NRA's chief lobbyist, James Jay Baker, wrote a letter to John Johnson indicating the NRA's support for collective bargaining; the letter was also forwarded to the bill's sponsors in the legislature, with the hope that it might influence some legislators. Johnson commented, "The NRA is pretty strong in rural Missouri," implying that rural legislators might feel pressure to support collective bargaining because the NRA favored it.[27] A minor controversy erupted when legislators complained about the NRA letter. The MAC denied any knowledge of it and distanced itself from the NRA on the issue.[28] The collective bargaining bill failed to pass, but it was clear that favors were exchanged between the NRA and rank-and-file police officers in 1999.

On the other hand, police brass tended to oppose Prop B. For example, the Missouri Police Chiefs' Association opposed conceal-and-carry and participated in the campaign against the referendum. The president of the organization, Hazelwood Police Chief Carl R. Wolf, asserted in January 1999 that if the law passed, "Missouri would have one of the most lax gun laws in the country," and that Proposition B was "so full of loopholes that it would be dangerous for people to carry concealed handguns in public and around our children."[29] The chief of police for Springfield, Lynn Rowe, argued that the training requirement of twelve hours was insufficient. He argued that twelve hours ". . . just scratches the surface on the basic mechanics of using a firearm. You can't teach judgment in 12 hours. It isn't adequate."[30] In addition, many law enforcement officials, even supporters of conceal-and-carry, worried about the impact on officers in the field. For instance, Christian County Sheriff Steve Whitney expressed concerns about determining who was legitimately carrying a concealed handgun and who was not. He said, "I'm not sure how to train officers to respond to good guys and bad guys with guns."[31] Another major organization representing law enforcement with an interest in Prop B was the Missouri Sheriffs' Association. The group was officially neutral on Prop B, but many individual sheriffs campaigned for or against it, as they saw fit.

Ted Boehm, the sheriff of Boone County, where the University of Missouri and the city of Columbia are, was the president of the Missouri Sheriffs' Association in 1999. He objected to Prop B because, in his opinion, it made too many convicted criminals eligible for permits. In an interview with the Associated Press he said, "This thing is so poorly written that I would have no choice but to issue a permit to someone so long as they had been law-abiding for five years," regardless of what they might have done before.[32] In addition, Boehm was annoyed by the perception the pro–conceal-and-carry side tried to generate that the law enforcement community generally supported Prop B. He argued, "These billboards say '2,300 law enforcement personnel support concealed carry.' Well, there's more than 17,000 officers in Missouri. What do the other 14,000 say?"[33] In fact, many police organizations opposed Proposition B, including the Greater St. Louis Police Chiefs' Association, the Missouri Peace Officers Association, the Missouri Police Chiefs' Association, the Kansas City Police Department, the St. Louis Police Department, many Kansas City and St. Louis suburban police departments, the Kansas City and St. Louis chapters of the National Organization of Black Law Enforcement Executives, and the Kansas City Metropolitan Crime Commission.

While many sheriffs supported conceal-and-carry in broad terms, several were leery about the specifics of Prop B. For instance, Steve Whitney, the sheriff of Christian County in southwest Missouri, where support for the proposition was much stronger than in Kansas City or St. Louis, shared some of Boehm's concerns about Prop B. Speaking at a SSWC press conference, he said, "There's not enough restrictions in Proposition B."[34] He was concerned about who might be eligible for a permit.

Other sheriffs from southwest Missouri who may have supported conceal-and-carry questioned the details of Proposition B, arguing it was too vague in parts. For example, Greene County Sheriff John Pierpont expressed concern about how the permit process would be administered when he said, "We've gotten no information on how to run it, have we?"[35] Another southwest Missouri sheriff, Doug Seneker of Lawrence County, who supported Prop B, still worried about how much discretion he would have to deny permits to certain people. He said, "Sometimes we know people and know things about people that would cause us in good conscience to have reservations about giving them a permit. But if it's not in the law, we probably have to," because the law would have allowed people to sue if they felt they had been denied a permit without justification.[36]

In addition to concerns about how to issue permits and how to approach people carrying concealed weapons, some law enforcement officers and other critics of Prop B were concerned about the number of hours of training required in order to receive a permit. HB 1891, which voters knew as Prop B, stipulated a minimum of twelve hours of training, but offered no specifics about what that training should entail. Some law enforcement officers, such as Lynn Rowe, the chief of the Springfield Police Department, suggested a minimum of forty hours would be necessary.[37]

Defending his bill, Wayne Crump argued that although the bill was not specific with regard to training, people should have faith in the Department of Public Safety to design a program that would train people to be responsible carriers of concealed weapons. Sheriff Seneker of Lawrence County concurred with Crump when he argued that people who suggested the Department of Public Safety wouldn't be able to come up with a good program were being unfair. He said, "That's saying the Department of Public Safety is stupid and would not come up with a reasonable course of instruction."[38] In addition to concerns about training, other aspects of the wording of HB 1891 were at issue throughout the campaign, especially claims that it was far too vaguely worded on key points such as who would be eligible for a permit.

Coming to the defense of his bill, Representative Crump argued it was left deliberately vague to grant counties leeway to implement their own systems of issuing permits. He suggested that if people had reservations about the wording of the bill, they should have spoken up sooner and said, "If it's not the best bill, a lot would lie on those who never made any input. I'm not ashamed of one thing in that bill."[39] He also argued that because the referendum was for a statute, not a constitutional amendment, the legislature would be able to fine-tune the conceal-and-carry law in later years to make up for any flaws in the original language. Crump asserted every law passed by the legislature is vague in some way and that the details of most laws are left to the bureaucratic agency, or agencies, that will enforce them, much as conceal-and-carry would be left to the Department of Public Safety.

Uncertainty about the impact of Prop B was exacerbated by the Department of Public Safety's reluctance to clarify prior to the vote any questions about how it would enact the law. A spokesperson for the department, Tami Holliday, said no guidelines would be prepared in advance, for two reasons. First, it would be inappropriate for the department to appear to be taking a position on Prop B, and second, department officials didn't want to waste money developing guidelines until they knew conceal-and-carry was a reality.[40] Of course, this created a dilemma for supporters of conceal-and-carry, who had to fight the criticism of opponents of Prop B. The vagueness of both HB 1891 and the Department of Public Safety gave ammunition to opponents such as Ted Boehm. While the department's officials claimed they didn't want to appear to take a position on Prop B, their refusal to take any action in advance of the vote might have had a real impact on the outcome of the election.

Throughout the campaign, Boehm was careful to qualify his statements, framing them as concerns about criminals being eligible for concealed weapons permits because of the wording of HB 1891. As the elected sheriff of a county that was home to a number of very powerful advocates of Prop B, he certainly had to worry about the effect an all-out stand against conceal-and-carry would have on his political future. Several other sheriffs, all from rural counties, were happy to make their views known. They appeared at the rallies with Charlton Heston, advocated the passage of Proposition B, and spoke out regularly. These included Sheriff Gary Starke of Pettis County, Sheriff Charles Heiss of Johnson County, Sheriff Dwight Diehl of Cass County, and Sheriff Duane Diehl of Bates County.[41] Missourians for Personal Safety listed on its Web site a total of thirty-two sheriffs who endorsed Prop B.[42] Many other sheriffs declined to take a public position. Sheriffs are elected officials, and in a great many Missouri counties, conceal-and-carry is very popular. While many sheriffs may have worried about the potential impact of conceal-and-carry permits, it would have been politically dangerous to take a public stance. Therefore, the Missouri Sheriffs' Association remained officially neutral on Prop B.

Other elements of the law enforcement community, however, were outspoken in their opposition to Prop B. For instance, St. Louis County Prosecutor Robert McCulloch challenged basic claims made by its supporters and said the proposed law was so ambiguous, "it might as well just say if you want a gun, carry one. There are, in effect, no regulations. To say that only law-abiding citizens get the permits is an out-and-out misstatement of the facts, or they are lying through their teeth."[43] McCulloch was joined in his opposition by Jackson County Prosecutor Bob Beaird.

Two federal prosecutors got themselves into hot water for voicing opposition to Prop B. The U.S. attorney for eastern Missouri, Edward L. Dowd, and western Missouri, Stephen Hill, were actively opposed to Prop B. Dowd, for example, expressed doubts throughout the campaign that were similar to those of McCulloch. In one interview, Dowd said, "The proposition is very poorly written. It's full of loopholes, loopholes that let anyone except convicted felons get weapons. The loopholes let the wrong people carry the wrong guns into the wrong places. If this passes, virtually anyone will be able to carry weapons virtually anywhere: banks, Wal-Marts, stadiums, bars, anywhere . . . The bottom line is that this is a boneheaded idea. The law prohibiting people from carrying guns around with them was passed in the 1800s, back in the 'Wild West' days. If it wasn't a good idea then, there's certainly no reason why it would be a good idea now."[44] In the heated atmosphere of the Prop B campaign, Dowd's and Hill's public stance against Prop B was not without consequence, as public officials who supported Prop B objected to the activities engaged in by the prosecutors.

An official complaint was lodged against Dowd and Hill by U.S. Senator Kit Bond and Ninth District Congressman Kenny Hulshof. In addition, the former Ninth District congressman and Prop B supporter, Harold Volkmer, was very angry about the prosecutors' involvement. Volkmer said, "To me, it's a misuse of funds. That isn't why we hire U.S. attorneys. That isn't part of the job. I still have some friends on the Hill. There should be a rider on the appropriations bill for the Department of Justice that no federal taxpayers' money or federal funds should be used to campaign for or against state issues."[45] Bond and Hulshof sent letters to the Department of Justice suggesting that Dowd and Hill had violated federal law by using tax dollars for purposes not authorized by Congress. Hulshof described his letter as a request to U.S. Attorney General Janet Reno for information about the law regarding political advocacy by U.S. attorneys. He said, "I felt it was appropriate to raise some questions."[46] Bond and Hulshof argued that it was inappropriate to use federal resources to defeat a state referendum and claimed that letters written by both men were illegally designed to promote public opposition to Proposition B.[47]

For his part, Dowd asserted he had a right to campaign against what he characterized as a bad law. He said, "Obviously as U.S. attorney it's absolutely proper for me to comment on a matter relating to law enforcement and public safety."[48] Dowd also suggested that the Second Amendment Coalition had acted improperly by distributing his office's toll-free number, intended for use by law enforcement officers, to supporters of Proposition B. The Prop B supporters, he claimed, flooded his office with calls, forcing him to shut down the phone line. If such a group could politicize his office, he seemed to suggest, then so could he.[49] For Bond and Hulshof, however, the toll-free number was part of the problem. They claimed it was being used to supply law enforcement officials around the state with anti-Prop B information at taxpayer expense.[50] In response to Bond's and Hulshof's complaints, Janet Reno directed the Justice Department's inspector general, Brian Steel, to investigate the prosecutors' involvement in the campaign.[51]

By autumn of 1999, Dowd and Hill were cleared by the Justice Department of any wrongdoing. The investigation concluded that Dowd and Hill were allowed to participate in the campaign because it involved an issue of public policy and was not a partisan political campaign. Further, it found that the prosecutors had actually asked for, and received, prior approval from the Department of Justice to get involved, even though they were not required to do so. However, after clearing the two men, Reno announced a new policy that mandated U.S. attorneys receive Justice Department approval before taking a public position on state or local legislation.[52] Senator Bond continued to complain about Dowd's involvement in the campaign after the Justice Department closed its investigation, despite the fact that Dowd soon left office to work under former U.S. Senator John Danforth on a Justice Department investigation into the disastrous government handling of the Branch Davidians.

Clearly, there were many people in Missouri, and outside the state as well, with an interest in the outcome of the Prop B campaign, and they had to make the issue relevant to average Missourians. This made for a campaign of statistics, fiery rhetoric, legal battles, and hard feelings. It seemed like everyone, including an economist named John Lott, had something to say about conceal-and-carry. As the campaign wore on, much was made of statistics and the meaning of state law on any number of topics, including the proper way to put a referendum on the ballot.

Chapter Ten

The Campaign of 1999—Interpreting
Statistics and the Law

John R. Lott, Jr.

The intellectual foundation of the pro-gun lobby's case for conceal-and-carry came from the work of John Lott, Ph.D., an economist who has devoted much of his research to gun laws and their impact on crime. During the Prop B campaign, he was referred to in at least one press report as "the intellectual godfather of sorts for proponents of Missouri's concealed weapons measure."[1] At the time of the Prop B debate, Lott was a professor at the University of Chicago's school of law. He is now with the American Enterprise Institute and is the author of numerous articles and books, many of which are about guns and the effect they have on crime. The pro–Prop B campaign relied heavily on Lott's best-known book, *More Guns, Less Crime*. The book's thesis is that laws allowing conceal-and-carry are an effective way to reduce crime. He supports this thesis with voluminous data showing that crime rates drop in states that adopt such laws. During the campaign, Lott wrote op-ed pieces advocating the passage of Prop B that appeared in both the *St. Louis Post-Dispatch* and the *Kansas City Star*. Late in the campaign, in an op-ed piece published in the *Kansas City Star*, Lott refuted several criticisms made of Prop B during the campaign. He wrote, "If passed, Missouri's rules will be among the nation's strictest. Only one other state requires a longer training period. The fee for a permit will be in the top third. Missouri will have the criminal background checks used in other states and will have a unique provision in none of the other right-to-carry states: the ability for police to deny permits to people who are 'known' drug users or criminals."[2]

In addition to writing editorials, Lott visited the Show-Me State several times during the campaign, in part as an effort to promote his book, but also to speak in favor of Prop B. While visiting St. Louis in late March, Lott said,

"Criminals tend to attack victims whom they perceive as weak, and guns can offset the differences in strength and serve as an important deterrent."[3] Lott was able to marshal many statistics to support his argument. Statistics, of course, are usually open to more than one interpretation, especially in an ideologically charged fight like the Prop B campaign. This made Lott an intellectual lightning rod in the showdown.

St. Louis County Prosecuting Attorney Robert McCulloch argued that Lott's statistics were misleading and dismissed him sarcastically when he said, "The problem is, he has a title, and that gives him instant credibility. But his statistics are laughable. You give them to any real statisticians and they'll giggle."[4] U.S. Attorney Edward Dowd was more substantive in his criticism when he argued that while Lott's statistics demonstrated a decrease in crime in states that adopted conceal-and-carry, the crime rates in those states were not as low as in states without conceal-and-carry. "In fact, FBI statistics show that in states that have strict laws against carrying concealed weapons, the numbers have dropped 25 percent since 1992, while states with laws that allow people to carry concealed weapons, they've dropped only 11 percent," he said.[5] Lott's interpretation of crime statistics and the impact conceal-and-carry laws have in reducing crime is very convincing. At the same time others, like the analysts who work for HCI, take the same data and come to the opposite conclusion. The truth is probably that concealed guns have a negligible effect on crime—they do not significantly increase or decrease crime—but it is impossible to convince the true believers on either side of the issue of that truth.

While Lott visited Missouri to urge voters to support Prop B, he was also critical of HB 1891, suggesting it was too strict to have the kind of dramatic effect on crime rates that states with more permissive laws had seen. For instance, he argued the fee was too high. He said the eighty-dollar fee would diminish the impact of conceal-and-carry on crime because "you're not going to be seeing as many poor people in urban areas that are particularly susceptible to crimes getting permits."[6] He also argued the minimum of twelve hours of firearms training mandated by the bill was too much and would dissuade many people from applying for permits. He suggested five to six hours of training as the optimal amount, in terms of encouraging enough people to get permits and, therefore, having the greatest impact on crime rates. Anything more than five or six hours, he said, would reduce the number of people who got permits and slow the decrease of the crime rate.[7] Lott was a critical figure in the Prop B fight, not because he was an especially dynamic campaigner or because he donated a great sum of money to MAC, but because his work gave intellectual ammunition to those wishing to enact conceal-and-carry in Missouri. Also, because of the often controversial nature of the statistics, it gave plenty of ammunition for those opposed to conceal-and-carry to fire back.

Legal Fights

In America, political issues rarely escape the courtroom. Alexis de Toqueville made this observation nearly two hundred years ago, and it remains true today. Not surprisingly, the courts played a prominent role in the Prop B campaign. Two significant lawsuits were filed in the months prior to the election, centering on the wording of the ballot. The wording of the summaries of referenda on ballots is often controversial because for many voters, the ballot is their first exposure to an issue. Most voters decide how to vote at the moment they read the ballot, without ever reading the law they are voting to enact. The wording on the ballot, therefore, can have a critical impact on the outcome, much as the wording of a question on a public opinion poll can dramatically affect the findings of a survey.

The first lawsuit was brought by a group of plaintiffs that included former Missouri Highway Patrol Superintendent Fred Mills; the president of SSM Health Systems in St. Louis County, Sister Mary Jean Ryan; and Chuck Keithley, a former sheriff of Taney County, which is in southwest Missouri. The plaintiffs were Proposition B opponents who sued over the ballot language included in Representative Crump's bill authorizing the referendum. According to HB 1891, the ballot was to read, "Shall state or local law enforcement agencies be authorized to issue permits to law-abiding citizens at least 21 years of age to carry concealed firearms outside their home for personal protection after having passed a state and federal criminal background check and having completed a firearms safety training course approved by the Missouri Department of Public Safety?" The plaintiffs claimed the ballot question was both too wordy and biased in favor of passage. A lawyer for the plaintiffs, Alex Bartlett, said that while the ballot wording implied that permits would only be given to "law-abiding" citizens, there was no such guarantee in the bill itself. The result, he argued, could be that people with serious criminal records or mental troubles could get permits and that it was misleading for the ballot language to imply strong protections were in place.[8] The judge, Cole County Circuit Judge Thomas Brown, avoided ruling on the wording itself by finding that the legislature had overstepped its bounds by writing the ballot language at all. He ordered the ballot to be rewritten by the secretary of state, as state law required, and further ordered that the state auditor was to supply an estimate of the cost of implementing the measure to be included on the ballot.[9]

Responding to the judge's order, Secretary of State Bekki Cook rewrote the ballot. On election day it read, "Shall sheriffs, or in the case of St. Louis County, the chief of police, be required to issue permits to carry concealed firearms to citizens who apply if various statutory requirements are satisfied?" Shortly thereafter, on January 25, 1999, State Auditor Claire McCaskill's office issued a cost estimate of the bill's fiscal impact on local governments. McCaskill's report indicated that the $80 application fee would cover the initial costs of issuing permits but the much lower $35 renewal fee would cost local governments as much as $1 million a year. Her office reported it could take as little as 1.35 hours to process each permit or as long as 2.95 hours per permit. McCaskill predicted that approximately 62,000 Missouri residents would apply for permits in the first three years and when their permits expired and they applied for renewal, local governments would incur significant costs.[10]

Before the ink was dry, the new ballot language and cost estimate brought objections from interested parties. For starters, pro–Prop B forces insisted McCaskill's office overestimated the costs of issuing permits.[11] Several different organizations tried to estimate the costs, and they all arrived at different conclusions. For example, the Missouri Sheriffs' Association said the proposition would cost $3.8 million to implement and would require the hiring of 150 new employees to process the applications and conduct background checks. On the other hand, the Missouri Division of Oversight estimated it would cost around $1.1 million and that sheriffs would only need 47 new workers, mostly in the St. Louis and Kansas City areas. While both the Division of Oversight and the Sheriffs Association used the state of Texas as their model, they arrived at significantly different estimates, with the state auditor's estimate being in the middle.[12]

Before long, a lawsuit was filed against both Bekki Cook and Claire McCaskill. The suit charged that the description of the law for the ballot was biased against passage and that the estimated cost of implementing the law was too high. The suit was filed by former Missouri Highway Patrol Captain Roy Bergman, who was a member of MAC and a paid consultant of the pro-gun Law Enforcement Alliance of America. Bergman's brief read, in part, "The official ballot title written by the Secretary of State fails to provide a fair notice of the substance, content and purposes of the proposed law and omits material facts necessary for voters to cast an intelligent and informed ballot."[13] The suit also alleged that Claire McCaskill's analysis overestimated the cost of Prop B to local governments. Finally, Bergman's brief also challenged the very authority of McCaskill and Cook to write the summary and cost estimate. The only thing that can be said with certainty about the wording of the ballot is that people assign different meanings to what they read and it was probably true that no matter how the ballot was written, it would have been objectionable to someone.

At the same time Bergman's suit was filed, another lawsuit was filed against Claire McCaskill, this one by Fred Mills, the former head of the Missouri State Patrol. In it, he claimed that the auditor had underestimated the proposition's potential cost and alleged there were several inaccuracies in McCaskill's cost analysis. He argued that sheriffs' workers would need to spend longer than three hours researching each applicant's background; that the number of residents seeking permits had been underestimated; that the cost of equipment, such as computers and other office supplies, had been neglected in the calculation; and that the estimate did not include the costs to be incurred by the Missouri Department of Public Safety in supervising the required weapons training courses.[14] As is true of many bills, the impact of Prop B was impossible to quantify before it was implemented, and the unknowns gave both sides room to maneuver in the courts. The fact that both sides filed suits over the cost estimate prompted Claire McCaskill to say, "If both sides are unhappy, it's probably a fair fiscal note. We will stand by the fiscal note. It's fair and accurate according to the way the law is written."[15] It was, of course, up to the court to make that decision.

Cole County Circuit Court Judge Byron Kinder ruled against the plaintiffs in both suits, ruling that the ballot description and cost estimates both provided accurate summaries of the bill voters would decide in April. While Mills, the anti–Prop B plaintiff, chose not to appeal the judge's decision, Bergman, the pro–Prop B plaintiff, did appeal. His case was heard by the Western District Court of Appeals in Kansas City.

In March, roughly a month before the election, a panel of three Court of Appeals judges agreed with Judge Kinder's ruling that the wording of the summary and the cost estimate were fair and accurate descriptions of the proposed law. They also rejected the claim that McCaskill and Cook did not have the authority to write the summary. They found that the legislature had previously given the secretary of state and the state auditor the authority to write the descriptions of referenda put on the ballot and that the legislature could not later write its own ballot language.[16] With this decision, the legal fights were over and the campaign continued.

As the campaign edged ever closer to election day, the importance of public relations and advertising became very clear to the advocates on both sides. Though the pro–Prop B advocates and the anti–Prop B advocates had very different resources, they both found effective ways to take their cases to the public.

Chapter Eleven

The Campaign of 1999—Funding and Advertising

The advertising during the Prop B campaign was almost all for the pro–Prop B side and was paid for, either directly or indirectly, by the NRA. The MAC began airing radio and TV ads in late February. In addition, the group also tapped the NRA's extensive grassroots network. As one reporter described, "The organization's well-funded get-out-the-vote apparatus has been calling registered voters at home throughout the state. People in some parts of Missouri reportedly have gotten as many as four telephone calls on the issue."[1] The activation of a grassroots network is a hallmark of a campaign coordinated with the aid of the NRA, which became even more effective with the advent of the Internet.

While the pro–Prop B forces began their broadcast campaign in late February, the opposition didn't begin running a TV spot until the end of March, and the ad they ran was fraught with controversy. The SSWC, which in January said it hoped to raise $2 million for its campaign, raised less than $1 million and spent $595,000 on the controversial television ad, produced by a Philadelphia ad agency, Shorr and Associates.[2]

The obvious funding imbalance was consistently highlighted by spokespersons for the SSWC, who argued the election was being bought and paid for by the NRA, which they accused of being an out-of-state carpetbagger. A member of SSWC, Fred Epstein, argued, "It's outrageous that the NRA is trying to buy victory. MAC is a thinly veiled front for the NRA. The gun lobby has flooded our community with an NRA-financed campaign."[3] Another representative of the SSWC, Gwen Fitzgerald, complained that the NRA would exit as soon as the election was over, leaving Missourians with the consequences. She said, "Their children and families won't have to deal with the potentially deadly consequences of this dangerous measure. The gun lobby is not spending millions of dollars because Missourians want concealed weapons. The gun lobby is spending millions of dollars because they are afraid Missourians do not want concealed weapons."[4] In another interview, Fitzgerald argued, "It's incredible. They are not even making a pretense of raising money in Missouri. The bigwigs at the NRA are pumping money out here as fast as possible to push their narrow agenda to do what's good for the NRA, not what's good for the people of Missouri"[5] Clearly, the opponents of Prop B were frustrated by the extent to which they lost the money war, often claiming they were being outspent by a rate of 10 to 1. Of course, their charges were a bit disingenuous. First, HCI, another outsider, was deeply involved in the anti–Prop B campaign, taking SSWC's side. Second, while HCI's resources were considerably less than the NRA's, there is little doubt that if the group had been able to give SSWC $3 million, the Missouri group would gladly have accepted.

That ratio was an exaggeration, but data from the Missouri Ethics Commission supported the conclusion that the NRA supported its Missouri affiliates well, giving them a spending advantage of about 5 to 1. On March 30, MAC reported receiving almost $3 million in cash donations, nearly all of it from the NRA.[6] The SSWC, the main opposition to Proposition B, reported raising $770,000. By election day, MAC reported $3.89 million in total money raised, with $3.8 million coming in donations from the NRA, including nearly $900,000 in the final days of the campaign. The last-minute NRA cash came in the form of loans and contributions to the campaign—$450,000 as a contribution for a telephone get-out-the-vote drive; a $200,000 loan; and in-kind contributions of staff and other services worth $112,000. This meant that the NRA was responsible for 97 percent of the money raised by MAC. The remaining 3 percent came from individual donations. In comparison, by election day, April 6, SSWC collected a total of $828,359, with approximately $150,000 coming from HCI. One analysis of the election estimated the pro–Prop B side spent $6 per vote, while the anti–Prop B side spent just $1.27 per vote.[7]

The financial resources of MAC were frustrating to SSWC, but MAC's money was also a rhetorical weapon SSWC continually used in its anti–Prop B campaign. Late in the campaign, for example, the group was considering a direct mail campaign, but spokesperson Gwen Fitzgerald reportedly was reluctant to discuss strategy because, as she said, "I don't want to say too much about what we're planning. Everything we do gets countered times three."[8] This was effective political rhetoric for SSWC, but the reality was that the NRA was simply doing in Missouri what it had been doing at the national level and in many other states for years. Opponents of Prop B were clearly offended by the NRA's money and they argued that Prop B was an issue of state policy that should be decided by the people of Missouri, but the proponents of Prop B could argue the same about HCI's involvement in the campaign.

For its part, the NRA was untroubled by SSWC's criticism. In a message to its members, the NRA rejected claims it was carpetbagging. The group claimed that a vote for Prop B would be "a shot across the bow of the anti-gun lobby," and that if Prop B was defeated, it would "weaken our Second Amendment rights in every state in the nation," clearly articulating why they felt justified becoming so involved in a "state" issue.[9] Brett Feinstein, a spokesperson for MAC, argued that the financial support of the NRA was nothing more than a reflection of the wishes of the Missouri members of the organization who, he claimed, totaled 103,000 people at the time. He said, "They can talk all they want about the big, bad NRA, but its members have banded together because they believe in the same things. Those 103,000 people can donate to us or to the NRA, but the result is the same."[10] He claimed that the Missouri members of the NRA paid $3.5 million in annual dues to the organization, plus whatever else they chose to donate, and he suggested, "The NRA hasn't polled its Missouri members, but it isn't going to go against their wishes. The vast majority support Proposition B."[11] Clearly, the organization was committed to victory in Missouri and, just as clearly, they were unconcerned with being branded as outside agitators.

No matter what SSWC said about the NRA, it had its own national organization working with it to oppose Proposition B. HCI was deeply involved rhetorically, if not financially. HCI certainly contributed money to the campaign, even if it was in a much smaller way, both proportionally and in real dollars. An assessment given by one spokesperson for the SSWC just three days before the election reiterated a familiar refrain: "The NRA has a built-in infrastructure that from day one was ready to turn out for this. We need to energize our supporters."[12] The implication in these kinds of comments seemed to be that the NRA's ability to mobilize voters was somehow a bad thing when, clearly, HCI and SSWC wished they could do the same. HCI gave $159,000 to the campaign, meaning that the NRA outspent it by a ratio of 20 to 1. HCI accounted for only 20 percent of the total spent in the anti–Prop B campaign, compared to the NRA's contribution of 97 percent of the Prop B campaign. Clearly, SSWC did not have the same financial advantages as MAC, which certainly had a powerful ally in the NRA. At the same time, however, 20 percent of SSWC's budget was from HCI, another out-of-state group, and there is nothing insignificant about 20 percent.

At the same time, SSWC could, and often did, claim its campaign was a homegrown affair compared to the pro–Prop B campaign. While nearly all the MAC money came from out of state, SSWC claimed twenty-two different, mostly local, contributors. Besides HCI, contributors to the anti–Prop B campaign included the Greater Kansas City Chamber of Commerce; James B. Nutter

Co., a mortgage company; Schnucks Markets, a grocery store chain from St. Louis; Silver Dollar City, an amusement park in Branson; Sprint, the long-distance telephone company, based in metro Kansas City; the Civic Council of Greater Kansas City; Hallmark Cards, Inc.; a Kansas City company called Utilcorp; the Kansas City Royals; the Kansas City Chiefs; the St. Louis Cardinals; and the St. Louis Rams.[13] According to the Missouri Ethics Commission, each of these organizations gave at least $5,000 and several gave as much as $25,000 to the campaign to defeat Prop B. Each company, incidentally, continued to be targeted by the NRA and some of its Missouri affiliates for boycott into 2004.

Because SSWC had significantly less money to spend, the group was forced to target its efforts more carefully than MAC, which relied on a broad multimedia campaign. SSWC focused on people it could rely on to stimulate the grass roots, trying to, as one reporter wrote, "run a more focused campaign emphasizing people who often deal with gun violence: health-care workers, teachers, the black community and church leaders. Safe Schools planned to hit all those groups this weekend with brochures or personal appeals. Ministers around the state have agreed to preach against Proposition B in today's Easter sermons."[14] To its credit, the SSWC was very effective operating with fewer resources. Of course, it really had little choice. With very little money for broadcast attacks on Prop B, the organization had to work at the grassroots level, and it did so to great effect.

When the NRA contributed an additional $900,000 to MAC in the last week of the campaign, the frustration of opponents of Prop B boiled over. In Jefferson City, a group of seven state legislators, including Representative Barbara Fraser, D–St. Louis, Representative Vicky Riback Wilson, D–Columbia, Representative Tim Harlan, D–Columbia, Representative Tim Van Zandt, D–Kansas City, and Senator Harry Wiggins, D–Kansas City, gathered for a press conference on March 31 to protest the NRA's level of involvement in the campaign. Barbara Fraser said, "These are paid for by people who won't have to deal with the consequences. They should keep their money in Washington, D.C., and leave Missouri alone," and complained that it was impossible to watch TV or listen to the radio without hearing a pro–Prop B ad.[15] Vicky Riback Wilson accused the NRA of acting without the approval of its Missouri members. She said, "I have spoken with many gun owners, many of whom are NRA members, who are opposed to Prop B."[16] To do her part to combat the NRA's action, Wilson said, she had contributed to SSWC.

Late in the campaign, anti–Prop B crusader Peter Herschend, the owner of Silver Dollar City, claimed, "When I look at the comparative budgets, that sets up the odds wrong and does not give us a true test of what Missourians want."[17]

Complaining about it didn't change reality, however. The anti–Prop B campaign was at a serious fiscal disadvantage, which was never more apparent than it was in the ad war.

The Campaign—Advertisements: In Favor of Prop B

Though they had a tremendous advantage in campaign resources, MAC spokesman Brett Feinstein was cautious, even pessimistic, in an interview with the *Kansas City Star* just days before the election. He said, "It is true that we have voters with a lot of intensity, but there are people on the other side who opposed us from the start, too. The question is: How energized are voters who have listened to both sides? I don't know where that gray middle is. This is a weird one."[18] MAC tried to minimize the uncertainty by using its financial resources to advertise heavily. The organization used its big budget to run a campaign that utilized many different advertising media, including the Internet, television and radio ads, newspaper ads, billboards, automated phone calls, one million direct mailings, half a million door hangings, and sixty thousand yard signs.[19] A common theme of the campaign was the suggestion that voters' civil liberties were at stake. On its Web site, the NRA addressed the Missouri election this way: "Welcome to Concord Bridge. On April 6, step onto that bridge at Concord, take up the musket of truth and help finish the fight for freedom."[20] The NRA used its Web site to mobilize the grass roots, telling its 103,000 Missouri members that it "can't stress enough the importance of this ballot referendum," and that they were to post notices of "grassroots elections seminars" to be held around the state.[21] These seminars were intended to not only rally support but also train grassroots leaders to be more effective campaigners.

As is true of any modern campaign, the most visible part of the MAC's efforts was on television. The group ran several spots, some tapping voters' emotions, others taking a slightly more intellectual approach. The first ads run by the MAC took a law and order approach, featuring two pro–Prop B spokespersons, John Johnson, the president of the St. Louis Police Officers Association, and O. J. Stone, the president of the Missouri Deputy Sheriffs' Association. In the ad, Johnson said, "Over 1,300 St. Louis police officers endorse the right-to-carry. We're on the street fighting crime every day, and we know right-to-carry works." Stone added, "We support Prop. B because in the 43 states with right-to-carry crime has gone down. That's why over 2,000 deputies and police officers across Missouri urge you to vote yes on Prop. B."[22] Obviously, the purpose of this and other ads featuring these same officers was to address one major concern head-on: the fear that concealed guns would lead to more crime, not less. By showing police as supporters, the MAC clearly hoped to allay such concerns. There was certainly nothing patently false in the ad, though it was clearly meant to give the impression that all police officers favored conceal-and-carry when, as Sheriff Boehm pointed out, that was not necessarily true. A "truth test" in the *St. Louis Post-Dispatch* pointed out some other flaws: "The ad is misleading because it incorrectly ties a drop in crime rates with implementation of concealed weapons law. Studies differ on whether concealed weapons increase or reduce crime . . . The ad also inaccurately states that 43 states have right-to-carry laws. About one-fourth of those states give authorities discretion over who can carry weapons, thus restricting the numbers of people who can carry concealed weapons."[23] In fairness, one must take the *St. Louis Post-Dispatch's* first critique cautiously. To say the ad was "misleading" implies an attempt to deceive. The truth about almost any statistic is that there may be dozens of ways to interpret it, as the debate over John Lott's data proved. A different interpretation doesn't mean there was an attempt to mislead.

In a second television ad, Johnson and Stone appeared again. Stone said, "Prop B, right-to-carry, will be one of the toughest laws in the country. Twelve hours of safety training, fingerprinting, criminal background checks by the Highway Patrol and the FBI. No one with a history of violence will get a permit. No felons. No wife abusers. No drug or alcohol addicts. Trust me, only law-abiding citizens will get permits. That's why over 2,000 deputies and police officers across Missouri urge you to vote yes on Prop. B."[24] In this ad, the intent was, once again, to build support for Prop B by showing that the law enforcement community supported it. It very specifically tried to address the complaints of some in the law enforcement community, like Sheriff Boehm, that the bill was too vaguely worded and that it contained too many loopholes that would allow people of questionable character to get conceal-and-carry permits. While the ad was truthful in saying that felons would be ineligible for permits, it also seemed to imply that absolutely no one with a criminal background would be able to get a conceal-and-carry permit, which was not true. Critics, like Sheriff Boehm, pointed out that people with serious misdemeanors on their records could still be eligible, as well as people who had committed felonies but had them plea-bargained down to misdemeanors.

A third ad shifted tactics, taking an emotional, demagogic approach. The spot featured Sue Kleeschulte, a victim of St. Louis's "Southside Rapist." It was different from the commercials featuring Johnson and Stone in the sense that it featured a "real person" to whom more people could relate. Clearly, the intent was to bring home to viewers the consequences of violent crime and to suggest that having a gun could prevent one from being victimized. In particular, MAC was trying to deliver a message to women, who polls found were significantly less supportive of Prop B than men. Obviously, MAC felt that featuring a woman crime victim might generate support among women voters.

Some suggested the ad was aimed at not only women but also urban voters to prove how Prop B could help them. Polls showed that urban voters were another group more likely to be opposed to Prop B. By showing a victim of crime from an urban area arguing that having a gun might have helped her, MAC was clearly trying to make Prop B more relevant to urban voters.

The ad attracted a great deal of discussion and controversy. Kleeschulte was initially reluctant to appear in the ad but was prompted to participate, she said, by her anger after viewing coverage of a press conference given by Clarence Harmon. During the press conference, the St. Louis mayor asserted that the proposition would allow gang members easier access to guns, angering Kleeschulte. She said, "They had mini Uzis on a table and proceeded to insult me as a citizen into believing that gang members would come down and apply for permits to carry these. The scare tactic that they used was an absolute insult to me as an adult woman. I was very angry."[25] She said that after seeing the report, she contacted MAC spokesperson Amy Pennington and told her she would do an ad in support of Prop B.[26]

Of course, one could argue that the MAC ad did exactly what Kleeschulte said made her so angry—try to scare people. In the ad, she appeared on camera and said, "You may have heard of the Southside Rapist. He raped women for a decade. I should know, I was one of his victims. So am I going to vote for Prop. B, the right-to-carry? Absolutely. I don't expect anybody to understand my position with Proposition B. It may not be something you would want to do, but I'm asking that you give me the right to protect myself. If I've learned one thing through all this, don't ever give up the right to protect yourself. Ever."[27] The implication, of course, was that maybe a concealed weapon would have prevented her attack. What the ad failed to mention, however, was that Missourians already had a legal right to keep handguns at home and to use them in self-defense.[28] Prop B would have done nothing to aid Sue Kleeschulte or any other victims attacked by the Southside Rapist in their homes. It wasn't inconceivable that a woman attacked outside her home could be aided by a concealed weapon, but that was not the type of attack featured in the ad.

The Kleeschulte ad became fodder for opponents of Prop B when a second victim of the Southside Rapist came forward after the Kleeschulte spot began to air. While she refused to divulge her identity, the woman said guns were not the answer to violent crime. She refuted the ad's implication that a gun would have made a difference in her attack when she said, "One of the first things he asked me was whether I had a weapon, and he checked."[29] Clearly, the Kleeschulte ad touched a chord with many on both sides of the issue, and certainly it had an impact on the campaign discourse. Whether it changed any voters' opinions is difficult to know.

The law enforcement community returned after the Sue Kleeschulte spot for a fourth MAC ad. In the spot, Major Stone said, "We can't always be there to protect the ones you love . . . That's why Missouri police officers overwhelmingly support Prop B." Sergeant Johnson added that more than a thousand members of the St. Louis Police Officers' Association supported the right to carry. Roy Bergman, the retired highway patrol captain, also appeared in the spot and said, "Retired police officers support it because FBI statistics show that violent crime rates are lower in right-to-carry states." Lastly, the Cass County prosecutor, Chris Koster, said, "The facts don't lie. In the 43 states with right-to-carry, crime has gone down."[30]

Again, the obvious intent of this commercial was to convince voters that conceal-and-carry was supported by the law enforcement community and persuade them that guns were an effective way to reduce crime. The same critiques of the earlier ad can be applied to this one: not all police officers in Missouri necessarily supported Prop B, and crime statistics were open to various interpretations. In addition, while Captain Bergman was in the ad to speak for retired officers, he neglected to mention why most retired officers really wanted Prop B to pass—so they could legally carry their own concealed weapons.

A final MAC TV spot generated considerable controversy when it tried to neutralize a common complaint about Prop B, that child molesters and stalkers could be eligible for permits to carry concealed weapons. In the ad, Major Stone said, "Trust me. Only law-abiding citizens will get a permit."[31] This went against the belief of many, such as Sheriff Boehm, and drew an angry response from the SSWC. They argued the ad was inaccurate in claiming that stalkers and child molesters would be unable to get permits under the law, and insisted that people convicted of misdemeanor stalking or child molestation would be able to get permits under the proposition, as would people with a history of violence more than five years old.[32] MAC refuted this, in part, by arguing that since HB 1891 would give sheriffs the right to deny permits to anyone who had displayed violent behavior in the past five years, molesters and stalkers could—and would—legally be denied permits on a case-by-case basis. MAC's Brett Feinstein said, "I hope the chiefs will place their trust in law enforcement continuing to protect the safety of Missourians," and suggested

Missourians should do the same.[33] The common theme of all the TV spots run by MAC was that Prop B was a sensible way to reduce crime, while opponents worried that passing Prop B would have the opposite effect.

In addition to television advertisements, MAC also used radio advertisements, newspaper ads, the Internet, direct mail, yard signs, door hangings, and phone banks to get out the vote. The group began its radio campaign in February with a series of ads featuring law enforcement personnel, including Sergeant Johnson and Major Stone.[34] Later in the campaign, MAC called on a U.S. senator for radio support. John Ashcroft appeared in a spot meant to assure voters that the law was strong enough to keep criminals from getting conceal-and-carry permits. Criminal background checks, he argued, would prevent criminals from legally carrying concealed weapons, but that wasn't enough protection for law-abiding citizens. In the ad, Ashcroft said, "As Missouri's former attorney general, I learned an important lesson. Criminals don't obey laws. Criminals don't get permits. And criminals don't get fingerprinted—not voluntarily."[35] The obvious message of the spot was that while law enforcement officials could prevent criminals from legally obtaining right-to-carry permits, it couldn't prevent them from illegally carrying guns. The only thing that could be done about that, therefore, was to give law-abiding citizens the chance to arm themselves.

MAC's campaign to win the Prop B vote was all-encompassing and the organization sought support from almost every imaginable constituency, especially those it could convince to worry about their personal safety. For urban residents, MAC wanted to show that crime was rampant in cities and that there was no reason criminals should be the only ones allowed to carry guns. MAC's ads on TV, radio, billboards, and in mainstream newspapers all made this appeal to voters in St. Louis and Kansas City. One of the most fascinating aspects of MAC's campaign was its attempt to capitalize on a wave of gay-bashing attacks to convince gays and lesbians that guns could protect them against violent hate crime. MAC had a two-pronged approach to gays and lesbians: running ads in so-called "alternative" newspapers and hiring a special consultant to speak to gay and lesbian audiences.

The consultant was a former Missouri prosecutor, Wood Kinnard. In 1999 he served as a board member of the national gay rights organization, the Human Rights Campaign. In meetings with gays and lesbians across the state, Kinnard argued that conceal-and-carry could prevent violent gay-bashing attacks. In an interview, he said, "It's an important issue. Ours is a community where choice and civil rights are key."[36] Similarly, ads run in "alternative" newspapers suggested hate crimes such as attacks on gays could be prevented by the right to carry. One ad featured photos of Matthew Shepard, James Byrd, Jr., and Billy Jack Gaither, with the tag line, "Hate or self-defense. Only one should be a crime." All three men were victims of hate crimes. James Byrd was killed by men with racist motives, but Matthew Shepard and Billy Jack Gaither were both gay, killed in separate incidents by men who claimed they were driven to violence after Shepard and Gaither made sexual advances on them. Shepard, a college student, was beaten and left to die outside Laramie, Wyoming, in October 1998. Gaither was a textiles worker in Alabama who was beaten and stabbed to death in February 1999.

Clearly, MAC wanted to convince the readers of the "alternative" publications that a concealed weapon, or the threat of a concealed weapon, could prevent such attacks. In addition to gays and lesbians, MAC also focused advertising at other specific constituencies, such as crime victims and women, with spots like the Kleeschulte commercial. In addition, they targeted ads at rural voters. Rural voters were the strongest supporters of Prop B, but MAC wanted to convince them that it was critical they actually get out and vote on April 6.

Billboards played an important part in the campaign. MAC erected a total of 131 billboards statewide.[37] Like much of the advertising in this campaign, the billboards generated controversy. Some members of the St. Louis Police Officers Association objected to the fact that the organization was listed on the billboards as a supporter of Prop B. The ubiquitous Sergeant John Johnson, the St. Louis Police Officers Association's president, asserted that a vast majority of members were in favor of the measure and that only four officers had actually complained. However, the controversy had legs because the vice president of the association, Sam Zouglas, was one of the officers to speak out. His chief complaint was that the training requirement in HB 1891 was insufficient. He said, "I don't believe 12 hours is enough, and I think the person should have to qualify like we do, twice a year."[38] His complaint echoed the concerns of Ted Boehm and others in the law enforcement community.

In addition to traditional media, MAC and its allies also relied on grassroots methods, such as Web sites, direct mail, e-mail, and phone banks. The members of groups such as the NRA, MAC, the Second Amendment Coalition, and Missourians for Personal Safety were "encouraged to register displeasure daily with opponents of concealed weapons and to write letters of support for Proposition B to local newspapers. They can react quickly. On Thursday, Missouri's pro baseball and football teams came out against concealed weapons. The next day, members got the message and the telephone numbers of the Cardinals, Rams, Chiefs and Royals to call to ask for reconsideration, 'talking points' included."[39] As is often the case when the NRA gets involved in campaigns, the rank-and-file were counted on to do their part to spread the word about Prop B.

The Opposition

While MAC had tremendous resources, the SSWC had difficulty raising money to pay for television ads, and when it finally did, the group produced a controversial spot that was factually inaccurate. The ad's visual featured an Uzi semi-automatic rifle, accompanied by voice-over narration that suggested Prop B would allow people to carry such a gun. "If Proposition B passes, Missouri's laws would be radically changed and someone convicted of assault, stalking—even child molesting—could legally carry one of these guns hidden beneath their clothes—in malls, stadiums, even school playgrounds," the ad said. "That's why Missouri's police chiefs urge you to vote NO on Proposition B."[40] Research shows that the visual element of a commercial, especially a political advertisement, is what people are most likely to remember.[41] This spot's visual image implied that passage of Prop B would make it legal to carry Uzis. The implied threat was inaccurate and, therefore, misleading. Prop B would never have allowed the carrying of a concealed Uzi because the Uzi in the commercial was not a handgun, and Prop B dealt with handguns. The gun in the spot was classified by the federal government as a rifle, even though it had a very short barrel. Furthermore, because of its short barrel, it was outlawed by the assault weapons ban passed by the U.S. Congress in 1994. Uzis are ugly, frightening-looking weapons with a fearsome reputation. Seeing it in a television spot would certainly concern those who were already inclined to oppose Prop B and might influence those who were previously neutral on the issue. The trouble is that by running such an ad, SSWC was not, according to its own standards, any better morally than MAC, which it often accused of unfair or dishonest campaign practices.

The reaction from Proposition B proponents was immediate and angry, and it had an impact on the debate. Responding to the controversy, NBC affiliate station KOMU TV, in Columbia, Missouri, refused to run the ad. The affiliate, owned and operated by the University of Missouri's School of Journalism, declared it was wrong to run a misleading ad.[42] Considering that much of the pro–Prop B campaign was headquartered in Columbia and that many powerful members of the state legislature supported Prop B, it is interesting that this particular station responded so quickly. It is very possible that KOMU and the university feared political repercussions from pro–conceal-and-carry legislators in the General Assembly. The station has occasionally run into trouble from the legislature, and since it is owned and operated by the university, anything it does that angers legislators could have a negative impact on the entire school.

Defending the advertisement, SSWC's spokesperson, Gwen Fitzgerald, apologized for the spot's use of the Uzi, but argued that the text was accurate and again pointed out that the pro–Prop B side was outspending its opponents by an estimated 10 to 1 ratio.[43] Of course, neither of these defenses erased the fact that SSWC was running a factually misleading advertisement. Robin Carnahan later blamed the ad on a production error by the Philadelphia company, Shorr Associates, that made the ad.[44] However, it was ultimately the responsibility of SSWC to run accurate advertisements, and three days after the ad began running the group changed the visual image, replacing the Uzi rifle with an Uzi pistol. The group explained that the commercial was always supposed to use the Uzi pistol and that using the rifle was an honest mistake.[45] MAC was not impressed with SSWC's explanation or the length of time it took to correct the error. MAC spokesperson Amy Pennington said her group had sent letters to all television stations running the ad to inform them they were responsible for broadcasting inaccurate information. She also accused SSWC of doing what SSWC also liked to charge MAC with—using demagoguery. She said, "I think they're trying very hard to scare the voters . . . and they've done it."[46] All in all, the ad was probably a winner for SSWC, despite the controversy surrounding it. There is little doubt that the controversial visual extended the shelf life of the one ad the group was able to afford, keeping it fresh in voters' minds.

Free media, even about a controversy, helped keep SSWC's message on TV. While the inaccuracy of using an Uzi rifle in the ad might have outraged proponents of Prop B, it certainly didn't dissuade opponents, and by giving the ad more exposure than SSWC could afford, it certainly helped spread the anti–Prop B message. As the famed Republican campaign consultant and current head of Fox News, Roger Ailes, once said, "You get a 30 or 40 percent bump out . . . by getting it on the news. You get more viewers, you get credibility, you get it in a framework."[47] Some evidence of the effectiveness of the controversy about SSWC's ad comes from MAC itself, whose own polling found a shift in popular sentiment about Prop B once SSWC started its television campaign. According to MAC's field coordinator, Whitney O'Daniel, MAC's tracking polls showed Prop B supporters in the majority until SSWC's television campaign began. At that point, MAC's polls found opinion began shifting against Prop B.[48] This admission by MAC only demonstrates a correlation between the start of SSWC's television campaign and a change in public opinion.

It is far from evidence of a causal relationship, but it suggests that a group with limited resources can have an impact if it times its spending just right. Of course, having a controversial ad doesn't hurt.

In lieu of money to pay for TV time, SSWC usually had to rely on other, less expensive methods of spreading their message. The group focused on specific constituencies, such as mothers who feared gun violence. For instance, in the final days before the vote, SSWC used a message taped by Hillary Clinton in phone banks targeted at women voters. In her message, Clinton argued that passage of Prop B would make Missouri more dangerous for families by increasing the number of guns in society.[49]

SSWC also relied heavily on free news media coverage to get its point across to the public. The group sponsored many media events and news conferences for opponents to present their concerns about Prop B. In Springfield, a stronghold of Prop B support, the committee sponsored news conferences in which county sheriffs, business leaders, and educators spoke out against Prop B. For example, on March 2 the committee sponsored a forum, led by Prop B opponent Pete Herschend, the co-owner of Silver Dollar City. The forum featured a wide array of opponents who argued that Prop B was a bad idea. Law enforcement officials at the forum reiterated familiar concerns about the training requirement and the fact that concealed guns could be allowed in bars and schools.[50]

In another Springfield event on March 31, the committee brought together the leaders of several school districts from southwest Missouri, all of whom expressed concern about how the law might affect their ability to keep guns out of schools. For example, the superintendent of the Nixa school district, Terry Reid, said, "We really think this is a step in the wrong direction in terms of providing safety for children. The fact that more people would have guns increases the likelihood that someone is going to get hurt."[51] Borrowing time-honored tactics of underfunded groups, SSWC created news events for the press to cover, getting the group media exposure it couldn't afford to buy.

Of course, Prop B opponents weren't the only people to recognize the power of a good media event. MAC had real star power on its side when the NRA President Charlton Heston made three appearances in Missouri to promote the proposition, and while many elected officials spoke out against Prop B, the referendum had many supporters in government as well. No supporters were as outspoken as Wayne Crump, the sponsor of HB 1891, but many Democrats from rural parts of the state joined Crump in favor of Prop B.

MAC felt a majority of Missourians supported conceal-and-carry, but at the same time, there was obvious concern among the organizers of the campaign for Prop B that St. Louis and Kansas City voters could kill the proposition.

Prop B had very strong support in public opinion polls in out-state counties, but MAC felt a genuine urgency to make sure those people voted. For that reason many rallies and forums were held around the state, especially in its southwest corner. Southwest Missouri is a conservative part of the state and its biggest city, Springfield, was considered an important pro-gun urban center. It was the largest metropolitan area with majority support for the referendum. Encouraging high turnout from this city and the surrounding area was a crucial part of the campaign. Few Democratic politicians were as supportive as Jim Kreider, D–Nixa, who later became speaker of the Missouri House of Representatives. Kreider drew considerable local media coverage when he sponsored a gathering in Nixa, giving supporters of Prop B an opportunity to express themselves. Kreider said, "This is a pretty important issue to me. It's a philosophical one. It's about freedom."[52] The forum and others like it were part of a concerted effort to bring out the vote in southwest Missouri.

As the election drew closer, the pace of pro–Prop B events accelerated in Springfield. On Friday, April 2, three women married to local law enforcement officers appeared at a news conference sponsored by MAC. Also on April 2, author John Lott, the intellectual leader of the concealed weapons movement, spoke in Springfield as part of his nationwide tour in support of his book, *More Guns, Less Crime.* On Saturday, April 3, MAC brought Gratia Hupp, a Texas state senator and a survivor of the Luby's Cafeteria shooting in Killeen, Texas, to speak in support of the referendum. Her visit to Springfield was paid for with two thousand dollars from the NRA.[53]

Hupp, whose parents were killed in the Luby's shooting, was elected to the Texas state senate after the murders. Speaking in Springfield, she argued, "A gun is a tool that can be used to kill a family, and it's a tool that can be used to protect a family," and asserted that if she hadn't been forced to keep her gun in the car, as the law in Texas required at the time, she might have been able to save her parents.[54] SSWC's Gwen Fitzgerald and Pete Herschend both criticized Senator Rupp's appearance as just another example of the NRA's using money to try to buy the election, a part of what Fitzgerald again called a "multimillion-dollar campaign to get Prop B passed."[55] Finally, on the fifth of April, the day before the election, Charlton Heston made his last visit to Missouri when he traveled to Springfield to rally supporters. Commenting on the visits of such high-profile supporters of Prop B, Fitzgerald again played the carpetbagger card. She said, "They've brought in Charlton Heston and John Lott, Washington, D.C., lobbyists...all advocates that won't have to live under the ramifications of this bill. We're a grass-roots organization, made up of Missouri leaders who know what it would be like in Missouri if this bill were passed. This is a terrible, terrible thing for us."[56] Whether it would be terrible, of course, was a debatable issue, but obviously, the anti–Prop B forces felt one of their best weapons was to play David to the NRA's Goliath.

While the groups supporting and opposing Prop B sparred with each other in the public spotlight, there was considerable maneuvering going on in Jefferson City as politicians tried to influence the outcome of the election. The actions of politicians on both sides brought charges of manipulation and intimidations. They also made for what was, at times, bizarre political theater.

Chapter Twelve

The Campaign of 1999—A Brawl

The Politicians Play Hardball

The public fight over concealed guns was certainly contentious. The skirmishes that took place in the background were, perhaps, even uglier. In the weeks prior to the vote, charges of intimidation were leveled against some members of the state legislature, especially the HB 1891 sponsor, House Majority Leader Wayne Crump. In March, Crump and House Minority Leader Delbert Scott, R–Lowry City, mailed a letter to lobbyists encouraging them to support Prop B. The mailing included a questionnaire to be returned to Crump that asked them to divulge their groups' positions on conceal-and-carry. The letters, according to Crump, were paid for by MAC, and he freely admitted that he intended to share the survey responses with that group. Of course, the letter and survey were more than a simple information-gathering tool. The majority leader and minority leader can both have tremendous influence on the legislative agenda, as both have procedural means of facilitating or blocking proposed legislation. Whatever Crump's and Scott's intent was, the letter and survey clearly had a chilling effect on any group or company with business before the legislature that might have opposed Prop B. The SSWC's spokesperson, Gwen Fitzgerald, accused Crump and Scott of trying to intimidate lobbyists, saying, "The undertones are pretty clear when people are asked to fill out their position and send it to a government office."[1] Most lobbyists, speaking off-the-record, seemed to agree with Fitzgerald. They said they recommended their clients remain neutral, under the principle that no good could come from stating a position on such a controversial issue.[2] Most companies seemed to agree with the lobbyists, as only twenty-two of the thousands of companies doing business in Missouri contributed to the SSWC.

Crump denied he was trying to intimidate anyone. He and several other legislators defended the letter in a press conference held in the capitol rotunda on March 11. They called the letter nothing more than normal political advocacy in a hard-fought campaign and denied intimidation was the intent. Crump was unapologetic for his association with MAC and said, "I'm working with them. It's no secret I'm in favor of it."[3] For Crump there was no impropriety in fighting hard for his own legislation, and he suggested that he wasn't doing anything different from the opposition.

Crump argued that when Robin Carnahan personally contacted lobbyists seeking contributions to oppose the referendum, she was the one trying to intimidate.[4] His implication was that Carnahan, as the governor's daughter, might coerce groups and companies to donate only because they didn't want to anger the governor. Robin Carnahan disputed this characterization, arguing, "That's like Goliath complaining about David fighting back. I'm a private citizen. I have no influence over lobbyists or legislation. They are powerful elected officials who are using their office to intimidate people."[5] The David and Goliath argument was a bit disingenuous on her part. Carnahan may, in fact, have been a private citizen, but she was undeniably the daughter of the most powerful elected official in the state, who was also outspoken in his opposition to conceal-and-carry. It does not stretch the imagination that when she spoke to lobbyists, they believed she could be speaking for her father. For Carnahan to suggest she was nothing more than a simple private citizen engaging in the political process was difficult to believe. What is certainly fair to conclude is that both Crump and Carnahan knew their names and positions were influential and hoped it would make a difference in the election.

In another interesting move, which Prop B opponents called heavy-handed, Wayne Crump used the legislature's work on the fiscal year 2000 budget to take a figurative shot at the governor. In late March he sponsored an amendment to eliminate $700,000 budgeted for the governor's ten-member Highway Patrol security detail and replace it with $160 for the governor and his wife, Jean, to apply for concealed weapons permits. Speaker of the House Steve Gaw tried to block the amendment, but was unable to, and the measure passed by a vote of 78–77, with nearly unanimous support from Republicans in addition to a few Democrats, including Crump. It was repealed thirty minutes later by a vote of 93 to 42 at Crump's request, but not before he'd sent a message.

Commenting on the maneuver, Crump suggested the fact that the governor opposed Prop B while benefiting from the protection of armed guards sent a mixed signal to the citizens of Missouri. He said, "I wanted to make a point today and I think the point's been made."[6] Chris Sifford, the governor's spokesman, said the action was typical of the NRA and its supporters' tactics: "If you don't agree with us, we're going to punish you."[7] He criticized legislators when he said, "If the legislature wants to eliminate the governor's security detail, the governor can deal with that. However, it does seem they have taken a cavalier attitude about the budget."[8] Only three Republicans voted against Crump's amendment, and two of them would play important roles in the post-1999 conceal-and-carry fight. Representative Jon Dolan, R–Lake St. Louis, who became a key figure in the override of Governor Holden's veto of conceal-and-carry in 2003, was critical of the vote. He said, "It makes for a few light moments, but it is a very serious subject. The chief executive of the state of Missouri must be protected."[9] Another Republican who voted against Crump's measure was Matt Blunt, R–Springfield, a supporter of conceal-and-carry and the Republican gubernatorial candidate in 2004. Blunt called Crump irresponsible for introducing the amendment, despite the fact that it was later repealed.[10]

This incident said a lot about Missouri politics. If anyone doubted the volatility of guns in Missouri, one didn't need to look further than this episode for evidence of how divisive the issue can be. The fact that guns prompted the Democratic majority leader to make such a direct attack against his Democratic governor graphically demonstrates that this is an issue which knows no partisan boundary.

The Companies—A Price to Pay

While many businesses in Missouri were reluctant to take a stand of any kind on the conceal-and-carry issue for fear of losing customers, there were a few businesses that took a public position against the right to carry. Why would businesses oppose the right to carry? An in-house memo written by the head of security of the Maritz Corporation in St. Louis, a corporate travel and market research company, became public and suggested that Maritz and other businesses should be opposed to Proposition B because it exposed employees and customers to danger in the person of a careless or angry gun carrier, and because it exposed companies to potential legal liability in shootings on their premises.[11]

A statement issued by the Greater Kansas City Chamber of Commerce in 1998 argued against concealed weapons and urged businesses to support the campaign against Prop B, as it expected that the NRA would contribute heavily to efforts to pass the referendum.[12] The Overland Park, Kansas, Chamber of Commerce, which is part of the Kansas City metropolitan area, also took a public position against conceal-and-carry.[13] When groups such as these opposed Prop B, it helped take pressure off their members to take a stand.

This does not mean there weren't some companies that went public with their opposition to Prop B. For example, Dee Wetzel, a spokeswoman for Schnucks Markets, Inc., a St. Louis grocery store chain, explained her company's opposition to conceal-and-carry when she said, "Our company wants to ensure a safe shopping environment for our customers and a safe workplace for our employees," reflecting the exact concerns expressed in the Maritz memo.[14] One businessman who took what was, perhaps, a surprising anti–Prop B position was Peter Herschend, the co-owner of Silver Dollar City amusement park near Branson. His public opposition was surprising because his business was located in the heart of a region with some of the state's strongest support for Prop B. In early March, Herschend led a news conference sponsored by the SSWC in Springfield designed to highlight the flaws in Prop B. He argued, "The law itself is just a hodgepodge of poorly written legislation."[15] He added, "The greater loss will occur when there is a shooting inside that business—it's a liability and a perception problem. Silver Dollar City is a very safe place today. Picture what one shooting would do."[16]

While the Kansas City Chamber of Commerce was clearly opposed to concealed guns, the question was murkier in St. Louis, where the St. Louis Regional Commerce and Growth Association (RCGA) became embroiled in a mid-campaign controversy about whether or not it endorsed or opposed Prop B. In early March, MAC issued a statement claiming the RCGA's official position was that it had not found a reason to oppose Prop B. This prompted Jim Farell, a spokesperson for RCGA, to say that MAC had combined information in a way that created a false impression of RGCA's support for Prop B. In fact, he said, the group had taken no position on Prop B and would not be taking a public position for several weeks, if at all.[17]

In its statement citing RCGA's support for Prop B, MAC quoted a member of RCGA's Public Policy Commission, Jonathan F. Dalton. What wasn't mentioned in the statement was the fact that Dalton was also the deputy treasurer of MAC and legal counsel and lobbyist for the NRA in Missouri. In denouncing MAC's statement, Farell added, "The RCGA's membership and volunteers are strongly divided on whether Proposition B would have an impact on the business community. In fact, they are strongly divided on their positions on Proposition B itself."[18]

MAC's spokesperson, Amy Pennington, tried to defuse the situation with a statement in which she took personal responsibility for the false impression created by the original press release. She said, "It was my mistake to quote him."[19] Meanwhile, SSWC expressed the expected level of outrage and issued a sharply worded press release that accused the MAC's original statement of being "riddled with loopholes," just like Proposition B itself.[20]

Backlash

The caution of many companies that decided not to take a position on Prop B was well advised, because the proponents of Prop B were particularly effective in organizing protests against anti–Prop B companies. During the campaign, the pro–Prop B side regularly called for customers of such businesses to protest against the companies' anti–Prop B stance. One media report noted, "Prop B proponents have encouraged economic sanctions against businesses that have contributed to the opponents' campaign. One of the proponents' committee's Web sites listed businesses that had contributed more than $5,000 to the opponents. The site said, 'Criminals get aid and comfort from Missouri businesses.'"[21] Pro–Prop B organizations publicized the names of companies that contributed to the campaign to defeat the referendum via mailings and on Internet sites and their targets included firms that were only tangentially involved. For example, the Ford Motor Company received many calls at its headquarters in Dearborn, Michigan, after the company's Jefferson City lobbyist suggested publicly that Prop B wasn't a good idea.[22] The proponents of Prop B also reacted quickly when the state's professional sports teams voiced opposition to the referendum, barraging team offices with phone calls.

Schools and educators were also targeted by proponents of Prop B. Many education groups opposed the measure. For example, Marlene Davis, the president of the St. Louis School Board, said, "I just don't want kids to believe that's the way we should live in society."[23] Brent Ghan, a spokesman for the Missouri School Boards Association, said, "There is a provision in that law that says the prohibition against possessing a firearm in a school zone does not apply if the person is licensed to do so by the state. If people are licensed to carry, they would be able to carry onto school grounds, and that would not be a violation of the gun free zones act."[24] Education groups opposed to Prop B included the St. Louis School Board; a group of school administrators from southwest Missouri cities including Springfield, Nixa, and Branson; the state Board of Education; the Missouri School Boards Association; and associations of principals, superintendents, and teachers. Proponents of Prop B responded to objections from educators with the same vigor they had for businesses opposed to Prop B. For instance, after two statewide organizations, one representing principals and the other serving superintendents, mailed a letter to schools throughout Missouri that argued Prop B would nullify the Gun Free School Zones Act of 1990, MAC contacted its grassroots followers to inform them what the principals and superintendents said, that it was untrue, and to urge them to contact principals directly.[25]

In Columbia, public school principals scheduled a press conference where they planned to stake out an anti–Prop B position. In a preemptive strike following the public announcement of the upcoming press conference, pro–Prop B forces mobilized members to call the principals of Columbia schools and the school district's administration, according to Greg Robinson, a spokesperson for Missourians for Personal Safety, one of the pro–Prop B groups based in Columbia.[26] The press conference was canceled, though the Columbia superintendent, Jim Ritter, denied it was because the principals were intimidated or the school district had ordered them to cancel it. Ritter said, "I certainly didn't feel intimidated by it. I am not going to allow anyone to intimidate us."[27] Ritter claimed the district had received half a dozen calls or fewer, though there is no way to verify that number. The official reason for canceling the gathering was that due to a scheduling conflict, one of the principals was unable to attend the event.[28] Regardless of these official comments, it still seems possible that intimidation played a role in canceling the news conference.

Peter Herschend, the co-owner of Silver Dollar City, reported receiving many phone calls from Prop B supporters. He responded defiantly, saying, "It may not be the nicest way to run a campaign, but the NRA knows how to organize in a powerful fashion. It can be effective because some people will give in to that. Not me."[29] Other companies that might have opposed Prop B were not as brave, however, and either refused to take a position or backed away from anti–Prop B statements after Prop B advocates responded. The supporters of Prop B proved themselves very eager to respond to any organization that spoke out against Prop B. Sometimes, they were a little too enthusiastic.

For example, one pro–Prop B group, the Second Amendment Coalition, urged its members to e-mail businesses such as NationsBank of Kansas City and Hallmark to express their displeasure with the companies' position on Prop B. In the case of NationsBank, however, the attack was misplaced. In March and April, the Second Amendment Coalition's Web page said, "Attention, NationsBank customers. Did you know that the CEO of your bank is giving money to the opponents of right-to-carry? That's right, the money your account earns him is being used to oppose your constitutional right."[30] However, it soon turned out that NationsBank had been attacked unfairly. The company was officially neutral on the proposition and never donated money to the SSWC's campaign.[31] The company's Kansas City division president, Bill Nelson, signed a fund-raising letter in support of SSWC, but neither he nor the bank gave any money to the group. A spokeswoman for NationsBank of Kansas City, Shirley Nova, reported that several branch managers received complaints from Prop B supporters who thought the chairman of NationsBank's parent corporation, BankAmerica Corp, had endorsed the SSWC.[32] That assumption was entirely untrue, but the damage was done before the truth was widely publicized.

After the Prop B campaign drew to a close, a hit list of other businesses that supported the SSWC was posted on the Second Amendment Coalition's Web site. In fact, as late as mid-2003 the list was still posted there. Following the campaign, supporters of Prop B were clearly upset with anyone who opposed them, from the governor to companies that donated to the anti–Prop B campaign. As MAC spokesman Brett Feinstein said, "They are taking customer money and using it for political purposes. It is my right, as a consumer, as to where I spend my money if I don't want to see my money funneled through a cause I don't want to participate in. It seems to me from a business standpoint that I would stay out because I don't want to alienate my customer base."[33]

Groups such as Missourians for Personal Safety posted lists of companies that opposed Prop B during the campaign and urged their members to boycott them. Missourians for Personal Safety's boycott list was still on the Web site sponsored by the group, www.moccw.org, in 2004. The site promised to let conceal-and-carry owners know who the opponents of Prop B were, how they made money, and who their competition was. The Web master of the site, Steve Jones, cited Schnucks Markets as an easy target that could be hurt by a boycott.[34] Greg Robinson, the treasurer of Missourians for Personal Safety, suggested that it was perfectly legitimate for supporters of conceal-and-carry to take drastic action against companies that contributed to the anti–Prop B campaign because there was so much at stake. He said, "They want to represent themselves as being good corporate citizens. But people who feel strongly about this aren't going to be going to Silver Dollar City. And I know people who have pulled money out of Commerce Bank. This is a civil rights action. If the NAACP was doing this to obtain their objectives, you would find nothing wrong with it."[35]

In 2003, the NRA posted a blacklist of what it called "anti-gun" organizations, news media figures, celebrities, and corporations. Of forty-four corporations the NRA asserted had "leant their corporate support to gun control initiatives or taken a position supporting gun control," twenty-six were based in Missouri and nearly all had opposed Prop B in 1999. The NRA list included the name and contact information for the chief executive of each corporation. The Missouri companies included on the list were: American Century, an investment company; AMC, a movie theater chain; Argosy Casinos; Blue Cross/Blue Shield of Kansas City; BJC Health Systems; Earthgrains, a commercial bakery; General American, an insurance company; Hallmark; Health Midwest; James B. Nutter, an investment company; the Kansas City Chiefs; the Kansas City Royals; Mallinckrodt, Inc, a clothing starch company; Maritz Corporation; Schnucks Markets; Silver Dollar City; Site Oil Company; Southwestern Bell, St. Louis; Sprint; SSM Health Systems, St. Louis; the St. Louis Cardinals; the St. Louis Rams; Saint Louis University; Sverdrup Corporation, an engineering firm; and Unity Health, St. Louis.[36] Clearly, posting the list of corporations was an attempt to achieve some measure of payback for the 1999 defeat of Prop B.

The NationsBank controversy was only a single example of the action taken against the banking industry in Missouri for lending support to the anti–Proposition B campaign. The Missouri Bankers Association took a public position against Prop B in December 1998 and sent letters to its member banks stating the group's position. However, in February 1999 the organization took a second vote and decided to adopt a neutral position on the issue. This switch was in response to the actions of pro–Prop B advocates, according to Max Cook, the president of the MBA. Cook said, "The next thing we knew, all heck broke loose, and we started getting phone calls and e-mails and faxes and what have you from the general public. They were saying 'Hey, what are banks doing getting involved in this issue' . . . We had a huge wave of communication from people saying how terrible we were. There was a period of 10 days to two weeks when we did nothing but respond to people."[37] The effective protest against the MBA's opposition to Prop B was coordinated by Fred Meyers, the campaign manager of MAC, who sent a mailing to supporters of Prop B calling on them to take action.[38]

The governor, not shy about expressing his opposition to Prop B, was angered by the actions of Prop B supporters. In statements to the press a week before the Prop B vote, Carnahan asserted that the pro–Prop B campaign had engaged in a "pattern of intimidation" against opponents of the proposition.[39] Carnahan also said, "I am very disappointed with the personal nature some of the proponents have gotten into on this, including Representative Wayne Crump."[40] However, from the perspective of Crump, Meyers, and other supporters of Proposition B, they were merely exercising their rights to participate in the political process. Crump said, "The NRA has 103,000 members who will take exception to any organization or business taking a stand in opposition to their feeling."[41] MAC spokesperson Brett Feinstein said the governor "can use whatever scare words he wants to. NRA members buy goods, they buy services, and if they are shopping places where the vendor or the store is working against something they believe in, they take their business someplace else."[42] Boycotts are seldom truly effective because it is hard to get large numbers of people to go along with the action, but the threats of boycotts can be enough to get a business's attention and make it change its behavior. The threat of boycotts from Prop B supporters clearly had an impact on many Missouri businesses because they believed the threat, perhaps because Prop B supporters were a unique group of people. What set Prop B supporters apart from the average citizen was their determination to follow through on the threats they made, both before and after the vote.

The objective, of course, was not just some simplistic desire for revenge. It was an attempt to send the message, "You won this battle, but the war is far from over." For the supporters of conceal-and-carry, the loss in 1999 was a setback, but was by no means the end of the debate. In fact, several years later, in 2003, after the legislature cleared the way for conceal-and-carry, businesses opposed to hidden guns continued to pay a price as pro-gun advocates still objected to companies that supported anti–Prop B efforts, but also turned their attention on businesses that wished to take advantage of the right the new conceal-and-carry law offered them to post signs notifying patrons that guns weren't allowed in their places of business. In response to this, longtime advocate Tim Oliver began to offer a printable card on his Web site, learntocarry.com, for gun carriers to give business owners that read, "No Guns, No Money," and said they would shop elsewhere if they couldn't carry their guns into the store.[43]

Anheuser-Busch and Its Support for Prop B

While few companies took a stand against Prop B, there weren't many companies that got involved in the pro–Prop B campaign either. One exception was the beer giant, St. Louis–based Anheuser-Busch. In early March 1999, the brewer effectively endorsed Prop B through a statement publicized by MAC that said, "This company has a long tradition of promoting responsible firearms ownership as well as shooting sports," and added that the company felt Proposition B was the "prudent" result of six years of debate on conceal-and-carry.[44]

As the only major company and a brewery, no less, to endorse the proposition publicly, Anheuser-Busch received instant criticism from opponents of Prop B. Sarah Brady, the president of HCI, said it was socially irresponsible for a producer of alcohol to support the proposition. She said, "Study after study has shown that in most violent events, both victims and offenders were drinking alcohol before the violent incident took place."[45] SSWC also condemned the endorsement, of course. Spokesperson Gwen Fitzgerald called the brewery socially irresponsible and added, "One of Proposition B's major loopholes is that it allows the carrying of concealed handguns into bars, restaurants, stadiums, casinos, and other venues where alcohol is served."[46]

In the face of such public criticism, a spokesman for the company tried to downplay its position by saying that while it had expressed support for Prop B it had not sought to place its support in the spotlight. The company's general counsel, Stephen K. Lambright, said the brewery "was approached by a local organization supporting this proposal, and we provided them with our opinion. They issued a news release to announce this. We have not provided any further support or assistance to this effort."[47] MAC's spokesperson, Amy Pennington, tried to aid Anheuser-Busch's public image when she argued that the company hadn't given any money for the campaign and that MAC didn't plan to use the endorsement in its advertisements. She said, "We absolutely recognize that firearms and alcohol don't mix, but this has nothing to do with that. This is a personal safety and personal rights issue."[48]

One might wonder why the company would take even a low-profile position on this issue. The decision by Anheuser-Busch seems to have been motivated by a concern about a preexisting public perception of the company as a supporter of gun control legislation. The corporation seems to have felt that such an impression was hurting sales among key segments of the beer-drinking population. In his statement, Anheuser-Busch's Lambright suggested the company's policy was a simple business decision. His statement read, "For several years, rumors have been perpetuated among consumers that Anheuser-Busch supports gun control legislation. In fact, we receive a steady number of calls or letters each month from consumers inquiring about our position on gun rights. For some consumers and retail customers, hearing this rumor is enough for them to boycott our products."[49] Of course, saying that the company was endorsing Prop B for economic reasons did nothing to reduce criticism from the opposition. The company's position was widely scorned by opponents of Proposition B, but that did not cause the group to change its position on conceal-and-carry. If anything, the brewery seems to have stiffened its resolve over the years.

In fact, guns seem to have led to the company's decision in 2003 to drop financial support for the reelection campaign of Governor Bob Holden. The company announced it was no longer supporting the incumbent and, instead, the brewery very publicly endorsed his Democratic primary opponent, State Auditor Claire McCaskill, and gave her a ten-thousand-dollar campaign donation, apparently in response to Holden's veto of the 2003 conceal-and-carry bill. At the time the company made its endorsement decision, a company spokesperson said the decision was made, in large measure, because it was important to the company's chairman, August A. Busch III. The spokesperson said, "This is a huge deal for Mr. Busch," because he was an avid sportsman with "strong concerns about personal security."[50] One reporter described the sequence of events in this way: "Before Holden vetoed the bill last summer, sources say, a brewery lobbyist showed up at the governor's office to tell him that such action would end the long-standing support he'd enjoyed from Anheuser-Busch and its executives. Holden confirmed that position later in phone conversations with Anheuser-Busch Cos. Chairman August A. Busch III and corporate group vice president Stephen K. Lambright."[51] The timing of events became a little uncertain several months later when the Holden campaign made the brewery's endorsement of McCaskill the subject of a campaign commercial and a brewery official stepped in to defend themselves and McCaskill. The official asserted its decision to support the state auditor had nothing to do with guns. In June 2004 Lambright said, "We made our decision to support Claire McCaskill before any discussions of her position on the concealed carry law. Our support for her is strictly due to her potential as a gubernatorial candidate for the state of Missouri."[52] In fact, McCaskill was on record at the time as saying that, had she been governor, she would also have vetoed the bill. Of course, since she wasn't governor at the time, she didn't have to, and when Holden lost the financial support of the brewery, it was costly, not just in financial terms, but also in terms of public relations.

The governor responded to the decision, saying, "Anheuser-Busch has indicated they are no longer supporting me . . . There's many people in that organization that wanted me to support the conceal-and-carry, and I said no."[53] Traditionally, Anheuser-Busch gives money to candidates of both parties, as any smart company doing business in Missouri would. According to state ethics records and the National Institute on Money in State Politics, the brewery has been the largest corporate donor to the two main political parties in Missouri over the past three elections. In those three elections, Anheuser-Busch gave a total of $371,600 to the Missouri Republican party and $352,650 to the Missouri Democratic party.[54] In 2004, while the company supported the candidacy of Claire McCaskill, it also supported the campaign of Matt Blunt, the Republican nominee for governor.

The brewery's decision to drop Holden and support his Democratic opponent was political fodder Holden tried to use against McCaskill during the 2004 primary campaign. McCaskill was quite outspoken in her opposition to conceal-and-carry as the Jackson County prosecutor in the mid-1990s. While Governor Holden clearly decided to appeal to his base by opposing conceal-and-carry in 2003, McCaskill remained quiet on conceal-and-carry, saying she preferred to focus on other issues. In an interview with the *Kansas City Star* in October 2003, she said guns and abortion were important issues but that they distracted the legislature too much, taking too much time and energy away from issues that were, in reality, more important for Missourians, such as transportation, education, and health care.[55] As the campaign heated up in the summer of 2004, guns were the focus of the most controversial television ad of the primary season in Missouri. The ad claimed, "Holden loses the support of Anheuser-Busch because of the veto. Three weeks later Claire McCaskill takes almost $10,000 from Anheuser-Busch and says 'my focus now has changed' on conceal and carry."[56] In response, McCaskill argued the ad took the quote out of context and reiterated that if she had been governor in 2003, she also would have vetoed the bill.[57] The ad was critiqued on many fronts, including the press, as a misrepresentation of McCaskill's true views, but the fact that events that really began in 1999 became a campaign issue in 2004 is no surprise. Where guns are concerned in Missouri, there are very few boundaries.

The fighting between advocacy groups and politicians was, of course, about one thing—influencing voters. As election day drew near, the advocates of Prop B had reason for encouragement, because polling numbers looked good. The campaign wasn't over until the last ballot was cast, however, and many, including the editorial writers of some of the state's largest newspapers, weighed in until the very end.

Chapter Thirteen

The Campaign of 1999—Public Opinion
and the News Media

As the campaign was fought, neither side could comfortably claim the public was on its side, though if anyone had reason for optimism, it was the pro–Prop B side. The *Kansas City Star*'s corporate parent, Knight-Ridder, conducted a public opinion poll of six hundred Missourians on the concealed guns issue in mid-March 1999. The poll found the vote was too close to call. With a margin of error of plus or minus 4 percent, the survey found that 42 percent of likely voters opposed Prop B, 39 percent supported it, and the rest, nearly 20 percent, were undecided. The poll found men were much more likely to support conceal-and-carry than women; that African Americans were much more likely to oppose conceal-and-carry than whites; and that urbanites were much more likely to oppose Prop B than rural respondents. In St. Louis, the poll found only one in five respondents favored the proposition, while one in three favored it in Kansas City.[1] This was similar to an earlier poll conducted by the *Star* at the end of February, which found that 60 percent of people in the Kansas City metropolitan area opposed Prop B while only 23 percent favored it.[2] The pro–Prop B advocate, Steve McGhee, president of Missourians for Personal Safety, seemed to reflect frustration in response to this soft support for conceal-and-carry. He said, "We have a lot of soft supporters who think it's a good idea but don't know whether they want everybody carrying guns . . . I say people already are carrying guns. They are called criminals."[3]

The *Star*'s mid-March poll also showed a slight majority favored conceal-and-carry in rural parts of the state. Interestingly, the poll found that even among supporters there was a great deal of ambivalence about concealed weapons. As the *Star* reported, ". . . substantial numbers of potential voters question whether concealed weapons play a role in reducing crime. Even among people who support concealed weapons, one in four said they don't. Close to half of the gun owners—45 percent—opposed the proposal."[4]

According to the poll, the clearest predictor of whether someone supported or opposed Prop B was if they hailed from St. Louis and Kansas City or from out-state. There clearly were important cultural differences at play. For rural Missourians, guns were a way of life. A gun was a tool, not a threat. For urbanites, guns held a sense of danger. Rural residents tended to favor guns because they'd always had a positive relationship with them. Urban residents opposed guns because of the violence and destruction criminals wrought with them in hand.[5]

Paralleling the difference between urban and rural voters was the difference between African Americans and whites. In both the *Kansas City Star* poll and another survey, conducted by the *St. Louis Post-Dispatch,* African Americans tended to oppose Prop B, while whites tended to be more favorable toward it.[6] As with the split between rural and urban Missourians, the difference is easily explained. Whites seemed to fear violent crime and wished to find a defense against it. African Americans tended to view guns as the cause of violent crime and sought a way to reduce the violence. At the same time, however, the *Star's* February poll found evidence to suggest that if conceal-and-carry did become legal, a greater percentage of African Americans, 30 percent, would apply for permits than whites, 15 percent. Explaining this, Emanuel Cleaver, Kansas City's mayor and a Prop B opponent, said, "We're the victims . . . African-Americans are disproportionately transported to funeral homes with gunshot wounds . . . African-Americans tend to be paranoid, with some justification, about not being able to protect themselves."[7]

Religious leaders, many of whom were pastors of largely African American, inner-city congregations, were outspoken in their opposition to Prop B. In an editorial published in the *Kansas City Star* in late March, a group of African American religious leaders from the Kansas City area wrote, "Most active law enforcement officers fear that Proposition B would force them to assume that 'everyone is packing' . . . The specter of walking through metal detectors at most public venues is unacceptable and a deleterious step in the wrong direction in our efforts to teach our children how best to build a civil society."[8]

Yet another statewide survey, conducted by William Woods University the week before the election, found a plurality of voters favored Prop B. In a survey of 513 registered voters, the school's survey found 41 percent of respondents supported the proposition, while 37 percent were opposed.[9] Neither the *Kansas City Star* nor the William Woods polls were conclusive, as both were within their margins of error and included large numbers of undecided voters.

In an earlier poll conducted by the *St. Louis Post-Dispatch* in 1998, 60 percent of St. Louis residents opposed the right to carry, while 54 percent of residents statewide were opposed. In late March 1999, however, the *Post-Dispatch* found opinion had changed to majority support for Prop B, with significantly fewer respondents claiming to be undecided.[10] It is possible that the difference in the number of undecided voters was the result of a blitz of late pro–concealed weapons advertising.

The *Post-Dispatch*'s poll, conducted by Zogby International, found that 53 percent of 605 likely voters favored the proposition, while 34 percent were opposed and just 13 percent were undecided, as opposed to the 20 percent who were undecided in the *Kansas City Star*'s poll just a week earlier.[11] The St. Louis poll had a margin of error of 4 percent. In breaking down demographic subgroups, the study found the strongest supporters were men, gun owners, and rural Missourians. In addition, Republicans were more likely to favor the proposition than Democrats. Interestingly, the survey, like the *Kansas City Star* poll, found the pro–Prop B campaign's favorite selling point that concealed handguns would reduce crime did not make a significant impression on voters, who didn't agree with the statement. In addition, just 32.7 percent of respondents indicated an intention to apply for a permit, while 66.1 percent said they would not.[12]

Many of the *Post-Dispatch*'s questions elicited results that were somewhat confusing, given the number who claimed to support Prop B. The poll found that only 23 percent of respondents felt concealed weapons would make their communities safer, 40 percent felt it would make their communities less safe, and 34 percent felt it would make no difference. Similarly, 48 percent indicated they didn't believe concealed weapons would deter crime, while 41 percent said they would. Finally, the poll found 45.2 percent of respondents felt gun control laws were not strict enough, 30.9 percent felt they were about right, and only 15 percent felt gun control laws were too strict. Another 8.9 percent were unsure.[13]

These findings, contrasted with majority support for Prop B, reflect a great deal of ambivalence about the issue and, more generally, demonstrate the dangers of relying too heavily on public opinion polls. We are, as a people, remarkably inconsistent in our opinions on almost every issue of public policy and political ideology, as can be demonstrated time after time.

John Zogby, the pollster who conducted the survey for the *St. Louis Post-Dispatch*, suggested his findings might have been influenced by the wording of the questions. His survey was worded this way: "Q. Proposition B on the ballot will ask: 'Shall sheriffs, or in the case of St. Louis County, the chief of police, be required to issue permits to carry concealed firearms to citizens who apply if various statutory requirements are satisfied.' How will you vote?" Zogby suggested that respondents indicating support for Prop B might have been influenced by the ballot language, arguing the wording of the proposition was confusing and probably led to higher support than one might normally expect. He said, "That's pretty confusing. The language is ambivalent. What it's saying is that by having police issuing permits, that kind of legitimizes the whole notion of carrying concealed weapons. The language itself is confusing because it could encourage people to do it."[14] Zogby's analysis rings true, but it also leads one to wonder why his pollsters didn't choose a different way to ask the question if they thought using the actual ballot language might give an inaccurate picture of people's true feelings. There are literally thousands of examples where the wording of a question influenced the findings of a survey. Sometimes simply changing one word can dramatically alter the responses to a question.

The Gender Gap

Women were seen as a critical audience throughout the campaign. As both the *St. Louis Post-Dispatch* and the *Kansas City Star* found, many women were skeptical about Prop B. In the *Kansas City Star* poll, for example, among men, 50 percent favored conceal-and-carry and 36 percent were opposed. Among women, only 28 percent supported the proposition, while 47 percent were opposed. However, an additional 22 percent of women were undecided, making them a target for appeals by both sides, with a couple of weeks left to go before the vote.[15] The *Star's* poll of the Kansas City area in February found that there were stark differences between men and women. The survey found that women opposed Prop B by a margin of five to one and that only one in thirteen women planned to apply for a conceal-and-carry permit if it passed.[16]

The safety of women was always a major talking point for the pro–Prop B campaign. In February, for example, Steve McGhee, the president of Missourians for Public Safety, claimed that women made up more than 80 percent of the students who took his firearms training classes, suggesting that women felt guns would provide them with an edge in the fight to protect themselves.[17] In the MAC ad featuring rape victim Sue Kleeschulte, she argued passage of Prop B would allow women to protect themselves against crime. Clearly, the ad was intended to shake women up and make them think of guns as a means of self-defense. Of course, the fact that the press pointed out that the ad was deceiving in suggesting Prop B would make it legal for women to do something it was already legal for them to do might have mitigated the impact of the spot, at least in the urban centers of St. Louis and Kansas City targeted by the ad. Other proponents of Proposition B also tried to emphasize women's safety as a reason to vote for the proposition.

John Hemeyer, the sheriff of Cole County, where Jefferson City is located, was a vocal supporter of Prop B. Hemeyer said he supported it as a way to give women additional protection against violent crime. In an interview with the Associated Press he said, "This is a choice I want my wife and daughter to have."[18] Not surprisingly, the NRA also argued that concealed guns protect women. The organization claimed 75 percent of women would be victims of at least one violent crime in their lifetime and that being allowed to carry handguns could help women change that statistic. A few women in the state legislature also promoted Prop B along similar lines. Suggesting that being a woman made her vulnerable, Representative Annie Reinhart, R–Liberty, said shortly before the Prop B vote, "I have to drive to Jefferson City, often at night. All it takes is one time for something to happen and I'm alone. The one thing I'm going to wish I had is a gun."[19] Another woman legislator, Representative Judy Berkstresser, R–Crane, said, "Girls and guns make a good combination for safety."[20] The safety argument was potent, but powerful arguments were also made by the other side.

Opponents of Prop B took issue with the suggestion that it would reduce violent crime against women, since women could already legally protect themselves with guns within their own homes. Others objected to what they viewed as a paternalistic attitude toward women. Rhonda Chriss Lokeman, the op-ed editor of the *Kansas City Star,* argued the entire premise used by the pro–Prop B side was offensive to women. She wrote, "Consider: While seeking to empower women, which they say Prop B's passage would do, they present sobbing women as distressed damsels who are sitting at home with the kiddies, while their unarmed hubbies go out to untold dangers on the urban landscape. Tear 'em down to build 'em up, you see. Who said chivalry was dead?"[21] This is an interesting perspective that is not immediately obvious to many, especially men. She argued that by claiming to help women, the supporters of Prop B could well have added to the popular perception that women are incapable of taking care of themselves—without a deadly firearm.

Many women's groups also argued that HB 1891 contained too many loopholes for men guilty of violence against women. It was widely suggested that the bill didn't provide the checks necessary to keep men with histories of domestic assault and stalking from getting conceal-and-carry permits. One legislator with a long history as a champion of legislation to protect battered women, Representative Vicky Riback Wilson, D–Columbia, said that over the years when conceal-and-carry was repeatedly considered, proposals to prohibit men with records of domestic violence from getting permits were thwarted by the pro–conceal-and-carry side. The gun advocates consistently refused to compromise, she said, because they claimed it would ban too many law-abiding people from carrying guns.[22]

Once, as Wilson described, legislators were making progress toward a provision in conceal-and-carry legislation that would prevent domestic abusers from ever being issued permits, but the compromise was derailed by a representative of the NRA who was present at negotiations. The NRA lobbyist, a woman from Washington, D.C., insisted Missouri's definition of domestic violence was "too liberal" and that such a provision would unfairly deny many people the right to carry. She urged the bill's sponsors to oppose such language, and they did. From Representative Wilson's perspective, a seemingly common-sense compromise was thrown to the side by the NRA's intransigence.[23] Clearly, from Wilson's perspective, Prop B would not have been a positive development for women. Like every other aspect of the Prop B fight, the battle for women's votes was heated. As the vote drew close, advocates of both sides tried to sway undecided women.

The Role of the News Media

While opponents of Prop B often complained about the imbalance of campaign funds and that most of the pro–Prop B money came from the NRA, Prop B's supporters were just as vocal with complaints about media bias against conceal-and-carry, arguing that the news media's condemnation of the proposition more than made up for an imbalance in paid media. An overview of media coverage of the campaign suggests the pro–Prop B forces may have had a legitimate complaint. From an editorial perspective, the state's three largest daily newspapers were all clearly opposed to Prop B. While an occasional editorial supporting Prop B was published, it was almost always an op-ed piece written by a guest contributor who supported conceal-and-carry, such as John Lott or Fred Meyers.

This section offers a brief sample of the kind of editorials published by the newspapers in the state's biggest cities. In all three cities, Kansas City, St. Louis, and Springfield, the editorial position of the papers was anti–Prop B. In Kansas City and St. Louis the papers' editors also made it clear in nearly every editorial on Prop B that they felt conceal-and-carry would be a moot issue without the contributions of the NRA.

The *St. Louis Post-Dispatch* was very forthright in its opposition to Prop B on the pages of its editorial section and was often quite critical of those who supported it. For example, the paper carried a withering criticism of Anheuser-Busch when the brewing company went public with its support of conceal-and-carry. An editorial on the topic with the rather incendiary title, "Fun With Guns and Beer," accused the company of taking the NRA's position to the point of endangering society. It read, in part, "The irresponsibility of this position is staggering. Alcohol and firearms are a deadly mix, and while Anheuser-Busch's statement on conceal-carry says it encourages drinking only after the day's hunting is over, it says nothing about drinking with a handgun hidden on one's person."[24] The apparent anger in this editorial shows how deep opposition to conceal-and-carry among the paper's editorial staff must have run, given that the paper was attacking St. Louis's biggest corporate citizen and, no doubt, one of the paper's biggest advertisers.

In an editorial published a few days before the election, the *St. Louis Post-Dispatch* echoed SSWC when it railed against the role played by the NRA in the campaign. The paper's editors expressed outrage at the fact that the NRA had come from outside to start a fight about an issue most Missourians didn't naturally care about. It called the NRA an outside agitator, acknowledging but dismissing the fact that many Missourians were NRA members. The editorial read, in part, "Of course, thousands of loyal NRA members don't perceive the NRA as an outside organization . . . There's nothing wrong with national groups weighing in on local political referendums, especially if their role is to educate and bring to the discussion a broader wisdom . . ." But the NRA, the editorial continued, was only worried about furthering its own agenda and was trying to do so by spending an enormous amount of money to scare the citizens of Missouri.[25] Like SSWC's officials often did, the *Post-Dispatch's* editorials explored the carpetbagger theme regularly. The paper's editorials repeatedly connected MAC to the NRA. The editors argued concealed weapons were being foisted on Missourians by forces outside the state, and suggested that without the actions of the NRA, Missourians might never have considered conceal-and-carry. This is misleading, of course, since opinion polls showed that, in fact, many Missourians supported conceal-and-carry. Perhaps not a majority supported it, but many did.

Following Prop B's defeat, the *Post-Dispatch* published editorials praising voters for casting a "vote for sanity," and asserted the defeat of Prop B sent a clear message to the rest of the country that the NRA couldn't just dump money into a state and buy an election. One such editorial concluded, "Outspent, outgunned and fighting one of the hardest fears to allay—the fear of crime—

opponents of the proposition squeaked through on good, old-fashioned common sense."[26] Clearly, the newspaper's editors had a strongly held objection to conceal-and-carry before, during, and after the election that might have reflected, but perhaps also influenced, the opinions of St. Louisans who read the paper.

Of course, the *St. Louis Post-Dispatch* was not the only newspaper to regularly campaign against conceal-and-carry and for gun control. Editorials in the *Kansas City Star* regularly critiqued the NRA and conceal-and-carry. Well before Prop B, during the 1996 Democratic primary for the seat of Sixth District Congresswoman Pat Danner, the *Kansas City Star* supported her unsuccessful opponent, Larry Kinnamon, Jr., of St. Joseph, citing Danner's support of the NRA as a major reason. The author of the editorial, Laura Scott, wrote, "Too often, she has preferred to go along with her campaign contributors rather than to vote in the best interests of constituents. The prime example of this is in her allegiance to the NRA."[27] As with the *Post-Dispatch,* the *Star's* editorial writers tried often to link guns in Missouri with the NRA.

Just days before the Prop B election, the editorial page editor of the *Kansas City Star,* Rich Hood, published an editorial that disputed many of the statistics provided by conceal-and-carry advocate John Lott in his own op-ed piece, printed in the *Star* on April 1, 1999. Hood wrote that Lott's data were misleading or inaccurate and suggested statistics showed that in Texas many violent crimes had been committed by people with legally obtained conceal-and-carry permits. He concluded by expressing concern about what he argued was the sloppy wording of HB 1891 and that there would be little penalty for those who violated it. He wrote, "If Missourians listen to the misleading promises of the gun lobby and pass this wrongheaded proposition, the least thing responsible businesses and institutions should expect is that violations of restricted-area laws would be severely punished."[28] The editorial was long, filled with statistics, and aimed to refute, point by point, every argument made by Lott in his own editorial. Editorials similar to Hood's followed in the pages of the *Kansas City Star* up to, and after, election day.

Even the *Springfield News-Leader,* located in the heart of Missouri gun country, took an editorial position opposed to Prop B, though the paper distinguished itself from its cousins in a couple of ways. First, it published far fewer editorials than the others, and second, it made slightly different, perhaps less shrill arguments that rarely invoked the NRA. For example, in an editorial published on March 31, 1999, the paper pointed to incidences of gun permit abuses in other states and how they might be repeated in Missouri, rather than raging about outside influences. The editorial provided this analysis: "Will cases like this come up every day? No. But they show that rather than wiping out crime, as supporters want us to believe, a concealed weapons law will legally put pistols in the cars, fanny packs, and pockets of people who have no business with a gun."[29] It concluded with the hope that Missourians would vote against the proposition.

In an editorial published on April 1, an editorial presented the argument that by passing Prop B, Missouri's citizens would be giving up in the war on crime. The editorial argued that putting more guns on the street was not a way to reduce crime and suggested that crime rates had fallen faster in states without conceal-and-carry laws. The editorial read, "A yes vote for Proposition B is no different than waving a white flag. . . . Don't let them do that to Missouri . . . We want a safer Missouri. Proposition B is not the way to get there."[30] It was a unique argument for the editorials against Prop B, not nearly as angry as many viewpoints expressed in other papers.

A couple of days before the election, the *News-Leader*'s editorial page editor, Robert Leger, took an analytical approach to the U.S. Constitution to oppose Prop B. He wrote that the Second Amendment did not guarantee an absolute right to carry guns and that even the words of HB 1891 proved the point because it would deny certain people the right to a concealed weapons permit. He wrote, "The supporters of Proposition B proudly tout provisions that would deny concealed-weapons permits to felons, drunks, drug-users and those who have exhibited violence in the past five years. Those arguments deny a constitutional right to bear arms. Here's why. A true constitutional right applies equally to everyone."[31] It was a reasoned argument much different in tone from editorials in the state's other big city dailies, though it was just as anti–Prop B as other editorials.

In the aftermath of the election, the Springfield newspaper continued to present the argument that guns were instruments of violence and that putting more of them on the street would do nothing to reduce violent crime. An editorial published the day after the election argued, "Proposition B lost overwhelmingly in St. Louis and Kansas City, where crime really is a problem. The people who know most about crime recognized that more guns and the threat of more violence is not the answer."[32] This editorial seemed especially aimed at disappointed supporters of Prop B who clearly felt that the election was something less than democratic, since virtually every county in the state except those around St. Louis and Kansas City voted for Prop B.

Clearly, the news media in Missouri's three largest cities contributed to the anti–Prop B campaign with their consistent calls to defeat the measure. It is impossible to say with certainty if they helped, or how much they helped, but Prop B lost in both Kansas City and St. Louis. The referendum did well in southwest Missouri, but who can say how its margin of victory there was affected by media coverage? Might it have garnered more votes if not for the *News-Leader's* cautionary tone? Wherever the actual truth lay, supporters of Prop B clearly blamed the media.

Many Prop B advocates commented on the tone of coverage that preceded the vote. One pro–conceal-and-carry advocate, Dale Schmid, the president of the Second Amendment Coalition, testified before the Missouri House of Representatives Sportsmanship, Safety and Firearms Committee, a special panel created specifically to address the concealed weapons issue, in April 2001. Schmid suggested the reason Prop B had done so poorly in the St. Louis area was due, in part, to biased coverage in the *St. Louis Post-Dispatch.*[33] A Kansas City area member of the NRA board of directors, Bob Hogdon, argued that the proposition had done less well than expected in northwest Missouri because of its proximity to the Kansas City media market which, he argued, editorialized against the referendum.[34] Wayne Crump asserted after the election that while the pro–Prop B campaign had raised five times as much money as the anti–Prop B campaign, it had actually been far outspent because of the free anti–Prop B coverage provided in the *St. Louis Post-Dispatch* and the *Kansas City Star.*[35]

It is difficult to say what impact news coverage had on the outcome of the election because comparatively few people read newspapers in this day and age, but opinion leaders certainly read newspapers, and if the coverage of the Prop B campaign affected them, it could also have trickled down to the people such opinion leaders influenced. The advocates of Prop B have a case in this sense: the editorial pages of three major Missouri papers gave the anti–Prop B campaign something it couldn't have paid for, a stream of arguments against concealed guns, sent directly to the homes of a large percentage of Missouri's eligible voters.

After months of angry campaigning, election day finally arrived. Voters went to the polls on April 6 and the proponents and opponents had little to do but sit back and nervously await the results.

Chapter Fourteen

The Campaign of 1999—Election Day

After a long, ugly campaign, Proposition B was defeated on April 6, 1999, seemingly bringing the conceal-and-carry debate in Missouri to an end. Surely, opponents of conceal-and-carry felt, such a defeat made it inconceivable for the state legislature to return to the issue after the people had spoken. Missouri, however, is a state where gun issues never seem to be settled, and the defeat merely set the stage for the first big political battle of the new millennium. While the opponents of Prop B celebrated, its supporters were angry but undeterred. For many pro–Prop B activists, the defeat was an affront to the Constitution and their civil liberties, not a legitimate outcome of the democratic process. With supporters adopting such an interpretation of the events of 1999, the question was not if conceal-and-carry would return, but when.

The vote on April 6 was very close, with Prop B losing by just 43,843 votes: 634,809 voted in favor of Prop B, while 678,652 voted against it, a 48.3 percent to 51.7 percent margin. The turnout of 1,313,461, 36 percent of registered voters, was significantly higher than the 25 percent predicted beforehand by the secretary of state.[1] Furthermore, turnout in many counties was significantly higher than the state average of 36 percent (see Table 1). That high turnout, combined with the fact that the proposition lost by just fewer than 44,000 votes, shows how prominent the Prop B campaign was to many voters and how closely divided Missourians were on the issue. As votes were being counted, it seemed things were going the way the opponents of Prop B wanted, but Fred Meyers suggested the opponents were getting excited too quickly because the early returns were mostly from St. Louis County, which everyone knew would go against Prop B. He said, "We know the out-state vote is where our people are." Wayne Crump reflected the same sentiment when he said, "I'm hopeful. The rural areas are still to come. They should put us over the top."[2]

Things didn't work out as Meyers and Crump hoped, of course, and one factor that might have been a warning to Crump on election day was the fact that turnout was significantly higher than the secretary of state had predicted it would be. In St. Louis County, which accounted for the most votes against Prop B, turnout was exceedingly high for an April election. As Table 1 shows, 43.41 percent of the county's registered voters turned out to vote. This compares with significantly lower turnout for the April 1998 election, when only 19.3 percent of registered voters turned out.[3] Much as it is impossible to prove that SSWC's ad campaign alone caused a significant shift in public opinion about Prop B late in the campaign, it is also impossible to prove that Prop B's presence on the April ballot, along with numerous high-profile local issues scattered around the state, affected turnout, but there was clearly some connection. Prop B supporters such as Crump had fought to get Prop B on the April ballot, thinking it would be a low-profile election day that would thus give them their greatest chance for success. It was interesting that a MAC official, Field Coordinator Whitney O'Daniel, tried to blame the April date for Prop B's loss, saying, "School board and local elections drive out different voters."[4] O'Daniel seemed to argue that because there were hotly contested local issues on many ballots across the state, turnout on April 6 was higher than normal in certain critical places such as St. Louis County. Once at the polls, O'Daniel apparently wanted to suggest, many of these voters, especially women, decided to vote against Prop B. At the same time, Robin Carnahan and opponents of Prop B argued it was the notion that legalizing concealed guns would make schools less safe that caused turnout to be higher than normal for an April election.[5]

In addition to local issues on ballots across the state, there was another statewide proposition at issue. Prop A would have instituted a fifty-cents-per-month fee on cellular phone bills to finance a new system that would have made 9-1-1 the statewide emergency number for cell phones. Like Prop B, this referendum also failed. Because of the tremendous attention drawn by Prop B, Prop A got very little attention before election day, but its presence on the ballot might have drawn at least a few voters to the polls who might not have voted otherwise. Clearly, there was some interplay between Prop B and the other issues on ballots across the state, but it is very difficult to say with certainty which influenced the other. In St. Louis County, however, where turnout in 1999 was so dramatically different from 1998, Prop B was almost certainly a factor behind the higher turnout.

Regardless, Prop B lost, and its opponents were jubilant in the days after the election. In their joy, they were, perhaps, not as mindful of the closeness of the election as they should have been. SSWC's Gwen Fitzgerald said, "It looks like common sense and public safety prevailed. It's a tremendous victory for the citizens of Missouri."[6] Carl Wolf, the chief of the Hazelwood Police Department and the president-elect of the Missouri Police Chiefs Association, argued, "I think the voters of Missouri have spoken—they don't want hidden guns."[7] Bob Clark, a member of SSWC and the president of the Clayco Construction Company in St. Louis, said, "We came in knowing we are being outspent. We've really gotten our message out that it's the people and common sense against the angry NRA. That's what is keeping us at the table."[8] While the opponents were jubilant, the defeat of Prop B was a blow to its supporters.

As HB 1891's sponsor, Wayne Crump was predictably disappointed with the outcome. Looking to assign blame for the loss, he later said he never would have proposed the public vote had he known that the governor would work so hard to defeat it.[9] He was also critical of the opposition and suggested the referendum failed because the anti–Prop B side ran a misleading campaign. He said, "I think it just shows where the ads and misinformation left people in doubt. If people in Missouri are in doubt, they are going to vote 'no.'"[10] On the day after the election, Crump suggested, "I don't think in the near future it will be resubmitted to voters," though he didn't say the issue wouldn't resurface in other forms, such as a bill in the legislature.[11] In fact, he suggested that changing the bill in certain ways, such as increasing the number of hours of firearms training, might make it more palatable—to legislators, not voters.[12] Later, while sponsoring a new concealed weapons bill in 2002, Crump suggested the referendum had failed because of Secretary of State Cook's ballot language and State Auditor McCaskill's overestimate of the cost of Prop B.[13] Crump's criticism of the ballot language was echoed by many other pro–Prop B activists in the days after the campaign.

Fred Meyers, the leader of MAC, argued the opposition's campaign was unfairly advantaged because the weight of the state and federal governments were brought to bear against Prop B. Meyers asked rhetorically, "How do you fight against the governor, first lady, and the Justice Department."[14] The NRA's chief lobbyist, James Jay Baker, echoed this complaint when he said, "Governor Carnahan injected his own personal views into this democratic initiative process."[15] Another representative of the NRA, Bill Powers, said of the governor, "He did everything he could do to defeat this measure. This crosses the line to where it becomes a mistrust of the people of the state."[16] Chris Sifford, the governor's spokesperson, dismissed these complaints when he said, "It obviously doesn't make a lot of sense for an organization in Fairfax, Virginia, to criticize the governor for being involved in a public policy issue in Missouri. This is a group that pumped millions of dollars into a Missouri campaign from out of state."[17]

The governor, who was gearing up to challenge John Ashcroft for his U.S. senate seat, said, "I think we've shown what's probably true in most states—that the majority of people are not in favor of concealed weapons. Interest groups led by the NRA have pressured legislators and governors to pass and sign legislation that is not favored by the majority of the people. I hope other states will take heed and show their resistance to this idea."[18] Joe Sudbay, a lobbyist for HCI, echoed the governor's criticism of the NRA when he said, "They knew they would have a low turnout and a lot of money. Their calculation backfired on them." He added, "Hopefully, it will show elected officials that the gun lobby's position is far more extreme than their average constituents," but he had to know better.[19] The proponents of Prop B had other complaints about the campaign.

For instance, Brenda Potterfield, the treasurer of MAC and a strong supporter of the NRA, was angry about the way the NRA had been characterized throughout the campaign. She said, "The NRA is behind it, but the NRA is him and me and everybody in this room . . . We are the NRA."[20] She seemed very interested in showing that NRA members were regular folks, not frightening militia members.

Fred Meyers blamed media coverage, what he called a negative, untrue ad campaign by SSWC, and predicted conceal-and-carry would be back, though he argued it would require a change in the state's political leadership. He said, "The people won't get the right-to-carry until there's a pro-gun governor," suggesting the issue would return with a different governor in office.[21] He added that while the national press might try to write off the NRA, the organization "will come back like the Energizer bunny."[22]

Meyers also attributed the defeat of Prop B to turnout in St. Louis County, where the proposition lost by more than a hundred thousand votes.[23] Following the tallying of the last votes, Meyers contradicted his earlier statement when he said opponents of Prop B shouldn't get too excited about early returns because they were all from St. Louis and didn't reflect an expected groundswell of support from out-state. "As soon as we got those numbers in we knew there was no way to recover," he said, and remarked that St. Louis voters had been frightened by SSWC's campaign.[24] Blaming St. Louis was another common theme of the pro–Prop B supporters. The leaders of MAC and vocal supporters of conceal-and-carry lost because of the concentrated "urban" vote, suggesting that two small geographic areas had denied the residents of the rest of a big state the right-to-carry.

Certainly, the vote in and around St. Louis and Kansas City was heavily anti–Prop B. The result in St. Louis City was 26 percent in favor versus 74 percent against. It was 30 percent in favor to 70 percent against in St. Louis County, and 44 percent in favor versus 56 percent against in St. Charles County. In Kansas City, the proposition lost by a margin of 42 percent to 58 percent. In the rest of the state, the vote was 61 percent in favor and 39 percent opposed, reflecting a dramatic difference of opinion between the urban and rural areas of the state. The referendum passed in 104 counties, almost all of which were rural, while it lost in 10 counties.[25] Most of the counties where Prop B failed surrounded the state's two biggest cities, but there were some other notable pockets of anti–Prop B voting. While the proposition passed in the state's third-largest city, Springfield, it wasn't by as large a margin as some expected, and the proposition lost in three other cities: Jefferson City, Columbia, and St. Joseph. Clearly, the pro–Prop B forces had been right to worry about urban voters, but they were also right when they said they needed to make sure that the supporters of conceal-and-carry in out-state Missouri understood that their votes were critical in winning the election. In St. Joseph and the rest of northwest Missouri, the supporters didn't do as well as they hoped. This delighted the opponents of the proposition, of course, and Lawren Massey, a spokesperson for SSWC, was sure to point out that her group had campaigned just as hard to convince rural voters conceal-and-carry was a bad idea as it did urban voters.[26]

Greg Pearre, a spokesman for MAC, said, "Last night was very disappointing to see the results. It was reassuring to win 104 out of 114 counties. I don't know how you do that and lose. It was very disheartening."[27] Like other disappointed advocates, he suggested the next goal would be to work to elect politicians who would pass conceal-and-carry, saying, "The chance of another referendum vote is not in the near future. We want to elect a pro-gun governor and put a good bill on his desk."[28] This sentiment was oft-repeated by concealed guns supporters in the years following the Prop B election, and it was clear they had no intention of giving up the fight for conceal-and-carry.

The Prop B vote was followed very closely by the tragic mass murder at Columbine High School in Littleton, Colorado. For a time, the killings put a stop to conceal-and-carry legislation pending in the Colorado state legislature, and seemed to have a chilling effect across the country. The exception was in Missouri, where conceal-and-carry was once again discussed in the state legislature as early as 2000. This early return of the issue was predicted by Representative Vicky Riback Wilson, D–Columbia, shortly after the Columbine tragedy. In late April 1999 she suggested guns would never go away as an issue in the Show-Me State. "Guns are one of those gut-reaction issues that define people politically" in Missouri, she said. "Many members, even if they are not bothered by the specific proposal, see any attempt to regulate guns as a step down the road to less access to firearms."[29] A representative on the other end of the political spectrum, Larry Crawford, R–Centertown, who would become the post–Prop B champion of conceal-and-carry, suggested Columbine would have little effect on the issue in Missouri, and like Wilson, he was correct.[30]

At the national level, pro–gun-control legislators suggested the defeat of Prop B would give momentum to federal gun control. Senator Dick Durbin, D–Illinois, said, "We can only hope this vote will convince some senators and congressmen that sensible gun control is not only good for law enforcement and children's safety, but also a safe political position." He added, "The NRA has had a lot of trouble in recent years. They clearly thought they could win a big victory in Missouri and turn around their fortunes. That didn't happen. This has to discredit their organization."[31] Not surprisingly, James Jay Baker, of the NRA, denied the defeat was anything more than a temporary setback in one state.[32] It didn't take long to discover whether Durbin or Baker was more prescient, because a narrow version of conceal-and-carry was back in Missouri as soon as 2000.

Before that, however, a second issue arose in Missouri's General Assembly as the Prop B campaign raged across the state. The issue was a proposal to grant liability protection to the gun industry, including manufacturers, distributors, and dealers, brought on by a lawsuit filed by the city of St. Louis against several different gun industry entities.

Table 1. Prop B County by County Vote Totals.

County*	Yes on B	%	No on B	%	Turnout**
Adair	2,925	0.625401	1,752	0.374599	25.49%
Andrew	2,705	0.505607	2,645	0.494393	55.11%
Atchison	907	0.532902	795	0.467098	37.68%
Audrain	3,576	0.58118	2,577	0.41882	38.61%
Barry	4,352	0.68331	2,017	0.31669	32.48%
Barton	2,209	0.693564	976	0.306436	40.49%
Bates	3,248	0.687698	1,475	0.312302	41.11%
Benton	2,911	0.697079	1,265	0.302921	36.99%
Bollinger	2,203	0.791023	582	0.208977	31.76%
Boone	14,164	**0.397888**	21,434	**0.602112**	**35.99%**
Buchanan	9,441	**0.42506**	12,770	**0.57494**	**42.53%**
Butler	5,919	0.790676	1,567	0.209324	23.03%
Caldwell	1,480	0.596053	1,003	0.403947	41.32%
Callaway	5,910	0.616524	3,676	0.383476	41.74%
Camden	5,944	0.622213	3,609	0.377787	38.79%
Cape Girardeau	8,871	0.608812	5,700	0.391188	29.31%
Carroll	1,798	0.601137	1,193	0.398863	37.95%
Carter	1,096	0.807069	262	0.192931	29.31%
Cass	11,201	0.576242	8,237	0.423758	40.31%
Cedar	2,666	0.672723	1,297	0.327277	39.23%
Chariton	1,625	0.615764	1,014	0.384236	35.78%
Christian	6,552	0.662688	3,335	0.337312	27.96%
Clark	1,625	0.658695	842	0.341305	51.19%
Clay	17,684	**0.432827**	23,173	**0.567173**	**34.52%**
Clinton	3,004	0.550889	2,449	0.449111	42.65%
Cole	9,667	**0.487101**	10,179	**0.512899**	**41.73%**
Cooper	2,519	0.564039	1,947	0.435961	42.65%
Crawford	2,981	0.684815	1,372	0.315185	27.78%
Dade	1,693	0.683212	785	0.316788	45.47%
Dallas	2,687	0.690036	1,207	0.309964	43.10%
Daviess	1,359	0.559029	1,072	0.440971	47.28%
Dekalb	1,734	0.575888	1,277	0.424112	51.62%
Dent	2,680	0.773895	783	0.226105	33.90%
Douglas	1,934	0.768986	581	0.231014	26.37%
Dunklin	4,009	0.627485	2,380	0.372515	29.89%
Franklin	14,358	0.597976	9,653	0.402024	41.38%
Gasconade	2,823	0.678932	1,335	0.321068	41.01%
Gentry	972	**0.476471**	1,068	**0.523529**	**40.21%**
Greene	23,647	0.530095	20,962	0.469905	27.37%
Grundy	2,254	0.571791	1,688	0.428209	54.01%
Harrison	1,439	0.528655	1,283	0.471345	42.62%
Henry	3,761	0.611445	2,390	0.388555	38.80%

County*	Yes on B	%	No on B	%	Turnout**
Hickory	1,776	0.763871	549	0.236129	39.05%
Holt	1,271	0.604375	832	0.395625	46.79%
Howard	1,924	0.58303	1,376	0.41697	50.54%
Howell	5,294	0.738663	1,873	0.261337	29.40%
Iron	1,693	0.696995	736	0.303005	35.04%
Jackson***	37,059	**0.47528**	40,914	**0.52472**	**33.83%**
Jasper	12,180	0.648942	6,589	0.351058	27.53%
Jefferson	25,487	0.573296	18,970	0.426704	37.07%
Johnson	5,455	0.590496	3,783	0.409504	34.66%
Kansas City****	16,455	**0.283922**	41,516	**0.716078**	**30.36%**
Knox	868	0.644395	479	0.355605	41.36%
LaClede	3,997	0.68736	1,818	0.31264v	30.11%
Lafayette	4,538	0.505401	4,441	0.494599	42.25%
Lawrence	4,574	0.655113	2,408	0.344887	33.66%
Lewis	1,805	0.65924	933	0.34076	40.64%
Lincoln	6,477	0.607485	4,185	0.392515	47.74%
Linn	1,976	0.546611	1,639	0.453389	35.11%
Livingston	2,014	0.538647	1,725	0.461353	38.02%
Macon	2,817	0.712623	1,136	0.287377	37.98%
Madison	1,599	0.658025	831	0.341975	26.19%
Maries	1,775	0.749261	594	0.250739	39.09%
Marion	4,166	0.559871	3,275	0.440129	40.03%
McDonald	2,371	0.751982	782	0.248018	22.04%
Mercer	813	0.757689	260	0.242311	44.78%
Miller	3,435	0.65466	1,812	0.34534	34.92%
Mississippi	1,860	0.658407	965	0.341593	26.26%
Moniteau	2,576	0.612022	1,633	0.387978	49.08%
Monroe	1,769	0.641174	990	0.358826	44.51%
Montgomery	2,536	0.611674	1,610	0.388326	51.61%
Morgan	2,935	0.676111	1,406	0.323889	36.34%
New Madrid	3,437	0.672734	1,672	0.327266	43.06%
Newton	8,237	0.696163	3,595	0.303837	33.09%
Nodaway	2,490	**0.431917**	3,275	**0.568083**	**45.25%**
Oregon	2,149	0.751136	712	0.248864	41.26%
Osage	2,523	0.619293	1,551	0.380707	48.11%
Ozark	2,033	0.802923	499	0.197077	33.03%
Pemiscot	2,313	0.668497	1,147	0.331503	21.36%
Perry	2,085	0.603998	1,367	0.396002	31.58%
Pettis	6,056	0.641865	3,379	0.358135	38.61%
Phelps	6,090	0.594494	4,154	0.405506	43.14%
Pike	3,211	0.622287	1,949	0.377713	45.33%
Platte	7,331	**0.437646**	9,420	**0.562354**	**29.84%**
Polk	3,642	0.663872	1,844	0.336128	30.34%

County*	Yes on B	%	No on B	%	Turnout**
Pulaski	4,336	0.677924	2,060	0.322076	36.45%
Putnam	986	0.692416	438	0.307584	34.51%
Ralls	1,914	0.70784	790	0.29216	35.85%
Randolph	3,583	0.644193	1,979	0.355807	34.70%
Ray	3,392	0.604742	2,217	0.395258	32.75%
Reynolds	1,697	0.787837	457	0.212163	32.55%
Ripley	1,952	0.812995	449	0.187005	25.31%
St. Charles	28,039	**0.438569**	35,894	**0.561431**	**39.78%**
St. Clair	2,211	0.728021	826	0.271979	44.61%
St. Francois	6,502	0.574432	4,817	0.425568	32.15%
St. Louis City	16,945	**0.259023**	48,474	**0.740977**	**29.24%**
St. Louis County	88,334	**0.304762**	201,512	**0.695238**	**43.41%**
Ste. Genevieve	2,419	0.556988	1,924	0.443012	41.20%
Saline	2,657	0.504941	2,605	0.495059	29.88%
Schuyler	1,046	0.735067	377	0.264933	41.98%
Scotland	961	0.696377	419	0.303623	43.68%
Scott	5,573	0.622821	3,375	0.377179	33.85%
Shannon	1,722	0.831884	348	0.168116	32.33%
Shelby	1,184	0.625793	708	0.374207	38.99%
Stoddard	5,007	0.684016	2,313	0.315984	37.43%
Stone	3,790	0.672463	1,846	0.327537	29.04%
Sullivan	1,656	0.680362	778	0.319638	49.30%
Taney	4,636	0.636638	2,646	0.363362	27.62%
Texas	4,827	0.732473	1,763	0.267527	44.03%
Vernon	3,080	0.6226	1,867	0.3774	39.16%
Warren	3,249	0.575452	2,397	0.424548	36.93%
Washington	3,375	0.723783	1,288	0.276217	31.66%
Wayne	3,008	0.782722	835	0.217278	37.91%
Webster	3,653	0.681912	1,704	0.318088	30.00%
Worth	383	0.536415	331	0.463585	39.19%
Wright	3,044	0.763864	941	0.236136	33.80%

*Counties where Prop B lost are in **bold**.

**Turnout is percentage of registered voters.

***Excluding Kansas City

****Data from Kansas City Election Board

Missouri Secretary of State, "Election Night Reporting, April 6, 1999," www.sos.mo.gov/enrweb/countyselect.asp?eid=8&arc=1. Registered voter data are from the University of Missouri Department of Economics, Economic and Policy Analysis Center, www.econ.missouri.Edu/eparc/SAM_2003?G/G23.pdf and the Kansas City Election Board, www.kceb.org/results/1999/040699.htm.

Chapter Fifteen

More in 1999—Missouri Takes on
Liability Lawsuits

Beginning in the late 1990s, several cities began legal proceedings against gun manufacturers, motivated in part by well-publicized shootings such as Columbine. A large part of the discussion after such shootings revolved around questions of where the shooters, who were often children, got their guns. The tragic shooting at Columbine High School in Colorado came just as several cities were beginning to sue gun manufacturers and dealers, accusing them of partial responsibility for the violent crime that racked their cities.

The NRA was prepared for these suits and reacted quickly. It had supported legislation calling for limits on liability suits against gun manufacturers in the late 1990s, regularly referring to them as "frivolous." In so doing, the NRA broke through a long-standing wall of separation between it and the gun industry. The NRA worked hand-in-hand with gun manufacturers, distributors, and retailers at the state and federal levels to get laws passed outlawing lawsuits against the gun industry for liability in crimes committed with their products. Why, after many years of claiming independence from the gun industry, did the NRA suddenly become its partner? Because the group came to see such suits as another potential step down the slippery slope that could, one day, lead to the outlawing of all guns. If the cities prevailed, the NRA argued, they could drive the gun industry out of business, making it impossible for people to buy and own guns. The NRA's perspective was that it wasn't fair to hold gun manufacturers responsible for how their products were used. Once the guns left the factory and were legally sold by a gun dealer, the group argued, the industry shouldn't be responsible for how they were used. As Charlton Heston said, the gun industry's fight "has become our fight . . . What is at stake is not just your livelihood but liberty."[1]

Lawsuits by governments against the gun industry became common beginning in 1998, when the city of New Orleans filed the first action. After New Orleans fired the first shot, thirty-three municipalities, counties, and states sued gun manufacturers. In response, several states adopted anti-liability legislation protecting the gun industry, and in April 2003 the U.S. House of Representatives began work on a bill that would give gun manufacturers and dealers federal immunity from lawsuits. If such protection was granted to the firearms industry by Congress, it would be the only industry to have such sweeping federal legal protection. Currently, thirty-three states have legislation barring such suits. In addition, gun manufacturers, with support from the NRA, have been very successful fighting suits in court.

Since these suits began to be filed in earnest in 1998, no government has won its case and most have been thrown out by judges. According to the NRA's Institute for Legislative Action, "... courts in numerous states have made it clear that these cases have no basis in law," and the group points to decisions in Ohio, Connecticut, Florida, Louisiana, and California in support of this contention.[2]

City-sponsored lawsuits against gun manufacturers and distributors were, no doubt, inspired by the successful campaign waged by state governments against the tobacco industry. Authors Peter Brown and David Abel portrayed attorneys involved in the tobacco settlements in heroic terms,[3] as crusaders for the public good, but these attorneys also made a tremendous amount of money, and there is little doubt they hoped to have similar success against the gun industry.

Predictably, the NRA and its allies saw these lawsuits as little more than immoral profiteering. In an editorial published in several newspapers around the country in December 1999, Eric V. Schlecht, the chief lobbyist of the National Taxpayers Union, suggested that such lawsuits were the brainchildren of greedy trial lawyers. He wrote, "... a group of the nation's richest trial lawyers met to determine how to follow up on their successful shakedown of the tobacco industry. Once they determined the gun industry was sufficiently susceptible, they began pitching their scheme to any mayor or attorney general who would listen. Not only did they listen: they jumped at the chance as city after city began filing lawsuits against gun manufacturers."[4] Clearly, it took no time for the rhetorical battle to heat up.

As city governments began to file lawsuits against the gun industry, calling them a strategy for reducing violent crime, the NRA responded by stepping up its effort in state legislatures. The liability protection movement has a long history. The first state to adopt a law granting gun manufacturers immunity from lawsuits was California, in 1982. Interestingly, California was also the first state in the country to establish a limit on damages in medical malpractice suits, a movement that also swept through state capitals and Washington in the late twentieth and early twenty-first centuries.

After many years of legal battles, the constitutionality of the California law was upheld by the state's Supreme Court in August 2001 when it held that it was the legislature's responsibility to "set California's public policy regarding gun manufacturers' liability under these circumstances. Given that public policy, plaintiffs may not proceed with their negligence claim."[5] The case at the center of the California Supreme Court's decision was filed by the victims of a 1993 mass shooting in a San Francisco law office who wanted to sue the manufacturer of the gun used in the shooting. They claimed the manufacturer had irresponsibly marketed the firearm and was therefore liable. In rejecting this claim, the California Supreme Court reflected the decisions of several state and federal courts on similar cases around the country, essentially finding that the manufacturers and distributors of a legal product couldn't be held responsible for an individual who chose to use the product improperly.

As cities began to file lawsuits against the gun industry, they followed two basic blueprints. The first, used by such cities as New Orleans and Atlanta, was to sue manufacturers under product liability laws, asserting that gun companies were selling dangerous, poorly designed products. The products were defective, the suits argued, because they did not include adequate child-safety locks and ways to prevent anyone other than the gun's owner from firing it when such technology was available.

The second type of lawsuit relied on a different legal principle and made the argument that gun manufacturers, through the sale of their products, were violating public nuisance ordinances. The first city to file such a lawsuit was Chicago, where the action was aggressively pushed by its mayor, Richard M. Daley. The suit's architect was a Temple University professor of law, David Kairys, who originally designed the lawsuit for the city of Philadelphia, which never filed it.

The legal argument, as described by Brown and Abel (2003), asserted ". . . the gun industry created a 'public nuisance' by flooding the city with 'an excess of handguns.' And this increased operational costs for the Chicago Police Department, Fire Department, and public hospitals."[6] Mayor Daley described the suit, saying, "Gun manufacturers and retailers know exactly what they're doing. They knowingly market and distribute their deadly weapons to Chicago criminals, refusing to impose even the most basic controls. Therefore, we are suing 22 manufacturers and four distributors, seeking tougher controls and $433 million in damages."[7] In its brief, the city detailed what it asserted were gun-related costs to the police department, the public health system, and so forth. The sale and ownership of handguns is illegal in Chicago, and the suit alleged that gun manufacturers and retailers deliberately worked around the prohibition by operating through gun dealers located in suburbs just outside the city limits.

Refuting the charges from the NRA and others opposed to the lawsuit, Josh Camper, a spokesman for Mayor Daley, asserted money had nothing to do with Chicago's reasons for filing the lawsuit. Camper said, "Chicago would not take a penny if we could just get the handguns off the street."[8] This attitude was echoed by gun control advocates. For example, Timothy Lytton, a law professor at New York University, said the goal of cities filing such lawsuits was to regulate the gun industry, not to collect big financial damages. "Unlike tobacco, plaintiffs aren't in this business to make money," Lytton said. "It gives the industry an incentive to regulate itself."[9] Of course, not everyone saw such pure motives behind the suits. A spokesperson for the NRA, Bill Powers, said the suits were frivolous and motivated by greedy trial lawyers. He said, "They are driven by attorneys looking to make money, promulgated by mayors who are looking for someone to blame for their problems, and pushed by anti-gun lobbyists to accomplish the kind of gun control they haven't been able to pass through state and federal legislatures. There are obviously a number of mayors judging whether to jump on this trendy bandwagon."[10] The gun industry's representatives generally agreed with the NRA's charges that there were impure motives for the lawsuits, but it also felt that even if the cities' motives were pure, attacking the gun industry was misguided.

Representatives of the gun industry argued that the industry was not able to control what people did with legally manufactured products once those products left the factory. Steve Sanetti, the vice president of gun manufacturer Sturm, Ruger and Co., said, "How can manufacturers control what law enforcement can't? That's what we're being asked here, and it's colossally unfair."[11] One analyst, Jeffrey Roth of the Urban Institute, suggested cities might have a hard time proving liability in court because less than 1 percent of gun dealers were involved in selling 70 percent of the guns used in crimes. He said, "That figure suggests that there are a small number of bad apples in the barrel, rather than a bad distribution system, and that seems to me to weaken the theory behind at least some of the lawsuits."[12] The success of suits against the gun industry would depend in part on the ability of cities to prove gun manufacturers knew their products were being irresponsibly distributed and chose to do nothing to prevent it. It was a difficult legal hurdle to clear.

The public nuisance argument was dealt a blow in October 1999 when a Cincinnati judge threw out a case filed by that city's government. Officials sought compensation for the cost of emergency services it was forced to supply in response to gun-related crimes. The case was also intended to force changes in the way guns were designed and marketed.

The judge, Robert Ruehlman, wrote that the city's claims were vague and unsupported by legal precedent. He threw out the city's claim that the gun industry created a public nuisance, writing, "Here, the nuisance is the criminal or reckless misuse of firearms by third parties who are beyond control ..." and added that because such misuse is out of the control of the gun industry, "nuisance does not apply." He addressed the city's attempts to force changes in the design and marketing of guns by saying that only the state legislature had the authority to create such laws. Finally, he rejected a claim by the city that the industry was liable because it had inadequately informed the public of the dangers guns can cause. He wrote, "There can be liability for failure to warn only if the risk is not open and obvious or a matter of common knowledge ... the risks associated with the use of a firearm are open and obvious and matters of common knowledge."[13]

The gun industry was quick to applaud Judge Ruehlman's decision and call it an important precedent for similar suits filed in other cities. The NRA's chief lobbyist, James Jay Baker, said, "This is a major victory for those who believe, as NRA members believe, that we must hold criminals accountable for their crimes."[14] In the American legal system, there is no requirement that one city or state honor the legal precedents of another city or state, but a court's decision can lend credibility to a given legal argument and make it easier for other judges to accept.

As city lawsuits proliferated, the NRA pitched in with legal advice and friend of the court briefs for the gun industry. The group also began to work feverishly in state capitals across the country, lobbying state legislatures to nip liability suits in the bud. For instance, just five days after the city of Atlanta filed its suit, the NRA was able to shepherd a bill through the Georgia state legislature that banned local governments from filing suits against gun manufacturers. The executive vice president of the NRA, Wayne LaPierre, said, "What the mayors are going to find out is that a direct attack on the freedom to bear arms is the toughest briar patch they can jump into. They think that there is no cost, and this is a way to a quick buck, like tobacco money. But their cost, politically and economically, is going to be high, because we're determined to expose this for the sham that it is."[15]

The NRA followed its victory in Georgia with a campaign in Louisiana, where LaPierre and Charlton Heston appeared at the state capitol to rally sympathetic legislators.[16] This was a surprisingly direct lobbying strategy for the NRA to take on any issue, but especially liability legislation, which they had largely left to the gun industry in the past. In Missouri, for example, the NRA had remained in the background until the Prop B campaign. As the former speaker of the Wisconsin House of Representatives, Tom Loftus, wrote in his book, the NRA is usually at its most effective behind the scenes, in committee and subcommittee meeting rooms. This is the kind of action that doesn't get much attention from reporters because the media don't cover what Loftus calls "process." By working behind the scenes, Loftus argued, the NRA can more effectively negotiate and/or pressure legislators.[17] In the case of "frivolous" lawsuits, however, the NRA leaders took an early position that was much higher-profile. This was certainly deliberate—Georgia and Louisiana were both states friendly to the NRA agenda and LaPierre knew he and Heston would be well received. By going to Louisiana, LaPierre and Heston were able send a message to other states where perhaps their direct interference might not have been as welcome.

Like Georgia, Louisiana quickly passed a "frivolous lawsuit" bill that retroactively made New Orleans's lawsuit illegal. The city sued the state over the new liability protection law, and the case made its way to the doors of the U.S. Supreme Court in October 2001. The court refused to hear the case, effectively upholding a Louisiana Supreme Court decision that found the new law to be constitutional. The U.S. Supreme Court's nondecision certainly had a chilling effect on prospective liability suits. If the court was unwilling to get involved, then state laws and state courts' interpretations of those laws would hold sway, and many state courts had already thrown out suits against gun manufacturers by late 2001 and upheld state laws limiting liability. This gave the NRA even greater incentive to pass anti–"frivolous lawsuit" bills in as many states as possible, including the Show-Me State.

Missouri

In March 1999 the city of St. Louis announced its intention to join several other cities in filing a lawsuit against gun manufacturers to seek damages for the cost of crimes committed with guns. In its suit, the city claimed gun manufacturers were guilty of promoting gun violence by deliberately selling a dangerous product.

The suit was filed against twenty-seven defendants, including gun manufacturers, distributors, and trade groups, in April 1999. The city accused gun manufacturers and dealers of profiting at the expense of public health and safety by refusing to do anything to better regulate the sale of guns and to improve gun safety, despite the fact that they knew their products were used to commit violent crimes. In the suit, the city alleged gun violence cost the city tens of millions of dollars in terms of law enforcement, investigation of violent crimes, and medical expenses. It also asserted that guns and gun crimes caused population loss, decreased property values, reduced tax revenues, and decreased worker productivity.[18] Bob Ricker, a spokesman for the American Shooting Sports Council, one of the suit's defendants, said, "It's absolutely ridiculous to try to blame gun manufacturers for the city's criminal justice problem."[19] Ridiculous or not, the city was not alone in pursuing this legal course.

With its action, St. Louis joined Chicago, Miami, Bridgeport, Detroit, and others on the list of cities that filed liability lawsuits against gun companies. St. Louis's decision to sue came in the wake of a failed attempt in August 1998 by the leaders of several cities and leading gun manufacturers to negotiate ways to ease gun violence. When the talks broke down, St. Louis proceeded with its legal action. St. Louis Mayor Clarence Harmon said, "The gun makers are aware that their products are used frequently in crimes and accidental shootings. It is time to place the burden of the problem firmly where it belongs."[20]

At the same time St. Louis officials filed suit, state legislators such as Wayne Crump suggested that a bill to shield gun manufacturers from such lawsuits was a possibility, though he admitted it would be difficult to do in the middle of the bigger fight over Prop B. One analyst with the Center to Prevent Handgun Violence, Dennis Henigen, agreed that the outcome of Prop B would have an impact on what the legislature did about liability protection. He said, "That would send a political signal that Missourians are not anxious to have more and more guns."[21]

Despite the distractions of the Prop B campaign, Crump introduced a liability protection bill in mid-April. Governor Carnahan promised to veto liability protection, just as he'd promised to veto conceal-and-carry. Crump's bill went nowhere in the house, but as time ran out on the session, Representative Jon Bennett, R–St. Charles, with support from Crump, proposed a liability protection amendment to a courts bill the house had just received from the senate. The amendment would have made it illegal for Missouri cities to sue gun manufacturers for damages.

Bennett, who denied being either a gun owner or a member of the NRA, said he proposed the amendment because liability lawsuits in general were out of control. He said, "Lawsuits are being filed not because these products are working defectively, but because defective people are working these products."[22] The amendment was adopted by the house, and the amended bill passed by a vote of 76 to 47 before being returned to the senate with just one day remaining in the session.

With more time, the bill may well have passed in the senate with the liability protection amendment attached. The amended legislation caused a flurry of last-minute negotiations between Bennett, Senator John Schneider, D–Florissant, who was the courts bill's original sponsor, and a few pro-gun senators. The senate voted to strip the amendment from the bill, which prompted the house to pass a resolution with an even stronger majority than the vote on liability protection, 85 to 47, to refuse to accept the bill without the amendment. This action seemed to be the final nail in liability protection's coffin for 1999, but it was briefly revived at the last moment by negotiations between Senator Schneider, who opposed the liability amendment, and Jon Dalton, an NRA lobbyist. The two men replaced the house amendment with a new clause that said cities would be financially liable for all court costs of liability lawsuits if a judge determined the suit to be frivolous. The senate passed the bill with this new compromise amendment and it was quickly returned to the house, which also passed it.[23] It was not the bill the NRA wanted, but it was an important first step.

Liability protection failed in Missouri in 1999, but what is most interesting about the legislative maneuvering is the fact that the final resolution of the dispute was brokered not by a legislator, but by a lobbyist for the NRA. In passing its resolution, the house said it would not accept the courts bill without the liability protection amendment, but when the NRA lobbyist said it would be OK to take a smaller step in the direction of the elimination of "frivolous lawsuits," the legislators went along with him. It was stark evidence of the kind of power Tom Loftus suggested the group had in Wisconsin and other state legislatures such as Missouri's.

The failure of the legislature to pass a bill outlawing liability lawsuits against gun manufacturers kept the city of St. Louis's litigation alive. While the case worked its way through the courts, St. Louis joined several other cities and the federal government in negotiations with the gun industry, but many gun manufacturers shunned the talks after they were condemned by the NRA and the even more strident Gun Owners of America. Only one company, Smith and Wesson, engaged in negotiations with cities, but in the end those did not bear much fruit for gun control advocates. Yet early in 2000, it looked like Smith and Wesson had reached a historic agreement.

When the settlement with Smith and Wesson was arranged, St. Louis Mayor Harmon said, "This is the breaking of the dam. We think we're beginning as a country to come to grips with the meaning of firearms in our society and how to control their use."[24] Smith and Wesson made several concessions, including a promise to sell handguns with trigger locks, to develop smart gun technology that would limit a gun's use to its owner, and to change the way it marketed its guns, which would prevent it from selling its guns through disreputable dealers and at gun shows. In return for these concessions, the cities agreed to drop their lawsuits against Smith and Wesson and also agreed to a "preferred buying program" to make Smith and Wesson the supplier of firearms for their police forces. As a party to the settlement, Mayor Harmon promised he would urge the St. Louis Police Department to contract with the company. He said, "We have an obligation to recommend policy that promotes the safety of our citizens, the effective operation of the Police Department and the best interest of the city's police force. Given the settlement offered, I believe giving preference to Smith & Wesson accomplishes all of these goals."[25] The preferred buying program was intended to help Smith and Wesson recover some of the financial losses it might incur from boycotts against it for signing on to the agreement. The company's reputation with gun owners and the rest of the industry took a severe hit. Smith and Wesson was immediately condemned by the NRA, the Gun Owners of America, and most gun manufacturers. The company found its products boycotted by members of the Gun Owners of America. In addition, several gun manufacturers responded with a lawsuit against the governments that were parties to the settlement, claiming the preferred buying program was illegal.

In response to overwhelming pressure from gun enthusiasts and the gun industry, Smith and Wesson began to reinterpret some of the key parts of the agreement, neutralizing most of the concessions it had agreed to. In the end, many of the cities that agreed to drop legal action against Smith and Wesson refiled their suits, arguing the company wasn't living up to its end of the bargain. As the state legislature reconvened in Jefferson City in January 2000, the city of St. Louis was still very much involved in legal action against the gun industry, and legislators were still very much involved in the question of conceal-and-carry. In January 2000, conceal-and-carry was back on the General Assembly's agenda.

Chapter Sixteen

2000—The Fight Continues with Elections
of a Different Sort: Ashcroft versus
Carnahan and Bush versus Gore

There were no conceal-and-carry bills introduced in the 2000 session of the Missouri General Assembly that would have given all Missourians the right to carry. However, bills were introduced in the house by Sam Gaskill, R–Washburn, and in the senate by Harold Caskey, D–Butler, to grant the right to carry to prosecutors and other law enforcement officials. Caskey's bill was voted out of the Civil and Criminal Justice Committee in February but never made it onto the senate calendar. Gaskill's bill was assigned to the Public Safety and Law Enforcement Committee in late April, but never made it out of committee. Neither bill made a real splash, but the fact that any legislator would flirt with any variation of conceal-and-carry so soon after Prop B was typical of Missouri politics.

While no legislators introduced sweeping conceal-and-carry legislation in 2000, pro-gun activists kept the issue alive. One group formed after the defeat of Proposition B, called the Vermont Project, began circulating petitions in February that called for two ballot initiatives. One would have allowed citizens to carry concealed weapons without a permit and the other would have forced the repeal of a state law requiring a permit for the sale or transfer of a conceal-able gun. The group adopted the name "Vermont Project" because there are no restrictions against concealed weapons in the state of Vermont and it hoped to persuade Missourians to adopt the same sweeping policy. A spokesman for the group, Stephen Umscheid, said, "This is a response to the ongoing problem that Proposition B was supposed to help us with. We are doing this to save lives, and that's the only reason."[1]

Not surprisingly, in the wake of Prop B, the NRA's reaction was lukewarm. The state's NRA lobbyist, Greg Pearre, commented, "It's not that we're against it, but it's not our deal. We will probably not get involved," and went on to add that while the NRA supported the right to carry, it also supported background checks, which were not part of the Vermont Project's proposals.[2] Steve Jones, of the Columbia-based group Missourians for Personal Safety, commented that most gun groups were steering clear of the proposal out of political pragmatism, in light of Prop B's defeat in 1999. He said that passage of an initiative like that proposed by the Vermont Project wouldn't be possible without "...years of voter education."[3] Without the support of these important organizations, the Vermont Project's petition drive for an initiative fizzled out.

Gun advocates rallied at the state capitol in Jefferson City in March to protest gun control measures at the state and federal levels and call for better firearms education. The argument commonly made by gun rights supporters was that restrictive gun laws weren't the solution to crime problems. Rather, a well-educated, well-armed populace was what was required. The official purpose of the rally, organized by Missourians for Personal Safety, was to promote the use of the NRA's "Eddie The Eagle" gun safety program by public schools, but the speakers spoke broadly in support of gun rights and against gun control. Addressing the gathering of roughly five hundred advocates, Steve Jones said, "Let's get volunteers into our schools and let's forget about ridiculous things our president recommends, such as trigger locks."[4] Of course, it wasn't just the president who supported trigger locks, and Jones certainly had more than just Bill Clinton on his mind. In 2000, State Senator Mary Bland, D–Kansas City, sponsored SB 1067, which would have required trigger locks for all assault weapons and concealable guns. The bill had sufficient support to be voted out of the Civil and Criminal Justice Committee in mid-March, but it went no further.

Kevin Jamison, of the Western Missouri Shooters Alliance, spoke at the rally and took the opportunity to criticize Governor Carnahan's involvement in the Prop B vote. He said, "We lost because the governor's faction decided they could lie faster than we could tell the truth."[5] The receptive audience enjoyed his incendiary words. With the stated goal of beginning to educate Missourians about guns, Michael Gordinier, a professor from Washington University, told the audience, "We're simply not perceived as mainstream normal any more," and that something needed to be done to change that impression for their message to gain ground.[6]

The gathering gave every appearance of a campaign rally. There was a drawing for free gun safes and several different groups, "ranging from the Boy Scouts to 'armed informed mothers,'" appeared at the rally. Finally, the organizers announced a new roadside sign campaign that was to be "...modeled after the old Burma Shave ads. Organizers asked landowners to permit the signs to be placed on their land. One example shown at the rally would use these five signs: 1) If guns; 2) cause crime; 3) matches; 4) cause arson; 5) Safewithguns.org."[7] The signs could still be seen on farms bordering Missouri highways in 2004.

The gun rally ended in controversy when it was followed by a group of 65 schoolchildren from St. Louis who filled a stage in the capitol rotunda with 729 pairs of shoes, meant to represent the number of people killed in gun-related incidents in 1998. The gun advocates did themselves no public relations favors when they harassed the students and their parents. Michael Gordinier, the Washington University professor, harmed his own attempt to make gun advocates seem more mainstream when he verbally attacked the schoolchildren, saying, "How dare they wallow in the blood of innocent victims to further their sick agenda?" and added that the children's "non-thinking soccer moms" were allowing themselves and their children to be duped by "a small group of anti-freedom zealots." He added, "Shame on the useful idiots that carry their water. And shame on the parents that raise their little sign carrying children to grow up to become unthinking bigots."[8] It was a vitriolic attack aimed at a group of children, and it certainly did nothing to promote the idea that gun advocates were "mainstream."

In addition to the shoe demonstration, gun control advocates from Missouri participated in national and state events marking the so-called Million Mom March in mid-May 2000. While delegations from around the state participated in the rally in Washington, D.C., there were also several local rallies. Fresh from the Prop B victory in 1999, Missouri supporters of gun control were ebullient in 2000.

Liability protection legislation was back, if only briefly, during the 2000 legislative session. It was sponsored in the house by Representative Jon Bennett, R–St. Charles, as HB 1671. One of the bill's cosponsors was, not surprisingly, Wayne Crump. The bill, proposed to retroactively make the St. Louis lawsuit illegal and prevent other local governments from filing similar lawsuits against the gun industry. Bennett presented his bill as a way to stop out-of-control litigation in general, not just as protection for the gun industry. He said, "Right now it's firearms manufacturers. Next it could be manufacturers of alcohol or fatty foods."[9] A spokesman for the NRA suggested that unless such "frivolous" suits were halted, they would bankrupt many gun manufacturers. Bennett's bill had a public hearing in the House Civil and Administrative Law Committee in late February, but went no further than that. Liability protection for the gun industry was back in 2001, however, with a new, powerful sponsor.

While most state lawmakers were hesitant to debate guns so soon after the Prop B election, one controversial anti-gun program masterminded by prosecutors in Jackson County went into effect in November 2000. It was designed to crack down on the use of guns and, at the same time, seemed to kick supporters of conceal-and-carry while they were down by increasing the penalties for carrying concealed weapons. Under the new plan, people convicted of carrying a concealed weapon the first time would receive a ticket and a fine. Second-time offenders would receive community service and a felony conviction on their records, and third-time offenders would be subject to a federal gun charge with a minimum penalty of five years in jail.[10] Spearheading the effort were Jackson County Prosecutor Bob Beaird and U.S. Attorney Stephen L. Hill, both of whom were outspoken opponents of Prop B.

The prosecutors claimed the program was intended to complement one begun in 1999 by Hill, called Project Felon, in which Hill charged any convicted felon caught with a concealed weapon with a federal gun charge. The new program, however, seemed to go much further and, again, was loaded with extra meaning in the wake of the Prop B vote. Hill commented that the get-tough policy was needed because "There's a big chasm out there where gun cases aren't being prosecuted in state court," prompting an angry response from the pro-gun community.[11] Kevin L. Jamison, of the Western Missouri Shooters Alliance, said it was going to make criminals out of people who were simply trying to protect themselves. He added, "They're trying to take a lot of people with no felony convictions and give them felony convictions. Project Felon was never intended to make felons out of people who were scared because the system can't protect them."[12] Hill and Beaird, while certainly wanting to reduce crime, probably drew satisfaction from taunting Jamison and other champions of conceal-and-carry.

Project Felon was still in effect several years later, though it became known as Project Ceasefire in 2003. The new U.S. attorney for Western Missouri, Todd Graves, reported that in 2003, prosecutions for gun crimes were up more than 30 percent. Explaining the increase, he said, "The statistics mirror a rising rate of gun prosecutions taking place nationally as part of the increased emphasis placed on the crime by federal officials."[13]

Campaign 2000

Guns were an issue in Missouri during the 2000 election season for reasons that should be obvious—the state was obsessed with them. Richard Gephardt, then the U.S. House minority leader, ran a campaign ad that attacked Bill

Federer's position on guns; Federer was his opponent for reelection. The visuals showed several images of Federer with guns, while a narrator said, "Does Bill Federer share our values? He opposes the Brady Bill—opposing a 5-day waiting period to buy a gun. He opposes the ban on assault weapons. He believes it should be legal for people to carry concealed weapons in Missouri, and tried to make it the law, letting people take guns, even semi-automatic weapons, into bars and into sporting events. Bill Federer. Too extreme for Missouri."[14] Clearly, Gephardt saw the value of making an issue out of guns in his metropolitan St. Louis district after the Prop B vote. Gephardt, relatively safe in his own district, also recognized that 2000 offered the chance for Democrats to retake control of the House, and Missouri was right in the thick of things, as always. Two districts became open seats in Missouri when the incumbents stepped down, one into retirement, the other to run for governor. They were both names familiar to observers of the Showdown: Democrat Pat Danner, from the Sixth District, and Republican Jim Talent, from the Second District. Of course, Republican leaders no doubt saw Missouri as a chance to pick up a seat and expand the party's 222–211 margin.

An old name resurfaced in 2000 when, on May 22, 2000, Danner, faced with treatment for breast cancer, decided to end her campaign for reelection and leave after eight years in Congress. Since Danner was expected to easily win reelection, there wasn't much interest in the race prior to her decision. Her withdrawal, just eight days before the May 30 deadline to file campaign papers, suddenly made the Sixth District one of the most competitive races in the country.[15] Four Democrats and four Republicans quickly joined the campaign, seeking party nominations in the August primary.

The instant front-runner among the Democrats was Steve Danner, Pat Danner's son, who had last run for elective office in 1994, when he lost to State Auditor Margaret Kelly. In the interim, he had worked as a lawyer and the owner of a hotel management and construction company. Danner was attacked almost immediately by Republican party officials for not being as conservative as his mother.[16] Where guns were concerned, Danner did, indeed, seem to be trying to put distance between himself and his mother, saying that he supported trigger locks and instant background checks for all gun sales.[17] This apparent pro–gun control stance was, perhaps, unexpected considering that his mother was regularly endorsed by the NRA and that he had sponsored conceal-and-carry legislation during his career as a state legislator.

Danner won the primary and faced off against Republican Sam Graves, a state senator who ran a very aggressive campaign. Despite winning the primary, Danner was unable to shake the attacks from the other side that he was significantly more liberal than his mother, especially in supporting tax increases. Danner often used the phrase "the acorn didn't fall too far from the tree" when comparing himself to his mother, but Graves said, "Steve Danner may say the acorn didn't fall too far from the tree, but when it fell, it rolled to the left."[18] A number of prominent Republicans came to stump for Graves, including Speaker of the House J. Dennis Hastert, Majority Leader Dick Armey, Congressman J. C. Watts, and Senator John McCain. Danner's main benefactor during the campaign was Dick Gephardt. In the end, Graves ran a more effective campaign and won by the healthy margin of 51 to 47 percent.

Guns were even more prominent in the gubernatorial election. The candidates for governor were Jim Talent, who left his safe Second District seat in Congress to seek the governor's mansion, and Bob Holden, the state treasurer. Early in the campaign, just after the Prop B vote, both politicians staked out very careful positions on concealed guns. For Talent, this was tricky. He was from a region of the state, suburban St. Louis County, which voted strongly against conceal-and-carry, but he was seeking statewide office and would need the votes of rural Missourians to win. With this in mind, Talent endorsed Prop B throughout 1999. Two days after the election, trying to play both sides of the issue, Talent said he wouldn't sign a bill passed by the legislature if it was identical to Prop B, but added, "I do think the Legislature could address the issues that were raised . . . We could write a bill that the majority of Missourians would be comfortable with."[19] On the other hand, Holden also tried to play both sides of the field, while leaning a little more to the gun control side. He said, "I think the people of Missouri decided the issue yesterday. They sent a pretty clear message."[20] At the same time, however, he refused to dismiss such a compromise out of hand.

Guns are not an issue on which a politician in Missouri can remain noncommittal, and both men solidified their positions as the campaign wore on. Holden maintained a firmer anti–conceal-and-carry stance, while Talent became more outspoken in his support of the right to carry, indicating his intention to sign it into law if a bill came to his desk as governor. In a state with so many single-issue voters on both guns and abortion, it is almost impossible for a candidate for statewide office to remain neutral on either issue, and neither did.

Meanwhile, the candidates for the state's U.S. Senate seat, incumbent Senator John Ashcroft and Governor Mel Carnahan, were also separated by guns. Both men campaigned actively in the Prop B election. In the immediate aftermath of the vote, both Carnahan and Ashcroft dismissed the suggestion that the campaign in 2000 would revolve around guns. Carnahan, for instance, when asked if Prop B would be an issue in the senate campaign, said, "It may be, but it will just be one of many. There are many contrasts between me and John Ashcroft, and this will simply be one of them."[21]

While Carnahan was right in saying guns weren't the only point of separation in the 2000 campaign, they were unavoidably a major campaign issue because the groups on both sides continued to make them an issue, becoming more active as election day drew near. According to FEC records, in 1999 and 2000 the NRA officially endorsed Ashcroft, gave him direct contributions from its various political action committees, and spent several hundred thousand dollars in independent expenditures on his behalf, paying for polls, phone banks, mailings, and advertisements.[22] Immediately after the Prop B election, James Jay Baker, the NRA's chief lobbyist, said, "The positive aspect of this for us is we have a very activated gun constituency in Missouri, and they have very long memories. We would certainly be opposing Governor Carnahan in any future office he chooses to run for."[23] In mid-October 2000 the NRA's Bill Powers promised the governor's role in the Prop B campaign would "come back to haunt him."[24] The other side also promised not to let the fires go out. SSWC's Gwen Fitzgerald said Ashcroft was an outspoken supporter of Prop B primarily because he feared the NRA's financial power, and Brian Morton, a spokesman for HCI, said, "We've always supported Governor Carnahan, and when he runs against Senator Ashcroft, if the NRA's involved, we'll be involved."[25]

Interest groups of all varieties were active in the Ashcroft-Carnahan race. A study conducted by Brigham Young University's Center for the Study of Elections and Democracy found that interest groups contributed about 62 percent of the money spent on Carnahan's behalf and 50 percent of the money spent for Ashcroft. Of the interest groups that contributed, Handgun Control Inc. was in the top four for Carnahan and the NRA was in the top three for Ashcroft.[26] The bulk of HCI's money, $360,628, was spent on anti-Ashcroft advertising, while $10,000 was given directly to the Carnahan campaign. For its part, the NRA spent $504,716—about 92 percent of its expenditures in Missouri in 2000—on behalf of John Ashcroft.[27]

Despite their early assertion that the campaign would not center on guns, neither candidate left gun issues out of the debate for long. Governor Carnahan attacked Ashcroft for his position on guns quite early in the race. This isn't surprising when one considers that his U.S. Senate campaign was managed by his former chief of staff, Marc Farinella, who served as the spokesman for SSWC before returning to work for the governor. With such an activist running the campaign, it was almost inevitable guns would play a major role.

At the St. Louis County Democratic party's annual Jefferson Days event in June 1999, several weeks after the Prop B vote, Carnahan accused Ashcroft of being a "tool of the NRA" who loyally supported the group in the Senate and in the 1999 Prop B campaign. In his speech, Carnahan referred to a *New York Times* article that portrayed Ashcroft as an important NRA ally and promised, "I will not be a captive of the NRA," adding, "I don't think we want anyone who is bought and paid for" to be representing the state.[28] John Hancock, the executive director of the Missouri Republican party, responded to this attack with a defense of the senator. He said, "John Ashcroft fully supports the gun laws that are on the books. It's the Carnahan administration's failure to enforce those laws that's the problem. It is not extreme to stand up for law-abiding citizens owning hunting equipment."[29] Of course, concealed handguns are rarely considered "hunting equipment," and the Carnahan campaign was quick to point that out. Carnahan reiterated his criticism of Ashcroft on guns throughout the campaign. For instance, in the days leading up to the pro–gun control Million Mom March in Washington, D.C., in May 2000, the governor criticized Ashcroft's votes on gun legislation in the U.S. Senate, commented on the money the NRA had donated to Ashcroft since 1994, and reminded voters of the senator's support of Prop B.[30]

HCI was very active in campaign politics in 2000, launching the biggest TV and radio campaign effort in its history. The group was heavily involved in the presidential campaign, running anti-Bush television ads in five major markets where it believed the gun issue could be decisive, including St. Louis. The group also continued to be involved in Missouri state politics. HCI produced an anti-Ashcroft TV spot, and in September 2000 the senator was number one on a list of legislators HCI called "The Dangerous Dozen." All twelve were Republicans and, according to the group, had the worst records in Congress on gun control. HCI's Joe Sudbay said, "The Ashcroft-Carnahan race is something we're taking very seriously," and suggested that the group would run anti-Ashcroft ads in the St. Louis television market because the senator had voted against all thirteen bills that HCI considered important.[31] Ashcroft's campaign responded to the attack by calling HCI a partisan organization that couldn't be relied on to report the facts in an objective way. HCI's anti-Bush and anti-Ashcroft TV spots both sparked a small campaign controversy, both nationally and in Missouri, when a St. Louis television station refused to air them.

HCI's anti-Bush ad suggested that if voters wanted to know Bush's position on guns, all they needed to do was examine his record in Texas, where he signed a law making concealed handguns legal. It claimed the Texas law allowed people to carry guns into places such as churches and amusement parks. The advertisement also included a quote from then-NRA First Vice President Kayne Robinson, who later succeeded Charlton Heston as president of the organization. Robinson was quoted as saying that if Bush won, "We'll have a president where we work out of their office." The comment came from remarks Robinson made to a closed-door meeting of NRA members. The speech, of course, was never meant for public consumption, but someone taped his remarks, and they ended up in the HCI ad. According to the *Washington Post,* what Robinson said in full was, "If we win, we'll have a president, with at least one of the people that's running, a president where we work out of their office. Unbelievably friendly relations."[32] The HCI spot concluded with the statement: "Say NO to the gun lobby. Tell George Bush handguns don't belong in our nursing homes and churches." Assessing the spot, an ad-watch report in the *New York Times* was critical of HCI when it suggested the organization was merely hoping to generate free media buzz with the ad. The reporter wrote, "By trying to depict Mr. Bush as a pawn of the N.R.A., the advertisement seeks to make him seem like an extremist on gun control issues . . . Also, it suggests that the governor is not his own man, that he is beholden to powerful right-wing interest groups. The advertisement is not being shown widely enough to affect many voters directly, but Handgun Control is clearly hoping that journalists in Washington and Texas will use it to write critical stories about Mr. Bush."[33] The Bush campaign argued that HCI was misinterpreting the Texas law and asserted that Bush would not pursue a similar law at the national level. The campaign also denied the NRA set the agenda for Bush as governor or would do so for a Bush White House. One of Bush's campaign spokesmen, who later became his White House press secretary, Scott McClellan, said, "Neither the NRA nor any special interest sets the governor's agenda. Governor Bush sets his agenda based on his priorities and principles."[34]

Defending himself, George Bush said, "I'll make the decisions as to what goes on in the White House. I'll make it clear what my positions are."[35] Clearly, Bush hoped to put out the flames sparked by Robinson's statement, though the NRA's response wasn't especially helpful to the candidate's efforts. James Jay Baker, the NRA's chief lobbyist, made no attempt to deny that Robinson was referring to Bush in his speech and said, "Kayne has a good relationship with the governor from their proximity for long periods in Iowa and we at the NRA have had very good relations with George Bush over his entire public life. Bush is very supportive of the rights of law-abiding gun owners, and he's followed his words with deeds."[36] The comments did nothing to alleviate the fears of the gun control lobby, and the Bush campaign felt compelled to continue to defend its record on guns, while HCI continued to defend the ad as fair and accurate.

Explaining the group's reason for running the ad, HCI's Joe Sudbay said, "What our people have learned is that if you want to change the gun laws, you've got to change the people making the gun laws. The race is very, very close. There are few that offer such a sharp contrast as this one."[37] As the politicians debated the ad, the local St. Louis CBS affiliate, KMOV, refused to run the ad and did not issue a public explanation of its decision.[38] This was frustrating to HCI, of course, and Joe Sudbay pointed out that no other television station had refused to run the ad because of its content.[39] This did nothing to prompt KMOV to run the ad, however.

A month later, KMOV also refused to run an HCI ad that criticized Senator Ashcroft. The spot referred to Ashcroft as "the best friend of the pro-gun interests."[40] This time, KMOV's general manager, Allan Cohen, explained the station's decision. He said, "We are allowed to cover controversial issues in a variety of ways. We choose to address this issue through news and public affairs."[41] Cohen added the station was within its rights to reject both the anti-Bush and Ashcroft ads because they were issue ads, not candidate ads.[42] This was certainly true—the station had no legal obligation to carry an interest group's advertisement. The station's parent network, CBS, made a similar decision in 2004 when it refused to sell airtime during the Super Bowl to the liberal advocacy group MoveOn.org, which wanted to run a so-called "issue ad" attacking the size of the federal deficit under the Bush administration. Explaining its Super Bowl decision, CBS said it simply chose not to politicize the game and issued statements explaining it never allowed political ads to run during the game.

The decision in 2000 by KMOV to reject the anti-Bush and Ashcroft ads raised some eyebrows, in light of the fact that the station was owned by a Dallas-based company, Belo Corporation, whose CEO, Robert Decherd, said he was a friend of George Bush.[43] This didn't change the legality of the station's decision not to run the ads, but it made KMOV appear partisan and, as is usually the case with such decisions, refusing to run the ads undoubtedly drew more attention to them than simply running them would have done. HCI's Joe Sudbay said, "It seems like the losers in all of this are the people of St. Louis who miss out on an opportunity to hear this debate."[44] It wasn't a major campaign scandal, but it was yet another flashpoint in Missouri's long, controversial history with guns as a political issue.

According to FEC records, HCI spent at least $215,000 in the 2000 Senate campaign in Missouri. In addition to the television campaign against Ashcroft, gun control activists remained involved in the races for senator and governor in more grassroots ways. HCI sent direct mail to gun control activists. According to the BYU study, "One mailing included an election guide, a list of candidates to oppose, and noted that Bush and Cheney are 'in a league of their own'" on guns.[45] These efforts certainly helped mobilize gun control advocates.

In early October 2000, for example, Missourians Against Handgun Violence held a rally outside a gun range in Talent's district, urging him to sign a pledge not to go against the will of the people, as expressed in the Prop B vote, if he was elected governor. A spokesperson for the group, Frieda Bernstein, said Talent had "...been in Washington too long sleeping with the NRA," and attacked his campaign position supporting conceal-and-carry.[46] It was a small rally of only about a dozen people, but it had the desired effect—getting coverage in the media, dramatically increasing the number of people who heard the protest. In addition to this rally, gun control advocates around the state also took the unusual tactic of passing out Talent's own campaign fliers to supporters of gun control in order to highlight Talent's pro-gun position.[47]

Not to be outdone by the gun control lobby, the NRA was very active in both the Missouri gubernatorial and U.S. Senate campaigns. In the Senate campaign, the group used television ads featuring Charlton Heston and billboards urging people to "Vote Freedom First." The group also paid for radio advertisements and direct mail encouraging gun rights supporters to vote for Ashcroft.[48] Again, according to FEC records, the NRA spent more than $550,000 on the Ashcroft-Carnahan race alone. In addition to the NRA's paid media efforts, gun advocates were also effective at the grassroots level.

In October the NRA ran phone banks and a direct mail campaign to stimulate single-issue voters to turn out and bring their friends and family with them. The NRA was, once again, demonstrating its understanding of the fact that many people in Missouri could be activated solely by the gun issue. Some of these voters were people who otherwise wouldn't vote, while others were people who would usually support a Democratic candidate, were it not for his or her position on guns. It is widely believed, for example, that many labor union members in Missouri who might be naturally inclined to support Democratic candidates don't do so if the Democrat is pro–gun control.

NRA spokesman Bill Powers commented on the organization's push into mid-October when he said, "This is the time in every campaign when everybody starts focusing on those activists. They're more important than the money we'll spend...we'd do skywriting if we thought it would work," and added, "We'll be very visible, very active."[49] The efforts of the NRA, both through paid media and the grass roots, were thrown into disarray shortly after Powers made this comment, however.

An accident of historic proportions intervened at the end of the Senate campaign, making it nearly irrelevant. On October 16, Governor Carnahan, his son, Randy, and his spokesman, Chris Sifford, were killed in a plane crash while flying from one campaign appearance to another. The governor's death brought many prominent national politicians to the state for the funeral, including

President Clinton, and had a chilling effect on the campaign of not only John Ashcroft but also the other Republicans running for statewide office in Missouri. The tragic deaths prompted the NRA to pull a final ad campaign attacking Carnahan and to cancel most of the campaign activities it had planned for the last days of the race.

In the wake of Carnahan's death, the races for senator, governor, state treasurer, lieutenant governor, and attorney general all went to the Democrats in 2000. The only statewide race won by a Republican was Matt Blunt's campaign for secretary of state. Earlier in the campaign, though most races were very tight, it seemed as though the Republicans were poised to claim the mantle of power in Missouri statewide offices. There was considerable speculation following the election that the Democrats' success in 2000 was at least in part attributable to the atmosphere following Carnahan's death. While he was alive, the governor had a tremendous impact on the fortunes of the Democratic party in Missouri politics. In 1988, Carnahan was the only Democrat to win a statewide election when he became lieutenant governor. By the time of his death in 2000, all five of the major statewide offices were held by Democrats, but Carnahan was locked in a very tight race with Ashcroft that he appeared likely to lose. Along with Carnahan, it appeared very possible that Jim Talent would beat Bob Holden. If that had happened, it meant at least three of the statewide elections in Missouri would have gone to the Republicans.

When Carnahan was killed just weeks before election day, most polls indicated he was trailing Ashcroft by a slight margin. After his death many political observers, both in Missouri and nationally, assumed the race would go to Ashcroft by default. However, there was a groundswell of support for the fallen governor that gave his campaign the push it needed to get over the top; other Democratic candidates on the ballot were probably helped as well. The pomp and circumstance of Carnahan's funeral had an undeniably Democratic tint and put Republicans in a very uncomfortable position. The BYU study described the celebrity-laden funeral in this way: "TV viewers were offered what amounted to a three-hour eulogy," and suggested it did much to advance his campaign.[50] When Carnahan died, it was too late to legally remove his name from the ballot. The Democratic lieutenant governor who succeeded him, Roger Wilson, announced that if Carnahan won the election, he would appoint Carnahan's widow, Jean, to serve in his place. Missouri law authorizes the governor to appoint an interim senator to serve until a special election can be held to determine who will complete the remainder of the term. This left Ashcroft and his allies with the unpleasant prospect of campaigning against a dead man and a widow.

Ashcroft and his supporters, including the NRA, responded to Carnahan's death by largely suspending the campaign from mid-October until election day. As the BYU study described the last days of the campaign, "... the NRA stopped all radio and television advertising for at least a week. The NRA had sent a bulk mailing to licensed hunters before the accident, but received negative phone calls about the mailer after Carnahan's death."[51] On the other hand, allies of Carnahan, especially labor unions such as the AFL-CIO, worked hard to get out the message that Carnahan was still on the ballot and that supporters could still vote for him. They used phone banks, door hangers, fliers distributed at work places, and direct mail to mobilize voters.[52]

The Ashcroft campaign's uncertainty allowed Carnahan supporters a wide open playing field. Jean Carnahan ran just one TV spot after her husband's death, a tribute to her husband's memory, but the campaign also sent a letter to almost a million Democratic voters urging them to support Mel Carnahan's legacy.[53] Bumper stickers emblazoned with the message "Still With Mel" appeared around the state, and his campaign continued in his absence.

The outcome of the election was both historically close and tainted with controversy. Carnahan won the race with 50.4 percent of the vote versus Ashcroft's 48.4 percent. The controversy came from St. Louis, where it was alleged that Democratic poll workers kept the polls open past the legal closing time. Seeing no advantage in fighting the result, Ashcroft opted to bow out gracefully and avoid an ugly court battle. Perhaps he knew an appointment to higher office was coming from George Bush, pending the outcome of the controversial presidential election, but he also undoubtedly knew there was nothing to be gained from appearing to be a poor sport in a loss to a dead man.

Election day culminated what had been, prior to Carnahan's death, an ugly, no-holds-barred campaign. The race broke along familiar lines for Missouri politics, with Carnahan winning heavily in St. Louis and Kansas City, while Ashcroft did well in the out-state regions. The NRA, according to the BYU study, used "Value messages ... aimed at both the rural vote and at some of the labor support in the metropolitan exurbs" to motivate voters to support Ashcroft at the polls.[54] The campaign seemed to be working prior to Carnahan's death, but the effectiveness of the NRA's efforts will forever be obscured by the tragic events of October 16.

As close as the Ashcroft-Carnahan race was, it was nowhere near as close as the gubernatorial election, which was decided by a razor-thin margin. Bob Holden beat Jim Talent by roughly thirty thousand votes; once again, in such a close race it is not unreasonable to suggest that the grief Missourians felt after the death of Carnahan helped pushed Holden into office. Like Carnahan,

Holden performed strongly in urban areas, winning in both St. Louis and Kansas City. Talent did well in rural areas, though Holden was not completely shut out in the rural counties. According to Missouri election records, Holden won in thirty-five counties, including seven of the ten that voted against Prop B in 1999. Talent won in eighty counties, including all of the counties that voted in favor of Prop B and three that voted against it.

In the aftermath of the 2000 elections, both parties argued guns had helped them in Missouri. For instance, Republicans claimed, and many Democrats agreed, that the gun issue helped George W. Bush win Missouri. Al Gore supported many federal gun control proposals, including trigger locks, licensing purchasers of new handguns, a ban on cheap handguns, and a limit on handgun purchases to one per month. He also opposed laws limiting the ability of local governments to sue gun manufacturers.[55] All of these proposals made Gore very unpopular with gun enthusiasts.

Speaking of Al Gore during the campaign, Bart Stupak, a Democratic congressman from rural northern Michigan, said, "To gun owners, he's already viewed as an extremist. If he wants to talk about safety measures, that's O.K. People see that as reasonable. If you talk about further layers, he'll lose voters in a minute. They're not comfortable with his position as it is."[56] Stupak was uniquely qualified to address guns and the impact they could have on a campaign. He served a district where views on guns and other social issues were very similar to those in out-state Missouri. Stupak was a conservative Democrat who was a longtime member of the NRA, and for most of his career he was given a grade of A by the NRA's Institute for Legislative Action, based on his voting record. However, in 2000 he became a target for defeat by the organization. The NRA dropped its support after Stupak cast a vote in favor of mandatory background checks at gun shows. The organization endorsed his opponent and pumped money into the district in an effort to unseat Stupak. This forced Stupak to hold town hall meetings across his district explaining his position on guns and to run television ads featuring the congressman with a shotgun. Stupak survived the race, but it had to be an eye-opening experience for him. Stupak was speaking from personal experience when he commented on Gore's liability on the gun issue, and the congressman's analysis accurately portrayed the views of many conservative, rural Democrats.

The NRA targeted Gore early in the campaign at the national level, as well as campaigning against him in Missouri. At the May 2000 annual NRA convention, the group officially declared its opposition to Al Gore. Charlton Heston, speaking to NRA members, said, "The N.R.A. is back. All of this spells very serious trouble for a man named Gore."[57] The NRA's convention was held just after the Million Mom March, a gathering of gun control advocates that Wayne LaPierre characterized as a Gore campaign rally organized by the White House.[58]

After the election, the NRA was quick to point out how effective it had been in the presidential race. As Dick Dahl wrote in the *Nation,* "The NRA claims that Al Gore lost the election on the gun issue . . . The conventional wisdom among the Democratic leadership has favored the NRA interpretation."[59] On the other hand, gun control activists agreed with the NRA about the importance of the gun issue, but argued that the reason Gore lost wasn't because he was anti-gun, but because he wasn't anti-gun enough. Dahl wrote, "Gun-control activists say that to the contrary, had Gore not backed off on the issue as his campaign progressed, he would have gotten more votes from suburban women who were inclined to vote for him based on that issue alone. They also point to the fact that seven of the nine House candidates who received the most NRA money lost, as did five of the seven top NRA recipients in the Senate."[60]

Scholars may argue about how important the issue of gun control was during the presidential race, but what can't be denied is that the 2000 presidential campaign was decided by a razor-thin margin. The balance in the Electoral College was tipped to Bush with victories in states that could just as easily have gone to Gore. These included West Virginia, Arkansas, Tennessee, and Florida. Like Missouri, each of these states has long had a significant level of support for the NRA and its agenda. Clearly the group's decision to "declare war" on Gore made some difference in the presidential election, even if it only moved a few thousand voters in each of the swing states won by Bush.

While the gun issue seemed to have hurt Gore, Missouri Democrats claimed it was a positive force in Bob Holden's defeat of Jim Talent, whose pro–conceal-and-carry position harmed him in his own home territory of suburban St. Louis, where Prop B lost overwhelmingly in 1999. In 2001, the executive director of the state Democratic party, B. J. Atwater, said, "I believe it was that same issue that defeated Jim Talent . . . Guns is a wedge issue, but for Republicans as well as Democrats."[61] The gun issue is something everyone in Missouri wants to claim, and it is an issue that can truly make a difference in elections in the Show-Me State, especially in races as close as those in 2000.

As 2000 drew to a close after an exhausting campaign season, there was no time to relax, because three special state senate elections loomed on the horizon. In two of them, guns promised to play a critical role. The elections were considered critical because the balance of power in the senate depended on their outcome. The Republicans emerged from the 2000 election with a majority in the Missouri Senate, but the outcome of the special elections left long-term control up in the air.

Chapter Seventeen

2001—Elections Begin to Make a Difference

Special Elections

As 2001 began, guns once again took center stage, first in the January special elections in three state senate districts. The districts were the Twelfth, in the state's northwest corner; the Eighteenth, in the state's northeast corner; and the Fourth, in the St. Louis area. In each of the three, the seats were left open by senators who were elected to higher office. In the Twelfth District, Republican Sam Graves was elected to the U.S. Congress. In the Eighteenth District, Democrat Joe Maxwell was elected Missouri's lieutenant governor. In the Fourth District, Democrat William Lacy Clay, Jr., was elected to the U.S. Congress. The vacancies left control of the state senate up in the air, and the political parties viewed the stakes in the special elections as incredibly high, especially in the Twelfth and Eighteenth Districts. The Fourth District received less attention because it was a safe Democratic seat. John Hancock, the chairman of the state Republican party, recognized the importance of the special elections, especially the Twelfth and the Eighteenth, when he said, "Ultimately, it's about who is going to control the state Senate—one-third of the governing power in the state capital."[1] With so much at stake, the elections drew an almost unprecedented amount of state and national attention.

Republicans won both the Twelfth and Eighteenth Districts, helping to ensure that the Republicans held the majority in the state senate for the first time since 1948. In both districts, guns and abortion dominated the debate. Prior to the special elections, the Republicans held an advantage of 16 to 15. According to State Ethics Commission records, the two parties combined to spend around $800,000 on the two campaigns, and considerably more was spent on the campaigns in total. One reporter wrote, "The four candidates for two Senate seats have gathered a total of $1.23 million in a fund-raising frenzy sparked by the virtually even split between Democrats and Republicans in the chamber."[2] The fact that more than a million dollars was spent in two state senate races is stark evidence of how critical their outcome was thought to be.

In the Twelfth District race, two state representatives faced each other. They were David Klindt, R–Bethany, and Randall Relford, D–Cameron. As state representatives, indicated by their records as legislators, both candidates supported conceal-and-carry. The NRA, however, endorsed Klindt, the Republican, because, it reported, he had also voted for the liability protection legislation that would have made it illegal for cities and counties to sue gun manufacturers. Klindt also received the support of pro-life groups even though both he and his opponent voted in support of a recent bill banning so-called partial birth abortions. Klindt got the nod from pro-life advocates because of objections to some amendments proposed by Relford that activists felt would have weakened the bill.[3] In the end, Klindt won the election rather handily, with 66.1 percent of the vote.

In the Eighteenth District election, John Cauthorn, R–Mexico, ran against State Representative Robert Clayton III, D–Hannibal. Cauthorn had never held elective office, though he was the former president of the Missouri Cattlemen's Association. Cauthorn pushed a hard-line conservative agenda. As was the case in the Twelfth District, guns and abortion were cornerstone issues, with advocates on both sides swamping the race with money and advertisements. Cauthorn's campaign was described as no-holds-barred. For instance, "Cauthorn's ads began the day after Christmas and were surprisingly harsh. He criticizes Clayton's support for abortion rights and implies that Clayton does not support gun rights. Clayton supported the concealed carry proposal in 1999, and has backed proposals to prevent cities from suing gun manufacturers."[4] The Republican party chairman, John Hancock, branded Clayton an "urban lawyer" who was not in synch with the members of the rural senate district, and argued guns and abortion were an important part of the strategy to defeat him.[5] During the campaign, the NRA was very active in its support of Cauthorn, ignoring Clayton's own strong record on gun rights. The group attributed its support for Cauthorn to an objectionable committee vote by Clayton and what it characterized as unacceptable answers on a candidate survey, but representatives of the group would not elaborate on its position when asked by reporters after the race.[6] Cauthorn won the election with 54.2 percent of the vote to Clayton's 45.8 percent. Cauthorn's victory gave the NRA a conservative ideologue who was committed to conceal-and-carry and increased the Republicans' majority in the senate.

The chairman of the state Democratic party, Joe Carmichael, suggested ads run by pro-life and pro-gun groups had been very effective in helping defeat Clayton. With regard to guns, he said the attacks on Clayton worked because his party wasn't able to convince rural voters that "Democrats don't want to take your guns away."[7] Once again, a top Missouri Democrat, Joe Carmichael, was alluding to what many Democrats felt was the Gore effect. Clearly, the "wedge" issues of Missouri politics played a critical role in the special elections of 2001.

In the third special election, held in the Fourth District, the race was easily won by State Representative Pat Dougherty, D–St. Louis, with nearly 84 percent of the vote. The striking difference between the three races was the turnout. In both the Twelfth and Eighteenth Districts, turnout was relatively high for a special election: 25,615 votes were cast in the Twelfth District race, while 34,160 were cast in the Eighteenth District. On the other hand, in the Fourth District election, where guns and abortion were hardly mentioned and the election of Dougherty was a foregone conclusion, turnout was just 7,796.

The gun issue was strangely quiet in three special state House elections held in August. Two of the races were in rural districts, while the third was in St. Louis. While both parties poured money into the races, the NRA officially stayed out of the campaigns. According to NRA spokespersons, the group found both the Democratic and Republican candidates acceptable. The very inaction of the NRA was fascinating, of course, because it pointed to the group's success in writing the rules for political success in rural Missouri. Chiefly, the rule was "if you're pro-gun control, don't bother running." The organization's inaction in the special elections may have contributed to a somewhat surprising outcome, however. The Democrats won two out of the three races, helping the party maintain a slender advantage in the house. The St. Louis race, to replace Pat Dougherty, was an easy victory for the Democratic candidate, Michael Daus.

In the other two races, in the Third and Seventh Districts, both in rural northwest Missouri, the Democratic candidates, Jim Whorton and Deron Sugg, took positions very similar to their Republican opponents, Roscoe Moulthrop and John Quinn, hoping to position themselves for victory. In both cases, the Democrats distanced themselves from Governor Holden, criticizing his positions on several issues, including guns, and avoiding appearances with him at campaign rallies. Both candidates were pro-gun and pro-life and suggested Holden was too interested in trying to please urban voters. Speaking of Holden, Sugg said, "He did very well in St. Louis. There almost seems like a quid pro quo with some of his decisions."[8] Whorton referred to Holden, a member of his own party, as "One Term Bob" on the campaign trail.[9]

The governor had no public response to these comments, nor did he participate in the campaigns. In fact, Holden was out of the state, attending the annual meeting of the National Governors Association, on election day. The Democratic candidates performed quite well. Whorton won his race by a slight margin, while Sugg lost, but very narrowly. Prior to the elections, the Democrats held a majority of 85 to 74, so control of the house wasn't at stake, but both parties hoped to position themselves for the upcoming 2002 elections, when ninety new members were to be elected, thanks to term limits. As evidence of the importance they assigned to the races, the parties together raised close to three hundred thousand dollars for the two elections.[10]

The chairwoman of the Republican party, Ann Wagner, complained about Whorton's conservative positions on guns and abortion. She said, "Those are our issues."[11] Certainly, Whorton and Sugg were both considerably more conservative than a Democrat from St. Louis or Kansas City would have been, but activists like those in the NRA simply made it necessary for Democrats to adopt such positions if they were to have a chance of winning the elections. The positions that candidates took on these controversial issues was sometimes a matter of region rather than of party. If the point was not clear beforehand, the Prop B fight in 1999, the elections of 2000, and the special house and senate elections of 2001 taught both Republicans and Democrats that Kansas Citians and St. Louisans vote one way on guns and out-state voters another. It also was made clear that many voters make their choices based on the gun issue, without regard for party label. Finally, the elections demonstrated that for many voters, guns are the only issue which motivates them to vote at all.

Ashcroft for Attorney General

Another "campaign" stirred pro- and anti-gun activists to action in early 2001, when George Bush nominated John Ashcroft to be his attorney general. Interest groups soon banded together both to support and to oppose his nomination, including organizations on both sides of the gun debate. The confirmation process took on a heated, ugly quality similar to the race between Ashcroft and Carnahan. In fact, Mel Carnahan's campaign manager in 2000, Marc Farinella, inserted himself into the middle of the fight when he leaked Carnahan campaign files of anti-Ashcroft material to the coalition of interest groups opposing Ashcroft's nomination.[12] Farinella claimed the decision to release the information was his alone but his mea culpa did little to reduce the controversy that spilled over on Senator Jean Carnahan. The forces favoring Ashcroft were outraged. David Israelite, a spokesman for the Republican National Committee, said, "It is unfathomable that opposition research files would be distributed without the express permission of the candidate, and in this case, clearly his wife is carrying on his political legacy."[13] What Israelite was suggesting, of course, was that Jean Carnahan had something to do with the release of the information.

Ashcroft was a socially conservative politician whose positions on issues such as guns, civil rights, and abortion had long drawn fire from liberal interest groups. Missouri politics were drawn into Ashcroft's nomination for many reasons. First, of course, Ashcroft was from Missouri and had been active in Missouri politics for three decades. Second was Ashcroft's decision in 2000 to block President Clinton's nomination of Missouri Supreme Court Judge Ronnie White to the federal judiciary. White was the Missouri House Civil and Criminal Laws Committee chair who had blocked conceal-and-carry in 1992. White was also African American, and Ashcroft's actions in opposition to his nomination sparked charges of racial bias. This was a campaign issue in 2000, and White was called to appear at Ashcroft's confirmation hearing for attorney general by the ranking minority member on the Judiciary Committee, Senator Patrick Leahy, D–Vermont. The Missouri judge gave riveting, harsh testimony about the former senator.

Ashcroft claimed his opposition to White was based on the Judge's liberal record as a jurist, not his race. In Ashcroft's defense, given his very conservative political ideals, he certainly objected to White's politics. There is no doubt Ashcroft would have opposed Judge White regardless of race. If anything, Ashcroft deserves credit for sticking to his beliefs, regardless of the consequences. He had to know his opposition to White would invite charges of racial bias that could become an issue in his campaign against Carnahan, yet he stuck to his ideological beliefs and opposed the nomination anyway. It may not have been a wise political move, but it was ideologically honest. One may also speculate, of course, that one of Clinton's reasons for nominating White in an election was that it would put Ashcroft in an uncomfortable position.

In addition to the race issue, interest groups opposed to Ashcroft found many reasons to object to his nomination. Ashcroft's strong pro-life stance activated pro-choice groups to resist his nomination and, of course, the former senator's position on guns was also an issue. The Million Mom March began a grassroots campaign urging its members to contact their senators and voice opposition to Ashcroft. HCI also denounced his nomination, and Michael Barnes, an official with HCI, questioned Ashcroft's ability to serve as the nation's leading law enforcement official. Barnes wondered aloud how Ashcroft could fully apply the nation's gun laws, since he consistently voted against gun control measures during his term in the U.S. Senate and campaigned heavily in support of Prop B. Barnes said, "He voted against common sense gun measures at every opportunity. How can we expect this man to support and defend laws he says have no value?"[14] There were certainly few groups more likely to oppose Ashcroft's nomination for Attorney General than HCI.

The NRA, on the other hand, supported his nomination, as it supported him throughout his political career. While the confirmation hearings were partisan and ill-tempered, Ashcroft's nomination was approved by the Republican-controlled Senate. In one of her first key votes as a senator, Jean Carnahan voted against Ashcroft, outraging many Missouri Republicans who felt she owed him her vote in light of the fact that he had bowed gracefully out of the Senate campaign rather than fight the voting irregularities in St. Louis, but Carnahan viewed it as a vote of conscience.[15] As gun control advocates feared, there was a great deal at stake for the proponents and opponents of gun rights with the appointment of John Ashcroft to the position of attorney general.

Very soon after taking office, Ashcroft indicated he was considering a major change in the Department of Justice's interpretation of the Second Amendment that would affect how it dealt with cases of alleged violations of federal firearms regulations. For roughly sixty years, regardless of which party held the White House, the Department of Justice had officially subscribed to the Supreme Court's opinion in *Miller v. United States* (1939), which held that the Second Amendment granted states a right to arm its militias but did not grant individuals the right to keep and bear arms.[16] In a May 2001 letter to the NRA, Ashcroft indicated the Justice Department was on the verge of a new position when he wrote, ". . . the individual rights view is embraced by the preponderance of legal scholarship on the subject."[17] This view may or may not have been embraced by the "preponderance of legal scholarship," as Ashcroft suggested, but it was certainly not a position embraced by the Supreme Court, which had declined to take any cases directly related to the meaning of the Second Amendment since the Miller decision in 1939.

Ashcroft officially changed the administration's interpretation of the Second Amendment later in the year. In a memo to all of the Department of Justice's U.S. attorneys on November 9, 2001, Ashcroft wrote he wanted to be apprised of all cases where the Second Amendment applied and suggested the department was adopting an individual rights interpretation of the Second Amendment. Ashcroft seems to have been influenced by the decision of the U.S. Fifth Circuit Court of Appeals in *Emerson v. United States,* which took a similar approach to the Second Amendment.[18] In his memo to the Department of Justice, Ashcroft wrote, "*Emerson* is also noteworthy because, in upholding this statute, the Fifth Circuit undertook a scholarly and comprehensive review of the pertinent legal materials and specifically affirmed that the Second

Amendment 'protects the right of *individuals*, including those not then actually a member of any militia or engaged in active military service or training, to privately possess and bear their own firearms.' The Court's opinion also makes the important point that the existence of this individual right does not mean that reasonable restrictions cannot be imposed to prevent unfit persons from possessing firearms or to restrict possession of firearms particularly suited to criminal misuse. In my view, the *Emerson* opinion, and the balance it strikes, generally reflect the correct understanding of the Second Amendment."[19]

This memo meant the Justice Department would change how cases of alleged firearms law violations were handled. Ashcroft's order meant the Department of Justice would consider gun ownership an individual right protected by the Constitution as opposed to a privilege that could be granted or taken away by the government. A reasonable comparison might be driving a car. There is no constitutionally protected right to drive a car. Most assume they have a right to drive when they reach the age of sixteen, but driving is a privilege one must earn by passing written tests, demonstrating driving proficiency, and maintaining a good driving record. It is also a privilege that can be taken away for several reasons. According to the Supreme Court's decision in *Miller,* gun ownership and usage are also privileges, but the Ashcroft memo meant that government regulation of gun ownership was being reconsidered.

Ashcroft didn't argue the new interpretation meant the right to keep and bear arms was absolute and that there could be no gun control laws. There were, he asserted, limits to the right to guns, just as there are limits on most of the rights guaranteed by the Constitution. The right of free speech, for example, doesn't give one a blank check to say anything one might wish. One cannot, for example, falsely yell "Fire" in a crowded movie theater, thereby causing a panicked stampede which results in the injury or death of audience members. Similarly, the Ashcroft position suggested there were some in society who had clearly forfeited their right to keep and bear arms. In his memo, Ashcroft wrote, "As I have stated many times, reducing gun crime is a top priority for the department. We will vigorously enforce and defend existing firearms laws in order to accomplish that goal."[20] Nevertheless, the Ashcroft memo was a significant change in policy because it meant the Department of Justice planned to change the legal status of gun ownership in the United States. From the department's perspective, the Second Amendment no longer merely gave permission for the states to create militias to protect themselves from an oppressive federal government—it now was officially interpreted to mean that individuals had the right to keep and bear arms.

Federal prosecutors throughout the system were expected to adopt the department's new interpretation of the law and, of course, the gun control lobby was very disturbed. The Brady Campaign against Handgun Violence, formerly HCI, was dire in its assessment of the policy change. In a press release, Sarah Brady wrote, "It appears that Attorney General Ashcroft has decided once again to do the bidding of the gun lobby, this time by jettisoning the long-standing position of the United States government on the meaning of the Second Amendment, only to replace it with the discredited interpretation held by the gun lobby... Indeed, the National Rifle Association (NRA) has openly stated that it will use a changed U.S. position to seek to challenge the constitutionality of common-sense gun laws."[21]

Jonathan Lowy, an attorney for the Brady Center for Gun Violence (HCI), argued, "Every federal gun law is now on the table."[22] Another spokesman for HCI, Daniel Vice, suggested that the new Justice Department policy would only help criminals. He said, "The practical effect is, in courts now, criminal defendants will be able to challenge their indictments under gun laws and the government will have to agree with the criminals in court: that there's a much stronger constitutional standard that makes it harder to defend our gun laws."[23]

The NRA, of course, was ecstatic about the change. In response to the new policy, a spokesman for the NRA, Andrew Arulanandam, said, "I don't have a crystal ball in front of me. However, without a doubt, we feel this affirmation of the Second Amendment is the precise interpretation."[24] Clearly, the department's new interpretation of the Second Amendment was a major change of policy. The Supreme Court, the final American arbiter of the Constitution, has yet to apply the Ashcroft opinion in a decision, but it reflects a shifting attitude in some lower courts.

Meanwhile, Back in the Show-Me State

By March 2001, the political atmosphere was different, both in Missouri and Washington. In Washington, the legislative and executive branches were both controlled by the Republicans for the first time since the Eisenhower administration, putting gun rights advocates back into play at the federal level. Gun control activists, who had enjoyed some legislative success in the wake of the Columbine attack, were back on the defensive in Washington and continued to face trouble in Missouri. The elections of 2000 and 2001 reiterated to most elected officials that a position taken against guns could be very hazardous to the health of a political career. Further, it showed that trying to find a path down the middle was no way to solve the problem.

For instance, the losers in the Twelfth and Eighteenth District special senate elections were pro-gun, but not pro-gun enough, while the winners were outspoken in their support of conceal-and-carry and the NRA. This atmosphere left the legislature ripe for the return of conceal-and-carry legislation in 2001. During the session a majority of legislators supported conceal-and-carry, and there were very few felt who felt politically safe enough to fight it.

There was new, pro-gun leadership in both houses. The speaker of the house, Jim Kreider, D–Nixa, and the house majority leader, Wayne Crump, were both pro-gun. The new senate president pro tem, Peter Kinder, R–Cape Girardeau, was also pro-gun. With pro-gun legislators holding the major legislative leadership positions, gun rights advocates had friends in high places. Speaker Jim Kreider addressed the guns issue directly when he argued rural Democrats favored conceal-and-carry because that is what their constituents wanted. He said, "The gun issue was big in last year's election. I think that's why Bush won Missouri. We Democrats have a tough time in rural areas because we were linked to the 'anti-gun Gore.'"[25] As Kreider began his tenure as speaker, he seemed determined to prove that rural Democrats had nothing to do with the "anti-gun Gore." One of his first actions as speaker was to create a special house committee for gun bills, the Special Committee on Sportsmanship, Safety, and Firearms, so the bills wouldn't be lost in the usual crush of legislation during Missouri's five-month General Assembly session. The chairman of the special committee was none other than Wayne Crump.

Gun rights supporters made themselves very visible during the 2001 legislative session. At a pro-gun rally at the state capitol in February, roughly two hundred advocates converged to lobby lawmakers. At the rally, Kevin Jamison of the Western Missouri Shooters Alliance said, "Tell them the gun nuts are here. They say we are dangerous. They say we are evil. The nicest thing they call us is a gun nut. All right, we're the gun nuts and we want a 'shall issue' license."[26]

By March, five different conceal-and-carry bills were introduced in the Missouri General Assembly. Of the bills introduced, the major contenders were SB 560, sponsored by Senator Caskey; HB 853, sponsored by Representative Crump; and HB 258, sponsored by Representative Don Koller, D–Summersville. HB 258 and HB 853 were later combined by the Special Committee on Sportsmanship, Safety, and Firearms and became known as HCS HB 853 & 258.

As the conceal-and-carry issue came storming back during the 2001 legislative session, St. Louis played host to a meeting of local anti-gun groups that came together to discuss strategy for defeating concealed handgun bills in Missouri. Stacey Newman, the spokesperson and copresident of the St. Louis chapter of the Million Mom March, spoke negatively about the revival of conceal-and-carry. She said, "I think it's really sneaky. The voters had their say. We're blown away that they are bringing it up again." She added, "The NRA has lost lots of money in Missouri, but they are not ready to quit. We aren't either."[27] Just as the pro-gun forces turned to the state legislatures in the early 1990s when Washington became less hospitable, gun control advocates had to refocus on the state level in the wake of Republican dominance following the 2000 presidential election. For instance, the Million Mom March, which had been regularly taking place in Washington, was canceled in lieu of events at state capitols.[28]

For its part, the NRA was enthusiastic about the changing political environment in both Jefferson City and Washington. At the federal level, the NRA focused on a federal liability protection law that would prevent state and local governments from suing gun manufacturers as well as several other legislative initiatives, such as the elimination of the federal ban on assault rifles. Never an organization to put all its legislative eggs in one basket, the NRA also pursued similar legislation at the state level, including Missouri. Gun control activists meeting in St. Louis, like Stacey Newman, were right to worry.

In Jefferson City, the conceal-and-carry bill leading the way out of the starting gate was Crump's HB 853. In an attempt to avoid the controversy of Prop B, the bill contained a provision calling for applicants to demonstrate a need for a permit, in an apparent attempt to avoid the criticism of Prop B that nearly anyone, including convicted criminals, would have been eligible for a concealed weapon under Prop B. The "need provision" was not well received by either side, however. For example, Kevin Jamison of the Western Missouri Shooters' Alliance said, "Need-based bills are prone to abuse. In other states, if you have political pull, you have a need. If you don't have pull, then you don't have a need."[29] On the other side, opponents complained that Crump defined need so broadly that virtually anyone would still be able to qualify for a permit.

As the legislature got to work on conceal-and-carry in earnest, it seemed it was not the only branch of government that was more receptive. For a time in early 2001, the climate also seemed to be more inviting at the governor's mansion.

For the full span of his eight years in office, Mel Carnahan promised to veto conceal-and-carry legislation. Bob Holden, the newly elected governor of Missouri, a rural Democrat from the southwest corner of the state, opposed concealed handguns for most of the 2000 campaign. However, in the spring of 2001 Holden seemed to moderate his position and opened the door for negotiation when he suggested he wanted to build a relationship with the new, rural, pro-gun legislative leaders. He said, "I'm willing to look at any proposal to see if there is room for compromise. But I will not back down on gun safety or good law enforcement."[30] Laying the groundwork for compromise, the governor's legal counsel, Glenn Norton, met with representatives of gun groups, such as the Second Amendment Coalition, and suggested the governor would consider signing a concealed handguns bill if it was reasonable. Any movement toward signing a right-to-carry bill was a dramatic shift from the steadfast promise of Governor Carnahan to veto any conceal-and-carry bill.

Norton, the governor's counsel, characterized Holden's new willingness to compromise as an acceptance of political reality. He said, "It seems to the governor and to me, if this bill is going to come and there's some chance that it's going to pass, it would be foolish for us not to be involved in the process . . . Without the appropriate restrictions, he would not be in favor of conceal-and-carry."[31] Following the meeting, Gil Pyles, a spokesman for the Second Amendment Coalition, asserted there was enough support in the legislature for the passage of concealed weapons legislation, but that "The devil is going to be in the details." He knew the governor would not sign just any conceal-and-carry bill.[32] Stacey Newman, the copresident of the St. Louis Million Mom March, was not happy with the governor's overture to pro-gun forces. She angrily said, "We mothers will not stand by and tolerate political arrogance from those legislators who are ignoring the state's majority vote. Don't they understand allowing concealed weapons will only worsen the epidemic of gun death in our state?"[33]

The possibility of compromise didn't last, however. Just a week later, the governor shifted tactics again and endorsed a second referendum on concealed weapons. He said, "The public needs to have a great deal of input into this." He also seemed to acknowledge his supporters in Kansas City and St. Louis when he said, "We've got to protect the safety of citizens and ensure the protection of law enforcement. It's a difficult issue for people in different parts of the state to address. I'm trying to work with all parties to try to find some common ground."[34] The referendum idea came from SB 629, sponsored by Ken Jacob, D–Columbia. A veteran and combative legislator, Jacob was frequently involved in legislative maneuvering through the years of fighting over conceal-and-carry. He offered bills and amendments several times with the ultimate goal of defeating the right to carry. Under SB 629, permits would have been issued by the Highway Patrol, not county sheriffs, and applicants would have been required to demonstrate a need for a concealed weapon. Explaining the bill, Jacob said, "If a person can't demonstrate why they have to carry one, I don't understand why they need to carry them. They have to show they are in danger."[35] While Jacob never supported conceal-and-carry, the new referendum was a way to reduce the pressure on the governor to act on conceal-and-carry if the legislature sent him a bill. If it was in the form of a referendum, Holden wouldn't have to choose to sign or veto it—it would be out of his hands. Certainly Jacob believed conceal-and-carry would fail again in a second public vote.

It is doubtful that such a bill would have saved the governor much stress, however. Had a referendum bill been passed by the legislature, it would have led to another lengthy political campaign. While Jacob thought a referendum would allow the governor to stay above the fray, Holden would inevitably have been drawn into the fight, and for much longer than it would take to sign or veto a bill. It is very possible a referendum campaign would have been much more politically damaging.

Of course, there was very little support for a referendum bill in the legislature, so Holden never really had to worry about it. For obvious reasons, supporters of conceal-and-carry, like the NRA and Wayne Crump, strongly objected to a second referendum. Opponents of conceal-and-carry might have welcomed a second referendum, confident that they could repeat the victory of 1999, but the costs of campaigning would have stretched their very thin resources to the breaking point. In the end, it didn't matter. Too many key players opposed a second referendum, and Jacob's bill was a nonstarter. The Civil and Criminal Jurisprudence Committee took no action on his bill.

While Speaker Kreider opposed Jacob's proposal, he suggested that there might be other ways to compromise. One possibility, he suggested, was to pass a conceal-and-carry law but allow local governments some choice. He said, "Certain counties could opt out of the provision and not allow concealed weapons in those counties."[36] At the time Kreider made his suggestion, no bills contained such a provision, but the speaker pointed out that Crump, the chairman of the Sportsmanship, Safety, and Firearms Committee, was working to find a compromise acceptable to everyone.

Of course, Crump was most supportive of his own bill, and he defended it against charges that it was undemocratic for the legislature to pass a law the people had rejected just two years earlier. He said that because HB 853 was more restrictive than Prop B with its "need provision," it wasn't a repudiation of people's wishes in 1999. He suggested the people of Missouri might have approved Prop B if it included a "need provision." In addition to the "need provision," Crump argued his bill placed more restrictions on where a concealed gun could be carried and offered increased penalties for those caught carrying a concealed weapon without a permit. His hope was that the legislature could settle on a bill that was open enough to win the support of gun rights advocates and restrictive enough for the governor to sign, avoiding the need to bring it to the people again.[37] Crump continuously discounted the notion that he and other supporters of conceal-and-carry were opposing the public will. He said, "We are doing the right thing addressing this again," and argued that he continued to fight because his constituents wanted the right to carry.[38]

Crump also denied accusations that the return of conceal-and-carry was the responsibility of the NRA, a charge made in a *St. Louis Post-Dispatch* editorial. The editorial read, "But the NRA shows great resiliency in ignoring the majority. On Wednesday a couple hundred self-proclaimed 'gun nuts' converged on the Missouri Capitol, demanding that legislators do an end-run around the Proposition B defeat and pass laws that would allow almost any adult to carry a gun. These protestors do not speak for a majority of people who voted on the issue in our state."[39] The tone of the editorial was red meat for opponents of conceal-and-carry, but the truth is that when there are massive swings in public opinion polls from one week to the next, Crump could have convincingly argued that it was impossible for the *Post-Dispatch* to say that the people wouldn't have voted differently in 2001.

In early April, the Committee on Sportsmanship, Safety, and Firearms approved a bill that combined elements of two conceal-and-carry bills: Crump's HB 853 and Koller's HB 258. The new bill, a committee substitute, was referred to as HCS HB 853 & 258. Crump's bill was the main body of the bill. Koller's contributions were several adjustments and refinements of Crump's version of conceal-and-carry. The committee reported the new bill to the full house, though the committee chairman, Crump, admitted it was probably too late for the bill to make it to a final vote in both chambers before the end of the legislative session in May. In an attempt to pressure the governor, Crump commented publicly that he had tried to contact Holden to negotiate on conceal-and-carry, but the governor hadn't responded. He said, "I think it's to the governor's benefit to look at this very seriously before he vetoes it."[40] The governor, however, did not seem to agree the bill was to his benefit. He made it clear the bill was not sufficiently different from Prop B, and if it didn't contain a provision for a public vote, he would veto it. Holden repeated, "If they want to send something to a vote of the people, I'll look at something like that. Right now I haven't seen anything that I think is really any different from Proposition B . . . The people spoke on that issue before, I would let the people speak again."[41]

While Crump certainly wanted conceal-and-carry to pass in 2001, he was willing to settle for a symbolic victory that he could build on in 2002. While he admitted the bill's fate was in doubt as time ran out on the legislative session, Crump felt that many legislators, especially Democrats who had been hurt by the gun issue in 2000, wanted the chance to take an initial vote on the bill so they could insulate themselves from an attack by the NRA in the 2002 elections. He also thought that the bill could still actually gain final passage if the senate added it to a major crime bill it was considering in April. He said, "The vehicle is there, and with the Republican controlled Senate being pro-gun . . .

I hope they'll put it on there. The Senate is more pro-gun than the House."[42] The senate did not adopt his bill as an amendment to the crime bill, however. As time ran out on the session, it seemed that time was also running out on conceal-and-carry once again.

Ever the cagey legislator, Crump didn't put all his conceal-and-carry eggs in one basket. Along with pushing HCS HB 853 & 258, Crump also proposed his own amendment to a big, omnibus crime bill, House Bill 835, in April. HB 835 was sponsored by Representative Phil Britt, D–Kennett. The amendment would have made it legal for people to carry concealed guns in their car without a permit. In the age of road rage, this may seem like a bad idea, but Crump said he simply wanted to legalize what he believed many Missourians were already doing, thanks to a longstanding ambiguity about the law. Many legal scholars believed that an old Missouri law which allowed travelers to carry firearms to protect themselves from highwaymen when traveling across the state on horseback also allowed people traveling across the state in automobiles to carry guns. Crump wished to clarify it and expand it to prevent local governments from passing ordinances against carrying concealed weapons in cars, because of a loophole in the 1984 preemption law.

The law passed in 1984 that prevented city governments from enacting their own firearms ordinances contained an exemption allowing them to limit "the open carrying of firearms readily capable of lethal use."[43] Needless to say, several cities, including the urban centers of St. Louis and Kansas City, enacted such restrictions on guns in cars. Crump complained that differences in the law from one jurisdiction to the next were too confusing to those from areas that had no limits on guns in cars, like his own district. In taking this position, Crump made the same argument adopted by the NRA to pass the preemption law in the first place.[44] This amendment, like the more general conceal-and-carry bill, failed to advance through the legislature in 2001, but the defeats did not crush the resilient Crump, who brought them back again in 2002.

While Governor Holden objected to Crump's bill and made it clear that he was not prepared to easily accept conceal-and-carry legislation, he received considerable criticism from gun control advocates and the St. Louis and Kansas City newspapers for not being opposed enough to concealed weapons. The *Kansas City Star*, for instance, criticized him harshly following a meeting between the governor and the paper's editorial board after the close of the legislative session in May. The *Star*'s editorial read, in part, "Holden also told the Editorial Board that the conceal-carry bill had at least 130 votes in the House and about two-thirds of the Senate. For this reason, the governor explained, it was best to take a low-key approach and not make any declarative statements on this contentious issue . . . In other words, Holden is attempting to take credit for helping to engineer the legislation's defeat. That's news to the foot soldiers in the war for more responsible gun control. To them, Holden missed the battle but is among the first in line for his medal."[45] The *Star* accused the governor of at best playing politics with the issue, and at worst lying about his own actions. It is difficult to understand the paper's position. After all, as a longtime opponent of concealed weapons, the paper's editorial staff got what it wanted: the defeat of conceal-and-carry in 2001. What the editors seemed to ignore was that Holden was truly in a precarious political position, having barely won election in 2000. He may genuinely have had no choice other than to play the issue coyly.

Liability Protection

Conceal-and-carry wasn't the only gun-related issue debated during the 2001 legislative session. Liability protection for the gun industry was back, this time under the sponsorship of a power player, new Senate President Pro Tem Peter Kinder. Kinder's bill was SB 123. A similar bill, HB 852, was sponsored in the house by Representative Crawford, though it was set aside early in the session in anticipation of Kinder's bill.

Kinder said lawsuits like one filed by the city of St. Louis, which alleged the gun industry cost the city money by refusing to more carefully distribute its products and by also refusing to work to develop new gun safety standards, were "frivolous and bogus." Further, he argued that suits against legal products were a danger to freedom and promised his bill would "stop cities from going down a ridiculous money trail."[46]

A leading opponent of Kinder's bill was Senator John Schneider, D–St. Louis, who had been instrumental in killing similar legislation in 1999. He was outspoken in his criticism of the bill and asserted that the legislature was being manipulated by the NRA. Another outspoken advocate of gun control, Senator Ken Jacob, D–Columbia, said, "It's amazing to me that we have to protect the manufacturers of guns, and we don't even have any of them in this state."[47] The most common criticism of the bill was reflected by an editorial in the *St. Louis Post-Dispatch* that argued the bill was "senseless and dangerous," and that it "undermined the most fundamental tent of justice, the right to your day in court" by making it illegal for localities to sue the gun industry.[48]

Regardless of its opponents in the legislature or the criticism from the press, Kinder shepherded his bill skillfully through the senate, blocking several amendments that would have altered the basic intent of SB 123, which was to keep governments from suing the gun industry for any issue "relating to the lawful design, manufacture, marketing or sale of firearms or ammunition to the public."[49] The bill also would have made any pending lawsuits, such as the one filed by officials in the city of St. Louis, retroactively illegal.[50] During debate on the bill, Kinder fended off no less than fifteen amendments, thirteen of which were sponsored by either Senator Jacob or Senator Schneider. The other two amendments were sponsored by another longtime gun control advocate, Senator Mary Bland of Kansas City.

During the floor debate on the bill, Kinder said, "This is the place to call a halt to bogus lawsuits," and argued that by passing his bill, the senate could help to keep governments from trying to put lawful industries out of business.[51] Kinder successfully guided his bill through the senate, which passed it by a vote of 22 to 11 on March 8. The bill was then forwarded to the house, where it was approved by Crump's Special Committee on Sportsmanship, Safety, and Firearms on May 2. After that, however, the bill languished on the calendar until the end of the session, never coming up for debate. Like conceal-and-carry, liability protection would have to wait for another year.

The NRA Comes to the Show-Me State

The 2001 legislative session made it clear that the conceal-and-carry issue still had strong legs, and gun rights received a booster shot of support in May 2001 when the NRA brought its annual convention, and nearly forty thousand members, to Kansas City. While the meeting's location had been scheduled several years in advance, Kansas City was almost certainly picked because Missouri is regularly such a battleground state for guns. An NRA spokesman, Bill Powers, said Kansas City would be a good place to discuss the group's success in the 2000 elections and added, "Our membership in Missouri and gun owners in general were very active and very motivated."[52] As the NRA prepared to come to Missouri, the Million Mom March and other activists promised to organize rallies to protest the meeting.[53] The Bush administration was represented at the NRA gathering by Gale Norton, the secretary of the interior, who addressed the convention.[54] During the meeting, Charlton Heston was reelected to his fourth term as NRA president. In a speech to the gathering, Heston congratulated the members for their role in the 2000 election of George W. Bush, reminding them that defeating Al Gore had been the NRA's number one priority. He said, "Liberty was on the line. And God bless you, you who made the difference, you who stepped forward to vote freedom first . . . You are of the same lineage as the farmers who stood at Concord Bridge."[55]

As the NRA convention proceeded, the Missouri Democratic party held its annual Truman Days gathering in Kansas City. This prompted the party's executive director, B. J. Atwater, to joke that she might attend the NRA gathering to clear up the group's distorted view of the party's position on guns. She said, "We're not out to take people's guns away. We're for gun safety."[56] She was not serous about attending the conference, but her comments reflected the continued frustration many Democrats felt about their perceived position on guns.

The Election Cycle Never Stops

A new political campaign started to take shape in late 2001, as Jean Carnahan and her Republican opponent, former gubernatorial candidate Jim Talent, began to jockey for position in the upcoming special election to choose someone to complete Mel Carnahan's term in the U.S. Senate. While Jean Carnahan had been chosen by Governor Roger Wilson to fill the office won by her husband, state law mandated that an election be held as soon as possible, and in 2001 Talent and Jean Carnahan began campaigning for a November 2002 election. By November 2001, Jim Talent was working hard to raise money for his campaign. Jean Carnahan had already banked close to $2 million to use in the campaign, though she didn't officially announce her candidacy until early 2002. As the campaign began to heat up in 2001, both candidates tried to maximize the lessons they had learned about guns in 2000.

As Carnahan and Talent campaigned, one thing was abundantly clear—they were determined to "out-gun" each other. This often made for silly political theater. In the U.S. Senate in November, for example, Jean Carnahan went out of her way to publicly praise a decision by the U.S. Fish and Wildlife Service to extend duck hunting season in several states. Her spokesman, Tony Wyche, explained that she wanted to recognize the move because she enjoyed hunting, though he admitted it also allowed her to rebut critics who said she was anti-gun. In an attempt to further diminish that impression, he added, "She does have a marksmanship certificate."[57] At the same time she was clearly trying to improve her image among gun owners, Carnahan also tried to bolster her credentials with "urban" voters by purchasing a residence in the St. Louis suburb of Clayton and continuing to express opposition to conceal-and-carry. She seemed to be trying to accomplish the Missouri politics equivalent of nuclear cold fusion: appear acceptable to both the out-state and St. Louis and Kansas City constituencies. Nuclear cold fusion, while theoretically possible, has proven to be quite illusive, and it is no less difficult to be equally appealing to rural and urban Missourians. Carnahan wanted to show she was fond of guns while still supporting several gun control measures, including background checks for gun purchasers, trigger locks for handguns, and the federal assault weapons ban. It was a tough sell, especially to the out-state voters.

Talent, the St. Louis County Republican, learned from the gubernatorial election in 2000 that he also had a gun dilemma. While he expressed support for instant background checks for gun purchasers and stronger penalties for crimes committed with guns as a congressman, he also voted against the federal ban on assault weapons and against waiting periods for gun purchasers, and he was a vocal supporter of Prop B. He lost his own county by about six thousand votes in 2002, and guns almost certainly played a part in that loss. Faced with rejection by the voters at home, he seemed to be positioning himself more for out-state voters in 2002. If Carnahan looked uncomfortable trying to play to both constituencies, Talent seemed equally out of place trying to be a good old boy. To handle the makeover, Talent hired an out-state Republican, Lloyd Smith, to run his campaign. Smith was an aide to U.S. Representative Jo Ann Emerson, from southeast Missouri, with a strong reputation as a Republican operative in Missouri's Boot Heel. Smith had worked hard to make the Republican party palatable to conservative, but longtime Democratic, out-state voters, much as Karl Rove is credited with doing throughout the state of Texas. Talent hoped Smith would work similar magic for his campaign.[58] It was no small part of Talent's plan to make sure he did better with rural voters in 2002 than he did in 2000, while holding onto the more conservative suburban voters around St. Louis and Kansas City.

As it turned out, 2002 was a good year not just for Talent but also for Republicans across the state. Republicans took over control of both houses of Congress in 1994, in what many called the Republican Revolution. While it took a few years longer in the Show-Me State, Missouri experienced its own Revolution in 2002.

Chapter Eighteen

2002—A Missouri Republican Revolution

Just as Cardinals fans see every April as the beginning of a glorious run to the World Series, supporters of conceal-and-carry saw 2002 as THE year Missourians would finally win the right to carry. The Vermont Project was back in 2002, collecting petition signatures to put an initiative on the November ballot that would bring Missouri conceal-and-carry with no restrictions. The Vermont Project still lacked the support of the NRA and other pro-gun groups and fell far short of gaining the necessary signatures to get on the ballot, but the group's founder, Steve Umscheid, was undaunted by failure. He saw his efforts as a movement for social change and said, "Our second attempt at collecting our signatures is almost certainly not going to happen... We need some kind of event to get these people off dead center... We're trying to get the problem solved here in Missouri. I consider it an opportunity. If I can leave this behind, it will have put a dent in the universe."[1] As was true in 2000, the Vermont Project's proposal lacked the support of the pro-gun community because it would require another expensive campaign. In addition, the very libertarian nature of the proposal, which advocated there be absolutely no limits on carrying guns, made even many gun rights supporters nervous.

As the 2002 legislative session began, Governor Holden, perhaps smarting from the criticism of gun opponents in 2001, was more outspoken in his opposition to conceal-and-carry and indicated he would veto any such legislation that landed on his desk. In an interview with the *Kansas City Star,* the governor said, "I'll veto it. The people of Missouri have spoken on that issue. If lawmakers want to put it to a public vote again, that's up to them."[2] In making this choice, Holden was clearly putting his fate in the hands of St. Louis and Kansas City voters, while writing off a sizable number of out-state voters. Holden's threats were a serious obstacle to conceal-and-carry because a veto would probably hold in 2002. The state's house of representatives was still in

Democratic hands, and getting enough votes to override the veto of a Democratic governor seemed unlikely. Rural Democrats wanted conceal-and-carry, but overriding their own governor would put everyone in a politically embarrassing spot in an election year. Of course, Holden's threats weren't enough to stop legislators from introducing conceal-and-carry legislation as the session got under way. In fact, such bills seemed to be growing on the trees that surround the capitol.

Jim Kreider, the speaker of the house, spoke out in favor of concealed weapons once again, saying, "A lot of representatives say it's their constitutional right. I think it promotes safety and it reduces crime. And I would like for law-abiding citizens not to have to break the law."[3] Kreider reestablished the Special Committee on Sportsmanship, Safety, and Firearms to devote special attention to conceal-and-carry. In 2002 the panel was chaired by Frank Barnitz, D–Lake Spring.

Early in the 2002 session, several conceal-and-carry bills were introduced in the General Assembly, including HB 1589, sponsored by the ubiquitous Wayne Crump. In the senate, committee hearings began on SB 938, sponsored by John Cauthorn, R–Mexico, who was elected in the special election of 2001. Cauthorn's bill proposed that county sheriffs be authorized to issue permits to persons twenty-one or older, providing they had not been found guilty of a crime punishable by more than a year in prison or been dishonorably discharged from the military. Applicants could also be excluded if they had a record of alcoholism, drug addiction, or mental incompetence. Persons wanting a permit would be required to demonstrate an ability to handle a firearm and had to complete an eight-hour training course.[4]

In late February, the House Special Committee on Sportsmanship, Safety, and Firearms approved two bills. The first was a merger of different conceal-and-carry bills, including Crump's HB 1589 and HB 1435, sponsored by Representative Larry Crawford, R–Centertown. The composite bill, HB 1729, had a libertarian bent. It required just four hours of firearms training for anyone seeking a permit, a total significantly less than that proposed in Prop B. It also would have allowed people previously committed to mental institutions to receive a permit, provided they hadn't been committed in the previous five years.[5] The bill passed out of committee by a vote of 9 to 1. The second bill voted out by the committee, HB 1344, was another repeat performer, also sponsored by Wayne Crump. Approved by a vote of 10 to 0, it would have allowed Missourians to carry concealed weapons in the passenger compartments of automobiles, including on the persons of the occupants, without requiring a permit. The bill also contained a provision that would allow retired police officers with at least fifteen years of service to carry concealed weapons.

Finally, it clarified existing law to say that active-duty officers were allowed to carry concealed weapons when off duty.[6] Once again, Crump argued the bill would decriminalize something his constituents and other out-state Missourians were already doing. Other supporters argued the bill was simply offering people a way to protect themselves against carjacking and other violent crimes.[7]

The car bill, HB 1344, received preliminary approval in the house in mid-March. It received final approval, by a vote of 104 to 46, on March 20. Upon getting news of this vote, Governor Holden again took the opportunity to reiterate his newly strengthened stance against conceal-and-carry. His spokesman, Jerry Nachtigal, said, "The governor feels the voters have spoken on this issue. He sees no reason to expand concealed carry. At this point, he would veto the bill."[8] It was a legitimate threat: with just 104 votes, the bill lacked the two-thirds support necessary to override a veto. In the house, 109 votes are needed for an override.

Crump countered that his bill simply filled a need, allowing drivers to defend themselves in their vehicles. Representative Chuck Purgason, R–Caufield, added that the law would prevent guns from being stolen from cars. The current law, he argued, already allowed people to carry guns in their cars, but required them to be kept in plain sight. He suggested that Crump's bill would allow people to hide the guns legally, making them much less vulnerable to theft.[9] Democratic legislators from Kansas City and St. Louis vehemently opposed the bill and offered several amendments to water it down. These amendments, including one that would have restricted guns from cars in which children were riding and another that would have required carriers of concealed guns to obtain special insurance for accidental shootings, failed.[10]

Much of the rhetoric in support of the bill suggested it was needed to protect women and children, reminiscent of the Prop B campaign in 1999. Beth Long, R–Lebanon, argued, "This is not about conceal-and-carry. This is about protection," and suggested that would-be attackers would think twice before attacking a lone woman in her car if they thought she might be armed.[11] For his part, Crump denied that the guns-in-cars measure was related to conceal-and-carry in any way, while opponents of the bill argued strenuously that its passage would open the door to allowing people to carry concealed guns on their persons.

Meanwhile, with the support of the NRA, the special committee's version of conceal-and-carry, HB 1729, was debated by the full house in April. Speaker Kreider was confident about the bill's chances of passage in the house, but less so about whether it would become law. He said, "The majority of the House believes in that fundamental freedom. I'm not too optimistic over in the

Senate."[12] The house bill was similar to Senator Cauthorn's bill, though it required just half the firearms training that the senator's bill did. During the house's debate of the bill, several options were considered and rejected that could have mollified the residents of counties where Proposition B failed in 1999.

One proposal that was quickly rejected was to hold another referendum. A second proposal, made by Catherine Hanaway, R–Warson Woods, the house minority leader, picked up on Kreider's suggestion that counties have the chance to opt out of conceal-and-carry. In Hanaway's proposal, conceal-and-carry would remain illegal for residents of counties that voted against Proposition B, while people from other counties would be allowed to carry their concealed guns anywhere in the state.[13] When this was proposed, it drew the ire of many state legislators, including opponents of conceal-and-carry from urban districts. State Representative John Russell "Russ" Carnahan, D–St. Louis, the son of the former governor, said it would turn people from St. Louis into "second class citizens" by establishing one standard for them and another for everyone else.[14] Other proposals, such as denying permits to anyone convicted of domestic violence or banning guns from churches, were also rejected.[15] As Kreider predicted, the bill passed in the house, though not with enough votes to overcome a gubernatorial veto. The vote was 99 to 50, and the bill gained the support of several Republicans from districts in the St. Louis area.[16] This reflected a shift in strategy, as even Republican legislators from suburban St. Louis had rejected conceal-and-carry in the past. In 2002, however, the Republican party's leadership understood guns could give them an advantage over Democrats and applied pressure to suburban Republicans to support conceal-and-carry. With work completed on guns-in-cars and conceal-and-carry in the house, the bills advanced to the senate.

In a poll of 802 likely voters commissioned by the *St. Louis Post-Dispatch* and conducted by Zogby International in late April 2002, the public opposed conceal-and-carry by a margin of 53 percent to 44 percent. The survey asked, "Do you strongly support, somewhat support, somewhat oppose, or strongly oppose a proposal to allow Missourians the right-to-carry concealed weapons?"[17] Statewide, 40.2 percent of respondents were strongly opposed, while 12.8 percent were somewhat opposed. On the other side, 25.3 percent of respondents strongly favored the right-to-carry, while 18.5 percent somewhat favored it. In St. Louis, 63 percent were opposed and 34 percent favored the idea. As was always true in public opinion polls on the issue, support for concealed weapons was significantly higher among Republicans and residents of out-state areas. It was also much higher, the poll found, among Republicans than Democrats.[18]

In the senate, John Cauthorn's bill was approved by a vote of 5 to 3 in the Senate's Pensions and General Laws Committee. Opposition groups testified at the hearing, again arguing that such a law shouldn't be passed because the question had been answered by the public in 1999. Opponents also argued a concealed weapons law would do nothing to decrease crime.[19]

Cauthorn's bill stalled after its committee vote, however, and little progress was made on conceal-and-carry in the senate until HB 1729 arrived from the house. In the senate, the bill was shepherded by Harold Caskey, D–Butler. Caskey spoke in rather grandiose terms of conceal-and-carry when he said, "God created man. Sam Colt made them equal."[20] With time running out on the session by the time the senate took up the bill, the bill was ill-fated, however. It was further harmed when it was amended in a way that made it unacceptable to many supporters of conceal-and-carry. The amendment, sponsored by Senator Doyle Childers, R–Reeds Spring, called for a second statewide referendum on conceal-and-carry.[21] In addition, the amendment called for counties with populations of greater than two hundred thousand to be exempt from conceal-and-carry.[22] Childers's amendment would have also allowed St. Charles County an exemption from the two hundred thousand population exemption. Childers claimed he had no idea what his amendment would do to the bill's likelihood of passage and added, "I'm not involved in strategizing. All I know is my constituents wanted us to look at it."[23] The amendment was adopted by a vote of 15 to 14 on May 14. Clearly, the hope was this amendment would neutralize the opponents of conceal-and-carry in St. Louis and Kansas City. Much as Catherine Hanaway's amendment failed in the house, however, Childers's amendment was unacceptable to many supporters of conceal-and-carry who didn't want two standards and who opposed a second statewide referendum. With the amendment attached to the bill, support withered, and the bill died as the session came to an end.

On a related note, lawsuit liability protection for the firearms industry was a nonstarter in 2002. Both Senator Peter Kinder and Representative Larry Crawford introduced such bills, SB 1027 and HB 1437, respectively, but neither bill made it out of committee. A third liability protection bill, HB 1680, sponsored by Representative Mark Hampton, D–Summersville, was approved by the Special Committee on Sportsmanship, Safety, and Firearms on April 23, but never appeared on the house calendar for debate.

As the legislative session drew to an end in 2002, supporters of conceal-and-carry lamented its failure. Some suggested its defeat was due to a lack of genuine support by Republican senators from metropolitan areas where Prop B failed in 1999, despite attempts by the party leaders to bring them into the fold. They claimed that such senators feared the reaction of so-called "soccer moms" opposed to conceal-and-carry. This claim may have been true, but if so, it is unfair to blame them for worrying. Guns clearly cost Jim Talent, the party standard bearer in 2000, votes in St. Louis and Kansas City. Why wouldn't suburban Republican legislators fear the same thing?

Other supporters blamed the NRA for not being more involved in the fight. Frank Barnitz, the chair of the Special Committee on Sportsmanship, Safety, and Firearms, said, "I don't know what happened to the NRA on this. They haven't been around much." He suggested that local gun groups didn't have enough clout to help get the bill passed without the help of the NRA.[24] Gary Davis, a spokesman for the NRA, suggested the governor's promise to veto the bill made it a fight not worth fighting in 2002. Instead, he said, the group preferred to focus its resources on the 2002 elections and getting more gun-friendly legislators elected. He said, "We still want to put it on his desk and see what happens," but only after electing more pro-gun legislators in November.[25] The implication was, of course, that the NRA wanted to make sure there would be enough votes to override a Holden veto. The most interesting thing about Barnitz's finger-pointing and the NRA's defense of its inaction is that it once again put in stark relief the significant role the NRA always played in the conceal-and-carry fight. When Barnitz, the main steward of the right to carry in the house in 2002 said, essentially, "with the NRA, all things are possible," it was hard to argue the group was anything but a key player.

For a short while in the summer of 2002, the governor was able to enjoy a victory on guns. With conceal-and-carry safely dead in the legislature for 2002, Jerry Nachtigal, the governor's spokesman, took the opportunity to express some political bravado. He said, "No matter what form it takes, any conceal-carry legislation is dead on arrival when it gets to the governor's desk. The citizens weighed in on this three years ago. We're not opposed to another public vote, necessarily, but to push through conceal-carry legislation is, in the governor's view, wrong."[26] The governor was able to gloat, once again, that conceal-and-carry had disappeared without his having to take any action on it. Somehow, despite enthusiastic support for conceal-and-carry in both chambers of the legislature, the issue died again in 2002, and all the government had to do was threaten a veto. Of course, no one, including the governor, believed the fight was finished. As disappointed as the supporters of conceal-and-carry were in May, they didn't despair. Like the NRA, the champions of conceal-and-carry anticipated an easier road to victory in 2003, after the November election.

The NRA's Gary Davis promised guns would be a major campaign issue in the fall. He said, "We're single-issue voters. It doesn't matter if you're a Democrat, Republican, Libertarian, if you support our issue, we'll vote for you."[27]

Davis was not the only activist to promise conceal-and-carry would be a big issue in the election. Echoing Davis's comments, Kevin Jamison of the Western Missouri Shooters Alliance promised his group would only support candidates strong on conceal-and-carry. He said, "We're picking and choosing politicians we think will help us with this issue in the future," and he also suggested party labels had little to do with who the group supported. A politician's party label, he asserted, was no guarantee of a pro–concealed guns stance.[28]

Likewise, opponents of conceal-and-carry understood there was a lot at stake in the upcoming election. In July, Richard Cook, the director of the Kansas City Metropolitan Crime Commission, an opponent of Prop B in 1999, warned that opponents of conceal-and-carry needed to be active during the campaign. He said, "Voters absolutely need to be aware of what candidates think because concealed weapons are such a hot button in the Midwest."[29]

Fighting for Votes—Campaign 2002

The campaign season revived the bitter feelings generated by guns in 2000. As voting drew near, both candidates for Missouri's seat in the U.S. Senate pandered for the support of gun advocates. In September the NRA endorsed Jim Talent, as it had in his previous campaigns for Congress and governor. Given Senator Carnahan's opposition to conceal-and-carry as well as her support for other gun control measures, the NRA's endorsement of Talent was a mere formality. Losing the NRA's endorsement didn't mean, however, that Carnahan gave up on the gun vote. In what was a painfully obvious appeal for gun votes, she appeared with her shotgun at a skeet shooting contest in southeast Missouri during Labor Day weekend. The move was immediately criticized by nearly everyone, including the Talent campaign, gun rights advocates, and gun control advocates.

Carnahan's campaign went into defense mode, denying the claims of critics who accused her of shamelessly pandering for votes. Her campaign staff and representatives of the state Democratic party asserted there was nothing unusual about her participation in the event, as she had been a lifelong shooter. Mike Kelley, the executive director of the Missouri Democratic party, said, "It's not like we have to invent that she's a sport shooter. She likes to shoot guns. Jean Carnahan was shooting guns before most people in this state with hunting licenses were even alive."[30] Such explanations did little to quell the impression that Carnahan's participation in the event was little more than a political stunt to make her more appealing to out-state voters, particularly men. Even the *St. Louis Post-Dispatch,* which endorsed Carnahan, took exception to the appearance in an editorial. It read, in part, "Ms. Carnahan, who boasts of a sharpshooter's medal in college, will be aiming her Browning Citori at clay pigeons because she's got a problem with male voters . . . Despite the political misdirection, the candidates' positions on guns are clear . . . It would make a good subject for a debate if Ms. Carnahan can find time in her busy shooting schedule."[31] It was easy to make jokes when Carnahan appeared in the news media brandishing a shotgun, but in a state with a proven record of gun trouble for political candidates, one could easily understand that the senator felt compelled to do something to appeal to gun-owning Missourians.

In an additional effort to bolster Carnahan's image with pro-gun voters, supporters of her campaign began to distribute "Sportsmen for Carnahan" bumper stickers, trying to demonstrate she could be both pro-hunting and anti-concealed handguns.[32] If nothing else, the bumper stickers annoyed the NRA. A spokesman for the group, Andrew Arulanandam, objected to the campaign's use of the word "Sportsmen." He said, "That moniker has been identifiable with the NRA for a number of years."[33] This complaint had no effect on Carnahan supporters who were distributing the bumper stickers, of course. They felt there were many gun owners who did not necessarily support conceal-and-carry, and they wanted Carnahan to establish rapport with those voters and show them she had no designs on taking their guns away.

The battle for gun voters turned ridiculous as the Carnahan campaign and the Talent campaign tried to out-sportsmen each other. In response to Carnahan's skeet shooting event and a suggestion from Mike Kelley that Jim Talent had never even fired a gun, Talent responded by saying that he had, in fact, fired guns, but preferred fishing. He claimed he had taken his son bass fishing over Labor Day weekend while Carnahan was skeet shooting. The Missouri Democratic party responded by digging through state records and finding that Talent had never gotten a fishing license. At best, the party insinuated, this meant Talent had fished illegally; at worst, it meant he lied about going fishing in the first place.[34]

Despite widespread criticism of campaign tactics like the skeet shooting appearance and the Sportsmen bumper stickers, the Carnahan campaign's actions seemed to work. While a Zogby poll in August found Carnahan trailing Talent by a percentage point, a new Zogby poll in September put Carnahan ahead by a margin of 47.6 percent to 40.3 percent, with a hefty number of undecided voters.[35] Her biggest gain was among male voters, and the skeet-shooting event had been aimed primarily at male voters. In August, Carnahan trailed Talent by thirteen points among men. By September she trailed only by a single point. As John Zogby said, "She stopped his momentum. She really bounced back among men. It looks like skeet shooting and a few well-placed ads did the trick."[36] In that one-month period, she also overtook Talent in the St. Louis metro area, where she trailed him by a point in August but led by twelve points in September.[37]

As the campaign heated up, interest group activities accelerated. Carnahan had long been endorsed by the Brady Campaign, the Million Mom March, and organized labor. In August the AFL-CIO began running ads attacking Talent as a friend of big business. At a convention of Missouri labor leaders in September, John Sweeney, the president of the AFL-CIO, appealed for Missouri members of the union to contribute to Carnahan and other Democratic candidates.[38] The support of the union was important to Carnahan, but it was far from guaranteed. Union members are traditionally Democratic voters, but they often vote Republican solely on gun issues in Missouri. The Democrats' Mike Kelley acknowledged that the gun issue sometimes hurt Democrats among union members. He said that up to 25 percent of families in Missouri were union households and that rank-and-file union members could be conservative on certain social issues, such as gun control.[39] Clearly, Carnahan's campaign hoped that an endorsement from the group's president would help.

Meanwhile, the NRA was extremely interested in knocking Carnahan out of office. As an analysis of the campaign by the *Nation* reported, "The NRA has identified Missouri, Georgia, Minnesota, and South Dakota as the pivotal states in which they will be focusing their efforts to win back the Senate for the Republicans. Even though Democrats in those states and elsewhere aren't talking about guns, the NRA is dredging up their 'antigun' voting records and pointing to such nefarious campaign contributors as the National Education Association."[40] In late September the NRA began a series of mailers supporting Talent and attacking Carnahan. The organization also sponsored a statewide series of election workshops designed both to rally support for its chosen candidates and to teach grassroots activists how to get involved in campaign activities such as running phone banks.[41] At these workshops, candidates were invited to appear and speak to gun rights supporters. At one such workshop in the St. Louis area, the NRA's Andrew Arulanandam tried to draw a clear line of distinction between the two candidates. He said, "During her short tenure as a U.S. Senator, Jean Carnahan has amassed a strong anti-Second Amendment voting record. In contrast, Jim Talent has proven himself in word and deed to be a strong supporter of the right of law-abiding Americans to keep and bear arms."[42] The Carnahan campaign responded to this by pointing out that the NRA was playing loose with the facts when it talked about her voting record on guns because there hadn't actually been any gun control votes in the Senate during her time in office.[43]

Both campaigns began trotting out celebrities in September. Talent, of course, had the ultimate celebrity pulling for him, President Bush, who appeared with Talent in Kansas City, Springfield, and St. Charles during the campaign. In addition, former senator and presidential candidate Bob Dole appeared on behalf of Talent in southeast Missouri.[44] In October, Kit Bond and his Senate colleagues Sam Brownback and Conrad Burns made campaign appearances on behalf of Talent, as also did Rudolph Giuliani, the former mayor of New York. In addition, Charlton Heston and Wayne LaPierre made a late October appearance with Talent at an NRA rally in Joplin. The Heston-LaPierre visit to Missouri was a stop on a twelve-state tour of political races the NRA considered critical. The tour was part of a change in campaign strategy by the NRA in which the group greatly reduced television advertising and relied more on grassroots methods to mobilize voters. Wayne LaPierre said, "It's moving real people to the polling booth."[45] In his speech in Joplin, LaPierre was sure to remind voters of conceal-and-carry when he said, "Thirty-three states now have a right-to-carry and we're not giving up on Missouri."[46]

The Heston appearance was emotional, as the NRA's president had just announced he was suffering from Alzheimer's disease and would soon be forced to cease his public involvement with the NRA. LaPierre said, "They also know what he's going through. They've all heard the announcements on TV, and they understand what an effort it took for Charlton Heston to be in their state and that it's not easy, and I think that motivates them further."[47] Clearly, the image of Heston, widely viewed as the man who saved the NRA during dark times in the mid-1990s, was a powerful weapon for candidates in nip-and-tuck races like the Missouri contest. Taking advantage of his chance to stand next to Heston, Talent spoke to the rally and urged them to "Go out and talk about all the differences in this race."[48]

Meanwhile, Donna Brazile, Al Gore's former campaign manager, appeared on behalf of Carnahan in St. Louis. Senator John Kerry, D–Massachusetts, campaigned with Jean Carnahan in Kansas City in late October, on a day between the two debates of the campaign. Together, they refuted accusations made by Talent and an ad sponsored by the Missouri Republican party and the Republican Senate Campaign Committee in the last days of the campaign. The ad was filled with images of the American flag and the message that Carnahan didn't support the president's plan for homeland security. It implied, Carnahan said, that she was unpatriotic for disagreeing with the president. The ad also accused Carnahan of being motivated by the "thousands" of dollars she'd received in campaign contributions from labor unions. In addition, the campaign against Carnahan emphasized an early vote against President Bush's missile defense system, again suggesting that the senator didn't have the nation's best interests at heart.

Crying foul, Carnahan said she had never voted against the creation of the Homeland Security Department and insisted she had supported the idea even before the president did. The difference of opinion, she said, was over labor issues. While Carnahan supported the creation of the department, she also cast votes in favor of provisions to extend civil service protections to department employees that President Bush didn't want. The president said he wanted flexibility to be able to make quick hiring and firing decisions in times of emergency, while Carnahan and other Democrats claimed it would make it too easy for him to hire and fire people. Debate over this issue caused the bill creating the department to get stymied in the Senate for a time, making it a powerful Republican issue.

Expressing anger over charges that she was unpatriotic became a major theme of the Carnahan campaign in the final days of the race. Speaking to members of the International Association of Firefighters Local 42, Carnahan said she just wanted to protect the future employees of Homeland Security from capricious hiring and firing. In what would become a parallel to his angry denunciations of ads questioning his service in Vietnam during his presidential campaign of 2004, John Kerry attacked the anti-Carnahan ad when he said, "So let me just give it to you straight: Jim Talent's attacks on Jean Carnahan's patriotism don't belong in this campaign. That commercial is a disgrace."[49] Thanks to the ad and to Carnahan herself, the issue of the senator's patriotism was brought up repeatedly in the last few days of the campaign.

Because guns were once again so important in 2002, the campaign was reminiscent of both the 2000 campaign and the Prop B vote for many reasons. The campaign themes were quite similar, of course, and there was also great disparity in the financial involvement of the gun lobbies. As in 1999, the NRA greatly outspent the Brady Campaign. According to Federal Election Commission records, the NRA spent $245,549 in independent expenditures and campaign donations benefiting James Talent. Meanwhile, the Brady Campaign spent just $37,032 in independent expenditures and campaign donations benefiting Jean Carnahan.[50]

As election day approached, the two candidates found themselves campaigning to what had become their bases of support. For her part, Carnahan focused on the urban centers of St. Louis and Kansas City, largely staying away from the rural parts of the state where her husband was raised. Meanwhile, Talent, who was born, raised, and educated in St. Louis, found himself campaigning in the rural parts of the state. Both candidates knew their chances for election lay with these key constituencies. As a spokesman for the Missouri Republican party explained, "That's why you're seeing him in the cornfields and the crop rows. Jim Talent knows that motivating the base is number one."[51]

In the final days of the campaign the candidates debated twice, and in both debates Carnahan seemed uncomfortable and poorly prepared. Throughout the campaign, both Talent and the groups supporting him played up the theme that Carnahan was inexperienced and ineffective as a legislator compared to Talent, who had served many years in the Missouri General Assembly and the U.S. Congress. Unfortunately for Senator Carnahan, the two candidates' performances in the debates did little to change that perception. Talent successfully exacerbated the perception that Carnahan was an accidental senator by refusing to refer to her as Senator Carnahan, referring to her instead as "Jean" or "Mrs. Carnahan."

The first debate pitted the two candidates against each other in the studios of the public television station KETC in St. Louis. The debate was broadcast live around the state on the evening of Monday, October 21. The debate ranged widely, covering topics as diverse as defense, trade, the state of the economy, Social Security and Medicare, stem cell research, and the environment. In most cases, Talent was on the offensive, questioning Carnahan's votes on a variety of issues. There was also a notable exchange on gun control in which the candidates largely talked past each other. Carnahan said, "It is important that we keep handguns out of the hands of children and criminals, we keep assault weapons from them. I favor background checks and bans on assault weapons."[52] In response, Talent said, in part, "How can we keep people safe? That's the issue. I don't think generally you keep people safe by restricting the access of law-abiding adults to the means of self-defense. Then the criminals know that the honest people cannot protect themselves."[53] While both sides were quick to claim victory after the first debate, it seemed clear that in its wake, the Talent campaign was more enthusiastic and confident. The comments from Carnahan's supporters seemed almost to admit defeat in the first debate as they suggested she would be very strong in the second meeting. The only way to interpret those comments is that they didn't think she had been strong in the first.

The second debate, on Thursday, October 24, included Talent, Carnahan, and two minor party candidates, Tamara Millay of the Libertarian party and Daniel Romano of the Green party. It was held in Columbia, on the campus of Columbia College. While the presence of the two minor party candidates was good for an occasional light moment, the focus was clearly on the exchange between Carnahan and Talent. Like the first debate, the topics were varied, including education, minimum wage, and the potential war in Iraq. An interesting moment came when the subject of John Ashcroft was broached. Explaining why she voted against his appointment to attorney general, Carnahan said, "I felt it was a vote of conscience," to which Talent responded, "This was an issue where Mrs. Carnahan did not cast a vote I think reflected Missouri values."[54] Just as Gore's ultimate loss in 2000 will long remain a bitter pill for Democrats in Florida and beyond, Ashcroft's loss in 2000 is still a source of anger for many Missouri Republicans.

In both debates, Carnahan's major strategy was to express anger at what she said was an attempt by Talent and the Republican party to paint her as unpatriotic for her votes on the creation of the Department of Homeland Security and missile defense. On missile defense, Talent criticized what he characterized as flip-flopping on the president's missile defense plan. Initially, Carnahan said she did not support spending as much on development of a missile defense plan as the president wanted, though she later changed her mind in votes after the September 11 terrorist attacks.

The real sparks, however, were generated by the Republican party's television spot that criticized Carnahan for her votes on the legislation creating the new Department of Homeland Security. This was the ad that Carnahan spoke out against in her Kansas City appearance with John Kerry after the first debate. During the first debate, Carnahan and Talent sparred over the issue. Talent claimed Carnahan's opposition to the president's wish to be able to make quick hiring and firing decisions had "deep-sixed" the homeland security bill.[55] He argued that Carnahan was misguided in her characterization of the president's motives and said the president wasn't anti-labor, but that he simply wanted flexibility in the name of national security. Talent said, "For example, intelligence finds out that terrorists are coming over the Canadian border. He wants to be able to move agents there quickly without having to post the job for a bid for 30 days. To me it's common sense."[56] The exchange was a bit heated during the first debate, but the more dramatic moments came during the second debate.

As the second debate drew to a close, Senator Carnahan said, "I resent being told that I'm unpatriotic by my opponent. I would not doubt your patriotism, nor would I doubt the patriotism of any member of the Senate." She then turned to Talent, shook her finger at him, and said, "I don't want you to doubt it again."[57] Apparently angered by Carnahan's repeated charge that he was painting her as unpatriotic, Talent said, "The most inaccurate statement about me so far in the election is that I'm questioning somebody's patriotism, or even their motives, when I'm talking about their votes."[58] Taking the offensive against Talent for attacking her patriotism was a strong gambit for Carnahan, but it wasn't enough to objectively judge her the winner of the debates.

Talent simply seemed more relaxed and better prepared in both debates. He was a veteran of many debates, including three during the gubernatorial campaign in 2000, whereas Carnahan had never participated in them. One thing seemed obvious after the debates—Talent was a natural politician, doing what he loved, while Carnahan, on the other hand, seemed out of place, honor-bound to carry on her family legacy. It was not at all clear as she campaigned that she wanted to be doing what she was doing, and as the campaign ended, Talent appeared to have important last-minute momentum.

On election day, Talent won a narrow victory over Carnahan, with 49.8 percent of the vote to Carnahan's 48.7 percent. He managed this victory despite the fact that, once again, he lost his own home county, St. Louis. Clearly, the strategy he and his campaign manager, Lloyd Smith, devised to appeal to out-state voters worked. The race was obviously significant to Missourians, but Talent's victory also had significant national implications as well, helping the Republican party regain the majority in the U.S. Senate.

Carnahan left elected office, but she remains an important figure in the Missouri Democratic party. Two of her children ran for high-profile elective offices in 2004. Robin Carnahan, who headed the anti-Prop B campaign, was elected secretary of state, while Russ Carnahan, a state representative from St. Louis, won a narrow primary victory in his campaign to replace Dick Gephardt in the Third Congressional District. In 2003, Jean Carnahan campaigned on behalf of Dick Gephardt's failed presidential campaign in Iowa on a number of occasions. She also worked as a fund-raiser for Gephardt and U.S. Senate Minority Leader Tom Daschle.[59] Finally, she was outspoken in her support of Governor Holden, who ultimately lost the Democratic nomination to Claire McCaskill in 2004.

The Historic Change in Missouri

While the Republicans regained their advantage in the U.S. Senate, the Republican party in Missouri made its own history in 2002 by taking over full control of the General Assembly. In 1992 Missourians adopted term limits via an initiative. The new law instituted an eight-year lifetime limit for both representatives and senators, with the clock beginning to run in 1994. This meant that in 2002 an enormous number of seats in the state legislature were up for grabs. In the house, 73 of 163 seats, or 45 percent, were open, with no incumbents running. In the senate, 12 of the 34 seats, or 35 percent, were open. In a state that was ever more leaning toward the Republicans, this large number of open seats provided the G.O.P. with an opportunity to increase its majority in the senate and regain the majority in the house for the first time since 1954. Following the election, the Republicans controlled both houses of the Missouri state legislature for the first time since 1947. The victory in the house elevated Catherine Hanaway to speaker, making her the highest-ranking woman in the history of the Missouri General Assembly. The significance of this Republican Revolution was considerable in many areas of policy making, but nowhere was it more important than in conceal-and-carry legislation.

The election of many new Republican members of the General Assembly was very significant for conceal-and-carry. While conceal-and-carry bills had usually had enough votes to pass in recent years, there were always a couple of obstacles. First, the majority in the house was never quite big enough to override a threatened gubernatorial veto. Second, in the senate, there were always enough senators willing to throw obstacles in the way of conceal-and-carry to prevent final passage. After the 2002 election, the situation was different: the leadership was more determined, and the rank-and-file were more supportive. 2003 genuinely seemed like it was going to be conceal-and-carry's year.

The election of 2002 was the payoff for many years of effort by the NRA, the election of more pro-gun legislators. It is instructive to examine the NRA Political Victory Fund's list of endorsed candidates in the 2002 Missouri legislative races. As it does in elections at all levels of government, the NRA gave grades to candidates in all of Missouri's legislative races. It also gave endorsements to candidates in some of the races. The grades, according to the NRA's Political Victory Fund, are based on "voting records, public statements and their responses to an NRA-PVF questionnaire."[60] In Missouri's U.S. House elections, the NRA endorsed candidates in seven of nine races. Of the seven, all of the endorsed candidates were Republicans, except for Ike Skelton in the Fourth District, who was an old ally of the NRA. All of the candidates endorsed by the NRA were also incumbents, except for Catherine Enz, who opposed Richard Gephardt in the Third District. All of the NRA's endorsees received grades of A. In the U.S. Senate race the NRA endorsed Jim Talent, giving him an A, while they gave Jean Carnahan an F.[61]

The organization claimed an 82 percent rate of success in the "thousands" of state legislative elections in which it gave endorsements during the 2000 election cycle.[62] In 2002 in Missouri, the organization officially endorsed candidates in twelve of seventeen state senate races. Of the twelve endorsements, ten were given to Republicans and two to Democrats. Of the ten Republicans, three were incumbents and seven were running in open races, two of which faced no Democratic opposition. Of the two Democrats endorsed, one was an incumbent and the second was the former speaker of the house, Jim Kreider. Only two candidates received grades of A+ from the NRA: John Cauthorn and David Klindt, the two men elected in those hard-fought special elections in 2001. The NRA described the recipient of an A+ grade as "An incumbent with not only an excellent voting record on critical NRA issues, but who has also made a vigorous effort to promote the Second Amendment."[63] Clearly, Cauthorn lived up to these criteria by reviving the conceal-and-carry issue in 2002 with his own right-to-carry bill.

There were three races in which the group gave both the Democrat and Republican candidates a grade of A. In two of these, the NRA endorsed the Democrats: Jim Kreider of the Twentieth District and Steve Stoll of the Twenty-sixth District.[64] Kreider was something of a special case. As the speaker of the house, he was a strong supporter of conceal-and-carry. In the third race, the NRA endorsed Jon Dolan of the Second District, who became a critical player in the 2003 veto session on conceal-and-carry.

In the Missouri house elections, the NRA officially endorsed candidates in 56 of the state's 163 districts. Of those, 39 endorsements went to Republicans, while 17 went to Democrats. Of the Democratic endorsees, 15 were incumbents, while 2 were running in open seats, 1 unopposed. Of the 39 Republicans receiving an NRA endorsement, 30 were incumbents. Of the remaining 9, 7 Republicans were running for open seats and 2 were opposing Democratic incumbents. In 4 of the open-seat elections, the Republican candidate had no Democratic challenger. In cases where the Democrat and the Republican in a race received roughly the same grade, the NRA endorsed 5 Democrats, all incumbents, and 5 Republicans, all incumbents. Interestingly, in 2 of the 5 endorsements of Democrats, the group endorsed the candidate with the slightly lower grade. The 2 Democrats had grades of A-, whereas their Republican challengers both had grades of A.[65] Clearly, the NRA preferred to back a likely winner who was, for the most part, ideologically acceptable to them.

In all of the races, even those in which the NRA did not give an official endorsement, grades were given to the candidates, ranging from A to F, with some receiving a grade of "?" because they failed to respond to an NRA survey. The organization described A and F grades in this way: "1) A—"Solidly pro-gun candidate. An 'A' incumbent who has supported NRA positions on key votes. May also describe a non-incumbent 'A' candidate who has previously held other office and cast consistent pro-gun votes, or an 'A' candidate who hasn't held office but has expressed strong support for NRA positions on Second Amendment issues. It should be noted that a 'non-incumbent' candidate may have been awarded the 'A' rating due solely to their responses on the NRA-PVF candidate survey." 2) F—"True enemy of gun owners' rights. A vehement anti-gun candidate who always opposes gun owners' rights and/or actively leads anti-gun legislative efforts, or sponsors anti-gun legislation."[66]

The grade of "?" was not as ambiguous as it might seem. In reality, receiving a question mark was a negative assessment. The grade of "?" was described in this way: "Failed to answer NRA-PVF candidate questionnaire, often an indication of indifference, if not outright hostility, to gun owners' and sportsmen's rights."[67] The description of these grades is instructive in understanding how seriously the organization takes its election activities, especially when they use words such as "enemy" to describe candidates who don't support the NRA agenda.

What can one conclude from the NRA's assessment of candidates for the Missouri General Assembly in 2002? First, the group tended to favor Republican candidates, but not to the complete exclusion of Democrats. In the Show-Me State, 72 percent of NRA endorsements went to Republican candidates in 2002. If all things were equal, the organization probably preferred to endorse Republicans, but when they had a reliable Democratic incumbent, they gave that candidate their support, even when they might actually have rated the challenger slightly higher. This shows that while the group may lean to the right on issues other than guns, it still places guns first in the list of criteria it uses to assess candidates. It reflects a degree of ideological honesty that many critics of the NRA have criticized and challenged over the years.

With the elections of 2002 in the history books, the time for conceal-and-carry's victorious return had arrived. As the 2003 session of the General Assembly began, the issue was at the top of the legislative agenda.

The Federal Government Weighs In?

As 2002 drew to a close, the U.S. Congress debated a bill that could have changed the tenor of the conceal-and-carry debate in Missouri. The Community Protection Act, cosponsored by Senator Orrin Hatch, R–Utah, and Senator Patrick Leahy, D–Vermont, would have allowed off-duty and retired police officers to carry concealed weapons anywhere in the country. The bill was intended to provide increased protection against crime, especially terrorism, and it would have nullified any conflicting state laws that banned such officers from carrying concealed weapons. The bill had wide support but, strangely, lacked the endorsement of the NRA. In addition, it was actively opposed by the more strident Gun Owners of America. The groups opposed the bill on the grounds that it was unfair because it gave the right to carry to some citizens but not to everyone. The Brady Campaign to Prevent Gun Violence, on the other hand, remained neutral on the Community Protection Act.

The bill was strongly supported by associations of rank-and-file police officers, but it was opposed by the International Association of Chiefs of Police. A spokesman for the chiefs said, "This really doesn't protect the safety of communities. Off-duty officers are just average citizens when they leave their jurisdictions. They have no more authority to enforce the law than any other civilians."[68] The proposal had the support of most of the Missouri congressional delegation but was ultimately defeated by two prominent legislators. In the House, the chair of the Judiciary Committee, James Sensenbrenner, R–Wisconsin, a strong supporter of gun rights, took the Gun Owners of America's position when he argued the bill was counterproductive to the wider fight for gun rights in the nation. He said, "Individual states have a right to determine their own 'right-to-carry' laws," and added that if the Congress adopted the Community Protection Act, it would harm arguments "that federal legislation regulating firearms is unnecessary. We need to be consistent in our arguments if we are to fend off the continuous assault on the Second Amendment."[69] As chair of the Judiciary Committee, Sensenbrenner had the authority to hold the bill in committee, and that is exactly what he did. In the Senate, the bill was killed by Ted Kennedy, D–Massachusetts, who amended it enough to make it unpalatable to many supporters.

The Community Protection Act could have had consequences in Missouri. In 1999, some of the strongest lobbies supporting conceal-and-carry were organizations of rank-and-file police officers. Many law enforcement organizations came to endorse the proposal, including the Fraternal Order of Police, the National Troopers Coalition, and Missouri organizations such as the Springfield Police Officers Association.[70] The organizations wanted conceal-and-carry for off-duty and retired officers. If the federal government passed a law granting that right, it would potentially neutralize a major pro–conceal-and-carry constituency in the state.

However, the Missouri Deputy Sheriffs' Association took the Gun Owners of America point of view and objected to the fact that the act would only give conceal-and-carry rights to some. Marco Tapia, a representative of the Missouri Deputy Sheriffs' Association, said, "There's fear of terrorism, fear of victimization. Who are they to deny individuals the right to protect themselves and their families while giving that right to themselves?"[71] It seems a bit unusual for a group representing officers of the law to be so strongly in support of conceal-and-carry for everyone, but by 2002 the group was so committed to the fight that its leaders might have felt they had no choice but to stay the course. It is also possible, though unknowable, that the group's enthusiasm for widespread conceal-and-carry might have waned if the Community Protection Act passed. Without the support of organizations representing police officers, it is conceivable that conceal-and-carry's fate could have been very different in 2003.

As happens with many pieces of legislation, the Community Protection Act hung around the halls of Congress for years and became law in 2004. The bill's final passage was hailed by Missouri's own Roy Blunt, the U.S. House majority whip. In a visit to Springfield, Blunt said, "There have been many instances where people in law enforcement have been injured because they either attempted to intervene in a situation and were not armed or somebody recognized them that they did not recognize . . . Crime does not go off duty. Having armed officers ready to answer the call to protect and serve 24 hours a day, here at home, or on the road, is a commitment that will serve the public well."[72]

As 2002 drew to a close, however, the federal legislation was in limbo, and the forces for conceal-and-carry smelled blood in the water in Missouri. Governor Holden appeared weak politically, and the Republicans had respectable majorities in both houses of the legislature. If there was ever a year for conceal-and-carry to succeed, it was 2003.

Chapter Nineteen

2003—Victory for Conceal-and-Carry

In 2003, pro-gun advocates finally had the legislators they had long wanted, and they were ready for action. Both the Special Committee on Sportsmanship, Safety, and Firearms and Representative Wayne Crump were relics of the past, but there was no shortage of legislators with conceal-and-carry bills. The main bill was HB 349, sponsored by Representative Larry Crawford, R–Centertown, though there were others, including HB 120, sponsored by the former chair of the special committee, Representative Barnitz, D–Lake Spring, and HB 328, sponsored by Representative Munzlinger, R–Williamstown. The bills were referred to the Crime Prevention and Public Safety Committee in February, where a great deal of testimony was heard from pro- and anti-gun forces. St. Louis–area resident Dale Schmid, the president of the Second Amendment Coalition, spoke before the committee. He said, "There is great comfort in the regular, the normal and the tried and true. It is safer by far to follow successful leaders, whether they are individuals, organizations or other states. Many of the new members of this body are under the impression that LTC [license to carry] legislation is something new, and therefore dangerous. Nothing could be further from the truth. Take comfort in this fact."[1] It is not clear who Schmid meant when he said there were many new members of the legislature who felt that conceal-and-carry legislation was dangerous. In fact, there was tremendous enthusiasm for conceal-and-carry in 2003. The committee combined all the bills into Crawford's HB 349 and easily approved it. The bill advanced to the house floor, where it faced little resistance. On March 6, HB 349 was given final approval by the house with a veto-proof margin of 111 to 42. The bill granted Missourians twenty-one and older not only the chance to apply for a permit to carry concealed weapons but also the right to transport concealed weapons in their automobiles without a permit, combining what had been separate bills in years past.[2]

The bill advanced to the senate under the management of Harold Caskey, D–Butler, who was the Democratic Caucus leader. It was referred to the Senate Pensions and General Law Committee in April, which approved it by a vote of 5 to 3 on April 14. The bill was then referred to the Senate Committee on Governmental Accountability and Fiscal Oversight, which approved the bill on April 16. The bill was then ready for debate in the full senate. The bill had to wait as the senate worked on the state budget, but it found its place in the sun during the first week in May.

Before the senate voted on the bill, there was some significant conflict among Democrats. The senate minority leader, Ken Jacob, D–Columbia, led a filibuster against the bill. During the debate, Jacob spoke of the son of the majority leader of the Idaho Senate, Bart Davis, whose son, Cameron, was shot to death during an argument at a party. Cameron Davis, Jacob said, was killed by a person who had held a conceal-and-carry permit for just two months. Jacob then talked about an incident involving his own son, Daniel. Following a confrontation, Daniel's opponent left, but promised to return with a gun. Senator Jacob suggested that if Missouri had conceal-and-carry permits, his son might also have gotten shot.[3] Jacob and his fellow opponents of conceal-and-carry intended to talk the bill to death, but the filibuster was abruptly cut off by Senator Caskey, a fellow Democrat.

Relying on a rarely used parliamentary procedure, Caskey and four Republicans made a motion that brought the debate to an end. The tactic had not been tried since 1977 and had not been used successfully since 1972. It is so rarely used, the senate's researchers only found nine instances of its use in the twentieth century.[4] In the Missouri Senate, a senator may speak indefinitely unless a senator moves for an end to debate and is seconded by four additional senators. The senate then votes on the motion. A simple majority vote is needed to stop the filibuster. Generally, no one does this, out of respect for a senator's right to hold the floor, even if there are enough votes to end debate.

The vote to end Jacobs's filibuster was 20 to 11. Interestingly, fewer senators voted to cut off debate than ultimately voted to pass the conceal-and-carry bill, perhaps because they feared that they were setting a dangerous precedent by cutting off the filibuster. For example, Jim Mathewson, D–Sedalia, the former president pro tem of the senate and a longtime proponent of conceal-and carry, voted against shutting off debate. He said, "When you support something, you've got to be awfully careful because next time they might do it to you."[5] Caskey's decision to force an end to debate angered his Democratic colleagues.

For example, Ken Jacob said, "Everybody was pretty shocked. He's our caucus chairman."[6] One senator, Mary Bland, D–Kansas City, was reportedly so angry over the maneuver that she violated senate rules by staying on the floor but refusing to cast a vote when the bill came up for final approval.[7] Caskey defended his maneuver by suggesting it was his final option to move the bill forward. He said he tried to compromise with his fellow Democrats, but when they refused, he felt he had no choice.[8] Peter Kinder, the president pro tem of the senate, sounded a neutral note in the aftermath of the vote to cut off debate. As president pro tem he was the final arbiter of parliamentary procedure in the senate. Kinder said, "It is explicitly contemplated in our rules but has been the custom not to use it frequently. I hope it will be a long time before it is used again."[9] Despite this public comment, Kinder no doubt relished the embarrassing defeat for the Democrats, especially Ken Jacob, with whom he had a contentious relationship. In 2004 the two men both campaigned for lieutenant governor, though Jacob lost the Democratic primary to former Secretary of State Bekki Cook.

With the option of filibustering lost to them, several senators opposed to conceal-and-carry attempted to amend the bill. Pat Dougherty, D–St. Louis, tried to change the age of eligibility to twenty-five. Maida Coleman, D–St. Louis, tried to include language that would require permit holders to inform business owners if they were carrying a gun when they entered a business establishment. Joan Bray, D–St. Louis, tried to amend the bill to require that a permit holder be charged with criminal negligence if the permit holder's child shot someone with his or her gun.[10] These amendments all failed, but the bill did not make it through the senate unscathed, as many proponents hoped it would.

The major change in the senate's version of conceal-and-carry was to raise the age for a permit from twenty-one to twenty-three. The amendment was proposed by Harold Caskey in an apparent gesture toward compromise. Strangely, however, the bill still allowed persons twenty-one or older to keep a gun concealed in the passenger compartment of an automobile, creating a loophole in the law.

Ken Jacob repeatedly questioned whether the legislature had the right to vote on conceal-and-carry at all, in light of the 1999 Prop B vote. He said, "There seems to be a lot of discussion about how people's minds have changed, but I don't see that. If a referendum clause were added, it would end the opposition."[11] Annoyed by this argument, Caskey responded, "Every one of my counties carried it. You talk about a 'majority,' and the voter turnout was less than 30 percent for that election. The majority chose not to vote."[12] The senate approved the bill by a vote of 23 to 7, with four Democrats voting for passage. Three of the four Democrats were not surprising—Steve Stoll of Festus, Harold Caskey, and Jim Mathewson, all of whom were outspoken supporters of conceal-and-carry. The fourth, however, was Ken Jacob, who voted strategically. He hoped to have a chance to move for reconsideration of the vote and, perhaps, kill the bill. Had he voted against the bill, he would not have had the right to make this motion. He never got the chance to bring the bill back for reconsideration, so he was guaranteed to vote against an override of the governor's expected veto. Twenty-three senators were needed to override a gubernatorial veto, but since at least one—Jacob—would obviously not vote to override, there was plenty of reason for supporters of conceal-and-carry to be concerned about the bill's fate. This would put enormous pressure on the one Republican senator who voted against it, the Republican floor leader, Mike Gibbons, of Kirkwood and, perhaps, the Democrats who voted for it.

Since the senate had adopted the amendment changing the age from twenty-one to twenty-three, the bill had to be returned to the house for further consideration. With only a couple of weeks left in the session, time was running short. As the house reconsidered the bill, Larry Crawford urged his fellow representatives to quickly accept the bill as amended.

There was some debate in the house about the change in age from twenty-one to twenty-three, especially regarding the strange loophole created by the different age for guns in cars. One representative opposed to conceal-and-carry, Barbara Fraser, D–St. Louis, said, "You think it's OK for a 21-year-old to have a gun concealed in a car in front of an amusement park, but that same person would have to wait two years until they get out of the car?"[13] This anomaly in the bill didn't make a lot of sense, but it was not a concern to the supporters of conceal-and-carry. Responding to Fraser's observation, Larry Crawford failed to address the loophole head-on. Instead, he repeated Wayne Crump's old argument that allowing people to conceal weapons in their cars was simply legalizing what many people already did. Legalizing concealed guns in cars, he suggested, would prevent guns from being stolen because people wouldn't have to keep them out in the open.[14]

There were supporters of conceal-and-carry who opposed increasing the age to twenty-three, but with time running out in the session, the bill's supporters knew that fighting the senate's change could, once again, kill the bill. If one chamber changes a bill and the other chamber objects, the two houses have only one recourse, a conference committee to work out a compromise. Then the two houses must again vote on the new bill. To avoid the time-consuming process of a conference committee, the house approved conceal-and-carry with the higher minimum age by a veto-proof vote of 111 to 43 on May 5. After the house voted, the bill was sent to Governor Holden, who had long promised to veto it.

The bill itself was similar to previous attempts to pass conceal-and-carry. It mandated that anyone with a conceal-and-carry permit be legally allowed to carry a concealed handgun and it required sheriffs to issue a permit to anyone over the age of twenty-three who fulfilled certain requirements. In addition, it allowed everyone over the age of twenty-one to keep concealed weapons in the passenger compartments of their vehicles without requiring a permit. The bill required that applicants for a conceal-and-carry permit pass a criminal background check, pay the county sheriff's department a fee not to exceed one hundred dollars for the three-year permit, and take an eight-hour firearms safety course. The bill prohibited carrying concealed weapons in certain places such as police stations, polling places on election day, jails, courthouses, airports, hospitals, and amusement parks, though it allowed permit holders to carry their guns into schools, churches, child-care centers, bars, and casinos with permission of the management. On the other hand, it provided business owners the opportunity to declare their establishments gun-free zones. It also mandated that persons holding valid permits from other states would be allowed to carry their concealed weapons in Missouri. The bill was to take effect almost immediately after passage. For a short time, applicants would be issued a paper permit by their county sheriff. Then, after a few months, a person's conceal-and-carry permit status would appear on his or her driver's license. The bill also made it illegal to make the names of permit holders public record.[15]

Liability Protection

The effort to provide the gun industry with immunity from most lawsuits by local governments also returned in 2003. Senator Kinder, who had previously championed liability protection, sponsored SB 13, which was quickly approved in the senate by a margin of 24 to 10. The bill was then forwarded to the house, where it was guided by Larry Crawford. The house took up the bill late in the session and approved it on May 14 by a vote of 113 to 30. Pro-gun advocates viewed the bill as an attack on "frivolous" lawsuits and felt it would prevent anti-gun government officials and others from using the courts to attack the gun industry.

In addition to preventing future lawsuits, the new law was designed specifically to address the suit filed by the city of St. Louis. In part, it mandated, "The general assembly hereby occupies and preempts the entire field of legislation touching in any way firearms, components, ammunition and supplies to the complete exclusion of any order, ordinance, or regulation by any political subdivision of this state. Any existing or future orders, ordinances or regulations in this field are hereby and shall be null and void . . . The lawful design, marketing, manufacture, distribution, or sale of firearms or ammunition to the public is not an abnormally dangerous activity and does not constitute a public or private nuisance. No county, city, town, village or any other political subdivision nor the state shall bring suit or have any right to recover against any firearms or ammunition manufacturer, trade association or dealer for damages, abatement or injunctive relief resulting from or relating to the lawful design, manufacture, marketing, distribution, or sale of firearms or ammunition to the public."[16]

The bill offered a level of protection to the gun industry that other businesses did not enjoy, and the governor vetoed the bill in July. In his veto statement, Governor Holden criticized the legislature for trying to prematurely end the ongoing St. Louis lawsuit and for trying to prevent other political subdivisions from ever suing the gun industry. He wrote: "It is similarly poor policy to dictate that political subdivisions cannot file a case at any time. The proper forum for determining the merits of causes of action and liability of the gun and ammunition industries is in our state's impartial courts, not the political forum of the legislature."[17] In his statement, Holden drew a parallel to the successful state action against the tobacco industry, suggesting there were positive public policy benefits to be gained from such suits. In addition, he suggested the bill was worded in such a way as to also make it illegal for individual citizens to sue gun manufacturers. He concluded by observing that the legislation was little more than a special favor to the firearms industry.

Holden's veto was not the final word on the issue, however. Since the regular session of the Missouri General Assembly always ends in mid-May and gubernatorial vetoes can come into the month of July, the constitution provides for a special session in September when legislators may attempt to override vetoes. During the annual veto session in September 2003, the legislature again took up the bill. During debate on the veto override, Senator Jacob suggested that if the gun industry knew it would never have to fear lawsuits, it would be much less worried about whom it sold guns to. Kinder's response to this objection was a barbed critique of lawyers, including Jacob. Kinder said, "Your answer to everything is to file a lawsuit."[18] Following the debate, the senate overrode Holden's veto 23 to 10. In the house, the veto was easily overridden by a margin of 113 to 36. With these votes, the governor suffered an embarrassing defeat and the firearms industry gained a unique level of legal protection in Missouri.

Following the vote, Larry Crawford praised the override and defended the gun industry. In his statement, he suggested that holding gun manufacturers liable for the criminal use of their products would be akin to holding pen manufacturers liable for bad checks. He also said, "Right now we need jobs . . . This will wipe out the ability to file frivolous lawsuits."[19] It was difficult to see what Crawford meant. Missouri is not a state known for its firearms manufacturing sector, so it was hard to see how the new law would protect jobs. It is possible Crawford was suggesting the bill would be a model for other liability protection laws, but he did not make that point clearly. There have been other liability protection bills introduced in the Missouri General Assembly, though none other than the gun bill have become law. In 2003, at the same time guns played such a dominant role, the legislature also passed a bill limiting medical malpractice liability. That bill was also vetoed by the governor, but the legislature failed to override. In 2004 the legislature again tried to pass a malpractice reform, as well as a bill that would have made it illegal to sue fast-food restaurants for making people overweight. The so-called "Common-sense Consumption Act," also known as SB 1185, passed in both houses of the legislature, unanimously in the senate.[20] Medical malpractice reform was again vetoed by Governor Holden, but it returned in 2005 and faced much better prospects with a Republican, Matt Blunt, in the governor's office.

On the other side of the issue, several legislators decried the veto override and suggested that providing blanket liability protection to any industry set a bad precedent. Representative Vicky Riback Wilson, D–Columbia, echoed the governor's veto statement when she said if a lawsuit truly was frivolous, as the sponsors of the bill suggested the St. Louis lawsuit was, the judge hearing the case would always have the discretion to throw it out.[21]

The St. Louis lawsuit against the gun industry was still making its way through the St. Louis County court when the veto was overridden. The city government vowed it would continue the suit. The city counselor, Patti Hageman, said, "I think the governor was well-advised when he vetoed it," and suggested the legislature did not have the constitutional authority to interfere in the legal process by passing such a law.[22]

Despite Hageman's confidence, the St. Louis lawsuit, which had languished in the courts since 1999, quickly suffered a setback. In October 2003, St. Louis County Judge Emmett O'Brien dismissed the suit, though he did not address the new law in his decision. The city, he suggested, was trying to blur the lines between product liability and public nuisance laws. In throwing the case out, he cited a recent precedent from a New York state appellate court which declared that allowing a public nuisance suit to proceed against the gun industry would precipitate many similar suits against different industries.[23] He suggested Missouri state law limited the regulation of manufacturing and sales to the state legislature and that the courts were an inappropriate forum.

He also suggested that if the suit was allowed to proceed, it would cause a flood of additional lawsuits and that "issues of both logic and fairness" pushed him to dismiss the case.[24] A spokesman for the National Shooting Sports foundation, an industry trade group, was happy with the dismissal. He said the suit was "a clear misuse of the true purpose of the legal system."[25] O'Brien's decision was not the final act for the suit, however.

In June 2004 the city asked a three-judge Missouri Court of Appeals panel to reverse O'Brien's decision and reinstate the suit. Arguing for the city, Jonathan Lowy, an attorney from the Brady Center, said gun makers should bear some responsibility for the social costs related to the violent and illegal use of their products.[26] Responding to this line of argument, one attorney involved in the defense, Lawrence Greenwald, said, ". . . The fundamental issue which cuts through this entire case is: Should the city, which is not a person who got shot, collect from gun makers, who didn't do the shooting? That is exactly what St. Louis is trying to do."[27]

In July, however, the Appeals Court ruled against the city, and this time the new state liability law was invoked by the judges. The court's ruling read, in part, "The enactment of this statute seems to be in response to suits like this one, which attempt to apply theories of tort liability to the significantly regulated industry of manufacturers, distributors, and dealers of firearms. Therefore, we find the city's claims are prohibited" by the amended statutes.[28] Responding to the decision, Chris Cox, the NRA's chief lobbyist, said, "This sound decision is a victory for gun owners and all who believe society must hold criminals accountable for their crimes . . . These baseless lawsuits have done nothing but squander taxpayers' money. Unfortunately, big-city mayors and money-hungry lawyers have played into the hands of gun-banners, who designed these suits to crush the American firearm industry under the weight of legal fees."[29] After the court issued its decision, the city of St. Louis did not take any further action, though city officials such as Mayor Francis Slay said they were weighing their options for appealing the case further.[30]

While the override of Governor Holden's veto of liability legislation was important to gun rights activists and the gun industry, the issue got very little attention statewide in 2003. To use what is probably an understatement, it was overshadowed by the fight over conceal-and-carry. After the legislature passed the conceal-and-carry bill, Governor Holden's veto was certain, and the activists on both sides of the issue prepared for a summer-long campaign leading up to the legislature's veto session in September.

Chapter Twenty

Conceal-and-Carry Veto Fight!

Perhaps the most interesting thing about the passage of conceal-and-carry in 2003 was that the national lobby groups on both sides of the issue were almost invisible to the public throughout the session. The NRA, which always tried to act as though conceal-and-carry was a homegrown issue driven by freedom-loving Missourians, was, as a rule, quite low-key every year but 1999. However, an examination of Missouri Ethics Commission records from 2003 shows that the group worked with a handful of key legislators, including Representative Larry Crawford and Senators Peter Kinder, Harold Caskey, John Cauthorn, and David Klindt, throughout the session. The ethics records show that NRA lobbyists spent just one thousand dollars on gifts and meals for the legislators and their staffs.[1] In this day and age, one thousand dollars doesn't seem like an earth-shattering amount of money, but it shows that the group was monitoring the legislature's progress on both conceal-and-carry and liability protection, and what the ethics records can never reveal is what the group's reps told members. The other thing to bear in mind, of course, is that during the regular session there was little need for the NRA to worry. With their allies in power, conceal-and-carry was a virtual lock. The veto session wasn't quite as certain, however, and the NRA spent the bulk of its money in September, during that critical week.

On the other side, the Brady Campaign might have seen the handwriting on the wall and chosen not to use its limited resources. One legislator who supported conceal-and-carry, Tom Villa, D–St. Louis, suggested, "The opposition wasn't nearly as visible this time around, because they believed they were going to get their ears boxed."[2] In 2003, with a regime change in the legislature, the debate over conceal-and-carry was relatively easy for its supporters, especially in the house.

After the bill's passage, Representative Crawford said, "It's time we join the

35 other states that . . . allow their citizens to protect themselves when they're outside their homes."[3] As the governor received the bill, advocates on both sides tried to influence him and urged followers to contact the governor. Regardless of how many calls and letters he received, Governor Holden's mind to veto the bill was certainly made up at the beginning of the session.

The passage of conceal-and-carry in Missouri was a historic turn of events, the culmination of thirteen years of work. For supporters, the governor was the only remaining hurdle. For many years, a threatened veto was enough to discourage many legislators. Just a year earlier, in February of 2002, the speaker of the house, Jim Kreider, had said that although he supported conceal-and-carry, the governor's promise to veto would give many Democratic legislators pause because they didn't like to challenge their own governor.[4] Before the major electoral changes of November 2002, the Democratic governor's promise to veto any bills significantly dampened·enthusiasm for conceal-and-carry in the senate, where the bill ultimately died several times over the years.

By 2003 the situation was dramatically different. The new Republican house leadership was more than eager to challenge the Democratic governor, and for his part, Holden seemed eager for the fight. Conceal-and-carry was just one contentious piece of legislation in a session filled with conflicts between the governor and the legislature. The governor vetoed a total of twenty-six bills from the 2003 legislative session, many of which the legislature didn't have enough votes to override. Conceal-and-carry was a different story, at least in the house. In May, months before the legislature's veto session, Speaker Catherine Hanaway promised there would be more than enough support for an override. She predicted there would be "in the neighborhood of 115 votes."[5] Conceal-and-carry passed in 2003 because many legislators supported it, but it also gave Republicans a chance to hand Holden a stinging defeat.

In May, Kelly Whitley, a spokesperson for the NRA, said, "Right now, we're going to focus on encouraging the governor to sign the bill," and seemed to be trying to imply a veto of conceal-and-carry would mark the beginning of the end of his political career in Missouri.[6] The governor, however, was not dissuaded from vetoing the bill by comments from the NRA or by the fact that the leaders of the legislature seemed to have enough votes to overturn him. There would be several months before the veto could be overturned, and the governor promised to spend the summer campaigning against the bill. Holden felt confident legislators would reconsider once they heard from their constituents, who he predicted would turn against conceal-and-carry when they learned the details of the bill.[7]

In truth, the governor had little choice but to follow through on his promise to veto the bill, given the way he had won election in 2000 by carrying

St. Louis and Kansas City, two areas very opposed to conceal-and-carry. Two years into his term, Holden had an image problem. To many Missourians, he was weak and wishy-washy. During the 2003 session, several Republican legislators took to wearing buttons that said "OTB," for "One Term Bob." Signing the bill might have gained him some votes from single-issue union members in 2004, but it would certainly have alienated voters opposed to conceal-and-carry. What boxed Holden in was the fact that he faced a challenge from within his own party. State Auditor Claire McCaskill was already positioning herself to seek the Democratic nomination for governor in May. If he alienated urban voters, they would have a ready alternative in McCaskill.

Veto

As promised, the governor vetoed the bill in early July, waiting until just three days before the bill would have automatically become law without his signature. Holden made quite a show out of the veto, holding a ceremony in the St. Louis suburb of Kirkwood. The ceremony was described in the *Springfield News-Leader* as "a symbolic stop . . . to pen the veto, playing to the urban voting bloc that was key in defeating a similar concealed weapons ballot question in 1999."[8] At the ceremony, Holden said, "This was really an attempt to overthrow the will of the people. This is about hiding guns, not about having guns."[9] The veto ceremony was ripe with political meaning. It was held in an area where there was a great deal of opposition to Prop B in 1999, and that was also the hometown of Senator Mike Gibbons, the Republican floor leader who was the only member of his party to vote against the conceal-and-carry law. Undoubtedly, Holden's ceremony in Kirkwood was meant to pressure Gibbons to hold the line against conceal-and-carry in the override vote.

The symbolism of the moment was heightened by the fact that the ceremony came just three days after a deadly workplace shooting in Jefferson City, where Jonathon Russell, a disgruntled employee of the Modine Manufacturing Company, killed three coworkers, wounded five others, and took his own life. The killings temporarily took the wind out of the sails of the pro-gun groups opposed to the governor's veto, which had planned demonstrations across the state on the day of the ceremony. The groups canceled, they said, out of respect for the victims of the shooting.[10]

The ill timing of the tragic events in Jefferson City was compounded by an embarrassing discovery after Russell's rampage. The weapon he used had been owned previously by the Missouri Highway Patrol. It had been legally purchased from a Jefferson City gun store, which acquired the gun from a dealer in Kansas City, and it was stamped with the Highway Patrol logo and the initials

MSHP. The Highway Patrol defended the practice of selling retired guns to help buy new ones by pointing out that many other state and city governments do the same thing. However, the underlying message promoted by opponents of conceal-and-carry was that if law enforcement agencies couldn't keep track of their own guns, how could they keep society safe in the era of conceal-and-carry?

Greg Pearre, the Missouri spokesman for the NRA, tried to address the situation when he said it was the same as trading in an old car when buying a new one and that there was nothing untoward about the transaction. He added the tragedy was the result of Russell's actions with the gun, not the gun itself. Nevertheless, the governor publicly suggested the Highway Patrol should reconsider the policy and destroy old guns rather than sell them.[11] While the shooting was certainly a tragedy, it also gave the governor new, potent political material as he signed the veto.

In his veto statement, Holden argued the bill violated the public trust by undoing a vote of the people just four years before. Further, he argued the bill was less restrictive and required less training than Prop B would have required. He wrote, "The citizens of Missouri have already clearly decided that they do not wish to authorize the carrying of concealed weapons in this state. In April of 1999, voters in this state defeated a conceal and carry proposition despite the fact that the proposition would have mandated more firearms training than this bill (twelve hours as opposed to eight), limited reciprocity of the right to carry a concealed weapon to states that had equal requirements for the issuance of a permit (whereas this bill accepts permits from other states regardless of the permit requirements in those states), retained a criminal penalty for armed trespass (as opposed to this bill, which declares that it is not a criminal act to carry a concealed weapon into a prohibited area), and allowed sheriffs to consider juvenile court records when considering an application for a permit (as opposed to this bill, which does not). Despite the fact that the 1999 conceal and carry proposition was more protective of public safety than this legislation, the citizens of this state voted it down."[12] Holden also asserted the law violated the Violence Against Women Act because it did not prevent men convicted of misdemeanor domestic violence from getting conceal-and-carry permits, as federal law required. He further suggested it would put people at risk in a wide variety of venues where concealed weapons would be allowed, such as Little League baseball games in small stadiums, day care centers, and schools.

The governor also objected to allowing permit holders to keep their identity secret, as the law allowed.[13] Larry Crawford defended the anonymity provision by saying he had included it because he wanted to protect gun owners against theft. He suggested would-be thieves could use a public list of permit holders to track down guns and steal them from their owners.[14] It was a strange explanation, however, since one of the major arguments in favor of conceal-and-carry was that it would make would-be criminals less willing to victimize someone if they feared they might be shot. It seems a thief who knew his would-be victim was armed would be less likely to act, not more. Perhaps sensing the weakness of this argument, Crawford also suggested that by keeping permit holders' names secret, it would protect them from tele-marketers and political campaigns trying to target gun owners.[15] But this explanation didn't make much sense either. Certainly there were many other ways telemarketers could target gun owners, such as membership in gun groups and purchases from gun suppliers. Some observers speculated the anonymity provision was intended to allow county sheriffs to keep secret lists of potential armed posse members, but it is impossible to say for sure why the provision was included in the bill, and opponents of the bill repeatedly raised it as an issue for concern.

House Speaker Pro Tem Rod Jetton, R–Marble Hill, responded to the gov-ernor's veto statement and attacked Holden's assertion that the legislature vio-lated the public trust by, in effect, repealing the Prop B vote. He also refuted the governor's charge that conceal-and-carry would make society less safe. He said, "We tried to make sure with this bill that no one who was a bad person was able to get a weapon. That went a long way to calm the fears of some of the urban and suburban people."[16] This sort of argument obviously had little impact on the governor's decision to veto.

Holden's vetoes, including the conceal-and-carry bill, the liability bill, and another bill that created a twenty-four-hour waiting period for abortions, set the stage for a September showdown in the Show-Me State. As expected, groups supporting conceal-and-carry were vocal through the summer. West-ern Missouri Shooters Alliance spokesman Kevin Jamison argued that even if the legislature was unable to override the veto, the issue would return quickly. He said, "You have the right to defend yourself, but not the right to the means of self-defense . . . The legislature took our right away from us in 1879, and we want it back." He seemed to suggest they would never stop fighting for it.[17] As September approached, if supporters of conceal-and-carry were nervous about the veto session, it was with good reason—there was a great deal of uncertainty about the coming vote. In the house, there was no doubt the veto would be overturned, but that was only half of the battle.

In the senate, there were only twenty solid votes in favor of the override, while twenty-three were needed. Four Democrats voted for the bill in the spring. As the veto session approached, only two of those Democrats were solid supporters of conceal-and-carry, Harold Caskey and Steve Stoll, who could be counted on to vote for an override. The Senate minority leader, Ken Jacob, a third Democrat who voted for conceal-and-carry in May, was a lock to vote against the override. Jacob was a longtime opponent of conceal-and-carry who only voted for the bill as part of a failed parliamentary maneuver to kill it. The fourth Democrat was Jim Mathewson, who, while being a strong supporter of conceal-and-carry, expressed indecision about voting to override a Democratic governor.

In addition to doubts on the Democratic side of the aisle, it seemed likely that one strong Republican supporter of conceal-and-carry would be unable to attend the session to cast his vote for an override. As the session approached, the senator, Jon Dolan, R–Lake Saint Louis, was out of the country serving as a major with the Missouri National Guard in Guantanamo Bay, Cuba. It was believed at the time that it was illegal for him to take leave to return to Jefferson City and vote. In the days before the vote, Dolan said, "I need to respect this mission and its requirements. I am focusing on my mission and the welfare of my troops."[18] Therefore, the supporters of conceal-and-carry seemed to be well short of the twenty-three votes they needed, as Kevin Jamison of the Western Missouri Shooters Alliance admitted on September 7, 2003.[19]

The situation wasn't entirely hopeless for the supporters of conceal-and-carry, however. Mathewson was not a guaranteed vote against overriding the veto; he was simply undecided. The one Republican who voted against conceal-and-carry, Mike Gibbons, seemed open to persuasion. Both senators felt tremendous pressure from their parties and the proponents and opponents of conceal-and-carry as the veto session approached.

Mike Gibbons represented a district that voted against Prop B in 1999 by a margin of 70 percent to 30 percent, and the pressure to vote against conceal-and-carry in 2003 was strong. In fact, Gibbons was not the only Republican from the area to feel it. In the house, Ninety-first District Representative Kathlyn Fares, from the St. Louis suburb of Webster Groves, faced pressure similar to Gibbons's. As legislators from suburban St. Louis, Gibbons's and Fares's votes were in line with public opinion in their districts, but at the same time the Republican leadership in both chambers wanted to pass conceal-and-carry. A second house Republican, Rob Schaff of the Twenty-eighth District, voted "present" on conceal-and-carry. The Twenty-eighth District includes St. Joseph, which voted no on Prop B in 1999. The difference between Gibbons's vote and those of the two representatives was that in the house, the votes made no difference to the bill's fate. There was plenty of support for the veto override without Fares and Schaff. In the senate, however, the supporters of conceal-and-carry needed every vote they could get.

There was plenty of pressure from the other side as well, beginning with the governor's veto ceremony in Gibbons's district. At the time, Gibbons complained the governor was trying to pressure him not to override the veto and hinted that he was, in fact, considering changing his mind. Organizations from around the state pressured Gibbons over his vote while criticizing the governor for doing the same. Clearly, both sides recognized that Gibbons's vote would be pivotal. As part of its campaign to win the override vote, the Second Amendment Coalition sent every Missouri senator, including Gibbons, a copy of John R. Lott's new book, *The Bias Against Guns,* in an attempt to convince them of the wisdom of conceal-and-carry.

As the day of the veto override approached, it seemed Senator Jon Dolan was not going to make it back to Jefferson City from Cuba for the vote. Gibbons continued to receive heavy pressure from the leaders of the Republican party, the gun lobby, and the opponents of conceal-and-carry. Jeanne Kirkton, of the Million Mom March and the League of Women Voters of Missouri, met with Gibbons to try to convince him to stick with his original vote. Speaking after the meeting, she seemed to feel sorry for him. She said, "He's between a rock and a hard place. His constituents voted more than 70 percent against and remain opposed. He is being pushed by the Republican Party to vote for it because it's in their platform. It really puts a lot of pressure on him. I just hope he does the right thing according to his constituents."[20] On the other hand, supporters of conceal-and-carry tried to apply their own pressure. Dale Schmid, for example, seemed to feel the veto ceremony was a stunt and wrote to supporters on the Second Amendment Coalition's Web site that the governor was unfairly pressuring Gibbons and trying to embarrass him.[21] The Western Missouri Shooters Alliance spokesman, Kevin Jamison, argued Gibbons's own discretion, not the opinion of his constituents, should be the deciding factor. He said, "A representative owes his people his own judgment. We've presented incontrovertible evidence that license to carry creates no problem in the 44 states that have it and almost certainly creates a reduction in crime. It's a law-and-order vote if you vote for it. We are hoping he would see the reason of this and vote our way."[22] It was, as presented by advocates on both sides of the issue, a classic dilemma of representative democracy. It was a question of delegate versus trustee; decision-making based on public opinion versus decision-making based on an official's own reasoned judgment.

Prior to the veto session, Governor Holden expressed confidence that his vetoes would be upheld. He said, "I believe they are sound and they will uphold them. I am encouraging lawmakers to vote their conscience, and if they do that I think we'll be OK."[23] Gibbons, who seemed overwhelmed, said, "I've got piles of material and e-mails and phone messages and I'm going through all of it and trying to figure out what's right. I want to make sure I understand the facts."[24] With the pressure clearly showing, Gibbons said, "For me, in my district, in my party, being pulled very strong in two totally opposite directions, it isn't any fun."[25] For Gibbons, who held the position of majority floor leader at the time of the vote, a decision on the veto override probably had implications for his future in party leadership, which, no doubt, added to the pressure he felt. Another Republican party leader from suburban St. Louis showed increasing support for conceal-and-carry as she rose through the ranks. Catherine Hanaway, the speaker of the house, became much more outspoken in her support of conceal-and-carry when she assumed the speakership. At the very least, in past years she'd been willing to negotiate on conceal-and-carry, as demonstrated by the compromise amendment she proposed in 2002. In 2003, however, she joined many of her suburban colleagues in dropping their previous opposition and voting in favor of conceal-and-carry with very few restrictions. Clearly, one could argue that Hanaway felt it was necessary to strengthen her position on conceal-and-carry as part of her ascension to speaker and to help her chances at gaining a higher, statewide office. It meant she had to choose between the people of her district and the fact that the guns issue was a wedge that could be driven into the growing out-state split within the Democratic party.

Hanaway explained her new position on conceal-and-carry in a different way, arguing that her views had simply evolved over time and that she and other suburban legislators were greatly affected by the terrorist attacks of September 11, 2001. She said, "People are more security conscious on all levels."[26] Hanaway's chief of staff, Chuck Caisley, said, "Republicans and Democrats that are pro-gun are winning in suburban areas. I would argue that concealed weapons are becoming more accepted."[27] This may have been true, but there also were clear strategic political reasons to switch her vote. Whatever her motive, the political reality was that she changed her position and became significant in aiding the passage of conceal-and-carry in 2003. The vote to override the veto passed in the house by exactly the margin she predicted in May, 115 to 39. Hanaway had fulfilled her half of the Republicans' promise to hand the governor an embarrassing defeat on conceal-and-carry.

In the senate, however, uncertainty was the rule. While the decision for Gibbons was one of party versus the opinion of his constituents, the dilemma was exactly the opposite for Jim Mathewson. The former president pro tem was a supporter of conceal-and-carry, as were many in his district. He voted in favor of conceal-and-carry in May, but as the veto session arrived, he was under tremendous pressure from the governor and the Democratic party to vote against the veto override. The supporters of conceal-and-carry certainly recognized the pressure that Mathewson and other Democrats were under. Pete Kinder, the Republican president pro tem, referred to Mathewson when he said, "The outcome of an override is in doubt . . . they don't want to embarrass their own governor."[28]

Prior to the 2003 legislative session, there had been only a handful of genuine veto overrides since Missouri had become a state. A major reason for this was that although legislators of the same party don't always vote in lockstep on bills, they generally vote the party line in veto override votes, regardless of their personal preference. For much of the post–World War II era, Missouri's legislature was solidly Democratic and legislators simply didn't override the vetoes of Democratic governors. For Mathewson, an old school Democrat, there was considerable pressure to observe this tradition. Before the veto session, Mathewson seemed to lean against an override. He was a term-limited legislator about to enter his last year in office, so he would face no retribution from conceal-and-carry supporters in his district if he voted the party line. He said, "I am still in the thinking process. I don't like overriding governors. They take it personal. They make a special list for people who vote against vetoes."[29]

As the senate took up the override, the capitol took on what was described as a "playoff-like atmosphere, with pep rallies and slogans on clothes and posters like 'Support Bob Holden,' and 'Guns save lives.'"[30] After months of being bombarded by supporters and opponents of conceal-and-carry, Senator Gibbons decided to go with his party, not his district, and voted to override the governor's veto. He justified his vote by saying that although opinion in his district was heavily against conceal-and-carry, he was really taking the interests of his district to heart. He said, "I'm doing the right thing for the people I serve," although a large majority of his constituents didn't agree.[31] Anticipating criticism, he said he voted to override because the law was "the last chance for a safe, restrictive law. If we wait until next year, we will have a watered down bill without the restrictions. I'm convinced this is the safest gun bill we are going to have."[32] Gibbons may have felt this was true, but it was certainly unsatisfying to opponents of conceal-and-carry. Gibbons went to some length as he cast his vote to override the veto to make it clear he was not buckling under pressure from his party. In a statement on the senate floor, Gibbons said, "First, I need to address a rumor that the Republican Party and my Senate colleagues have pressured me, threatening my leadership position or any future that I may have. These rumors are absolutely false. I must admit that I expected there might be some of that, but I am proud to report that there has been no such threat. My Republican colleagues and the Party have never pressured me and have left me alone to resolve this issue as I see best to do the right thing for the people I serve."[33] These comments notwithstanding, opponents of conceal and carry no doubt believed Gibbons's decision was tilted by the tremendous pressure he felt from his party leadership—and his desire to remain part of that leadership.

While Mathewson might have been genuinely worried about the governor's anger, it wasn't enough to keep him from voting to override the veto in the end. Mathewson's explanation of his decision to override was, no doubt, unsatisfactory to the governor. He said, "I want to get rid of the damn issue because I'm tired of it. If we don't deal with it today, in January we'll be back here dealing with it again. It will never go away."[34] This was an interesting statement that was unsatisfactory for the governor and opponents of conceal-and-carry. To Mathewson, about to enter his last year as a senator, he might genuinely have wanted to put the thorny issue aside to leave more time for other issues. For opponents of conceal-and-carry, of course, such pragmatism was entirely misplaced. But for Mathewson, who expressed concern about angering the governor during the summer, there was little reason to worry about retribution from his party. First, he was term-limited and leaving office. Second, his constituents supported it. The truth was that Mathewson was a long-time supporter of conceal-and-carry. He wanted it to become law, he had an opportunity to ensure that it would, and perhaps he never felt as much indecision as he indicated prior to the vote.

This meant three of the four senate Democrats who voted for conceal-and-carry in May also voted to overturn the governor's veto. Harold Caskey of course was the sponsor of the bill in the senate, and Steve Stoll received an "A" and an endorsement from the NRA in the 2002 campaign. Caskey, Stoll, and Mathewson also voted to override the governor's vetoes of Kinder's liability protection bill and the twenty-four-hour abortion waiting period. They were joined in the abortion vote by Senator Pat Dougherty, D–St. Louis.

Gibbons's and Mathewson's votes gave the pro–conceal-and-carry side twenty-two votes, one short of an override. However, Jon Dolan, the senator serving with the National Guard, was able to get last-minute leave from his duty in Cuba and returned to Jefferson City just in time for the veto session. He voted to overturn the veto and, by a vote of 23 to 10 on Thursday, September 11, helped make conceal-and-carry the law of the land in Missouri.

Given the critical role he played in overturning the governor's veto, Dolan's surprise return to Missouri was controversial. Throughout the summer it appeared army regulations would prevent Dolan from taking part in the veto session, so when he was able to come home, it raised the eyebrows of conceal-and-carry opponents. In late September the Southern Command of the U.S. Army announced it was investigating the senator's leave, thanks in part to a request from Democratic Congressman William Lacy Clay, Jr.[35] Dolan was granted leave by his commanding officer after just two weeks of active duty, while army regulations stated that a soldier had to complete two months of active duty before being eligible for leave. His commanding officer, Lieutenant Colonel Pamela Hart, granted him six days of leave, however, because she said his presence was not critical to her mission in Cuba.[36]

In addition to the question of whether or not he got leave too early in his tour of duty, there was another possible problem with his vote in September. A Department of Defense directive stated that National Guard soldiers were prohibited from carrying out functions of political office when called up for a tour of duty longer than 270 days. This includes obvious duties such as voting on bills, but also prohibits any contact with legislative staff or constituents.[37] The reason for this regulation, according to Lieutenant Colonel Ellen Krenke, a spokesperson for the Department of Defense, is that "The military is supposed to remain apolitical . . . When you exercise the duties of an elected office, you are no longer apolitical, even if your actions are not directly related to the military."[38] The trouble in Dolan's case was that he was called up for a period "not to exceed 365 days," which could be more or less than 270 days, of course. Both the army's rule about leave and the Department of Defense directive about political action were open to interpretation. The wording of both was vague enough to give Dolan a plausible legal loophole. The senator contended the rule against political activity should only take effect after a soldier has been on duty for 270 days. He also asserted that nothing exceptional was done to grant him early leave to return to Missouri for the vote.[39]

In January 2004 the U.S. Army found Dolan had violated the directive banning National Guard members from performing political functions while on a tour of duty, but investigators concluded he had violated the rule unknowingly. Because the rule was vague enough that both he and his superior officers had misunderstood it, Dolan was only given a minor punishment in the form of a "letter of admonition." Dolan said, "I'm pleased that a fair resolution was made in the matter and that I can complete a tour of duty at Joint Task Force Guantanamo, as well as still serve the people of the Second District."[40] However, Dolan was also ordered by the military to either cease all political activities or resign from active military duty. Faced with this choice, Dolan resigned. He returned to Missouri in time for the start of the 2004 legislative session, where he served as the chair of the Transportation Committee.

The incident prompted the military to clarify its rules. In the future, officeholders who are also members of the National Guard will be advised clearly of the need to suspend political activities while on active duty. For his part, Dolan felt that a valuable connection between elected officials and constituents had been hurt by the army's decision. He said, "We must have our mayors and our state legislators serving with our citizen soldiers . . . You have to have your community going to war together."[41] In addition, he was harshly critical of the vague nature of the army's regulations and insisted they needed to be fixed. He said, "The Army is failing, in the middle of a war, to fix things for their citizen soldiers . . . The Army, by their inability to grasp their responsibility here, is not helping civil officers comply, and they need to get on it and get it accomplished. We will be starting a campaign to highlight this inequity."[42] He also claimed he was the victim of a partisan political attack instigated by Democrats such as Congressman Clay because they were angry he had voted to overturn Holden's veto. While Dolan's career with the Missouri National Guard was over, his political career was alive and well, and he was able to give the Republican leadership a critical vote on September 11, 2003. Without his vote, the legislature would have been forced to debate conceal-and-carry again in 2004.

Pro–conceal-and-carry forces were, as was to be expected, jubilant in the aftermath of the veto override. Senator Dan Clemens, R–Marshfield, from southwest Missouri, claimed the legislature took a step in "taking back individual rights" with the override.[43] Speaker Hanaway suggested the passage of conceal-and-carry after so many years was made possible by new leadership in the legislature that was willing to challenge the governor. After the veto session she said, "The House was pro-gun and pro-life before Republicans took over. What did change is that the bills went all the way through the process."[44] They went all the way, she implied, because the Republican leadership had no qualms about challenging the governor. In fact, they relished it.

Another legislator, Representative B. J. Marsh, R–Springfield, said the override votes on guns and abortion demonstrated that the governor was vulnerable. Marsh said, "Especially in southwest Missouri, on both issues Holden's just out of touch with reality."[45] Greg Jeffrey, the legislative director of Missourians for Personal Safety, called the override a victory for civil liberties and said, "After 13 years of struggle, we finally got for the citizens of Missouri one simple thing: the ability for honest citizens to ask for the permission to carry a concealed firearm if they are qualified."[46] Kevin Jamison, of the Western Missouri Shooters Alliance, called the victory a miracle and argued, "Perhaps people have finally realized what we've been saying for many years is true. In the states that have it, there haven't been any problems with it . . . People want to have the right to defend themselves or the means to protect themselves."[47]

Chris Cox, the NRA's chief lobbyist, lauded the victory in a press release. He wrote, "The NRA would like to thank representatives and senators who voted for the override. They recognize the right of law-abiding Missourians to carry a firearm for protection . . . Governor Holden's indifference on the issue of self-defense and the right of Missourians to protect themselves and their loved ones outside of the home was careless. The big winners today are the law-abiding citizens who will reap the benefit of this Right-To-Carry law. The streets of Missouri just became safer for everyone, except criminals."[48] Locally, the Second Amendment Coalition of Missouri, the Western Missouri Shooters Alliance, and other organizations also exulted in the good news on their Web sites.

On the other side, Senator Joan Bray, D–St. Louis, commented on the senate's actions in both the gun and abortion bills, suggesting there was a double standard at play. She said, "At one level it's saying we want the government to be terribly involved in very personal decisions of women. And then we don't want government involved in the use of lethal weapons."[49] Frieda Bernstein, a spokeswoman for Missourians Against Handgun Violence, said it was a sad day for Missouri and that increased carrying of guns would lead to increased numbers of children hurt and killed.[50] She added, "The NRA has brainwashed so many people that it will be a more polite society if everyone has a loaded gun on his hip. That's pretty sad."[51]

By overriding the governor's vetoes of the two gun laws and the twenty-four-hour abortion waiting period, the Missouri General Assembly handed Governor Holden the single biggest legislative defeat a governor of Missouri has endured in almost 150 years and increased the total number of meaningful veto overrides since the Civil War by almost 50 percent. The last time the legislature overrode a veto was when it rejected Governor Carnahan's veto of a bill making it illegal to perform partial-birth abortions in 1999. Prior to that, there had not been a veto override since 1980, when the legislature turned back Governor Joe Teasdale's veto of funding for the Truman State Office Building in Jefferson City.[52]

Despite the historic defeat, in his comments to reporters the governor was philosophical about the losses. He said, "I stood for things I believe in. I'll stand for them every day. This was an unfortunate day for people who have fought for choice and for those who have fought against gun violence. I think the rights of women have been compromised. I don't think gun legislation makes us safer as a state. I think it puts some people in harm's way. But the legislature has spoken."[53] The longtime contract lobbyist, John Britton, a household name around the capitol, tried to explain the historic override session. Britton said, "When you look back on this, I think you will see the influence of term limits. You will see the effect of the more organized aggressive campaigning done by the Republican Party." He said the governor ". . . just didn't like conceal-and-carry, and his position on the abortion issue has always been abundantly clear," but Holden was simply unable to hold back the tide.[54] Guns and abortion are arguably the most contentious issues in Missouri politics, and the 2003 legislative session seemed to signal a break in the dam that had blocked action on them for years.

The veto overrides signaled political trouble for the governor and raised questions about his ability to lead even the members of his own party. Shortly after the veto session, the governor was faced with what people had long anticipated, the official announcement by State Auditor Claire McCaskill that she was challenging Holden for the Democratic nomination. Representative Bob Johnson, R–Lee's Summit, commented on the fact that many Democrats in the house voted to overturn the governor's veto. He said, "This sends the message that he has lost the respect of a lot in the Democratic Party, especially in rural areas. It tells me that a lot of them have decided they are going to be challenged and they don't want to explain those issues to people in their area."[55] Holden's public response to the overrides and McCaskill's announcement was calm, though he had to be furious. He said, "I'll leave it to others to analyze the politics of this. I did what I thought was right."[56] Part of his statement was certainly true—others analyzed the politics of his choice and didn't agree.

In the aftermath of the defeat, the governor suggested he would throw his support to any citizen-sponsored initiative to repeal the new law. The governor's spokesperson, Mary Still, said, "We would be active. He would play whatever role the sponsors would need him to play."[57] Interestingly, while Claire McCaskill picked up the support of Anheuser-Busch because of the governor's opposition on conceal-and-carry, she said she would have vetoed the bill in May and also said she would support an initiative to overturn the law, though in saying so, she also critiqued the governor. She said, "I am opposed to concealed carry, and I would support every effort to reverse this law and will work to tighten the restrictions to make them meaningful. I am disappointed in the leadership that got us here."[58] While the critical comment was good sound bite material, it is hard to imagine how McCaskill could have changed the outcome, given the changed landscape in the legislature and the determination of the new Republican leadership to score a victory. She may have been more effective in communicating the importance of holding a firm party line to the Democratic senators who broke with Holden in the veto override, though that is only speculation now.

The Democratic governor was not the only politician to face political repercussions from the conceal-and-carry fight. Clearly, one of the races in which guns had the biggest impact was the reelection campaign of Senator Gibbons, who was challenged by Jeanne Kirkton, the same gun control advocate who seemed sympathetic of Gibbons's dilemma in the months before the veto session. She was not as sympathetic after his vote. During the 2004 legislative session, as the General Assembly revisited conceal-and-carry following a Supreme Court decision impacting its implementation, Gibbons seemed to be feeling some election-year regret about his vote. Responding to concerns about conceal-and-carry expressed by St. Louis–area law enforcement officials, Gibbons said, "Law enforcement has raised a lot of questions, and there is a tremendous amount of emotion out there. At some point when we revisit the law, we should revisit all of the issues that are out there."[59]

As the reality of the situation sank in, advocates on both sides began to prepare for the 2004 elections. Anti-gun protestors began to demonstrate at appearances made by Matt Blunt, Missouri's secretary of state and the Republican candidate for governor. Blunt supported conceal-and-carry, and protestors suggested his position would come back to haunt him in the governor's race. Meanwhile, pro–conceal-and-carry forces, led by groups such as the Western Missouri Shooters' Alliance, promised to support candidates who supported them in the conceal-and-carry fight.

Meanwhile, of course, the fight over conceal-and-carry was not over; it was simply shifting from one venue to another. With the override of Governor Holden's veto, the long legislative fight was over and the scene shifted, inevitably, to the courts, where opponents of conceal-and-carry sought to block the law's implementation. At the same time, the sheriffs who were charged with the duty of issuing concealed weapons permits scrambled to get ready for the late-October date when the law was to take effect.

Chapter Twenty-One

Legal Questions—Conceal-and-Carry
Gets Its Day(s) in Court

As the dust in Jefferson City settled, counties and municipalities around the state began to prepare for the new conceal-and-carry law. At the county level, sheriffs were now responsible for processing permits, and they had to set up ways to do that. One of the great concerns local law enforcement officials had about the new law was how much it would cost, in both dollars and time, to process permits and run background checks. The law was scheduled to take effect on October 11, 2003, which gave sheriffs only a month to get their systems in place. Under the new law, fingerprints taken by the sheriffs would be processed by the Highway Patrol and sent to the FBI for a background check. The state anticipated there would be as many as sixty thousand conceal-and-carry applicants in the first year the law was in effect.[1]

Among other things, there was uncertainty about how to determine who was qualified to teach certification courses. In an interview with the *Kansas City Star,* John Hemeyer, the Cole County sheriff and a supporter of conceal-and-carry, said he was an NRA-certified instructor, but even that organization's courses didn't cover every part of Missouri's law on the permissible use of force.[2]

The law was confusing for many who needed to make decisions about how to enforce it. Several apparent inconsistencies were scattered throughout the legislation, and in places the law was simply vague. Larry Crawford argued any major flaws could be fixed with future legislation, but as far as he was concerned, the law was in better shape than he'd expected it to be. This assertion was challenged by Todd Elkins, a minister from Independence and the chairman of an anti–conceal-and-carry religious group called Missouri Impact. He argued that the bill was poorly written, with little regard for public safety, thanks to pressure from the NRA and other pro-gun groups. He said, "The attitude was that any amendment was a stalling tactic or an attempt to kill the bill. So the details were never up for discussion. The restrictions that are in the bill are there just to defuse criticism. There was no real attempt to develop good public policy. The goal seemed to be, 'How can we write it so we can tell people it's a safe bill,' rather than 'How do we write a safe bill?'"[3] What this and other comments show is that opponents of conceal-and-carry were being forced to deal with the reality of a law they had spent many years successfully defeating.

Various critics argued that the law's vagaries and inconsistencies included the following: 1) The law provided a thousand-dollar fine and a one-year jail term for anyone who disclosed the name of a person with a permit. However, at the same time, the law also allowed members of the public to challenge a person's right to a concealed guns permit. How would it be possible to challenge someone's right to a permit if a criminal charge could be filed against anyone who revealed a permit holder's identity? 2) The law provided a sentence of fifteen days and a fine of three hundred dollars for any instructor who falsified an applicant's training record. Given the potentially serious consequences of such fraud, the penalty seemed small and rather out of balance with the penalty for revealing the identity of a permit holder. 3) The law required a background check to get a permit, but it also mandated that applicants be given their permits within forty-five days of applying, even if the background check was not complete. If the background check later came back showing there was reason to revoke the permit, it could be revoked, but to opponents of conceal-and-carry, this set up a dangerous opportunity for criminals to receive legal permits. 4) The law required a background check to receive a permit, but there was no provision for a new background check when renewing the permit after three years. 5) The law was unclear as to whether some government institutions, such as public libraries, would be able to prohibit the carrying of concealed weapons on their premises, because they are generally governed by a form of local government known as special districts and special districts were not mentioned in the conceal-and-carry law at all. The law said the state, courts, and any county or municipality could restrict guns in government buildings, but special districts were not included. 6) While the law adopted by the legislature in 1984 greatly restricted municipalities' ability to pass gun laws contrary to state laws, the conceal-and-carry law specifically allowed cities and counties to extend bans to government-owned or leased facilities. However, many local governments were trying to figure out how to take advantage of this right because the law also appeared to allow elected officials to carry concealed weapons while conducting government business. As James F. Shrewsbury, the president of the St. Louis Board of Aldermen, said,

"One of the most glaring loopholes in this already flawed state legislation is that it makes exemptions for elected officials. The bill I'm introducing this week will require everyone entering a city building to either leave their weapons at home or have them confiscated at the front door."[4]

The potential impact of the government's right to limit concealed guns was further limited, opponents claimed, by the fact that the law mandated that permit-holding violators of the law could be asked to leave, but they could not be charged with a criminal violation. If a licensed bearer of a concealed weapon refused to leave, he or she could be escorted from the building and issued a citation and fined up to one hundred dollars for a first offense, but it was not to be called a criminal violation. This clouded the legal picture a bit, because as some legal analysts observed, the issuance of a citation usually accompanies a criminal charge.[5] To aid cities that wanted to keep guns out of city halls and other government buildings, the Missouri Municipal League wrote a model ordinance for cities to adopt, but there was no guarantee this would solve cities' many potential legal pitfalls. This is just a sample of the many complaints about the new law. More extensive lists of alleged inconsistencies in the law can be found in many places, such as the lawsuit filed against the state by Kansas City Mayor Pro Tem Alvin Brooks and others.[6]

Governor Holden also made news in this area in mid-October when he issued emergency executive rules barring the carrying of concealed weapons into state buildings and facilities, including the capitol, state office buildings, state psychiatric facilities, the state fair complex, and other state-owned or leased property. He made the order, he said, to lessen the danger of conceal-and-carry. The conceal-and-carry law gives certain institutions of state government, such as the state legislature and the Missouri Supreme Court, the right to ban concealed weapons from government-owned buildings. However, the governor's actions extended the ban to all state government buildings, and the law did not specifically give the governor this authority. His rules faced review by Secretary of State Matt Blunt, as well as a joint legislative committee tasked with the job of reviewing executive orders made by the governor. The move was immediately criticized by Larry Crawford. Crawford suggested that contrary to the governor's claim that the ban would make government buildings safe, it would do exactly the opposite. Crawford asserted that the governor did not do a good job keeping government buildings safe and implied that until the governor improved security, state employees were well justified in carrying weapons to use for self-defense.[7]

In the end, some of the governor's bans stuck and others did not. In August 2004, for instance, the State Fair Commission voted to allow concealed weapons on most of the grounds during the 2004 Missouri State Fair. The only place they imposed a ban on guns was in places where alcohol was served, such as the Grandstand, where concerts and other events took place. The director of the fair, Mel Willard, said, "The thinking was, if their sheriff says they are law-abiding citizens, who are we to say they are not law-abiding and responsible citizens?"[8]

In a similar move, the Missouri Gaming Commission adopted a rule allowing guns in casinos, though this commission was much more reluctant than the Fair Commission. Only because the new conceal-and-carry law left it up to the management of individual casinos to decide if a person may enter with a concealed weapon did the commission change its rules, which previously banned all guns from casinos' premises.[9] While it is not expected that casinos' management will suddenly begin allowing people to carry guns into their facilities, it clearly rankled the Gaming Commission to have to change its policy.[10]

Court Fight

Many legal questions surrounded the new conceal-and-carry law as the state waited for it to take effect. In October 2003 a group of ten plaintiffs filed a lawsuit in St. Louis Circuit Court against several defendants, including the state of Missouri and its attorney general, Jay Nixon. The plaintiffs were Kansas City councilman and Mayor Pro Tem Alvin Brooks; Democratic state senators Joan Bray, Maida Coleman, and Rita Heard Days; a Jackson County legislator, Scott Burnett; a St. Louis city alderman, Lyda Krewson; the chief of the Hazelwood Police Department, Carl Wolf; Bishop Willie James Ellis of the St. Louis Clergy Coalition and the New Northside Baptist Church; Pastor B. T. Rice of the St. Louis Clergy Coalition and the New Horizon Christian Church; and a nonprofit group with the "mission of public advocacy for alternatives to violence and injustice," the Institute for Peace and Justice.[11] The case was heard in the courtroom of Judge Steven Ohmer, and when he issued a temporary injunction against the law, pending a hearing on a permanent injunction, Larry Crawford said, "Carjackers and gang bangers are out there holding hands and clapping over this decision today."[12]

The plaintiffs were represented by Burton Newman of Clayton and Richard C. Miller of Kansas City, and they challenged the conceal-and-carry law's constitutionality on a number of grounds. First and foremost, they asserted the law violated Article I, Section 23 of Missouri's current constitution, which was adopted in 1945. The section reads, "That the right of every citizen to keep and bear arms in defense of his home, person and property, or when lawfully summoned in aid of the civil power, shall not be questioned; but this shall not justify the wearing of concealed weapons." This is very similar to wording from Article II, Section 17 of the state's previous constitution, adopted in 1875. It read, "That the right of no citizen to keep and bear arms in defense of his home, person and property, or in aid of the civil power; when thereto legally summoned, shall be called in question; but nothing herein contained is intended to justify the practice of wearing concealed weapons." The plaintiffs' brief asserted that the 1875 constitution clearly banned concealed weapons and the newer constitution strengthened the ban. They argued, "The 1945 Constitution, by reason of the addition of the word 'exception' made it clearer that concealed weapons were prohibited and not part of the limited right to bear arms. Further, the exception itself is more stringent, as the phrase 'intended to justify the practice' was changed to read 'shall not justify the wearing of concealed weapons.'"[13]

The plaintiffs argued that the state's constitution clearly made the wearing of concealed firearms illegal and that the law should be struck down on that basis alone. They asserted that the new law was "unconstitutional because its reach is overly broad and extends beyond rights expressly limited by the Missouri Constitution."[14] The supporters of conceal-and-carry, on the other hand, argued the phrase merely meant the legislature could outlaw concealed guns if it wished, not that concealed guns were expressly forbidden under any circumstances.

The basic constitutionality of concealed weapons was not the plaintiffs' only avenue of attack, however. The plaintiffs' second argument against the bill relied on the Hancock Amendment, Article X, Section 21 of the Missouri Constitution. The Hancock Amendment mandates that state support for local governments may not be reduced and extra activities and services may not be imposed on local governments without full state funding. It reads, "The state is hereby prohibited from reducing the state financed proportion of the costs of any existing activity or service required of counties and other political subdivisions. A new activity or service or an increase in the level of any new activity or service beyond that required by existing law shall not be required by the general assembly or any state agency of counties or other political subdivisions, unless a state appropriation is made and disbursed to pay the county or other political subdivision for any increased costs." This is a prohibition against what politicians at both the state and local level like to refer to as "unfunded mandates." State officials often complain that the federal government requires too much of them without providing adequate funding, and local officials often make the same complaint about state governments.

In the conceal-and-carry case, the plaintiffs argued that forcing counties to conduct background checks and issue permits required them to provide a "new service" that the state had not adequately funded. The conceal-and-carry law allowed sheriffs to charge a permit fee of up to one hundred dollars as part of the application process. However, the plaintiffs argued the fee was insufficient because the law stated that revenue from the fees could only be used for "training and equipment," and not for expenses related to the processing of conceal-and-carry permits. For instance, sheriffs must pay the Missouri State Highway Patrol a thirty-eight-dollar fee for the processing of fingerprint checks, according to testimony given by sheriffs' representatives from four counties during the hearing in Judge Ohmer's courtroom. Since the processing of fingerprints didn't count as "training and equipment," it couldn't be covered by the permit fee and, therefore, it constituted a violation of the Hancock Amendment, according to the plaintiffs.[15]

That the plaintiffs were able to make this claim must have been a bitter pill for supporters of conceal-and-carry, because the only reason the law mandated that permit revenue be used only for training and equipment was because the lobbyist for the Missouri Sheriffs' Association requested such language be included. The reason for this, according to Jorgen Schlemeir, the association's lobbyist, was because sheriffs believed it would cost far less than the hundred-dollar permit fee to process applications and they wanted to be able to keep the additional revenue. Sheriffs worried the excess funds would be taken by county government officials and used to pay for other county services. Schlemeir argued that the intent of the provision was only to limit the use of extra money, not to say the fee couldn't be used for permit processing, but it provided opponents of conceal-and-carry with what proved to be a powerful weapon.[16] The plaintiffs argued the fee couldn't be used for permit processing and Mel Hancock, the creator of the Hancock Amendment, agreed with the claim. While Hancock was a supporter of conceal-and-carry, he said he believed that as the conceal-and-carry law was written, it created an unfunded mandate that made the new law unconstitutional.[17]

The third part of the plaintiffs' case against the conceal-and-carry law was that it violated Article I, Section 1 of the state constitution, which reads: "That all political power is vested in and derived from the people; that all government originates from the people, is founded upon their will only and is instituted solely for the good of the whole." The plaintiffs argued "the people" had expressly rejected conceal-and-carry in a statewide vote in 1999 and claimed the legislature was usurping the power of the people by passing conceal-and-carry just four years later.[18]

The plaintiffs' fourth claim was that the conceal-and-carry law violated the separation of powers, as expressed in Article II, Section 1 of the constitution. They argued that by granting the right to conceal and carry firearms, the legislature had gone "beyond the police power of the legislature to secure the general peace, comfort, safety, health and welfare of the people of the State of Missouri."[19]

Fifth, the plaintiffs argued the law should be found unconstitutional because it was insufficiently detailed. The lawsuit listed twenty-three separate phrases the plaintiffs claimed were too vague or that provided loopholes in the law. They argued, "The language specified below as used in the law does not convey to a person of ordinary intelligence sufficiently definite meaning when measured by common understanding and practices . . . These constitutionally vague terms render the entirety of the conceal-and-carry law unconstitutional because the statute lacks coherent meaning after the vague terminology and phrases are severed from the law."[20] The vagaries the plaintiffs detailed seemed compelling on paper, but defenders of the law would undoubtedly argue that a similar charge could be made against nearly every piece of legislation. Laws are, by nature, often vague. Legislators can be unclear for any number of reasons. Sometimes they pass laws about technical matters of which they have no real knowledge and leave room for professional administrators to fill in the details. Other times legislatures are deliberately vague to avoid being pinned down by angry interest groups or constituents. Finally, sometimes lawmakers are vague purely by accident. The point is, the charge of being too vague may have been accurate, but it wasn't unusual and was unlikely to sway the court.

Attorney General Jay Nixon defended the law while also expressing reservations about it. He classified his concerns as civil liberties–based and argued that a conceal-and-carry law would prompt more traffic-stop searches of motorists by the police.[21] Anticipating such a concern, Kevin Jamison of the Western Missouri Shooters' Alliance said, "There will be a certain period of hysteria . . . and in that six months there may be officers who are overly cautious, but I doubt very much that it's going to last very long. They are going to determine that this is really not changing anything. The guys who will take advantage of this law are not a threat to officers."[22] In addition to his concern about searches, Nixon reiterated a common complaint about the law that Governor Holden expressed in his veto statement, that the law would prompt sheriffs to keep confidential lists of permit holders, allowing them to, as he asserted, form secret armed posses.

The secrecy issue was controversial throughout the 2003 legislative session and continued after it was over. Senator Ken Jacob breathed new life into the dispute during the 2004 legislative session when he proposed an amendment to a bill designed to make changes to Missouri's Open Records and Meetings Law. The bill was SB 1020, and Jacob's amendment would have changed the conceal-and-carry law's prohibition against making public the names of permit holders and would have required county sheriffs to keep lists of permit holders available to the public. In addition, the amendment would have required sheriffs to sign sworn statements for each permit issued affirming that the proper background checks had been conducted.[23] Jacob argued it should be no different than having a hunting or fishing license, which are part of the public record. He said, "Citizens have a right to know when the government permits another citizen to have a permit to carry a concealed weapon."[24] The amendment was defeated in the senate by a vote of 19 to 13, after a debate in which the same unusual defenses of secrecy were presented. For example, Senator Harold Caskey suggested making permit holders' names public would potentially endanger their safety, which was reminiscent of Larry Crawford's comments during debate on the bill in 2003, when Crawford said, "I didn't want these people with conceal-carry endorsements to be a target for thieves."[25] Peter Kinder argued the names of permit holders simply weren't anyone's business. He asserted it was analogous to a person's medical records, which also remain confidential. He said, "That to me is not an issue of the public accountability—which is what I'm getting at . . . that's personal information."[26]

Regardless of his true feelings, Nixon's constitutional obligation was to defend the state law, and he did so vigorously. Politics often makes strange bedfellows, and Nixon was joined in defending the conceal-and-carry law by the NRA, which submitted legal arguments in favor of the new law. In deciding to allow the organization to participate as a friend of the court in the case, Judge Ohmer wrote, "This is an important case. This court welcomes as much information as it can achieve."[27] Both Nixon and the NRA disagreed with the plaintiffs' argument that Article I, Section 23 of the constitution banned concealed weapons. Stephen Halbrook, an attorney for the NRA, argued, "It's always been a matter of legislative discretion to regulate concealed weapons in public—who can carry them, who cannot."[28]

Supporters of the new law argued Article I, Section 23 did not prohibit the carrying of concealed weapons but left the decision up to the state legislature. As the clause was worded, it was possible to argue convincingly for either side in the dispute, and Judge Ohmer's task was to decide whose interpretation was right. It was a thankless task, of course, because whatever he decided, his finding would be immediately appealed.

Regardless of which higher court might eventually decide the case, Ohmer's job was to decide what the words of Article I, Section 23 meant. There was very little public debate recorded on the issue in either 1875, when the clause was originally written, or in 1945, when the state's current constitution was adopted. The constitution clearly gives citizens the right to bear arms in the name of self-defense and in the service of the government. The chair of the committee that wrote the provision on concealed weapons in 1875, Thomas

Gantt, a St. Louis judge with the Missouri Court of Appeals, addressed the issue during the constitutional convention. He said,

> Then this provision goes on and declares, that the right of every citizen to keep and bear arms in support of his House, his person, and his property, when these are unlawfully threatened, shall never be questioned, and that he shall also have the right to bear arms when he is summoned legally or under authority of law to aid the civil processes or to defend the State. There will be no difference of opinion, I think, upon that subject; but then the declaration is distinctly made, Mr. President, that nothing contained in this provision shall be construed to sanction or justify the wearing of concealed weapons. I need not call the attention of my brethren of the Bar to the fact that in one, at least, of the states of the Union, the decision was made that a provision in the Constitution declaring that the right of any citizen to bear arms shall not be questioned, prohibited the Legislature from preventing the wearing of concealed weapons. The wearing of concealed weapons is a practice which I presume meets with the general reprobation of all thinking men. It is a practice which cannot be too severely condemned. It is a practice which is fraught with the most incalculable evil. The committee desired me to say in reference to this provision that they gave no sanction to the idea which is sometimes entertained, not however by our Supreme Court, that the right to bear arms shall not [sic] include the right to carry a pistol in the pocket or a bowie knife under the belt.[29]

It is believed Gantt felt that concealed weapons were bad in part because at the time of the constitutional convention, Jesse James and men of his ilk were running roughshod over the countryside.[30] In addition, the historical record also suggests Gantt's views were influenced by his role in helping to end a long period of bloody street riots between anti-immigrant gangs and Irish immigrants in St. Louis. He seems to have genuinely feared the damage concealed weapons of any sort could do and was troubled by the violence that racked his city.[31] Of course, if this was true, it could lend credence to the claims of conceal-and-carry supporters that the 1875 provision was anti-immigrant and racist. Gantt's words are the only record of the debate on the clause, and they seem to indicate that the clause was included in order to make concealed weapons unconstitutional, but it is impossible to know this with certainty, just as it is impossible to know what motivated the other convention participants.

The plaintiffs, of course, were enthusiastic supporters of Gantt's apparent anti–conceal-and-carry position. The plaintiffs' attorney, Richard Miller, said, "The intent is absolutely clear. Don't you think if they intended for the Legislature to have the right to allow concealed carry, they would have at least mentioned it? There is no mention."[32] Miller was convincing, but it is easy to put an entirely different spin on the words of the constitution. The supporters of conceal-and-carry argued that Miller's interpretation had to be wrong, based on the history of gun laws in Missouri since 1875.

Proponents of conceal-and-carry said that if the plaintiffs' interpretation was correct and the legislature did not have the right to pass laws allowing the carrying of concealed weapons, then not even police officers would be allowed to carry hidden guns when on duty. In their briefs, both the NRA and the attorney general's office pointed to several other laws passed by the legis-lature—some immediately after the adoption of the 1875 constitution that allegedly forbade such concealed weapons—that regulated the wearing of concealed weapons. They argued that if concealed weapons were completely banned by the constitution, there would be no need for the state legislature to regulate them. For example, in 1879, the legislature passed a law banning everyone except law enforcement officers and "persons moving or traveling peaceably through this state" from carrying concealed weapons. The law also allowed anyone charged with violating the law to defend himself by demon-strating "that he has been threatened with great bodily harm, or had good rea-son to carry the same in the necessary defense of his home, person or prop-erty." This was the law that served as the basis for Wayne Crump's support for concealed guns in cars, and both the NRA and Nixon argued that if the claim of the conceal-and-carry opponents was true, then the legislature should never have needed to make this law. Further, it would mean law enforcement officers had been violating the constitution for more than one hundred years.[33]

The NRA's brief suggested the constitutional provision was merely meant to assure legislators "that they are not violating the constitution when they enact regulations specifying the circumstances under which concealed weapons may or may not be carried."[34] In other words, the clause was intended to let everyone know there was not an absolute right to carry concealed weapons and that the legislature could regulate them. This was diametrically opposed to the plaintiffs' interpretation of the clause.

The plaintiffs denied the defendants' claim that if the constitution truly banned the carrying of concealed weapons it meant officers of the law had been violating the constitution for the past century. Rather, the plaintiffs argued the clause's use of the word "citizen" clearly made a distinction between officers of the law and average Missourians. The constitution, they asserted, banned the carrying of concealed weapons by citizens, not by law enforcement officials. Therefore, it was incorrect to argue that their interpretation meant law enforcement personnel had been breaking the law since 1875, because they are not typical citizens.[35]

The sponsors of the law were clearly angered by the suit. Both Senator Caskey and Representative Crawford characterized the suit as a pathetic, last-ditch attempt to forestall the inevitable. Caskey said the constitutional claims had no legal merit and called the lawsuit "a desperate attempt to prolong the issue."[36] This was a harsh criticism and probably an unfair one. There was enough ambiguity in the constitution to justify the legal challenge—but it is also easy to understand Caskey's frustration. Larry Crawford also derisively dismissed the plaintiffs' claims when he said they were "whining that their way wasn't the way of the people who were elected."[37]

The lawsuit was originally delayed by a procedural question. The case was filed in St. Louis County, and the attorney general asked that it be moved to Cole County Circuit Court because the state capitol is in Cole County and therefore was the proper venue for suits against the state. Ultimately, Judge Ohmer kept the case in St. Louis County because the plaintiffs added the St. Louis County sheriff, James Murphy, as a defendant in the suit, clearly giving Ohmer's court jurisdiction. Next, Ohmer issued a temporary injunction on October 10, 2003, preventing the law from taking effect. Responding to the injunction, Kevin Jamison of the Western Missouri Shooters Alliance insisted the judge's ruling would be overturned. He argued, "The plaintiffs went judge shopping and they found what they wanted. Their petition is unbelievably frivolous. It shows a complete misunderstanding of the law."[38] He further argued that the constitutional clause in question was meant only to say there is no guaranteed right to concealed guns, not that concealed guns are unconstitutional. Therefore, Jamison asserted, it was perfectly legitimate for the legislature to approve.[39] The attorney general immediately appealed the restraining order, but the appeal was rejected by both the Eastern District Court of Appeals and the Missouri Supreme Court. It would have been very unusual had either appellate court overturned Judge Ohmer's order so early in the legal process.

On November 7, 2003, the judge announced his decision in the case and issued a permanent injunction against the law, finding it violated Article I, Section 23 of Missouri's Constitution of Missouri. He rejected the rest of the plaintiffs' arguments, including their claim that the law violated the Hancock Amendment, despite the evidence about unfunded costs presented by sheriffs' departments from four counties. Addressing Hancock, Ohmer wrote, "It is certainly questionable whether this law establishes a new activity on the part of existing Sheriffs' duties. However, there is no evidence to support the proposition that the law will result in increased costs to the Sheriffs' offices of the State. It is clear that the One Hundred Dollar ($100.00) application fee will be more than adequate to cover any increased costs. Therefore, this funding mechanism of the application and renewal fees under the law adequately satisfy the Hancock Amendment. Accordingly, Plaintiffs' challenge to the law under the Hancock Amendment—Article X, Section 21 is hereby DENIED."[40] For Ohmer, the specific wording of the law, which required the one-hundred-dollar fee only be used for training and equipment, was not problematic. This part of his decision would be revisited by the state's supreme court.

While Ohmer rejected nearly all of the plaintiffs' claims, he accepted the most significant one, that the new law violated Article I, Section 23 of the constitution. In his opinion, he explained the difficulty of his decision, writing, "The words of Article I, Section 23 of the Missouri Constitution are simple and easily read, but what do they mean? Also, what are the 'plain and ordinary' meaning of the words? That is not so simple. While the words are simple and clear, their meaning in the context of the Constitution is not definitive. This Court never said or implied anything to the contrary. Consequently, this Court must review a variety of sources and historical material in order to determine the meaning of these words in their constitutional context."[41] In his decision, Ohmer reviewed the wording of other state constitutions, relevant precedents, previous laws passed by the General Assembly of Missouri, and the 1875 constitutional debates. After reviewing other state constitutions, he suggested that while they were informative, they had no relevance for the law in Missouri. As for precedents, he concluded that none of the cases he reviewed came close enough to the current case and wrote, "The issue before this court is one of first impression."[42]

In the third part of his analysis, he concluded that laws previously passed by the legislature involving the carrying of concealed weapons were immaterial to answering the basic constitutional question in the case. What he meant was that it wasn't possible to change the meaning of the constitution by violating it a few times. Just because no one had challenged such violations in the past did not mean they weren't violations.[43]

Having exhausted these avenues of inquiry, Ohmer was left with trying to determine the intent of the people who wrote the constitutional clause. He wrote, "Finally then, where the language of a constitutional provision is clear, resort to the constitutional debate is not necessary. In light of the lack of a clear and definitive interpretation or meaning of the words of the Constitution, this Court must turn to the constitutional debates in order to decipher the meaning of Article I, Section 23 of the Missouri Constitution."[44] Since there was no record of debate on the clause in 1945, he determined that Article I, Section 23 was basically the same as the clause in the 1875 constitution and turned his analysis to that debate. In his analysis of the record from 1875, Ohmer concluded, "It seems clear from this history that the intent of the framers and the people who adopted the Constitution were to not justify the wearing of concealed weapons."[45] While Article III, Section 1 of the Missouri Constitution, he wrote, clearly gives the legislature the ability to regulate the right to bear arms, it must be done "under the limitation of Article I, Section 23 . . . To read the Constitutional provision and to find otherwise would make the words of the second clause of Article I, Section 23 a nullity."[46] Ohmer's decision was that the constitution meant the legislature could allow persons to carry weapons, but not to carry them concealed on their persons.

The defendants were quite unhappy with Ohmer's decision, of course. Attorney General Nixon immediately appealed to the Supreme Court of Missouri. He said, "We will be asking the Missouri Supreme Court to expedite this matter so we can have a full and final decision on this important public policy issue."[47] Nixon asked for a supreme court hearing on December 3, 2003, prompting the plaintiffs to complain they wouldn't have enough time to fully prepare their case if it was heard that quickly. Attorneys Newman and Miller argued they needed time to be ready to argue not only the provision the judge cited but also to re-argue the other four points they'd made in their lawsuit that the judge rejected. They complained that the attorney general was trying to rush the case and that his greater resources, including the NRA, gave him an unfair advantage if the schedule was rushed.[48] The court ultimately delayed the case's hearing until the end of January.

Governor Holden not surprisingly supported Judge Ohmer's ruling. He said, "Today's ruling will help protect the people of this state who voted against conceal-and-carry in 1999."[49] He added, "I didn't think the law was constitutional. That's the reason I vetoed it."[50] One of the plaintiffs, St. Louis Alderman Lyda Krewson, said she was pleased "that the constitution continues to protect the citizens of the state of Missouri from people who have concealed weapons in their purses, jacket pockets and glove compartments."[51] One of the plaintiffs' attorneys, Burton Newman, said, "Our ultimate goal has always been a determination with the Missouri Supreme Court that conceal-and-carry is unconstitutional."[52] If nothing else, Ohmer's decision was a bit of sunshine for the gun control side after a bruising defeat in the legislature.

On the other side, the NRA's attorney, Stephen Halbrook, reiterated his argument that the constitutional provision wasn't intended to make concealed handguns illegal and suggested the supreme court would arrive at the same conclusion. To support this, he again argued there were already exceptions to Article I, Section 23 allowing the police to carry concealed weapons and citizens to conceal weapons in their homes. He said, "Ever since Missouri has been a state, the legislature has decided when and where to either allow or prohibit concealed weapons."[53] Halbrook also suggested the plaintiffs' case was without precedent and, as such, had no chance to survive the supreme court. He said, "This is the first time anyone in American legal history has ever argued that a state bill of rights outlawed concealed weapons," as if to suggest such a notion was completely incomprehensible.[54] Of course, new precedents are made in every case; that is what supreme courts are for.

The bill's house sponsor, Larry Crawford, who was originally derisive in his dismissal of the suit, changed his tone following Ohmer's decision and said he had always expected the issue to end up before the Missouri Supreme Court. He also said, "If there was any issue to go to the Supreme Court on, this is the one I would want. This puts us in the best position to win."[55] He suggested it was appropriate for the court to make the final decision, and he was clearly confident the judges would rule in favor of conceal-and-carry.

The editors of the *St. Louis Post-Dispatch,* who had long opposed conceal-and-carry, took a surprisingly critical position against Ohmer's decision. An editorial argued that Ohmer had misinterpreted Gantt's words, and the paper largely adopted the NRA's position on Article I, Section 23. The editorial read, in part,

> Judge Gantt said wearing concealed guns was 'fraught with the most incalculable evil.' But he went on to say that the committee that wrote the wording 'gave no sanction to the idea . . . that the right to bear arms shall not include the right to carry a pistol in the pocket or a bowie knife under the belt.' Judge Ohmer points to Judge Gantt's double-negative statement as clear proof that the intent was 'to not justify the wearing of concealed weapons.' The words say quite the opposite—that hidden knives and guns are allowed. If the constitution meant what Judge Ohmer says it means, a century of laws that permit prison guards to carry concealed weapons would be unconstitutional. But no one ever argued that. Nor did gun opponents or Gov. Bob Holden suggest the law was unconstitutional during legislative debate— even though the governor revised history last week by saying he had vetoed the bill because it was unconstitutional.[56]

The editorial was perhaps an attempt by the paper to demonstrate some level of fair play, but it was wrong in this regard: Despite the *Post-Dispatch's* argument to the contrary, the wording of constitutions is rarely crystal clear, and in this case, there was certainly room for debate.

After Ohmer's decision, the status of the conceal-and-carry law in Missouri was as ambiguous as ever. An editorial in the *Springfield News-Leader* argued it was appropriate for the issue to end up with the Missouri Supreme Court after such a long, tortured history. The author expressed hope that "[o]nce conceal-and-carry makes it through all branches of government, there may be greater clarity and unanimity about its legitimacy."[57] The editorial was right; it was certainly appropriate for the courts to weigh in on the issue. The question in Missouri, however, was whether the supreme court would really resolve the issue, or whether its ruling would just be another stop in a never completed journey.

In a precursor to the hearing before the supreme court hearing, on December 18, 2003, Judge Ohmer rejected a second claim that the concealed weapons law violated the Hancock Amendment. He rejected this claim in his original November decision, but at the same time he told the plaintiffs' attorneys he would reconsider the argument. The second time around, the plaintiffs claimed not only that the law created an unfunded mandate but also that by using the fees to cover departmental expenses for equipment and training, sheriffs' departments would be using the money for things that would otherwise require a tax. This was, they argued, also a violation of the Hancock Amendment.[58] The attorney general's office argued that this claim of a violation of the Hancock Amendment had no legal merit; for the second time, Judge Ohmer agreed.

Developments Near and Far as Conceal-and-Carry Awaits Its Day in Court

As the conceal-and-carry law waited to appear before the Missouri Supreme Court, the state of Ohio became the thirty-seventh state to adopt a so-called "shall issue" conceal-and-carry law. When Governor Taft signed the bill on January 7, 2004, it allowed the NRA to claim that more than half of the American population now lived in states with the right to carry.

Also while the conceal-and-carry law awaited its day in court, another state was embroiled in a fight very much like the Show-Me Showdown. Wisconsin has had a long, ugly struggle over conceal-and-carry very similar to Missouri's fight. As Missourians waited for the state's supreme court to weigh in, Wisconsinites watched a titanic struggle between their governor and their legislature. The parallels between the two states are quite striking. The battle dragged over many years in both states, and in 2003 both states had divided governments, with a legislature controlled by the Republicans and a Democratic governor. When Wisconsin's legislature passed conceal-and-carry in late 2003, its governor, Jim Doyle, quickly vetoed the bill, complaining about the NRA's influence over the legislature. He said, "The legislative leadership had really totally been taken over by the NRA on this one. The NRA was even scheduling the time for votes on this measure. It really was a great example where special interests were just trying to roll over the will of the people here—and on a very important issue."[59] The legislature attempted to overturn the Democratic governor's veto in early February 2004.

The Wisconsin Senate voted to override, with five Democrats siding with eighteen Republicans, but in the house, the tally was 65 to 34, one vote short of the total needed. Symbolically, the override vote came down to one representative, Democrat Gary Sherman, much as the veto override symbolically came down to Jim Mathewson in Missouri. Sherman was a ruralite, an NRA member, and a cosponsor of the conceal-and-carry bill. Those characteristics should have added up to an easy decision to override the veto, but Sherman was angry with the Republican leadership of the house. He argued the veto override was simply an attempt to embarrass the governor, and he suggested Republicans were unwilling to compromise in ways that might have made the veto fight unnecessary.[60] Rather than give the Republicans a chance to embarrass his governor, Sherman, unlike Mathewson in Missouri, voted against the override. The Republicans and the NRA promised Sherman would pay a political price and set their sights on the 2004 election, when they planned to get more pro-gun legislators elected. Because Sherman chose party over guns, the issue is still unsettled in Wisconsin, where the two sides will continue to badger each other for at least one more legislative session.

As Missourians waited for their supreme court to decide the constitutionality of conceal-and-carry, yet another state was engaged in debate about the right to carry—Missouri's neighbor, Kansas. Like Missouri and Wisconsin, conceal-and-carry has been an oft-repeated issue in the halls of Kansas's state capitol in Topeka. In 2004, as legislators pushed to pass a conceal-and-carry bill, Democratic Governor Kathleen Sebelius promised, as her counterparts in Missouri and Wisconsin did, to veto it. Throughout the legislative session, Sebelius said things like, "Our crime rates are better than any of the surrounding states with conceal-and-carry," and "I am not a fan of conceal-and-carry measures, and while I have not seen the final bill, unless there's something in it I don't understand, it would be my intention to veto it."[61] And veto it she did. Unlike Missouri, where there were enough votes to override the veto, and Wisconsin, where supporters were just one vote short of an override, Sebelius had a more comfortable margin. Supporters of conceal-and-carry in Kansas would have to wait at least one more year. They promised to put all their energy into getting more pro-gun legislators elected in 2004, but they will have to deal with Governor Sebelius until at least 2006.

In January 2004 the Missouri Supreme Court heard the appeal of Judge Ohmer's decision on conceal-and-carry. In February they issued their opinion, and while they answered many of the questions about the legality of concealed weapons under Missouri's constitution, they raised a different objection that left people on both sides of the issue scrambling.

Chapter Twenty-Two

The Supremes Have Their Say and the Issue Is Settled—Sort Of

The week before the case was heard by the Missouri Supreme Court, the New Mexico Supreme Court issued a decision that was directly relevant to the case in Missouri. Gun control plaintiffs in New Mexico filed a suit to block that state's new conceal-and-carry law. Much like the suit in Missouri, the plaintiffs invoked a state constitutional clause. Article I, Section 23 of the Missouri Constitution contains the phrase "... but this shall not justify the wearing of concealed weapons," whereas the New Mexico Constitution reads, "... but nothing herein shall be held to permit the carrying of concealed weapons." The New Mexico Supreme Court found the state's conceal-and-carry law did not violate the constitution. Rather than interpreting the phrase to mean concealed weapons could never be legal, the court decided that the constitution merely meant concealed weapons were not a right, but a privilege to be regulated by the legislature.[1] This was precisely the argument made by the supporters of conceal-and-carry in Missouri, and prompted them to suggest the New Mexico decision was a good omen for the Show-Me State. There is no legal requirement that one state supreme court follow the precedents of another state supreme court, but Attorney General Nixon said, "The constitutional provision is similar, the argument is similar, and the justices on the New Mexico Supreme Court rejected that argument. This court in New Mexico has further given credence to our boring, yet reasonable argument."[2] It was powerful medicine for the defenders of conceal-and-carry and was probably discouraging for the other side.

The Missouri case was heard by the Missouri Supreme Court on January 22, 2004. During the hearing, the judges heard conflicting testimony from attorneys on the meaning of Article I, Section 23 of the Missouri Constitution, and many of the judges' questions centered on the meaning of the word "justify."

The justices pressed the plaintiffs to define the word, and attorney Burton Newman said it meant "allow."[3] With this definition, Article I, Section 23 would read ". . . but this shall not allow the wearing of concealed weapons," and would therefore mean concealed weapons were meant to be unconstitutional, according to Newman.

Arguing the state's case, Paul Wilson, a deputy attorney general, cited the state legislature's long history of regulating concealed weapons and said the new law was no different. Echoing the arguments made by many proponents of conceal-and-carry, he said, "No state in the country has bought the argument they're bringing to you today."[4]

For all the emphasis in the press about the meaning of Article I, Section 23, however, it wasn't the part of the case that captured the imagination of the judges. The judges seemed most interested in the allegation that the law violated the Hancock Amendment, which Judge Ohmer rejected twice. The judges asked several questions seeking further elaboration on the Hancock Amendment's role in the dispute. If the law did violate Hancock, as the plaintiffs claimed, it could lead to lawsuits against the state from sheriffs' departments, or suits against county governments by interested citizens. The judges spent most of the thirty-minute hearing on Hancock.

Approximately a month passed following the hearing before the court issued its decision. Several days before the court announced its finding, Representative Crawford made an unusual request of the supporters of conceal-and-carry. Speaking at a pro-gun rally in Jefferson City in late February, Crawford warned supporters not to harass the supreme court justices as they made their decision. He said, "The court's decision cannot be rushed . . . We certainly would not want to harm the outcome by inappropriate words or actions."[5] Clearly, Crawford and the gun lobby wanted its rank-and-file followers to understand that grassroots tactics such as calling and e-mailing that were usually so effective on legislators wouldn't work on the members of the Missouri Supreme Court.

The court issued its opinion on February 26, 2004. In a 5 to 2 vote, the judges affirmed Ohmer's decision in part and reversed it in part. The majority opinion was written by Judge Stephen Limbaugh. Most important for the supporters of conceal-and-carry, the court reversed Ohmer by finding Article I, Section 23 was not a prohibition of concealed weapons. They found that the clause merely granted the legislature the right to decide if concealed weapons would be legal and, if so, for whom and under what conditions. Explaining this portion of the decision, Judge Limbaugh first engaged in an examination of common dictionary definitions of the words in the clause and concluded the words should be read differently than Judge Ohmer read them. The common meanings of certain phrases were included in brackets by Limbaugh to illustrate what the majority felt was Article I, Section 23's true meaning. He wrote, "... but this [the right of every citizen to keep and bear arms ...] shall not justify [shall not warrant, shall not furnish grounds or evidence for, shall not support, or shall not provide sufficient legal reasons for] the wearing of concealed weapons."[6]

This did not mean Missourians had a right to carry concealed weapons, but it did mean the legislature had the right to decide who would be granted the privilege of carrying them. Limbaugh wrote, "In short, the words used are plain and unambiguous. There is no constitutional prohibition against the wearing of concealed weapons; there is only a prohibition against invoking the right to keep and bear arms to justify the wearing of concealed weapons. Consequently, the General Assembly, which has plenary power to enact legislation on any subject in the absence of a constitutional provision ... has the final say in the use and regulation of concealed weapons. Accordingly, this Court holds that the Concealed-Carry Act is not unconstitutional under article I, section 23."[7] With this finding, Ohmer's sole reason for imposing an injunction against the act was overruled. This was, in theory, exactly the decision the supporters of conceal-and-carry hoped to get.

The supporters of conceal-and-carry got more good news when Limbaugh affirmed two conclusions reached by Judge Ohmer, ruling that the claims of the plaintiffs "merit little attention." First, he found there was no merit in the plaintiffs' claims that the law violated the will of the people by reversing the Prop B vote. He wrote, "No court, at least in this state, has ever so held, and obviously, to do so would be to call into question the entire concept of representative democracy."[8] Second, he rejected the claim that the law was too vague. He wrote, "... plaintiffs contend that the Act is unconstitutionally vague because it fails to provide adequate notice of the prohibited conduct and set standards for its fair enforcement. Plaintiffs' sole support for their argument, however, consists of nothing more than a series of far-fetched hypotheticals. This approach is inconsistent with the long-standing rule in addressing such claims that 'it is not necessary to determine if a situation could be imagined in which the language used might be vague or confusing; the language is to be treated by applying it to the facts at hand.' At some time in the future plaintiffs' hypotheticals might arise as actual disputes; however, at this time they are merely conjecture."[9] As is true with most courts, the Missouri Supreme Court was not going to issue a peremptory strike against a possibly vague piece of legislation. So far, the forces defending the right-to-carry had won every battle, as the court threw out each of the plaintiffs' objections and said the law was constitutional. However, the court then created an unexpected obstacle to the implementation of the new law by reversing another part of Ohmer's decision. Ohmer twice found there was no merit in the plaintiffs' claim that the new law violated the Hancock Amendment. The judges of the supreme court had a different perspective, however.

The court found that for at least four counties—Camden, Cape Girardeau, Greene, and Jackson—the conceal-and-carry law violated the Hancock Amendment ban on unfunded mandates. This did not mean all conceal-and-carry laws would violate the amendment, or that the law couldn't be fixed, but in its current form, it violated Hancock. Before explaining how the new law violated Hancock, Limbaugh first refuted the state's assertion that the plaintiffs did not have legal standing to bring a case based on Hancock. Limbaugh wrote, "In the Hancock context, standing is conferred not by case law, but by the Constitution. Article X, section 23 states '. . . any taxpayer of the state, county or other political subdivision shall have standing to bring suit in a proper venue . . . to enforce provision of sections 16 through 22 inclusive of the article . . . ' Under section 23, plaintiffs claim taxpayer standing to enjoin enforcement of the Act statewide. At first glance, though, challenge is to a fee imposed only on the county level, which means that standing can be met only by individual taxpayers within each county. However, by directing that the sheriff in each county *shall* charge a fee of up to $100 for the issuance of each permit, it is the state that is imposing the fee, and it is doing so on a statewide basis. As such, plaintiffs have taxpayer standing to challenge the Act statewide, but, as will be discussed, a statewide remedy is inappropriate."[10]

Having established the plaintiffs' right to sue under Hancock, Limbaugh explained why the new conceal-and-carry law created an unfunded mandate. He wrote, "On the merits of plaintiffs' claim, the question is whether the provision for a sheriff's fee of up to $100—assuming the fee is otherwise constitutional—is sufficient to fund the increased costs in each county. The fee cannot be used to offset costs directly, but must be credited to the sheriff's revolving fund, section 571.094.10, which can be used only for training and equipment, section 50.535.2. Although some of the increased costs may be incurred for training and equipment and properly reimbursed from the fund, substantial costs may be incurred for other purposes, as well. If so, there is an unfunded mandate."[11] Part of the application process involved a fingerprint check. The "substantial cost" Limbaugh referred to was the thirty-eight-dollar fee sheriffs would pay the Highway Patrol for each fingerprint check.

Finally, Limbaugh explained why the court found that the law violated Hancock for only 4 of Missouri's 114 counties. He suggested Hancock might affect every county in the state, but at the time of the decision the court only had evidence from Camden, Cape Girardeau, Greene, and Jackson Counties because they were the only counties to present evidence during the original trial. Limbaugh wrote,

> As noted, the testimony regarding anticipated activities and costs in implementing the Act pertained to only four counties—Jackson, Greene, Cape Girardeau, and Camden. The evidence from Jackson County, all uncontroverted, was that costs of approximately $150,000 will be incurred in the first year alone to provide the personnel to fingerprint and conduct background checks on applicants and to otherwise process the permit applications. That projection was based on an estimated 5,000–6,000 applications, which in turn were based on county population and the fact that under existing law, approximately 5,000 firearms transfer permits are issued in the county each year. Testimony was also presented that in addition to the $150,000 cost for personnel, it would be necessary to engage the Missouri State Highway Patrol to conduct fingerprint analysis at $38 per case. Although there was little evidence to show the estimated number of permit applications in each county, it is not disputed that there will be more than a few. The fact remains, though, that even if there are only a few, for each one the increased cost to the county will be at least $38, and as a result, the case is ripe in each county... This conclusion, of course, governs application of the Act in all of Missouri's counties, but, in this case, specific evidence of increased costs was indeed presented for the four counties at issue. In fact, the same evidence that makes the case ripe for adjudication as to those counties—the costs for personnel in Jackson County and for the Highway Patrol fingerprint analyses in all four counties—is the same evidence that proves the Hancock violation on the merits of the case. This Court holds, therefore, that the Act constitutes an unfunded mandate in Jackson, Cape Girardeau, Green, and Camden Counties for which an injunction will lie prohibiting enforcement by the state... These counties are not required to comply with the Act to the extent that it mandates them to expend funds for that purpose.[12]

Since no other sheriff's departments presented evidence in Ohmer's courtroom, the supreme court concluded it was premature to conclude Hancock would be violated in any of the state's other counties, but Limbaugh predicted similar claims could be made if evidence was provided.

Interestingly, the sheriffs of the four counties did not necessarily agree with the court's decision. John Page, the sheriff of Camden County, said, "I don't see it as an unfunded mandate; never did," and explained he would get around the expense of processing application by having applicants pay the Highway Patrol directly, which would keep his office out of it. Sheriff Page also suggested any administrative costs of issuing permits could be paid for by the tuition for the county's firearms training course.[13] Despite the court's finding, three of the four counties, Camden, Cape Girardeau, and Greene, were accepting applications for conceal-and-carry permits by April 2004.

Responding to the supreme court's ruling, the Attorney General's Office immediately produced a short model bill for the legislature. Jay Nixon suggested the simple fix would eliminate the flaw cited by Limbaugh. Understanding that the problem should be relatively easy to fix, several legislators quickly introduced legislation to correct the flaw. Senator John Cauthorn introduced SB 1341, which would have changed the conceal-and-carry law to allow the permit fees to be used for the processing of applications. As it was passed, the law read, "This fund shall only be used by law enforcement agencies for the purchase of equipment and to provide training." Cauthorn's bill would have changed it to read, "This fund shall only be used by law enforcement agencies for the purchase of equipment and to provide training; and any reasonable expenses related to accepting and processing the application required pursuant to section 571.101, RSMO."[14] The bill was introduced on March 1 and went to the Senate Judiciary and Civil and Criminal Justice Committee on March 8, where it was eventually folded into SB 1332, sponsored by Senator Harold Caskey. This bill would allow sheriffs to use their sheriff's revolving funds to pay for all expenses related to the processing of conceal-and-carry permit applications.[15] It would also have allowed sheriffs to charge more than the one-hundred-dollar limit stipulated in the original legislation if they could demonstrate it was necessary to charge more. As the session ran toward its end, however, the bill seemed likely to run out of time.

Like Cauthorn and Caskey, Representative Larry Crawford sponsored a bill to fix conceal-and-carry in the house. His bill, HB 1565, would also allow sheriffs to use the permit fees to cover the expenses of issuing permits. The bill would add the following language to the existing act: "This fund shall only be used by law enforcement agencies for the purchase of equipment and to provide training; and any reasonable expenses related to accepting and processing such applications."[16] The bill was voted out of the House Crime Prevention and Public Safety Committee on April 13, but as of the end of April it still had not been added to the house calendar for a perfection vote. As with the senate bill, however, as the session ran out of time, the legislature failed to address the flaw in 2004.

In his decision, Limbaugh also assessed the possibility that the counties might be able to voluntarily raise money to pay for the expenses related to processing conceal-and-carry permits. He concluded that they may not. He wrote,

> ... the parties do not raise, nor do we address, the question of whether a county's governing body can still elect to fund the increased costs on a

voluntary basis from other county revenue sources that are not dedicated for some other mandated use. In any event, that portion of increased costs attributable to training and equipment can still be recouped by imposition of a sheriff's fee, again assuming the fee is constitutional. However, in the event the fee charged exceeds the amount of estimated actual costs of training and equipment necessary for processing the permit applications, as has been proposed by the three sheriffs testifying in this case, that excess cannot fairly be characterized as a permissible "user fee." Instead, it falls within Article X, section 22 of the Hancock Amendment, which, as explained, prohibits counties and other political subdivisions from levying any "tax, license or fees" without voter approval.[17]

Therefore, the counties that wished to find a way around the Hancock amendment because the citizens of those counties want to get conceal-and-carry permits might be precluded from doing so without first seeking the approval of all the counties' voters. Judging from the results of the Prop B election in 1999, where all but ten counties voted yes, passing such fees would be pro forma in most counties, but it would force them to jump an additional, costly, legal hurdle.

Not all of the law was affected by the Hancock problem. For instance, Limbaugh found no problem with the right for those twenty-one years and older to keep a concealed gun in their car, since no permit was required; the right to use a firearm in self-defense; and the prohibition of concealed weapons in certain areas and locations. Another part of the law Limbaugh determined was untouched by the Hancock Amendment was a clause that made it legal for people with conceal-and-carry permits from other states to carry their concealed guns in Missouri.[18]

Since the Hancock ruling caused many Missouri counties to delay the issuing of permits out of fear of being sued, many frustrated gun advocates began to apply for permits from states that grant permits to nonresidents such as Florida, Pennsylvania, and Utah, because the new law in Missouri granted reciprocity to other conceal-and-carry states, meaning out-of-state permits are honored in Missouri. Not every state with conceal-and-carry honors permits from other states and, in fact, there are many states, such as Texas, whose officials have said they will not honor conceal-and-carry permits from Missouri, but ensuring such reciprocity across the country is one of the current goals of the NRA. If Missourians were able to get out-of-state permits, they would be able to legally carry a concealed gun in Missouri. One state that was especially popular for Missourians in the spring of 2004 was Pennsylvania, because it issued permits to nonresidents for only twenty dollars and the application could be done over the Internet.

For example, Centre County, Pennsylvania, had an on-line permit application that was bombarded by Missouri residents after the county's Web address
appeared on the Web sites of pro-gun groups in Missouri. The sheriff of Centre County, Denny Nau, said, "The last few weeks have been overwhelming
from Missouri. All of a sudden, we were getting 200 a day."[19] Overwhelmed,
the sheriff finally stopped accepting applications for permits from Missouri residents, saying it was because he was uncertain about the legal status of conceal-
and-carry in Missouri. He said, "I'm still confused. I read one day that all
counties but four can get a license to carry, but then I turn around and see the
attorney general saying, 'I don't want anyone issuing.' Another day I see where
so-and-so can get a license to carry."[20]

An entirely different interpretation of the Hancock Amendment was suggested in the dissenting opinion of Chief Justice Ronnie White—the same
Ronnie White who helped kill conceal-and-carry legislation in 1992 and was
involved in John Ashcroft's tumultuous confirmation hearing. The Hancock
Amendment requires that any new mandate imposed on local governments
must be "fully financed." Judge Limbaugh's analysis assumed that if the sheriffs were allowed to use the one-hundred-dollar fee to cover their processing
expenses, Hancock would be satisfied. White, however, argued that making
the counties collect a fee to pay their own expenses was itself a violation of
Hancock.

In White's estimation, the Hancock Amendment demanded the state fully
fund any new requirements it made of the counties. Allowing the county to
collect a fee, no matter what it may be used for, was not the same thing as
providing full funding. He argued that if the state was going to authorize
conceal-and-carry permits and require the county sheriffs to process the permits, the state must reimburse the counties for any expenses related to that
new duty. Therefore, White asserted, the court's majority was wrong to limit
its finding of a Hancock violation to just four counties.

In his opinion, White wrote,

> Hancock requires full state funding, period. Full state funding means fund-
> ing from state revenue, and the $100 license fee authorized by the Act for
> county revenue is totally irrelevant. All of Missouri's remaining counties will
> incur an unfunded mandate to satisfy the Act's requirements for background
> checks, fingerprint analysis, and the associated administrative labor costs
> and record keeping each time an applicant applies for a license to carry a
> concealed firearm. The state essentially concedes this point and does not
> argue that the Act does not create additional services and activities increas-
> ing county expenditures, but rather urges that the evidence presented at
> trial demonstrates that the application fee authorized by the legislature will

pay for those additional expenses . . . Hancock requires that the State, and only the State, fully fund this mandate. The individual counties do not have legal authority to saddle their taxpayers with the unfunded mandate by drawing funds from other sources of county revenue. Any money diverted and expended by a county or political subdivision to finance the implementation of the Conceal and Carry Act, that is not provided directly from state revenue by a state appropriation, is money directly taken from the county taxpayers, each of whom has independent standing for injunctive relief . . . I would hold that until a specific appropriation is made by the state to cover the unfunded mandate imposed by the Act that no county need comply with implementing the Conceal and Carry Act.[21]

For White, the case was simple, based solely on the Hancock Amendment. In fact, he argued, the court didn't need to address Article I, Section 23 at all since the law blatantly violated Hancock. His opinion was not binding, but it certainly could be the basis of a new challenge to the law somewhere down the line.

In addition to the many implications of the court's decision for conceal-and-carry, some suggested it could have a much broader impact on state and local government relations. While the court's decision was not as strict as Justice White suggested in his dissent, the opinion was still a fairly hard-line interpretation of the Hancock Amendment, and many state officials feared it could have implications for other requirements the state makes of local governments. Larry Crawford said, "The ruling is going to make the counties and local governments more aware that we do put unfunded mandates on them."[22] With this precedent on the books, local government officials could begin to challenge many laws they felt place unfunded mandates on their governments. Senator Wayne Goode, D–St. Louis, suggested the ruling could cause a great deal of trouble, especially in a time of state budget shortages, when one option is to pass some of the costs of state programs down to the counties. He said, "If there was a very strict interpretation of Hancock, it would be very, very difficult to find funding for whatever would be included."[23] It is difficult to predict how successful local governments would be suing the state government, but this decision by the court could help them, unless the state legislature did something to rectify the problem.

When the court handed down its decision, the state legislature was already in session. When the champions of conceal-and-carry, like Larry Crawford and Harold Caskey, read the court's opinion regarding the Hancock Amendment, they tried to move quickly to fix the problem. What they found, however, was that even with majority support for conceal-and-carry in the legislature, what seemed like a simple issue to fix wasn't simple at all.

Chapter Twenty-Three

In the Aftermath of the Court's Decision

The implications of the Missouri Supreme Court's decision were significant for conceal-and-carry. While the court gave the champions of conceal-and-carry an incredibly important victory by finding it was constitutional for the legislature to create the right to carry, at the same time, the judges opened an enormous can of worms with their Hancock finding. First of all, the decision meant individual legal challenges could potentially be mounted in each of Missouri's 114 counties. Attorney General Jay Nixon predicted legal chaos in the wake of the decision unless something was quickly done to fix the law. He said, "Until the legislature passes the simple, quick Hancock fix that needs to be done, we can expect a continuous litigation rodeo throughout Missouri."[1] Without a change in the wording, he warned, lawsuits based on the court's finding could swamp county sheriffs, tax the legal system, and keep conceal-and-carry in limbo for some time.

The Lawsuits Begin

The first Hancock-based lawsuit was filed in March 2004. Ignoring Nixon's warning, Larry Crawford and his wife applied for, and were granted, conceal-and-carry permits. On March 1 the Crawfords apparently became the first Missourians to receive permits. They were issued by the sheriff of Moniteau County, Kenny Jones, after the Crawfords paid sixty-eight dollars each with their applications, writing separate checks to the Highway Patrol for the fingerprint checks and to Sheriff Jones for processing, in an attempt to create a precedent around the supreme court's decision. The checks were thirty-eight dollars for the fingerprint checks and thirty dollars for processing costs.[2] Speaking of being the first in the state to receive a permit, Crawford said, "I've been talking with sheriffs all around the state and gun movement people. I don't actually know that I am, but I haven't heard of anyone else, and people are saying 'You're probably the first.'"[3] He sought the first permit because he sponsored the bill. He said, "I'm more interested in going through the process than carrying right now."[4] Sheriff Jones said, "It was only fitting that he got the first one."[5] It was a symbolic moment for the advocates of conceal-and-carry, but if Crawford applied for the first permit to test the process for problems, he found one, because his permit led to legal action.

On March 11, 2004, the same lawyers who represented the plaintiffs in the Davis case, Burton Newman and Richard Miller, filed a lawsuit for Robert Barry, a resident of Moniteau County, against Sheriff Jones, Moniteau County, and the state government. Jones was subsequently dropped as a defendant, but the suit continued against the other defendants.[6] Barry's contention, expressed through his lawyers, was that by granting the permit to the Crawfords, the county "incurred costs not provided for by the state and used local money for a purpose not approved by local voters, both in violation of what is known as the Hancock Amendment to the Missouri Constitution."[7] The blueprint for this argument, of course, was drawn for the anti–conceal-and-carry forces by the opinion of Judge Limbaugh, though the suit went further than Limbaugh's opinion and borrowed from Chief Justice White's dissent by suggesting "that the fee should have been approved by local voters and that the law is unconstitutional statewide because it depends on a local fee instead of a direct payment from the state."[8] In other words, Barry's suit said that since the legislature did not provide the county with funds to pay for the processing of applications, the permits were given in violation of the Hancock Amendment because they created an unfunded mandate. Attorney Newman said, "The taxpayers of Moniteau County and any other county where permits are being issued are going to have to bear the burden of these increased costs because the legislature has not complied with the Hancock Amendment."[9] In June a Moniteau County judge denied Attorney General Nixon's motion to dismiss the lawsuit.[10]

In response, Larry Crawford said of Miller and Newman, "The plaintiff's attorneys seem to be very diligent in causing trouble."[11] However, he also said, "These lawsuits may actually help us get something fixed that I said we need to fix quickly," urging the legislature to get into gear on amending the law.[12] Of course, the bills sponsored by Crawford, Caskey, and Cauthorn did not address the Hancock problem as defined by Chief Justice White. While he wasn't named by Newman and Miller as a defendant in the lawsuit, Crawford asked the court to include him as a party in the case because the suit called for the nullification of his permit, as well as others issued in Moniteau County.

His request was granted. Explaining his action, Crawford said, "I'm really doing this for all Missourians. To me, this is sort of a civil rights lawsuit."[13]

At the same time they filed the new lawsuit, Newman and Miller also requested that Nixon investigate the legality of the Crawfords' conceal-and-carry permits, because of the speed with which they were issued by Sheriff Jones. The couple got their permits just four days after the court rendered its decision. Newman and Miller suggested the couple received their permits in much less time that it ordinarily takes the Highway Patrol to process fingerprint checks. Therefore, Miller and Newman argued, Sheriff Jones must have failed to follow procedure for issuing permits. The law, they asserted, required the sheriff to issue a permit only after receiving a completed background check. If Jones issued the permits before receiving a report back from the Highway Patrol, then there was no completed background check.[14]

At issue was the question of how extensive a background check needed to be if the sheriff knew the applicant(s) personally. Those arguing for quicker processing of permit applications suggested that the only purpose served by fingerprint checks was to establish the identity of the applicant with certainty. If the sheriff knew an applicant personally, they argued, the fingerprint check was unnecessary because the law states: "The sheriff shall make only such inquiries as he or she deems necessary into the accuracy of the statements made in the application."[15] Newman and Miller, on the other hand, argued a fingerprint check was an integral part of a complete background check under any circumstances and a background check couldn't be considered complete without one.[16] Nothing serious came from this inquiry, and while the legal wrangling continued, the state legislature tried to eliminate it by addressing the Hancock loophole.

Meanwhile, in the General Assembly

The need to fix the flaw in the conceal-and-carry act created the possibility for yet another all-out war between the legislature and the governor and cast a shadow over the 2004 legislative session. Early on, the governor indicated he would veto any legislation meant to patch the Hancock hole in the conceal-and-carry bill. As Mary Still, Holden's spokesperson, said, "The governor has said the law is so fundamentally flawed that there are only two ways to fix it. Either repeal it or take it to a vote of the people."[17] This made the leaders of the legislature less than enthusiastic to push the issue forward, knowing the fight would be divisive and that during an election year the votes might not exist to override a veto as they had in 2003. In theory, the problem with the conceal-and-carry law could be easily eliminated by passing a bill making some simple wording changes to allow counties to use the fee to pay their permit processing expenses. Nothing is simple about conceal-and-carry in Missouri, however. A new bill would give the governor an opportunity to use the veto again, and during the 2004 session he was clear in his intention to do just that.[18] An editorial in the *Springfield News-Leader*, which opposed Prop B in 1999, called on sheriffs to wait for a legal fix and also criticized a possible veto by Holden before the fact. The editorial read, in part, "The governor could veto it, but that would be foolish. This is a technical fix to a law that has been upheld as constitutional; it merely gives counties the means to recoup their expenses. Vetoing it would be childish and would be answered by an almost immediate override."[19] Such criticism was unlikely to influence the governor, of course, who by this point had made opposition to conceal-and-carry a major part of his platform for reelection. Given the embarrassment of the veto overrides in 2003, and with 2004 being an election year, Holden had little choice but to threaten to veto the bill—if the legislature could find time to pass it.

As the session wore on in 2004, it became doubtful lawmakers would finish in time, and many expressed frustration with the lack of a fix. For instance, late in the session, Jim Vermeersch, the executive director of the Missouri Sheriffs' Association, argued something needed to be done because without a fix, sheriffs were in an untenable legal position. He said, "It makes it a Catch-22, with the threat of litigation no matter what they do. Do they go ahead and issue and violate Hancock and suffer those consequences, or do they not issue and then try to justify how they're complying with the law?"[20]

In early March, Senator Harold Caskey introduced a bill in the senate that would have changed the conceal-and-carry law to allow sheriffs to use permit application fees for all the costs of processing applications.[21] Following the bill's introduction, conceal-and-carry foe Ken Jacob said, "I can't imagine it will sail through."[22] The first negative prediction from conceal-and-carry boosters came from Peter Kinder as the state legislature left Jefferson City for Spring break at the end of March. He suggested there would not be enough time to address the flaw during the 2004 session, which would leave the door wide open for lawsuits. Explaining the lack of movement, Kinder said, "As I travel around Missouri and visit with folks, I'm told that it's OK to let that lie ... This can be addressed county-by-county. It's in the courts, and the Legislature can tackle this in January... Generally, that's the sense I get from the public ... I'm not getting beat on to pass this in the remaining weeks of the session."[23]

Still fearing an avalanche of lawsuits that his office would have to defend, Jay Nixon criticized the legislature for its inaction. He said, "All of this stuff could be easily solved by the three sentences we gave to the Legislature within

72 hours of the Supreme Court decision... I am just disappointed that the Legislature has not stepped up to the plate and gotten this job done. They are leaving the sheriffs high and dry."[24] Later in the session, in early April, Kinder was more upbeat about the bill's chances. Speaking to a group of sheriffs who visited the capitol seeking clarification from the governor's office and lawmakers, he said the bill had passed out of committee and promised a vote on it before the end of the session.[25]

Expressing the frustration of that group of sheriffs with whom Kinder met, Marion County Sheriff John Waldschlager echoed the executive director of the Missouri Sheriffs' Association when he said, "I have no right to, nor will I, collect a fee that has not been voted on and violate the Hancock Amendment. That would open the door for major litigation against the county and I'm not going to subject them to that... It's a Catch-22 for sheriffs. We can be sued if we do and if we don't. House and Senate leaders, as well as the governor, need to step up to the plate and fix this mess instead of leaving the sheriffs and their county governments open to expensive litigation."[26]

House Speaker Catherine Hanaway, on the other hand, was less optimistic. When she met with the same group of sheriffs, Crawford's bill had not yet been reported out of committee, and she indicated that even if it was, she didn't know if there would be enough time left in the session to get it on the house calendar.[27] She also suggested that part of the reason she was reluctant to move forward with the bill was because it was unclear whether the governor would sign or veto it. She said, "If we had some glimmer of hope the governor was going to sign this thing, it would make things easier."[28] After the bill was finally voted out of the House Crime Prevention and Public Safety Committee on April 13, Larry Crawford urged the house to get moving on his bill. He said, "This is just cleanup, and we need to do it for our sheriffs. This is not about concealed weapons. That is the law of the land."[29] Crawford's comment was accurate, but to opponents of conceal-and-carry, the bill was much more than clean-up, it was a chance to derail concealed weapons for another year. For his part, Attorney General Nixon remained critical of all the players in this legislative game throughout the session. In May he criticized the governor for saying he would veto such a bill, and he criticized the legislature for not finding the time to debate the bills. He said, "If we're going to have this, we ought to do it right. Right means: Whatever county you are driving through, the rules are the same."[30]

A bill should have been easy to pass in both the house and the senate, but neither chamber's leader wanted to make room on the calendar for it. Both seemed to feel it wasn't worth the time because the real trouble would come when the bill reached the governor's desk. Assuming he would veto it, the real fighting would begin when it became necessary to override the governor's veto. This would not be a problem in the house, but in the senate, where the first veto was overturned with precisely the twenty-three votes necessary, anything could happen. Perhaps Senator Mathewson would change his mind and decide to support his governor. Perhaps in an election year Senator Gibbons, challenged by a gun control advocate for his seat, would decide he might lose his seat if he cast another vote allowing conceal-and-carry to take effect. In April, even Larry Crawford admitted that in an election year there might be Democrats who were less willing to embarrass the governor by overturning his veto.[31]

In what turned out to be little more than a footnote by the end of the session, but symbolic of the lingering anger over the passage of conceal-and-carry in 2003, Senator Ken Jacob introduced three bills that would have altered the new law. His goal, of course, was to reopen much of the conceal-and-carry debate from the year before. He said, "I will attempt to do the same thing we tried to do . . . pass a bill that makes sense and ensures the safety of Missouri's citizens."[32] His bills proposed that permits be required for carrying a concealed weapon in an automobile, that it be illegal to carry concealed weapons with permits from other states, and that guns be banned from a variety of places, such as public libraries, banks, and schools.[33] Speaking of the bill banning out-of-state permits, he said, "We want to make sure that anybody who carries a concealed weapon in this state has gone through proper training."[34] Of course, if the state was unable to pass a fix for the flaw in the conceal-and-carry law, Jacob's bill could have cut off a major alternate way for Missourians to get permits. In a way, even though his proposal to ban out-of-state permits bill failed, Jacob no doubt got some satisfaction when the state of Texas announced in July 2004 that it would not honor concealed-weapons permits issued in Missouri. Texas's reason for this policy decision was what it deemed a fundamental flaw in Missouri's law: as detailed earlier, even if a background check has not been completed, sheriffs in Missouri must issue permits to all applicants after forty-five days. If the background check later reveals a reason why someone should not have received a permit, then the permit can be revoked, but to Texas, that was like closing the barn door after the horses have escaped. One Texas official, Assistant Attorney General Becky Pestana, said, "With no way to distinguish between those Missouri concealed-handgun licenses issued in accordance with what Texas law requires and those issued under other circumstances, it is not possible at this time to effectuate reciprocity."[35] Supporters of conceal-and-carry downplayed the development, saying it was simply a matter of time, but such a public repudiation clearly pleased people such as Ken Jacob and Governor Holden.[36]

In addition, Jacob introduced a constitutional amendment that would have made it illegal for legislators to pass laws similar to proposals that had already been put to a public vote.[37] The obvious statement Jacob wanted to make with this, of course, was that the legislature had violated the will of the people, as expressed by the Prop B vote, when it approved conceal-and-carry in 2003. While the proposed amendment didn't go anywhere, Jacob undoubtedly felt he was speaking for a number of citizens distressed by the new conceal-and-carry law.

By the end of the session, nothing had been done to alter the conceal-and-carry law in Missouri. Jacob's bills, of course, went nowhere, but neither did the attempts in the house, sponsored by Crawford and Caskey, to change the law to avoid the Hancock Amendment troubles. Jim Vermeersch, the executive director of the Missouri Sheriffs' Association, lamented, "Without cleanup legislation, the sheriffs are in a real quandary out there."[38] Both Caskey's and Crawford's bills made it out of committee, but neither moved beyond that point. Explaining the lack of action on the legislation, Peter Kinder again placed blame on Governor Holden. He said, "What is the point of our taking up precious floor time when we need to do lots of other important issues on a measure which the governor said he would veto?"[39]

Moving Forward

In the wake of the supreme court's decision and despite Attorney General Nixon's admonitions against granting permits before the law was fixed, many counties decided to proceed with their plans to issue conceal-and-carry permits. As it became more clear the legislature wasn't going to bail them out, most counties developed plans they thought would comply with the court's decision and the Hancock Amendment and moved forward on their own.

For some large counties, known as "first-class" counties, the Limbaugh opinion pointed to a loophole that could provide a way around the prohibition against using application fees to process permits. Limbaugh wrote, "This Court also notes that under section 50.535.3, sheriffs of first-class counties have the option to 'designate one or more chiefs of police of any town, city or municipality within such county to accept and process [concealed-carry permit applications and then] reimburse such chiefs of police, out of the moneys deposited into [the sheriffs revolving fund] for any reasonable expenses related to accepting and processing such applications.' In theory, this provision allows some sheriffs to defer most, if not all, of their increased activities and costs under the Act."[40] Under the court's interpretation, this gave first-class counties a way around the Hancock problem. There are presently sixteen first-class counties in the state of Missouri, though it is predicted that three more counties will soon join their ranks. There are three classifications of counties, first through third. The classification is based on a county's property valuation. Under a law passed in 2004, all counties with a property valuation of $600 million or greater can become first class. In general, a county's classification affects the number of elected officials a county may have and the salaries of those officials. First-class counties may have home rule charters, and they may also have the opportunity to determine their own maximum tax levy.

In some first-class counties, sheriffs chose this option to legally begin issuing permits and made arrangements with local chiefs of police to reimburse them for issuing permits. In Boone County, for example, the cities of Hallsville and Ashland began issuing permits in May 2004. The sheriff of Boone County, Ted Boehm, who was an opponent of Prop B in 1999, said he chose this route because the Boone County legal counsel, John Patton, advised the sheriff against issuing permits himself. Boehm recounted his discussion with Patton: "If you do it, Boehm, you're in clear violation of the constitution, you will be sued, and you will lose'... So many people think that this piece of legislation is very up-front and simple ... But there's so many different variations within that statute that if you don't read every one of them you're not going to abide by that law. That's why you call in attorneys."[41] This part of the law resolved the issue for some counties, but since 98 of Missouri's 114 counties are not first-class, the solution was limited. In addition, if Chief Justice White's much more far-reaching interpretation of Hancock was ever adopted by a majority on the court, the loophole would solve nothing.

Not all first-class county sheriffs chose to use this option. Nowhere in the state was opposition to conceal-and-carry higher than in St. Louis, and the St. Louis County Police Department was not willing to allow local police departments to issue permits. The department's position was made clear in a press release that read, in part, "St. Louis County Police Department is receiving many inquiries concerning the February 26, 2004 Supreme Court of Missouri Opinion on House Bills 349, 129, 1236 and 328, commonly referred to as the concealed-carry act. Although some counties in Missouri may accept applications, the Office of the County Counselor has advised that they have prepared a challenge to the issuance of concealed-carry endorsements in St. Louis County. This decision, based on the Hancock Amendment means that the St. Louis County Police Department will not be accepting applications to obtain the Concealed Carry Endorsement."[42] On the one hand, the county's position was cautious from a legal perspective, but it could also be viewed as defiant. The county's policy gave it a further opportunity to delay what many felt was a bad policy. The county's refusal to issue permits—if inconsequential—was a bit of legal and political theater.

Dale Schmid, the president of the Second Amendment Coalition, lived in the St. Louis County city of Manchester. He asked the St. Louis County Police for a conceal-and-carry permit application and was told the county did not have applications and would not until the uncertainty caused by the supreme court was resolved. Schmid responded by preparing and attempting to submit his own application, which was rejected by the county police. The conceal-and-carry law provides an opportunity for persons denied a permit, or denied the right to apply for a permit, to challenge the county's decision in court. The law reads, "A denial of or refusal to act on an application for a certificate of qualification may be appealed by filing with the clerk of the small claims court a copy of the sheriff's written refusal . . . If at the hearing the person shows he or she is entitled to the requested certificate of qualification for a concealed carry endorsement, the court shall issue an appropriate order to cause the issuance of the certificate of qualification for a concealed carry endorsement . . . Any person aggrieved by any final judgment rendered by a small claims court in a denial of a certificate of qualification for a concealed carry endorsement appeal may have a right to trial de novo as provided in sections 512.180 to 512.320, RSMo."[43]

After being refused by the county, Schmid filed a petition in small claims court alleging the St. Louis County Police Department illegally denied him the right to submit a conceal-and-carry permit application. Named in the petition were St. Louis County Police Chief Ronald Battelle; Lieutenant Chris Stocker of the St. Louis County Police; and Patricia Redington, the St. Louis County counselor. Explaining his decision to file the petition, Schmid said, "They have been dragging their feet and pontificating against license to carry . . . it's dangerous for a police chief to pick and choose which laws he likes and dislikes and use his official capacity to do something about it."[44] Schmid's case was scheduled for a hearing on April 28, but he withdrew the petition shortly after he filed it.

Schmid went to great lengths on the Second Amendment Coalition Web site to explain why he changed his mind. Without naming names, he claimed he was contacted by state legislators and other advocates of conceal-and-carry and urged to drop his lawsuit. He said they told him it was a mistake to allow another St. Louis County judge the opportunity to make an anti–conceal-and-carry ruling because it would further delay implementation of the law.[45]

In dropping the suit, Schmid argued he'd already won because his action garnered a tremendous amount of positive media attention and had already achieved the impact he desired.[46] Schmid's action drew the ire of some fellow conceal-and-carry proponents, perhaps the people Schmid referred to on the Second Amendment Coalition Web site. For example, Greg Jeffrey, a longtime advocate for conceal-and-carry, used the Western Missouri Shooters Alliance Web site to condemn the lawsuit, characterizing Schmid's action as ill-conceived and potentially damaging to the long-term interests of the conceal-and-carry cause. Jeffrey also said that the suit was dropped thanks to pressure from a "national group," presumably the NRA.[47] While Schmid's action was not especially noteworthy from a legal perspective, it created, or at least exposed, a bit of division among members of the usually unified gun lobby in Missouri. The hullabaloo had no effect on the St. Louis County Police Department, however, which continued to refuse to grant conceal-and-carry permits.

While the first-class county stipulation provided a solution for some counties, others simply decided to roll the dice and proceed with issuing permits, despite the supreme court's decision and Nixon's admonition. In St. Charles County, a first-class county that could have used the loophole in the law, the sheriff's department instead began issuing permits in March. County Sheriff Tim Swope followed a plan he said could serve as a model for every county in Missouri. The St. Charles County Commission approved a plan to allow the sheriff to charge twenty-five cents for equipment and training. Equipment and training, of course, were the only areas for which the law and the supreme court's interpretation allowed the county to collect revenues, so they made up the difference with a ninety-five-dollar user fee for the expenses of processing applications.[48] Rather than call it an application fee, the county called it a user fee, a semantic difference they believed would allow them to get around the court's Hancock ruling. They were allowed, county officials argued, to use their authority under existing state law and the St. Charles County charter to create the fee to pay for "specific police services to individuals."[49] Explaining the strategy, St. Charles County Executive Joe Ortwerth said taxpayers wouldn't be forced to pay any expenses related to issuing permits and added, "We could have challenged this in court and asked Jefferson City to send us the money but that would have come from taxpayers, too."[50]

St. Charles County's forge-ahead attitude was part of the beginning of a trend. By September 2004 nearly every county in Missouri was taking applications for conceal-and-carry permits, despite the fact that the legislature had failed to act. The only exceptions were the state's major urban centers of Jackson County, St. Louis County, and St. Louis City.[51] Early on, as they began to take applications, many counties waited to actually issue permits because they continued to hope for a solution from the legislature, but since the law requires permits to be issued within forty-five days of an application being filed, counties were forced to move forward. By late Summer 2004, about eight thousand permits had been issued by sheriffs.[52] Similarly, the Missouri Department of Revenue moved forward, complying with the law by creating a conceal-and-carry endorsement to appear in the upper-right corner of driver's licenses. After July 1, anyone receiving a permit from a county sheriff was required to apply for a new driver's license with the endorsement within seven days of receiving the permit.[53] The last county outside of Jackson and St. Louis to begin issuing permits was Osage County, in the heart of Lake of the Ozarks country. The county had delayed issuing permits for fear of legal complications, but in the end it decided legal challenges were not a serious threat. In October the Osage County sheriff, Carl Fowler, said that in speaking with sheriffs from other counties, "I kind of got the impression they weren't really having any problems in issuing the permits."[54]

A Legal Victory for Opponents of Conceal-and-Carry

While Attorney General Nixon seemed to ignore this inquiry, the lawsuit against Sheriff Jones and Moniteau County proceeded and was joined by another suit. While the Moniteau County lawsuit filed by the anti–conceal-and-carry attorneys Newman and Miller plodded through the courts into the fall of 2004, a second suit marked a victory for opponents of conceal-and-carry. In this suit, filed in Cole County, St. Louis County officials followed through on their promise to take the state to court and sought a ruling that they did not have to issue conceal-and-carry permits. The county's argument, again borrowing from the supreme court's decision, was that since the state did not cover the costs of issuing permits, the law amounted to an unfunded mandate and was therefore illegal under the Hancock Amendment.[55] The county's lawyers argued that issuing permits would cost taxpayers seventy-one dollars more than the law allowed the St. Louis County Police Department to charge for permits.[56] In June, Nixon asked for the St. Louis case to be dismissed; as was the case in Moniteau County, his motion was rejected.[57] In October, Cole County Circuit Judge Thomas J. Brown decided in St. Louis County's favor when he agreed that the conceal-and-carry law imposed an unfunded mandate, illegal under the Hancock Amendment, on the county.[58] While the state weighed its decision of whether or not to appeal the decision, Nixon again took the opportunity to express his frustration with the fact that the legislature had not fixed the conceal-and-carry law's Hancock problem. He said, "When it comes to something like concealed weapons, we don't need different rules in different jurisdictions in Missouri . . . This would not be necessary if the Legislature had come back and done the fixes we asked them to do."[59]

In February 2005, Jackson County joined the ranks of those issuing conceal-and-carry permits, following a move by the county legislature to appropriate forty-eight thousand dollars for any overtime costs incurred by the sheriff's office in processing applications.[60] This left St. Louis City and County as the only remaining jurisdictions in Missouri to refuse to issue conceal-and-carry permits to their residents. By March 2005 roughly sixteen thousand permit applications had been made statewide.[61]

Conclusion

So, what did the legal and legislative wrangling mean? The only thing that can be said with certainty is that while the supreme court's decision was important, it was not the final word. Many predicted the court's decision would not be the end of the conceal-and-carry game, and that has certainly proved to be true. No matter which way the court decided, it was unlikely to settle anything permanently. The new leaders of the legislature promised that addressing the conceal-and-carry law's Hancock problem would be a priority in 2005, but that remains to be seen.

Chapter Twenty-Four

Conclusion

At least for the short term, the Showdown in the Show-Me State is nearly over. Conceal-and-carry passed in both chambers of the Missouri legislature in 2003 and supportive legislators overcame a gubernatorial veto. Needing further validation in the face of continued opposition, conceal-and-carry then traveled to the Missouri Supreme Court, which found that the state constitution did not prohibit the legislature from granting Missourians the privilege of carrying concealed weapons. Mission accomplished. In May 2005 supporters of conceal-and-carry could claim almost total victory. The only fly in the ointment for them was that permits were not being issued in two key jurisdictions—notably, places where Prop B had gone down in flames—St. Louis City and County. This meant that while it was legal to issue conceal-and-carry permits in nearly every square mile of the state, it was still illegal for a large percentage of Missourians to carry concealed weapons.[1] All Missourians were allowed to carry concealed weapons in their cars, and people issued permits elsewhere could carry their weapons in the St. Louis area, but that was certainly not enough for the many conceal-and-carry advocates living there who wanted their own permits.

The ability of St. Louis—city and county—to hold out against issuing permits disappeared by the end of the 2005 session of the state legislature. In March, House Bill 365, which fixed the unfunded mandate problem, passed by a vote of 142–7. From there the bill moved to the senate, where it was also expected to pass easily. The bill was sponsored by Representative Brian Munzlinger, and one of the cosponsors was Kenny Jones, the former sheriff of Moniteau County who had been named in the lawsuit protesting the issuance of conceal-and-carry permits to Representative Larry Crawford and his wife. Crawford was term-limited out of office, and Jones now holds his seat in the 117th District. The bill was passed by the full legislature in May and will knock down the reason expressed by St. Louis City and County for not issuing permits. It should also prevent gun control activists from filing dozens of lawsuits against the state and each county that granted permits, as Attorney General Jay Nixon predicted would happen without a fix by the legislature.

The passage of corrective legislation in 2005 seemed anticlimactic after the final divisive year of Bob Holden's tenure as governor. The legislature had the opportunity to fix this potential problem in 2004; for some reason, the fix failed to come to a vote. In their defense, the legislators got a late start, as the court did not issue its decision until late February, when the five-month legislative session was more than a month old. Curiously, however, this wasn't the excuse that conceal-and-carry proponents offered when they tried to explain the legislature's lack of action on the matter.

For its part, the legislature's leadership attributed the failure to fix the Hancock problem to the governor. Both Peter Kinder and Catherine Hanaway said the reason there was no fix for the flaw in the law was because it would have been a fruitless exercise with a threatened veto in the offing. This explanation, however, is not terribly compelling, given the tremendous success the supporters of gun rights had in overriding the governor not once, but twice, in 2003. There was no reason to believe a gubernatorial veto of a fix for the Hancock problem would stand any better chance of surviving than Holden's vetoes of conceal-and-carry or liability protection did. In the senate, the margin of victory was razor-thin in 2003, to be sure, but 2004 was a different year. Would Democrats Jim Mathewson, Harold Caskey, or Steve Stoll change their votes in 2004? Not likely, since Mathewson and Caskey were both being term-limited out of office and Steve Stoll was considering making a career change. They simply would not have felt any political pressure to pacify the governor. Senator Dolan spent the entire session in Missouri in 2004, so there was no doubt he would be around to support any conceal-and-carry-related measures. As for Mike Gibbons, he was criticized in his home district for his vote to override the governor, but would it have been enough to make him suddenly cast a vote against his party in an election year, even if he did suggest during the 2004 session that aspects of the law needed to be revisited? It seems very unlikely, because the pressure on him to toe the party line would have been tremendous. Of course, he never had to make the decision because it did not come to a vote.

As for the house, there were more than enough votes in that chamber to override Governor Holden in 2003. Maybe some Democrats who voted for conceal-and-carry and for the override in 2003 would have had second thoughts about overriding the governor in an election year, but would they have been more worried about the governor's fortunes, or their own? Democrats are already close to an endangered species in the General Assembly. It seems far from certain that they would have voted against a veto override just because they didn't want to embarrass a governor who, at the time, looked like he might not even be the Democrats' nominee for 2004. As it turned out, he wasn't.

So, while it was convenient for the leadership to blame Holden for a veto he never even got the chance to make, it doesn't seem like the only explanation for the failure to produce a fix in 2004. In simple terms, it just was not the right time for another gun bill. No doubt there were, as Peter Kinder suggested, other important things to handle. In addition, it is clearly possible that as legislators saw most county governments were pushing ahead without a fix, they concluded that new legislation was not urgent and simply did not want to get into a time-consuming—and potentially damaging—fight over it in an election year.

Holden clearly liked to fight about guns, so much so that he challenged not only the Republican legislators but also his Democratic primary opponent on the issue, accusing Claire McCaskill in a television ad of opportunistically changing her position on conceal-and-carry to take advantage of financial support from Anheuser-Busch. The issue came up in the first of their two pre-primary debates when, speaking of the gun lobby, Holden said, "I stood up . . . and she blinked."[2] This was an interesting charge to make against a woman who, throughout her career, repeatedly spoke in favor of gun control and against conceal-and-carry. To be sure, McCaskill fought back hard, calling the ad hypocritical, false, and misleading. She also said, "I have said I would have vetoed concealed weapons, and I have the same position he does."[3] Clearly, Holden was trying to appeal to his core constituency, St. Louis and Kansas City Democrats, but the strategy didn't work. Even in an election with a constitutional amendment on the ballot to define marriage in Missouri as between a man and a woman, which should have drawn lots of liberal Democrats to the polls, Holden was unable to win his party's nomination for 2004. McCaskill beat him, and she did it by winning big in out-state Missouri and performing respectably in St. Louis and Kansas City. Undoubtedly, Holden's decision to go the anti–conceal-and-carry route hurt him badly in rural parts of the state. Even if he won the nomination, he would likely have been in serious trouble in the general election, since Jim Talent showed in 2002 that St. Louis and Kansas City aren't enough to win statewide office in Missouri. During the general election campaign for governor, which pitted McCaskill against Matt Blunt, guns were not a commonly debated subject, and McCaskill attempted to blunt her past record of opposition to conceal-and-carry with a promise not to interfere with the legal right of Missourians to own firearms.[4]

At the same time the governor and the legislature postured over a fix for conceal-and-carry's Hancock problem, Missouri experienced its first legal shooting with a concealed weapon. In March, Bryan Rutherford, a St. Louis County resident, was approached in the parking lot of a condominium complex in Clayton by two men who brandished a weapon and robbed him. Rutherford got his gun from his pickup truck and shot a reported seven times, wounding one of his assailants.[5] Being the first shooting of this type since the law took effect, the incident drew wide attention and elicited many comments from both sides of the debate. To proponents, the incident was a graphic demonstration of the good concealed weapons can do. If he hadn't had the gun, what might have happened to Rutherford or someone else in that parking lot? To critics of conceal-and-carry, there were extenuating circumstances that deserved attention. First, what of the fact that it turned out the robbers were armed only with a BB gun? Does it matter it was only a BB gun? Does it matter that they carried only a BB gun? If the assailants intended for Rutherford to think it was a real gun, as he clearly did, is there a difference? Not according to the law, but since no one was killed, it may be easier to dismiss this reality. Second, what of the fact that only one of Rutherford's bullets hit an assailant and the others went flying around the complex? No one else was injured, but critics argued that it was mere luck. Rutherford was not charged with any crimes, but had he wounded an innocent bystander, who is to say what the St. Louis County prosecutor, Robert McCulloch, would have done?[6] McCulloch declined to charge Rutherford, but still the incident breathed new life into the fears of some in the law enforcement community. Days after the incident, McCulloch said, "Any law that would allow my 21-year-old daughter, who has never carried a gun, to carry one concealed in her car is a bad law."[7] His sentiment was echoed by the chief of the St. Louis County Police, Ron Battelle, who said, "Police work is a risky business at best. This just makes it riskier."[8] Clearly, there are strong points to be made on both sides of this case, just as there are strong arguments to be made about conceal-and-carry in general. As the prosecutor of neighboring Jefferson County, Bob Wilkins, said, "It's the perfect case for both sides of the argument. Each side can make their argument using the same set of facts."[9] Wilkins's statement nicely summarizes much of what has happened in Missouri.

The fight has been a long one since conceal-and-carry surfaced as a serious issue in the General Assembly in the early 1990s. The legislature has changed a great deal, going from many decades of Democratic control to a new Republican majority; from a majority that might have wanted to pass conceal-and-carry but feared the governor to a new majority that relished the chance to challenge the governor... at least in 2003. Now the Republicans firmly control the three major elective branches of Missouri's government. Since the legislature fixed the Hancock problem in the 2005 session, does that mean there will be no more gun politics in Missouri? Certainly not. Other issues will arise because Missourians, elected and otherwise, don't seem to know what to do without guns to fight about.

Lest one think this is peculiar to the Show-Me State, in 2005 Americans continued to rage on both sides of the gun issue at the national level as well. In September 2004 the U.S. Congress allowed the assault weapons ban, adopted in 1994, to expire, giving the NRA a victory in a fight that was waged for as long as Missouri's showdown. John Kerry criticized George W. Bush for allowing this to happen, saying Bush had made the world an easier place for terrorists and criminals to live in, but it was ultimately Congress that let the ban expire. For its part, the NRA once again strongly supported the president. The group attacked John Kerry as a "Second Amendment phony" and said that for two decades in the Senate he had consistently voted against the right to bear arms.[10] The group promised to spend $20 million in 2004, in addition to establishing its own broadcast network, beefing up its already legendary grassroots network, and airing a thirty-minute infomercial in battleground states in which Wayne LaPierre, the group's executive vice president, said, "Senator Kerry, how can you talk out of both sides of your mouth and keep a straight face?"[11] The NRA clearly had an impact in battleground states in 2000, and with voters just as closely divided in many of those same states in 2004, the group planned to have as much influence again. Certainly the results of the election, in which Bush won both the popular and Electoral College votes and improved his performance in battleground states where the organization was especially active, suggest the NRA did indeed have an impact.

In Missouri, some pro–conceal-and-carry politicians were successful in their aims for higher office. Peter Kinder was elected lieutenant governor, Matt Blunt was elected governor, and Mike Gibbons was reelected to the Missouri Senate, defeating gun control advocate Jeanne Kirkton. Gibbons, the majority floor leader, was subsequently chosen by his fellow Republicans in the senate to replace Kinder as the president pro tem. Perhaps the most interesting statewide race, from a conceal-and-carry perspective, was for the office of secretary of state. The race pitted Robin Carnahan, the leader of the fight against Prop B, against Catherine Hanaway, the speaker of the house who brokered the final passage of conceal-and-carry in 2003 in the house. During the race, in ads and debates, the two candidates both attempted to portray themselves as pro-gun. This was harder for Robin Carnahan to do, obviously, but Catherine Hanaway was also forced to address her pre-2003 record of voting against conceal-and-carry. Carnahan also made a point of explaining that her campaign against Prop B was a bipartisan effort.[12] In the end, Carnahan's name recognition probably allowed her to carry the election, despite the fact that she had never before held elective office. In April 2005, President Bush nominated Hanaway to be the next U.S. attorney in Missouri's eastern district. In the state legislature, Republicans and, presumably, pro–conceal-and-carry legislators increased their majorities in both the house and senate, paving the way for the fix of Missouri's conceal-and-carry law in 2005.

America is a nation with a complicated relationship with guns. It is, in a very real way, a nation built with guns. At the same time, it is a nation whose biggest cities are racked by gun violence every day. Missouri is a microcosm of that reality, with a long rural gun tradition and two major metropolitan areas whose violent crime rates regularly rank among the nation's worst. As America's most typical state, a state which sided with the winner in every presidential election of the twentieth century except for a single misstep when Missourians said "Show me!" to Adlai Stevenson instead of Dwight Eisenhower in 1956, it is no surprise that just as gun battles always rage at the federal level, they do the same here.

Notes

Chapter One

1. Fred W. Lindecke, "Hopefuls Wade into Gun Mire."
2. For an extensive record of the proceedings at the 1875 constitutional convention, please see Isidor Loeb and Floyd C. Shoemaker, eds., *Debates of the Missouri Constitutional Convention of 1875,* 12 vols.

Chapter Two

1. James Trefethen and James Serven, *Americans and Their Guns: The National Rifle Association's Story through Nearly a Century of Service to the Nation,* 130.
2. National Rifle Association, "Firearms Preemption Laws," www.nraila.org/Issues/FactSheets/Read.aspx?ID=48, accessed in 2004.
3. National Rifle Association, "Protecting the American Firearms Industry from Junk Lawsuits," www.nraila.org/images/lsprem.jpg, accessed in 2004.
4. National Rifle Association, "Range Protection Laws," www.nraila.org/Issues/FactSheets/Read.aspx?ID=49, accessed in 2004.
5. For example, see the National Opinion Research Center's 1999 National Gun Policy Survey, www.norc.uchicago.edu/new/gunrpt.htm, accessed in 2004.
6. National Rifle Association, www.nra.org, accessed in 2004.
7. Tom Loftus, *The Art of Legislative Politics,* 93.
8. Anthony Downs, *An Economic Theory of Democracy.*
9. *Quilici v. Village of Morton Grove,* 695 F.2d 261 (7th Cir. 1982).
10. Loftus, *The Art of Legislative Politics,* 93.
11. National Rifle Association, "Firearms Preemption Laws."
12. Missouri Revised Statutes. Title III, chap. 21, sec. 21.750.
13. Mark Schlinkmann, "Harmon Will Challenge State Restriction on City Gun Rules."
14. "Guns," *St. Louis Post-Dispatch.*

Chapter Three

1. John Ross, "Missouri Gun Laws Help Criminals."
2. Ibid.
3. Virginia Young, "NRA Led Blitz on Concealed Weapons. Legislators Cite calls from Constituents."
4. Robert Koenig, "Anti-Handgun Group Is Scoring Victories. Organization's Resources Are Dwarfed by Those of the NRA."
5. Ibid.
6. Fred Lindecke, "Police Chiefs Oppose Gun Bill."
7. Ibid.
8. Laura Scott, "Ashcroft's Risky Bet on Guns."
9. "As Governor, Ashcroft Had 'Grave Concerns' about Concealed Guns."
10. Young, "NRA Led Blitz on Concealed Weapons."

11. Ibid.

12. Ibid.

13. Peter Hernon, "Tired of Vulnerability, Say Gun Law's Backers."

14. Virginia Young, "House Approves Concealed Guns. Critics Lament 'License to Kill.'"

15. Ibid.

16. Ibid.

17. Ibid.

18. Fred Lindecke "State Senate Panel Rejects Concealed-Weapons Bill."

19. Ibid.

20. William Lhotka, Kim Bell, and Virgil Tipton, "Man Kills Wife in Court. 5 Wounded as Rampage Erupts in Divorce Case."

21. Joan Little and Terry Ganey, "Victim Rips Concealed Arms Bill."

22. "Lessons from Courthouse Rampage."

23. Little and Ganey, "Victim Rips Concealed Arms Bill."

24. William Lhotka, "Gunman Struck While Panel Was Discussing Security."

25. Little and Ganey, "Victim Rips Concealed Arms Bill."

26. Ibid.

27. Jim Mosley, "Armed: Concealed-Weapons Law Leaves Many Doors Ajar."

28. Laura Eardley, "Most in Survey Want No Change in Gun Law."

29. Martha Shirk, "Fresh Fight on Guns. Child-Safety Measures, Zones Around Schools Face Stiff Opposition."

30. Gregory Freeman, "Gun-Lock Bill Could Prevent Tragic Deaths."

31. Shirk, "Fresh Fight on Guns."

32. Barry Goldwater, "Acceptance Address at the Republican National Convention."

33. Shirk, "Fresh Fight on Guns."

34. Ibid.

35. Andrew Miller, "NRA Ads Attacked Candidates. More Than $100,000 Spent in Regional Races."

36. Bob Adams, "NRA Had Hand in Defeat of Two Incumbents."

37. Ibid.

38. Ibid.

39. Jake Thompson, "Danner Undecided on Whether She'll Back Brady Bill. Gun Lobby Supports Her House Campaign and Rates Her Highly."

40. Ibid.

41. Ibid.

42. Adams, "NRA Had Hand in Defeat of Two Incumbents."

43. Ibid.

44. Ibid.

45. Ibid.

46. Lindecke, "Hopefuls Wade into Gun Mire."

47. Ibid.

48. Ibid.

49. Mark Schlinkmann, "State's Defeat of 2 Congressmen Last Occurred in '52."

50. Jo Mannies, "Anti-Gun Lobby Fires Broadside at Volkmer."

51. Robert Koenig, "Folksy Style Helps Volkmer Survive."

Chapter Four

1. Gregory Freeman, "Handguns Kill Their Owners."

2. Ibid.

3. Kevin Murphy, "Gun-Control Issue Not Dead, Carnahan Says. Governor Wants to Let K.C., St. Louis Impose Tougher Regulation."

4. Fred Lindecke, "Concealed-Guns Debate Rages."

5. Ibid.

6. Fred Lindecke, "House Passes Weapons Bill. Concealed Gun Amendment Attached to Anti-Crime Bill."

7. Virginia Young, "Concealed-Gun Bill Loses Round One in Missouri Senate."

8. Terry Ganey and Virginia Young, "Concealed Gun Bill Reappears. State Senator's Plan Jeopardizes Crime Bill."

9. Ibid.

10. Young, "Concealed-Gun Bill Loses Round One in Missouri Senate."

11. Ibid.

12. Ibid.

13. Ibid.

14. Ibid.

15. Murphy, "Gun-Control Issue Not Dead, Carnahan Says."

16. Jean Haley, "Concealed Weapons Checked."

17. Joe Lambe, "Battle Rages on Concealed Guns. Foes Call Idea 'Idiocy.' Backers Contend It Would Cut Crime."

18. Ibid.

19. Murphy, "Gun-Control Issue Not Dead, Carnahan Says."

20. Ibid.

21. Ganey and Young, "Concealed Gun Bill Reappears."

22. Ibid.

23. Kevin Murphy, "Senate Says No to KC Gun Rules."

24. Ibid.

25. Ibid.

26. Jean Haley, "Gun Safety Postponed."

27. Robert Koenig, "Harold L. Volkmer."

28. Steve Kraske, "Rothman-Serot Leaves the Fray. Disillusionment with Politics Intensifies Her Calls for Finance Reform."

29. Jo Mannies, "Senate Hopefuls Debate Crime, Health. Democrats Criticize Rep. Alan Wheat's Absence from Forum."

30. James Kuhnhenn, "Issues Narrow Opponents' Contrast."

31. Jo Mannies, "Jim, Sarah Brady Back Wheat, Laud His Gun-Control Stance."

32. Kuhnhenn, "Issues Narrow Opponents' Contrast."

33. James Kuhnhenn, "Ashcroft and Wheat Trade Jabs. Crime Bill Isn't Tough Enough, Republican Says. But GOP's Danforth Backed It, Democrat Notes."

34. Ibid.

35. Kathleen Best, "Crime Bill Leaps Hurdle: 6 in GOP Join Democrats."

36. Kuhnhenn, "Ashcroft and Wheat Trade Jabs."

37. Virginia Young, "Danner Looks for Opening to Press His Challenge."

Chapter Five

1. Lewis Diuguid, "Concealed-Weapons Law Wouldn't Make Everyone Feel Safer."

2. Virginia Young, "Concealed-Weapons Supporters Vow They'll Try Again."

3. Ibid.

4. Virginia Young, "NRA Doesn't Want Vote on Gun Bill."

5. Ibid.

6. Kevin Murphy, "Battle Heats Up over Vote on Concealed Guns. Missouri Would Be First State to Let Its Citizens Decide Issue if House Follows Senate's Lead."

7. Ibid.

8. Joe Holleman, "Most Oppose Law to Allow Concealed Handguns."

9. Murphy, "Battle Heats Up over Vote on Concealed Guns."

10. Leo Fitzmaurice, "Brady Calls for 'Burial' of Concealed Weapons Plan."

11. Young, "NRA Doesn't Want Vote on Gun Bill."

12. Virginia Young, "Sen. Banks Takes on Concealed Weapons. Senate Majority Leader Launches a Filibuster."

13. Young, "Concealed-Weapons Supporters Vow They'll Try Again."

14. Ibid.

15. Virginia Young, "Jet Banks Says His Gun Stance Provoked Death Threat."

16. Young, "Sen. Banks Takes on Concealed Weapons."

17. Young, "Concealed-Weapons Supporters Vow They'll Try Again."

18. Young, "Sen. Banks Takes on Concealed Weapons."

19. Ibid.

20. Ibid.

21. Ibid.

22. Kevin Horrigan, "Who Will Have the Courage to Face Up to the Gun Lobby?"

23. Young, "Jet Banks Says His Gun Stance Provoked Death Threat."

24. Ibid.

25. Young, "Concealed-Weapons Supporters Vow They'll Try Again."

26. Ibid.

27. Ibid.

28. Ibid.

29. Ibid.

30. Kevin Murphy, "Hidden-Weapons Bill Falls. '95 General Assembly Ends without Vote on Issue."

31. Young, "Concealed-Weapons Supporters Vow They'll Try Again."

32. Ibid.

33. Murphy, "Hidden-Weapons Bill Falls. '95 General Assembly Ends without Vote on Issue."

34. Ibid.

35. Young, "Concealed-Weapons Supporters Vow They'll Try Again."

36. Ibid.

37. Robert Sigman, "More Threats from the Gun Fringe."

38. Ibid.

39. Young, "Concealed-Weapons Supporters Vow They'll Try Again."

Chapter Six

1. Terry Ganey, "Public Vote Acceptable to Sponsor of Gun Bill. Concealed Weapons Proposal Is Up for Debate This Week."

2. Ibid.

3. Will Sentell, "Concealed Guns Measure Declared Dead in Missouri."

4. Ganey, "Public Vote Acceptable to Sponsor of Gun Bill."

5. Ibid.

6. Sentell, "Concealed Guns Measure Declared Dead in Missouri."

7. Ibid.

8. Ibid.

9. Terry Ganey, "Just a Good Ol' Boy from Ozarks, Danny Staples Is a Force in the Senate."

10. "No Support from NRA on Concealed Weapons," *St. Louis Post-Dispatch.*

11. "House Committee Kills Concealed-Guns Measure," *Kansas City Star.*

12. Ibid.

13. Ibid.

14. For an excellent treatment of this subject, Elizabeth Drew, *Whatever It Takes: The Real Struggle for Political Power in America.*

15. Fred Lindecke, "Horn Counts on Mood Swing by Voters in 2nd District."

16. Fred Lindecke, "Horn Objects to Rival's Appeal for GOP Voters."

17. Ibid.

18. Julie Hirschfeld, "Ross Puts $50,000 of His Own into 2nd District Campaign."

19. Fred Lindecke, "Political Circuit."

20. Lindecke, "Horn Objects to Rival's Appeal for GOP Voters."

21. Laura Scott, "Kinnamon for Democrats."

22. Guy Gugliotta, "Blue Dog Democrats May Have Their Day in a Kinder, Gentler Congress."

23. Bill Lambrecht, "Republican 'Blue Dogs' Organize."

24. David Goldstein, "Blue Dogs Gain Force."

25. Philip Dine, "Labor Upbeat Despite Losses. Business, Other Special Interests Gleeful about Perceived Gains."

Chapter Seven

1. Kevin Murphy, "Measure Would Allow Concealed Guns for Some Missouri Prosecutors, Plus Retired Judges and Officers, Would Be Covered."

2. Kim Bell, "House OKs Vote on Weapons if Senate Approves, Referendum in '98."

3. Ibid.

4. Terry Ganey, "NRA Gives $75,000 to Support Gun Bill in Missouri."

5. Will Sentell, "Weapons Supporters Don't Want Referendum. Missouri House Bill Would Legalize Concealed Guns."

6. Ibid.

7. Kim Bell, "Bill Would Put Weapons Issue Before Voters."

8. Sentell, "Weapons Supporters Don't Want Referendum."

9. Bell, "Bill Would Put Weapons Issue Before Voters."

10. "Missouri Capitol Briefs," *St. Louis Post-Dispatch.*

11. Tim Bryant, "Clergy, Elected Officials Gather Here to Denounce Concealed Weapons Proposal as Dangerous."

12. Kim Bell, "Concealed Guns Protect Public, Ex-Officer Says. Senate Panel Backs April Vote on Issue."

13. Terry Ganey and Kim Bell, "Concealed Carry Will Make Missouri Safer or It Will Make the State a Scarier Place to Live. Voters Will Decide the Issue Tuesday."

14. HB 1891. www.house.state.mo.us/bills98/bills98/hb1891.htm, accessed in 2004.

15. Mark Schlinkmann, "Federer Will Challenge Gephardt, Ross Will Face Talent in November."

16. Ibid.

17. Ibid.

18. "House Races Include Some Libertarians, Taxpayers. Many Candidates Raise Issues of Taxes, Schools. Terms Are for Two Years."

19. Ibid.
20. Ibid.

Chapter Eight

1. Jennifer Barnett, "Conceal-and-Carry: The People Speak."
2. Kit Wagar, "Stakes High in Gun Debate. Missouri Campaign Is Expected to Be Costly, Emotional."
3. Ibid.
4. Terry Ganey, "NRA-Led Supporters of Concealed Weapons Are Fast and Flexible. Their Weapons Range from 'Fax Alerts' to Mass Mailings."
5. Scott Charton, "Missouri to Vote on Concealed Guns."
6. Kit Wagar, "Battle over Guns: Amid Heated Rhetoric, Missourians Face Vote on Concealed Firearms."
7. James Madison, Federalist Paper no. 10.
8. David Broder, *Democracy Derailed*, 5.
9. Steven L. Piott, *Giving Voters a Voice*, 75.
10. Ellis, Richard J. 2002. *Democratic Delusions: The Initiative Process in America*, 38.

Chapter Nine

1. Terry Ganey, "Brady Lobbies against Concealed Weapons, Will Greet Pontiff."
2. Yuki Noguchi, "Anheuser-Busch Support of Gun Measure Is Called 'Irresponsible.' Sarah Brady Assails What Brewer Says Was Only Its Opinion Given to Group."
3. Donald Bradley, "Warning of Guns' Danger. Brady Joins Concealed-Weapons Vote Fight."
4. Kim Bell, "Heston Urges OK of 'Sane, Sensible' Concealed-Gun Law."
5. Lee Hill Kavanaugh, "Show Business Role in Firearms Issue. Charlton Heston Seeks Proposition B Votes."
6. Bell, "Heston Urges OK of 'Sane, Sensible' Concealed-Gun Law."
7. Oscar Avila, "Many Officials Quiet So Far on Gun Plan."
8. Wagar, "Battle over Guns."
9. Ibid.
10. Ganey, "NRA Gives $75,000 to Support Gun Bill in Missouri."
11. Rudi Keller, "Urban Voters Send Gun Measure Packing."
12. Paul Dialing, "MidwayUSA Business Plan Hits Bull's Eye."
13. Larry Potterfield, "NRA Support."
14. Jo Mannies, "Fight against Prop B Pushed Robin Carnahan into Spotlight."
15. Jennifer Portman, "Loopholes Not Real, Author Says."
16. Kit Wagar, "Money and Messages Flow as Gun Campaigns Near End."
17. Ganey, "NRA Gives $75,000 to Support Gun Bill in Missouri."
18. Portman, "Loopholes Not Real, Author Says."
19. Kit Wagar, "Pro-Gun Forces Get More NRA Funds."
20. Wagar, "Money and Messages Flow as Gun Campaigns Near End."
21. Ganey, "Brady Lobbies against Concealed Weapons, Will Greet Pontiff."
22. Laura Bauer Menner, "Weapons Measure Flawed."
23. Terry Ganey and Bill Bryan, "Some in Police Group Oppose Weapons Plan. They Say Billboards Touting Concealed-Carry Plan Mislead. Board Voted 12–1 to Back Measure."
24. Kit Wagar, "Prop B Roused Intense Drive. But Will Voters' Zeal Match Campaign's?"

25. Ganey and Bell, "Concealed Carry Will Make Missouri Safer or It Will Make the State a Scarier Place to Live."

26. Ibid.

27. Ganey and Bryan, "Some in Police Group Oppose Weapons Plan."

28. Ganey and Bell, "Concealed Carry Will Make Missouri Safer or It Will Make the State a Scarier Place to Live."

29. Ganey, "Brady Lobbies against Concealed Weapons, Will Greet Pontiff."

30. Susan Wade and Dean Curtis, "Training an Emotional Issue."

31. Laura Bauer Menner, "Police Split on Concealed Guns."

32. Scott Charton, "Missouri to Vote on Concealed Guns."

33. Wagar, "Battle over Guns."

34. Menner, "Weapons Measure Flawed."

35. Laura Bauer Menner, Jennifer Portman, and Bob Linder, "Conceal-and-Carry: The People Speak. How Would It Work?"

36. Susan Wade and Christina Dicken, "Conceal and Carry: The People Speak."

37. Wade and Curtis, "Training an Emotional Issue."

38. Ibid.

39. Portman, "Loopholes Not Real, Author Says."

40. Menner, Portman, and Linder, "Conceal-and-Carry: The People Speak. How Would It Work?"

41. Kavanaugh, "Show Business Role in Firearms Issue."

42. The Missourians for Personal Safety Web site is www.moccw.org.

43. Terry Ganey, "Concealed-Gun Backers Say Foes Are Using Fear Tactics."

44. Gregory Freeman, "U.S. Attorney Takes Dead Aim against Concealed Weapons."

45. Ganey, "NRA-Led Supporters of Concealed-Weapons Are Fast and Flexible."

46. Rudi Keller, "Governor, NRA Up Ante on Prop B."

47. Ibid.

48. Tim Bryant and Bill Lambrecht, "Justice Looks into Dowd's Campaign against Prop B."

49. Ibid.

50. Keller, "Governor, NRA Up Ante on Prop B."

51. Bryant and Lambrecht, "Justice Looks into Dowd's Campaign against Prop B."

52. M. W. Guzy, "When Money Talks, Politicians Listen."

Chapter Ten

1. Kim Bell, "More Guns Equal Less Crime, Prof Says."

2. John Lott, "False Alarms Are Being Sounded on the Conceal-Carry Issue."

3. Bell, "More Guns Equal Less Crime, Prof Says."

4. Ibid.

5. Freeman, "U.S. Attorney Takes Dead Aim against Concealed Weapons."

6. Ibid.

7. Ibid.

8. Kit Wagar, "Concealed-Weapons Proposal to Be Rewritten in Missouri."

9. Terry Ganey, "Concealed Weapons Foes Get Change in Wording on Ballot."

10. Terry Ganey, "Former Highway Patrol Chief Sues Auditor over Wording of Concealed Weapons Measure."

11. "Concealed-Gun Costs Are Called Hard to Predict. Spending Could Be More in Later Years, McCaskill Says."

12. Will Sentell, "True Costs Still Anyone's Guess."

13. Terry Ganey, "Officials Are Sued over Concealed Weapons Ballot Measure."

14. Ganey, "Former Highway Patrol Chief Sues Auditor over Wording of Concealed Weapons Measure."

15. Ibid.

16. Terry Ganey, "Court Upholds Wording of Weapons Measure."

Chapter Eleven

1. Terry Ganey, "Concealed Guns Measure Has Substantial Backing Statewide, Poll Indicates Support Is Strong among Men, Current Owners of Weapons, Undecided Voters Are Called Key."

2. Kim Bell, "New Ad Uses Wrong Weapon to Urge Opposition to Concealed-Gun Measure."

3. Tim O'Neil, "NRA Is Trying to Buy Victory on Proposition B, Opponents Say."

4. Terry Ganey and Kim Bell, "NRA Boosts Weapons Measure Effort by $650,000."

5. Kit Wagar, "NRA Boosts Yes-on-B Campaign. Gun Rights Group Gave $2.2 Million."

6. Terry Ganey, "Concealed-Carry Backers Outspend Foes by 3–1. Most of Money Touting Plan Comes from Outside Missouri, Records Show."

7. Terry Ganey, "Proponents Paid Out $3.8 Million for Prop B."

8. Wagar, "Battle over Guns."

9. Ibid.

10. Wagar, "Pro-Gun Forces Get More NRA Funds."

11. Ibid.

12. Wagar, "Prop B Roused Intense Drive."

13. Wagar, "NRA Boosts Yes-on-B Campaign."

14. Wagar, "Prop B Roused Intense Drive."

15. Wagar, "Pro-Gun Forces Get More NRA Funds."

16. Keller, "Governor, NRA Ante Up on Prop B."

17. Traci Shurley, "Sides Make Points on Gun Issue."

18. Wagar, "Prop B Roused Intense Drive."

19. Ganey, "Concealed-Carry Backers Outspend Foes by 3–1."

20. Derrick Z. Jackson, "Missouri Smites 'Moses.'"

21. Ganey, "NRA Gives $75,000 to Support Gun Bill in Missouri."

22. Terry Ganey, "Post-Dispatch Ad Check (Proposition B)."

23. Terry Ganey, "Supporters of Concealed Guns Begin Ad Campaign."

24. Ganey, "Post-Dispatch Ad Check."

25. Terry Ganey, "Rape Victim Makes Ad in Favor of Gun Measure."

26. Ibid.

27. Ibid.

28. Ibid.

29. Terry Ganey, "Second Rape Victim Speaks—Against Concealed Weapons."

30. Kim Bell, "Post-Dispatch Ad Check (2 of 2 articles)."

31. Tim O'Neil, "Missouri Proposition B: Concealed Weapon: Two Area Chiefs Object to Ad, Say It Overstates Police Power."

32. Ibid.

33. Ibid.

34. Ganey, "Supporters of Concealed Guns Begin Ad Campaign."

35. Terry Ganey and Kim Bell, "Concealed Guns Is a Dead Heat, Poll Shows; Undecided Voters Are Key Factor."

36. Wagar, "Prop B Roused Intense Drive."

37. Ganey, "Supporters of Concealed Guns Begin Ad Campaign."

38. Ganey and Bryan, "Some in Police Group Oppose Weapon Plan."

39. Ganey, "NRA-Led Supporters of Concealed Weapons Are Fast and Flexible."

40. Kim Bell, "Post-Dispatch Ad Check. (1 of 2 articles)."

41. Darrell M. West, *Air Wars: Television Advertising in Election Campaigns, 1952–2000,* 6.

42. Bell, "New Ad Uses Wrong Weapon to Urge Opposition to Concealed-Gun Measure."

43. Ibid.

44. Mannies, "Fight against Prop B Pushed Robin Carnahan into Spotlight."

45. Kim Bell, "Opponents of Proposition B Replace Misleading Ad."

46. Ibid.

47. David Runkel, ed., *Campaign for President: The Managers Look at '88,* 142.

48. Jo Mannies, "Parents, Women Are Credited with Defeat of Prop B."

49. Jo Mannies, "Talent Says He Would Not Sign Gun Measure as Governor."

50. Laura Bauer Menner, "Weapons Measure Flawed, Leaders Say."

51. Jennifer Barnett, "Educators Speak against Concealed Guns."

52. Claudette Riley, "Rep. Jim Kreider, D–Nixa, Held Forum to Answer Questions and Get Feedback."

53. Ganey, "Proponents Paid Out $3.8 Million for Prop B."

54. Shurley, "Sides Make Points on Gun Issue."

55. Ibid.

56. Lee Hill Kavanaugh, "Texas Legislator Speaks in Favor of Proposition B."

Chapter Twelve

1. Terry Ganey, "Two in House Ask Lobbyists to Disclose Clients' Positions on Weapons Issue. Opponents Say It Is Attempt to Intimidate."

2. Ibid.

3. Ibid.

4. Ibid.

5. Ganey, "Concealed-Gun Backers Say Foes Are Using Fear Tactics."

6. "Capitol Briefs," *St. Louis Post-Dispatch.*

7. Ibid.

8. Will Sentell, "Missouri House Challenges Governor over Gun Measure."

9. Ibid.

10. Ibid.

11. Robert Sigman, "Opinion: Why Many Business Groups Fear Prop B. Executives Worry about On-Premise Shootings and Legal Liability if Concealed Carry Passes in Missouri."

12. Ibid.

13. Ibid.

14. Wagar, "Prop B Roused Intense Drive."

15. Barnett, "Conceal-and-Carry: The People Speak."

16. Portman, "Loopholes Not Real, Author Says."

17. Terry Ganey, "RCGA Unit's Stance on Gun Bill Is Misstated by Backers of Ballot Measure."

18. Ibid.

19. Ibid.

20. Ibid.

21. Ganey and Bell, "NRA Boosts Weapons Measure Effort by $650,000."

22. Ganey, "NRA-Led Supporters of Concealed Weapons Are Fast and Flexible."

23. Rick Pierce, "School Officials Denounce Proposition B, but Columbia News Conference Is Canceled."

24. Ganey and Bell, "Concealed Guns Will Make Missouri Safer or It Will Make the State a Scarier Place to Live."

25. Ganey, "NRA-Led Supporters of Concealed Weapons Are Fast and Flexible."

26. Pierce, "School Officials Denounce Proposition B, but Columbia News Conference Is Canceled."

27. Ibid.

28. Ibid.

29. Ganey, "NRA-Led Supporters of Concealed Weapons Are Fast and Flexible."

30. Second Amendment Coalition. 2003. www.sacmo.org.

31. Wagar, "Prop B Roused Intense Drive."

32. Wagar, "Money and Messages Flow as Gun Campaigns Near End."

33. Rudi Keller, "Prop B Backers Seek Retribution for Prop B Loss. Website to List Opponents Contributors." See also Terry Ganey, "Carnahan, NRA Square Off After Gun Vote Fails. Governor Hopes Other States Will Hear Voters' Message. Opponents Object to Carnahan's Role."

34. Ibid.

35. Ibid.

36. National Rifle Association, "National Organizations with Anti-Gun Policies." www.nraila.org/Issues/FactSheets/ Read.aspx?ID=15.

37. Ganey, "NRA-Led Supporters of Concealed Weapons Are Fast and Flexible."

38. Ibid.

39. Pierce, "School Officials Denounce Proposition B, but Columbia News Conference Is Canceled."

40. Keller, "Governor, NRA Up Ante on Prop B."

41. Ibid.

42. Pierce, "School Officials Denounce Proposition B, but Columbia News Conference Is Canceled."

43. Tim Oliver, www.learntocarry.com.

44. Ganey, "RCGA Unit's Stance on Gun Bill Is Misstated by Backers of Ballot Measure."

45. Noguchi, "Anheuser-Busch Support of Gun Measure Is Called 'Irresponsible.'"

46. Ganey, "RCGA Unit's Stance on Gun Bill Is Misstated by Backers of Ballot Measure."

47. Noguchi, "Anheuser-Busch Support of Gun Measure Is Called 'Irresponsible.'"

48. Ibid.

49. Ganey, "NRA-Led Supporters of Concealed Weapons Are Fast and Flexible."

50. Jo Mannies, "A-B Drops Support of Holden over Guns. Concealed-Weapon Veto Was Key, Sources Say."

51. Ibid.

52. David Lieb, "Holden Ad Twists McCaskill's Words on Concealed Guns."

53. David Lieb, "Anheuser-Busch Dumps Holden, Backs McCaskill."

54. Lieb, "Holden Ad Twists McCaskill's Words on Concealed Guns."

55. Steve Kraske, "Gun Battle Key in Fight for Governor."

56. Lieb, "Holden Ad Twists McCaskill's Words on Concealed Guns."
57. Ibid.

Chapter Thirteen

1. Kit Wagar, "Voters Split on Concealed-Gun Issue. Statewide Poll Shows Proposition Is a Toss-Up."
2. Kit Wagar, "Gun Proposal Lacks Support in City. Poll Shows 60% in KC Oppose Measure That Would Legalize Carrying a Firearm."
3. Ibid.
4. Wagar, "Voters Split on Concealed-Gun Issue."
5. Ibid.
6. Ganey, "Concealed Guns Measure Has Substantial Backing Statewide"
7. Wagar, "Gun Proposal Lacks Support in City."
8. Wallace Hartsfield, Robert Lee Hill, Patrick J. Rush, and Michael Zedek, "Faith Leaders Oppose Prop B."
9. Wagar, "Prop B Roused Intense Drive."
10. Ganey, "Concealed Guns Measure Has Substantial Backing Statewide."
11. Ibid.
12. Ibid.
13. Ibid.
14. Ibid.
15. Wagar, "Voters Split on Concealed-Gun Issue."
16. Wagar, "Gun Proposal Lacks Support in City."
17. Ibid.
18. Charton, "Missouri to Vote on Concealed Guns."
19. Wagar, "NRA Boosts Yes-on-B Campaign."
20. Wagar, "Prop B Roused Intense Drive."
21. Rhonda Lokeman, "Why Do Gun Backers Hide behind Women? Empowerment Doesn't Involve Packing a Piece."
22. Author interview with State Representative Vicky Riback Wilson, November 2003.
23. Ibid.
24. "Fun with Guns and Beer," *St. Louis Post-Dispatch.*
25. "Buying New Laws," *St. Louis Post-Dispatch.*
26. "A Vote for Sanity," *St. Louis Post-Dispatch.*
27. Scott, "Kinnamon for Democrats."
28. Rich Hood, "The Gun Lobby's Misleading Promises. A Look at the Results of Concealed Carry in Texas Should Give Pause to Those Inclined to Vote 'Yes' on Proposition B."
29. "Hidden Guns Add to Risks," *Springfield News-Leader.*
30. "More Guns Not the Answer," *Springfield News-Leader.*
31. Robert Leger, "Rights to Guns Not Absolute."
32. "Issue's Defeat Cause for Pride," *Springfield News-Leader.*
33. Terry Ganey, "Panel Is Expected to OK Concealed Weapons Bill but Time Is Running Short for State House Proposal to Reach a Final Vote."
34. Kit Wagar, "Rural Support Wasn't Enough for Gun Forces. Each Side Seeks Validation After Voters Sound Off."
35. Christen Bertelson, "Win, Lose or Draw—It's Over."

Chapter Fourteen

1. Data from Missouri Secretary of State, "Election Night Reporting, April 6, 1999 Special Election," www.sos.mo.gov/enrweb/statewideresults.asp?eid=8&arc=1 and from University of Missouri Department of Economics, Economic and Policy Analysis Center, www.econ.missouri.Edu/eparc/SAM_2003?G/G23.pdf, accessed in 2004.
2. Kit Wagar, "Firearms Proposition Failing in Partial Vote. Support Strong in Rural Areas."
3. Mannies, "Parents, Women Are Credited with Defeat of Prop B."
4. Ibid.
5. Ibid.
6. Terry Ganey and Kim Bell, "Urban Voters Defeat Prop B; Voter Turnout Hits a Record. Rural Support for Gun Measure Wasn't Enough."
7. Laura Bauer Menner, "Voters Veto Concealed Guns."
8. Ibid.
9. Terry Ganey, "Holden Says He Supports a Public Vote on Concealed Weapons. A Compromise Is Being Discussed in Legislature."
10. Ganey, "Carnahan, NRA Square Off After Gun Vote Fails."
11. Menner, "Voters Veto Concealed Guns."
12. Ganey, "Carnahan, NRA Square Off after Gun Vote Fails."
13. Terry Ganey, "Concealed Weapons Bill Approved by House. Measure Faces More Opposition in Senate."
14. Scott Charton, "Missouri Keeps Ban on Concealed Weapons."
15. Ganey, "Carnahan, NRA Square Off After Gun Vote Fails."
16. Wagar, "Rural Support Wasn't Enough for Gun Forces."
17. Ibid.
18. Ganey, "Carnahan, NRA Square Off after Gun Vote Fails."
19. Ibid.
20. Keller, "Urban Voters Send Gun Measure Packing."
21. Ganey and Bell, "Urban Voters Defeat Prop B; Voter Turnout Hits a Record."
22. Ibid.
23. Ibid.
24. Ibid.
25. See the Web site of the Missouri Secretary of State for election return data, www.sos.mo.gov/enrweb.
26. Wagar, "Firearms Proposition Failing in Partial Vote."
27. Greg Koehler, "Officials Say Proposition B Helped Boost Turnout in Several Counties."
28. Ibid.
29. Kit Wagar, "Pro-Gun Attitude Retains Strength. Littleton, Colorado Has Little Effect on Missouri View."
30. Ibid.
31. Deirdre Shesgreen, "Measure's Defeat Could Aid Gun Control."
32. Ibid.

Chapter Fifteen

1. James Bandler, "Under the Gun."
2. National Rifle Association, "Key Talking Points on S.659/S.1805."
3. Peter Brown and David Abel, *Outgunned: Up Against the NRA—The First Complete Insider Account of the Battle over Gun Control*, 1.

4. Eric Schlect, "Trial Lawyers Want to Profit from Anti-Gun Sentiments."

5. "Gunmakers Can't Be Sued over Crimes, Court Rules. Decision in California Denies Trial for Survivors of Massacre in 1993," *St. Louis Post-Dispatch.*

6. Brown and Abel, *Outgunned,* 21.

7. Ibid.

8. "Gun Groups Take Stand against Lawsuits. Makers, NRA Ask States to Stop Cities' Litigation," *Kansas City Star.*

9. Yuki Noguchi, "City's Suit Includes Arguments Used in Cases by Other States, Cities."

10. Yuki Noguchi, "St. Louis Plans to File Suit against Gun Manufacturers. City Would Be 6th Seeking to Recoup Costs of Crimes."

11. "Gun Groups Take Stand against Lawsuits."

12. Noguchi, "St. Louis Plans to File Suit against Gun Manufacturers."

13. "Judge Throws Out Cincinnati's Lawsuit against Gun Industry, Calling Claims Vague," *St. Louis Post-Dispatch.*

14. Ibid.

15. "Gun Groups Take Stand against Lawsuits."

16. Brown and Abel, *Outgunned,* 10.

17. Loftus, *The Art of Legislative Politics,* 93.

18. Mark Schlinkmann, "St. Louis Files Lawsuit against 27 Defendants in Gun Industry."

19. Ibid.

20. Ibid.

21. Noguchi, "St. Louis Plans to File Suit against Gun Manufacturers."

22. Terry Ganey, "Measure to Bar Cities from Suing Gun Makers Advances."

23. Terry Ganey, "Measure Outlawing Suits by Cities against Gun Industry Dies."

24. Deirdre Shesgreen, "Smith and Wesson Will Redesign Guns, Marketing; 30 Cities, Counties Agree to Drop Their Lawsuits."

25. Mark Schlinkmann, "Smith and Wesson Reaps Reward for Gun Safety. 29 Cities, Counties Will Give Preference to Company, Others Following Its Lead."

Chapter Sixteen

1. Jo Mannies, "Group Petitions for Concealed Weapons."

2. Ibid.

3. Virginia Young, "500 Rally at Missouri Capitol to Support Teaching of Firearm Safety to Youngsters. Afterward, Children from St. Louis Area Protest Gun Violence."

4. Ibid.

5. Ibid.

6. "Progress Amid the Rhetoric," *St. Louis Post-Dispatch.*

7. Young, "500 Rally at Missouri Capitol to Support Teaching of Firearm Safety to Youngsters."

8. "Progress Amid the Rhetoric."

9. "Metrowatch," *St. Louis Post-Dispatch.*

10. "Getting Tough on Crime," *Kansas City Star.*

11. Ibid.

12. Joe Lambe, "County Toughens Gun Stance. Repeat Offenders Face Five Years under New Plan."

13. "Project Ceasefire Gains in Missouri," *Jefferson City News Tribune.*

14. Eric Stern, "Post-Dispatch Ad Check."

15. Mike Rice, "6th Race Attracts National Spotlight. Danner Withdrawal Brings a Big Field."

16. Ibid.

17. Ibid.

18. Mike Rice, "Danner, Graves Square Off in Closely Watched Race."

19. Mannies, "Talent Says He Would Not Sign Gun Measure as Governor."

20. Ibid.

21. Ibid.

22. Deirdre Shesgreen, "Judge White Agrees to Testify at Hearing, Panel Aide Says."

23. Mannies, "Talent Says He Would Not Sign Gun Measure as Governor."

24. Jo Mannies, "Debate over Social Issues Heats Up as Election Nears."

25. Mannies, "Talent Says He Would Not Sign Gun Measure as Governor."

26. Martha Kropf et al., "The 2000 Missouri Senate Race."

27. Federal Election Commission. Records for Ashcroft and Carnahan. See www.fec.gov.

28. Jo Mannies, "Democrats Assail GOP as Pawns of the NRA. Carnahan, Party Leaders Hold Jefferson Days Here."

29. Ibid.

30. Jo Mannies, "Carnahan Attacks Ashcroft on Gun Control Record, His Donations from NRA."

31. Clayton Kale, "Organization That Advocates Gun Control Targets Ashcroft, Says He Has Worst Record in Congress. Senator Is No. 1 on Group's 'Dangerous Dozen' List."

32. John Mintz, "In Bush NRA Sees White House Access."

33. James Dao, "The 2000 Campaign: The Ad Campaign; Portraying Bush as a Pawn of the N.R.A."

34. Mintz, "In Bush NRA Sees White House Access."

35. CeCi Connolly and Terry Neal, "Bush Denies He'd Toe the NRA Line."

36. Mintz, "In Bush NRA sees White House access."

37. Terry Ganey, "KMOV Rejects Anti-Bush Ad from Group Promoting Gun Control."

38. Mannies, "Debate over Social Issues Heats Up as Election Nears."

39. Ibid.

40. Kropf et al., "The 2000 Missouri Senate Race," 82.

41. Terry Ganey, "KMOV Won't Show Ad That Criticizes Sen. Ashcroft."

42. Ibid.

43. "A Bad Call by KMOV," *St. Louis Post-Dispatch.*

44. Ganey, "KMOV Won't Show Ad That Criticizes Sen. Ashcroft."

45. Kropf et al., "The 2000 Missouri Senate Race," 82.

46. Eric Stern, "Gun-Control Advocates Gather at Pistol Range to Protest Talent's Support of Concealed Handguns."

47. Mannies, "Debate over Social Issues Heats Up as Election Nears."

48. Kropf et al., "The 2000 Missouri Senate Race," 81–82.

49. Mannies, "Debate over Social Issues Heats Up as Election Nears."

50. Kropf et al., "The 2000 Missouri Senate Race," 75.

51. Ibid., 76.

52. Karen Branch-Brioso, "Soft Money Did the Hard Work in Elections, Study Says."

53. Kropf et al., "The 2000 Missouri Senate Race," 76.

54. Ibid.

55. James Dao, "In Hunters' Havens, Gun Control Is Risk for Gore."

56. Ibid.

57. James Dao, "NRA Leaders Cast Gore as Archenemy."

58. Ibid.

59. Dick Dahl, "NRA Sees Room to Grow as Faithful Adjunct to the GOP."

60. Ibid.

61. Jo Mannies, "Gun Enthusiasts Here Plan to Flock to Convention in KC. Politics Will Be Prominent Topic at NRA Gathering."

Chapter Seventeen

1. Bill Bell, "Power Struggle for State Senate Includes Fight in 12th District. Race in Northwest Missouri Gets Extra Attention."

2. Kit Wagar, "Senate Skirmish Getting Expensive. Control of Chamber at Stake for Parties."

3. Bell, "Power Struggle for State Senate Includes Fight in 12th District."

4. Eric Stern, "Senate Race in Northeast Missouri Focuses on Guns, Abortion."

5. Jo Mannies, "GOP Picked Up Two Seats by Pushing Key Issues, Observers Say."

6. Ibid.

7. Ibid.

8. Eric Stern, "Holden May Be a Handicap for Rural Democrats. Two Candidates in Special Elections Have Declined to Campaign with Governor."

9. Jo Mannies, "A Little Governor Bashing Gets Results for Democratic Candidates."

10. Tim Hoover, "House Races Generate Extraordinary Interest."

11. Mannies, "A Little Governor Bashing Gets Results for Democratic Candidates."

12. Shesgreen, "Judge White Agrees to Testify at Hearing."

13. Ibid.

14. Ibid.

15. "Excerpts from the Forum," *St. Louis Post-Dispatch.*

16. *U.S. vs. Miller,* 307 US 174.

17. Karen Branch-Brioso, "Justice Department Footnote Marks Policy Reversal."

18. Ibid.

19. John Ashcroft, "Emerson v. United States, DOJ response."

20. Ibid.

21. Sarah Brady, "Press Release."

22. Rick Montgomery, "New Government Stance on Gun Rights Stirs Cheers, Fears."

23. Branch-Brioso, "Justice Department Footnote Marks Policy Reversal."

24. Ibid.

25. Kit Wagar, "Gun Bills Back in Missouri Politics."

26. Terry Ganey, "Gun Advocates Swarm Capitol to Back Bills. One Measure Would Allow Carrying of Concealed Weapons."

27. Wagar, "Gun Bills Back in Missouri Politics."

28. Deirdre Shesgreen, "Gun Control Advocates Turn Efforts from National to Local Government."

29. Wagar, "Gun Bills Back in Missouri Politics."

30. Ganey, "Gun Advocates Swarm Capitol to Back Bills."

31. Terry Ganey, "Holden's Lawyer Meets with Backers of Concealed Arms."

32. Ibid.

33. Ibid.

34. Ganey, "Holden Says He Supports a Public Vote on Concealed Weapons."

35. Ibid.
36. Ibid.
37. Ganey, "Gun Advocates Swarm Capitol to Back Bills."
38. Ganey, "Panel Is Expected to OK Concealed Weapons Bill"
39. Terry Ganey, "House Panel OKs Concealed Weapons Bill. Legislator Says Bill Differs from One Rejected by Voters in Missouri."
40. Ibid.
41. "Lawmakers Attempt to Hide Concealed Guns," *Kansas City Star.*
42. Ibid.
43. Missouri Revised Statutes. Title III, Chapter 21, Section 21.750.
44. "Lawmakers Attempt to Hide Concealed Guns."
45. "Officials Breathe Easier over Failure of Hidden Guns, but Issue Isn't Dead," *Kansas City Star.*
46. Ganey, "Gun Advocates Swarm Capitol to Back Bills."
47. Terry Ganey, "Senate Votes to Prohibit Suits against Gun Makers. Missouri Legislators Want to Bar State, Cities from Seeking Damages."
48. "Ambushing Voters," *St. Louis Post-Dispatch.*
49. Peter Kinder. Senate Bill 123.
50. Ibid.
51. Ganey, "Senate Votes to Prohibit Suits."
52. Mannies, "Gun Enthusiasts Here Plan to Flock to Convention in KC."
53. Matt Campbell, "Heston, NRA Set for KC Meeting."
54. Matt Campbell, "Events Include Speech by Interior Secretary Gale Norton."
55. "Heston Predicts at NRA Convention That He Will Be Re-Elected President," *St. Louis Post-Dispatch.*
56. Mannies, "Gun Enthusiasts Here Plan to Flock to Convention in KC."
57. Jo Mannies, "Events on Same Day Illustrate Carnahan's, Talent's Strategies."
58. Ibid.

Chapter Eighteen

1. Anne Wallace Allen, "Drive for Another Concealed Weapons Vote Is Falling Short."
2. Kit Wagar, "Weapon Bills Likely to Get a Major Push. Concealed-Carry Plans Offered in Missouri."
3. Ibid.
4. John Cauthorn, SB 938.
5. Frank Barnitz, HB 1729.
6. Wayne Crump, HB 1344.
7. Bill Bell, "House Votes to Ease Law on Guns in Cars. Gov. Holden Vows He'll Veto Measure if It Passes Senate."
8. Ibid.
9. Kit Wagar, "Concealed-Gun Bill Advances. House Gives Initial OK to Missouri Drivers."
10. Wayne Crump, HB 1344.
11. Kit Wagar, "Concealed-Guns Bill Passes House. Senate Gets Weapons-in-Vehicles Measure."
12. Terry Ganey, "Gun Bill Proposal Could Mean New Vote Here. Missouri House Debates Concealed-Weapons Options."
13. Larry Crawford and Wayne Crump, HB 1729.

14. Ganey, "Gun Bill Proposal Could Mean New Vote Here."

15. Ibid.

16. Ibid.

17. Terry Ganey, "Majority in Poll Are Opposed to Concealed Guns. Result Reflects Result against Weapons Proposal of Three Years Ago."

18. Ibid.

19. John Cauthorn, SB 938.

20. Karen Culp, "Bill to Carry Concealed Guns Stalls in Senate."

21. John Cauthorn, SB 938.

22. Eric Stern, "Senate Tentatively OKs New Statewide Vote on Guns."

23. Culp, "Bill to Carry Concealed Guns Stalls in Senate."

24. Rick Montgomery, "Gun Forces Shift Focus from Bills to Ballots."

25. Ibid.

26. Culp, "Bill to Carry Concealed Guns Stalls in Senate."

27. Montgomery, "Gun Forces Shift Focus from Bills to Ballots."

28. Linda Mann, "Concealed Weapons: How Do They Stand?"

29. Summer Harlow, "Candidates Speak on Concealed Weapons."

30. Jo Mannies, "Carnahan's Skeet Shoot Points Up Guns' Role in Senate Race."

31. Jeannie Oakley, "Jeannie Oakley."

32. Jerry Berger, "Talent's Campaign Uses 9–11 Observance to Drum Up Support for Senate Hopeful."

33. Jo Mannies, "NRA Boosts Talent at Workshop, Gun Rights Group Offers Election Aid to Activists."

34. Jo Mannies, "It's No Fish Story, Missouri Democrats Insist: Talent Doesn't Have a Permit."

35. Jo Mannies, "Carnahan 'Bounces Back' in Latest Poll."

36. Ibid.

37. Ibid.

38. Jo Mannies, "Democrats Make Pitch at Labor Conference, AFL-CIO President Praises Carnahan."

39. Jo Mannies, "In Countdown to Election, Parties Shun Undecideds, Concentrate on Loyalists."

40. Dahl, "NRA Sees Room to Grow as Faithful Adjunct to the GOP."

41. Mannies, "Democrats Make Pitch at Labor Conference."

42. Mannies, "NRA Boosts Talent at Workshop."

43. Ibid.

44. Mannies, "In Countdown to Election, Parties Shun Undecideds, Concentrate on Loyalists."

45. Sharon Theimer, "Special Interests Spend Millions to Influence Vote. Groups Are Focusing on 'Moving Real People to the Polling Booth.'"

46. Ibid.

47. Ibid.

48. Deirdre Shesgreen, "Republican Jim Talent's Campaign Is Upbeat after Debate with Carnahan."

49. Steve Kraske, "Carnahan Blasts Talent for GOP Ad on Homeland Security."

50. Federal Election Commission. www.fec.gov.

51. Mannies, "In Countdown to Election, Parties Shun Undecideds, Concentrate on Loyalists."

52. "Debate Excerpts," *St. Louis Post-Dispatch.*

53. Ibid.

54. "Excerpts from the Forum."

55. Ibid.

56. Ibid.

57. Kraske, "Carnahan Blasts Talent for GOP Ad on Homeland Security."

58. "Excerpts from the Forum."

59. Jo Mannies, "Carnahan Holds on to Her Influence in Democratic Party."

60. National Rifle Association, "Political Victory Fund."

61. Ibid.

62. Ibid.

63. Ibid.

64. Ibid.

65. Ibid.

66. Ibid.

67. Ibid.

68. Rick Montgomery, "Concealed-Carry Proposal Divides Congress, Gun Groups."

69. Ibid.

70. "Blunt: Federal Concealed Weapons Law Is Long Overdue," *Jefferson City News Tribune.*

71. Montgomery, "Concealed-Carry Proposal Divides Congress, Gun Groups."

72. "Blunt: Federal Concealed Weapons Law Is Long Overdue."

Chapter Nineteen

1. Dale Schmid, "Crime Prevention and Public Safety Committee Testimony."

2. Larry Crawford, HB 349.

3. Tim Hoover, "Concealed-Carry Bill Clears Senate."

4. Bill Bell, "Missouri Senate Backs Concealed Carry Bill as Democrats Split."

5. Marc Powers, "Missouri Senate Breaks Tradition to End Filibuster."

6. Bell, "Missouri Senate Backs Concealed Carry Bill as Democrats Split."

7. Hoover, "Concealed-Carry Bill Clears Senate."

8. Bell, "Missouri Senate Backs Concealed Carry Bill as Democrats Split."

9. Powers, "Missouri Senate Breaks Tradition to End Filibuster."

10. Larry Crawford, HB 349.

11. Hoover, "Concealed-Carry Bill Clears Senate."

12. Ibid.

13. Tim Hoover, "Concealed Guns Bill Advances to Holden. Fight Looms in Fall over Promised Veto."

14. Ibid.

15. Larry Crawford, HB 349.

16. Peter Kinder, SB 13.

17. Bob Holden, "SB 13 Veto Letter."

18. Bill Bell, "Gun Makers Get Shield from Suits as 3rd Veto Is Rejected."

19. Ibid.

20. Kelly Wiese, "Missouri Lawmakers Pass Ban on Obesity Lawsuits."

21. Bell, "Gun Makers Get Shield from Suits as 3rd Veto Is Rejected."

22. Ibid.

23. Tim Bryant, "Lawsuits against Gun Makers Are Misuse of System, Spokesman Says."

24. "Appeals Court Eyes Legalities of Lawsuits against Gun Makers," *Jefferson City News Tribune.*

25. Bryant, "Lawsuits against Gun Makers Are Misuse of System."

26. "Appeals Court Eyes Legalities of Lawsuits against Gun Makers."

26. Ibid.

27. Ibid.

28. Jim Suhr, "Appeals Court Rejects St. Louis City's Lawsuit against Gun Makers."

29. Ibid.

30. Ibid.

Chapter Twenty

1. Missouri Ethics Commission. www.moethics.state.mo.us, accessed in 2004.

2. Jo Mannies, "Attention Turns to Political Fight after Holden's Expected Veto."

3. Hoover, "Concealed Guns Bill Advances to Holden."

4. Wagar, "Weapons Bill Likely to Get Major Push."

5. Mannies, "Attention Turns to Political Fight after Holden's Expected Veto."

6. Ibid.

7. Ibid.

8. Aaron Deslatte, "Holden Vetoes Concealed-Gun Bill."

9. Ibid.

10. Ibid.

11. Paul Sloca, "Old Law Enforcement Guns Often Are Sold to Pay for Upgrades. Highway Patrol Once Owned Gun Used in Jefferson City Shooting."

12. Bob Holden, "Conceal-and-Carry Veto."

13. Terry Ganey, "Override of Gun Bill Veto Seems Destined for Defeat. Legislature Will Convene This Week to Consider a Number of Holden Vetoes."

14. Hoover, "Concealed Guns Bill Advances to Holden."

15. Ibid.

16. Deslatte, "Holden Vetoes Concealed-Gun Bill."

17. Kit Wagar, "Merits of Concealed Weapons Debated. Forum Draws Both Sides on Issue."

18. Ganey, "Override of Gun Bill Veto Seems Destined for Defeat."

19. Ibid.

20. Ibid.

21. Dale Schmid, "Messages from the President."

22. Ganey, "Override of Gun Bill Veto Seems Destined for Defeat."

23. Paul Sloca, "Guns, Abortion Likely to Top Veto Session."

24. Ibid.

25. Tim Hoover, "Lobbying Intensifies as Gun Vote Nears. Missouri Senate Focus of Veto Battle."

26. Mannies, "Attention Turns to Political Fight after Holden's Expected Veto."

27. Ibid.

28. Ibid.

29. Hoover, "Lobbying Intensifies as Gun Vote Nears."

30. Aaron Deslatte, "Override Effort Fails on Foster Care Veto."

31. "Black Thursday," *St. Louis Post-Dispatch.*

32. Kit Wagar, "Missouri Overrides Holden Vetoes. Way Cleared for Concealed Guns."

33. Mike Gibbons, "Remarks on the Floor of the Missouri Senate on the Occasion of the Veto Override Attempt (HB 349)."

34. Ibid.

35. Kathleen Hunter, "Warrior-Legislators Face Dilemma: Give Up One Job?"

36. Philip Dine, "Army Will Investigate Senator's Leave for Vote. Missouri Legislator Left Cuba for Vote on Gun Bill."

37. Hunter, "Warrior-Legislators Face Dilemma."

38. Ibid.

39. Dine, "Army Will Investigate Senator's Leave for Vote."

40. David Lieb, "Military Says Dolan Didn't Knowingly Engage in Wrong Doing."

41. Hunter, "Warrior-Legislators Face Dilemma: Give Up One Job?"

42. Lieb, "Military Says Dolan Didn't Knowingly Engage in Wrong Doing."

43. Aaron Deslatte, "Senate Overrides Gun, Abortion Vetoes."

44. Aaron Deslatte, "Vetoes Leave Holden in an Odd Spot."

45. Ibid.

46. Kit Wagar, "House Overrides Gun and Abortion Vetoes. Missouri Senate to Vote on Both Today."

47. Terry Ganey, "House Overrides Gun, Abortion Vetoes. Senate Gets Measures Today."

48. Chris Cox, "Press Release."

49. Deslatte, "Senate Overrides Gun, Abortion Vetoes."

50. Ganey, "House Overrides Gun, Abortion Vetoes."

51. "Black Thursday."

52. Scott Charton, "Carnahan Explains Why He'll Veto Abortion Bill. Proposal to Create Crime of Infanticide Goes Too Far, He Says. 8th Override in History Is Possible."

53. Wagar, "Missouri Overrides Holden Vetoes."

54. Deslatte, "Vetoes Leave Holden in an Odd Spot."

55. Kit Wagar and Steve Kraske, "Analysis: Holden Faces More Obstacles. Veto Overrides Hurt Governor, Critics Say."

56. Ibid.

57. Jo Mannies, "Governor Says He Would Back Bid to Reverse Concealed Guns Law. Opponents Are Expected to File Lawsuit Today."

58. Ibid.

59. "Protect the Police," *St. Louis Post-Dispatch.*

Chapter Twenty-One

1. Bill Bell, "Law Does Not Require Permit to Have Concealed Gun in Car, Group Says."

2. Tim Hoover, "Sheriffs Prepare to Issue Gun Permits."

3. Kit Wagar, "New Gun Law's Details Perplex Some. Opponents Say Disclosure Needed."

4. Bill Bell, "Sheriffs Meet to Iron Out Plans for Concealed Guns. System Would Check Up on Weapons Trainers and Who Has Had the Training."

5. Ibid.

6. Circuit Court of the City of St. Louis. *Alvin Brooks et al. vs. State of Missouri, et al.*, Cause No. 034–02425.

7. Tim Hoover, "Guns Banned in Public Buildings. Holden, KC-Area Counties Act before Law Takes Effect."

8. Scott Charton, "Concealed Guns Not Banned from Fairgrounds."

9. David Lieb, "Gaming Commission Relaxes Rule on Concealed Guns in Casinos."

10. Ibid.

11. *Alvin Brooks et al. vs. State of Missouri, et al.*

12. Tim Bryant, "Gun Law Is Contrary to State Constitution, Judge Says."

13. *Alvin Brooks et al. vs. State of Missouri, et al.*

14. Ibid.

15. Ibid.

16. "Sheriffs' Request Spurs Turmoil over Weapons," *Columbia Daily Tribune.*

17. "Hancock Doubts Law's Viability," *Columbia Daily Tribune.*

18. *Alvin Brooks et al. vs. State of Missouri, et al.*

19. Ibid.

20. Ibid.

21. David Lieb, "Nixon Voices Personal Concerns about Concealed-Carry Gun Law."

22. Ibid.

23. Terry Ganey, "Senate Vote Keeps Gun Permit Files Confidential. Concealed Carry Records Are Not Open to Public."

24. Ibid.

25. Hoover, "Concealed Guns Bill Advances to Holden."

26. "Senate Backs Gun Owners' Privacy," *Columbia Daily Tribune.*

27. "Gun Law Deserves Full Court Debate," *Springfield News-Leader.*

28. Peter Shinkle, "NRA Brief Supports Concealed Gun Law. St. Louis Judge Who Blocked Measure Will Hold a Hearing This Week."

29. *Alvin Brooks et al. vs. State of Missouri, et al.*

30. Peter Shinkle, "19th Century Lawyer Is a Big Gun in Concealed Carry Battle."

31. Ibid.

32. Ibid.

33. Tim Hoover, "Judge Delays Ruling on Gun Law. Temporary Injunction Still in Place."

34. Shinkle, "NRA Brief Supports Concealed Gun Law."

35. Ibid.

36. David Lieb, "Opponents to File Lawsuit against Concealed-Guns Law."

37. Ibid.

38. "Judge Delays Weapons Law," *Jefferson City News Tribune.*

39. Ibid.

40. *Alvin Brooks et al. vs. State of Missouri, et al.*

41. Ibid.

42. Ibid.

43. Ibid.

44. Ibid.

45. Ibid.

46. Ibid.

47. Tim Bryant, "Judge Permanently Blocks Missouri's Concealed Guns Law."

48. Terry Ganey, "Concealed Weapons Opponents Seek to Delay Appeal before State High Court. Nixon Wants Hearing on Dec. 3, but Challengers Say They Need More Time."

49. "Ruling Sets Up Appeal on Gun Law," *Columbia Daily Tribune.*

50. Bryant, "Judge Permanently Blocks Missouri's Concealed Guns Law."

51. Ibid.

52. Ibid.

53. Ibid.

54. "Conceal-Carry Boosters Point to New Mexico Court Ruling," *Columbia Daily Tribune*.

55. Kit Wagar, "Judge Blocks State's Gun Law. Concealed-Carry Ruling Is Appealed."

56. "The Road to Hell," *St. Louis Post-Dispatch*.

57. "Judicial Review of Laws Warranted," *Springfield News-Leader.*

58. "Gun Case Remains on Track," *Columbia Daily Tribune*.

59. Steven Walters, "Threats, Switches Mark Wisconsin Gunfight."

60. Ibid.

61. Jim Sullinger, "Sebelius Vows Veto of Concealed Carry."

Chapter Twenty-Two

1. *State ex rel. N.M. Voices for Children, Inc. and Dr. Victor LaCerva v. Denko.*

2. "Conceal-Carry Boosters Point to New Mexico Court Ruling."

3. "Gun Law Foes, Supporters Get Day Before High Court," *Columbia Daily Tribune.*

4. Ibid.

5. "Gun Rights Backers Eager for Decision. Courts Won't Rush Ruling, Official Says," *Columbia Daily Tribune.*

6. Limbaugh, Stephen N., Jr., *Alvin Brooks, et al. v. State of Missouri.* SC85674."

7. Ibid.

8. Ibid.

9. Ibid.

10. Ibid.

11. Ibid.

12. Ibid.

13. Josh Flory, "Gun Issue Unresolved."

14. John Cauthorn, SB 1341.

15. Harold Caskey, SB 1332.

16. Larry Crawford, HB 1565.

17. Limbaugh, *Alvin Brooks, et al. v. State of Missouri.*

18. Ibid.

19. Tim Hoover, "Sheriff Halts Weapons Permits."

20. Ibid.

21. Ronnie White, *Alvin Brooks, et al. v. State of Missouri.* SC85674.

22. "Gun Ruling Raises More Mandate Issues," *Columbia Daily Tribune.*

23. Ibid.

Chapter Twenty-Three

1. "Gun Foes File Lawsuit over Funding Issue," *Columbia Daily Tribune.*

2. Tim Hoover, "Lawsuit Pulls Sheriff into Concealed Weapons Saga."

3. "Lawmaker Receives Gun Permit," *Columbia Daily Tribune.*

4. "Gun Foes File Lawsuit over Funding Issue."

5. Steve Rock, "Gun Ruling Stymies Counties. Funding Issue Is Unresolved."

6. "Sheriff Dismissed from Concealed Guns Lawsuit," *Jefferson City News Tribune.*

7. Terry Ganey, "Law's Sponsor Gets Permit. Crawford Wanted to Test Process, Look for Problems."

8. "Gun Foes File Lawsuit over Funding Issue."

9. Hoover, "Lawsuit Pulls Sheriff into Concealed Weapons Saga."

10. "Concealed Guns Cases Allowed to Proceed," *Jefferson City News Tribune.*

11. Ibid.

12. "Gun Foes File Lawsuit over Funding Issue."

13. David Lieb, "Crawford Allowed to Intervene in Concealed Guns Lawsuit."

14. Steve Rock, "Concealed-Carry Investigation Sought."

15. Larry Crawford, HB 349.

16. Terry Ganey, "Concealed Weapon Law Faces New Lawsuit."

17. Tim Hoover, "Fixes for Gun Law Languishing. Inaction Would Leave Sheriffs in Tight Spot."

18. Marc Powers, "Lawmakers Urge Action on Fix for Concealed Weapons Law."

19. "Sheriffs Should Wait on Gun Permits," *Springfield News-Leader.*

20. Hoover, "Fixes for Gun Law Languishing."

21. Tim Hoover, "More Battles over Guns Expected This Year."

22. Ibid.

23. Terry Ganey, "Lawmakers May Delay Changes in New Concealed Weapons Law."

24. Ibid.

25. Danny Henley, "Sheriffs in No-Win Situation."

26. Ibid.

27. Ibid.

28. Bob Watson, "Sheriffs Seek Help to Fix Concealed Weapons Law."

29. Powers, "Lawmakers Urge Action on Fix for Concealed Weapons Law."

30. Hoover, "Fixes for Gun Law Languishing."

31. Powers, "Lawmakers Urge Action on Fix for Concealed Weapons Law."

32. Hoover, "More Battles over Guns Expected This Year."

33. Ganey, "Law's Sponsor Gets Permit."

34. Hoover, "More Battles over Guns Expected This Year."

35. "Texas Rejects Missouri Concealed-Gun Permits," *Kansas City Star.*

36. Ibid.

37. Senator Jacob's bills were as follows: SB 1356, banning guns in cars; SB 1357, banning out-of-state permits; SB 1358, banning guns in certain locations; and SJR48, a constitutional amendment banning laws already voted on by the people. They may be read at www.house.state.mo.us.

38. Hoover, "Fixes for Gun Law Languishing."

39. Ibid.

40. Ganey, "Concealed Weapon Law Faces New Lawsuit"; Hoover, "Lawsuit Pulls Sheriff into Concealed Weapons Saga."

41. Josh Flory, "Permits on Hold in Boone."

42. St. Louis County Police Department, "St. Louis County Police Not Accepting Applications to Obtain Concealed Carry Endorsement."

43. Larry Crawford, HB 349.

44. Terry Ganey, "County Resident Sues to Carry Concealed Gun. No Formal Application So He Brought His Own."

45. Dale Schmid, www.sacmo.org, accessed in 2004.

46. Ibid.

47. Greg Jeffrey, Schmid Lawsuit.

48. Ganey, "Lawmakers May Delay Changes in New Concealed Weapons Law."

49. Mark Schlinkmann, "Gun Permit Applicants May Face Line."

50. Ibid.

51. Information compiled by conceal-and-carry advocate Tim Oliver on www.learntocarry.com, accessed in 2004.

52. Matt Schmitz, "Thousands Still Need Revenue Department's Endorsement for Conceal-Carry."

53. "Metropolitan Area Digest," *St. Louis Post-Dispatch.*

54. David Lieb, "Osage County Begins Issuing Concealed Gun Permits."

55. Limbaugh, *Alvin Brooks, et al. v. State of Missouri.*

56. "Concealed Gun Cases Allowed to Proceed."

57. "Sheriff Dismissed from Concealed Guns Lawsuit."

58. Heather Ratcliffe, "St. Louis County Wins in Court."

59. Ibid.

60. "Metropolitan Area Digest," *St. Louis Post-Dispatch.*

61. Clay Barbour, "Refusal to Give Gun Permits May End."

Chapter Twenty-Four

1. Lieb, "Holden Ad Twists McCaskill's Words on Concealed Guns."

2. Kit Wagar, "Holden, McCaskill Trade Criticism."

3. Lieb, "Holden Ad Twists McCaskill's Words on Concealed Guns."

4. Matthew Franck, "Social Issues Such as Gay Marriage Separate Blunt, McCaskill."

5. Jeremy Kohler, "Conceal-Carry Bullet Landed in Nearby Condo. Neighbors Say Incident Raises Questions about Consequences of Law."

6. Ibid.

7. "Protect the Police," *St. Louis Post-Dispatch.*

8. Ibid.

9. Kohler, "Conceal-Carry Bullet Landed in Nearby Condo."

10. Jeffrey Birnbaum, "In Swing States, Kerry Reaches for the Gun Votes."

11. Ibid.

12. "Missouri Offices," *St. Louis Post-Dispatch.*

Bibliography

"A Bad Call by KMOV." *St. Louis Post-Dispatch,* September 11, 2000.

"A Vote for Sanity." *St. Louis Post-Dispatch,* April 7, 1999.

"Ambushing Voters." *St. Louis Post-Dispatch,* March 2, 2001.

Adams, Bob. "NRA Had Hand in Defeat of Two Incumbents." *St. Louis Post-Dispatch,* November 13, 1992.

Allen, Anne Wallace. "Drive for Another Concealed Weapons Vote Is Falling Short." *St. Louis Post-Dispatch,* January 27, 2002.

Alvin Brooks et al. vs. State of Missouri, et al. Circuit Court of the City of St. Louis. Cause No. 034–02425. October 2003.

"Appeals Court Eyes Legalities of Lawsuits against Gun Makers." *Jefferson City News Tribune,* June 10, 2004.

"As Governor, Ashcroft Had 'Grave Concerns' about Concealed Guns." *St. Louis Post-Dispatch,* April 11, 1999.

Ashcroft, John. "Emerson v. United States, DOJ response." www.usdoj.gov/osg/ briefs/2001/0responses/2001–8780.resp.html. 2001.

Avila, Oscar. "Many Officials Quiet So Far on Gun Plan." *Kansas City Star,* February 20, 1999.

Bandler, James. "Under the Gun." *Boston Globe Magazine,* May 9, 1999.

Barbour, Clay. "Refusal to Give Gun Permits May End." *St. Louis Post-Dispatch,* March 25, 2005.

Barnett, Jennifer. "Conceal-and-Carry: The People Speak." *Springfield News-Leader,* March 28, 1999.

———. "Educators Speak against Concealed Guns." *Springfield News-Leader,* April 1, 1999.

Bell, Bill. "Gun Makers Get Shield from Suits as 3rd Veto Is Rejected." *St. Louis Post-Dispatch,* September 13, 2003.

———. "House Votes to Ease Law on Guns in Cars. Gov. Holden Vows He'll Veto Measure if It Passes Senate." *St. Louis Post-Dispatch,* March 21, 2002.

———. "Law Does Not Require Permit to Have Concealed Gun in Car, Group Says." *St. Louis Post-Dispatch,* September 20, 2003.

———. "Missouri Senate Backs Concealed Carry Bill as Democrats Split." *St. Louis Post-Dispatch,* May 3, 2003.

———. "Power Struggle for State Senate Includes Fight in 12th District. Race in Northwest Missouri Gets Extra Attention." *St. Louis Post-Dispatch,* January 22, 2001.

————. "Sheriffs Meet to Iron Out Plans for Concealed Guns. System Would Check Up on Weapons Trainers and Who Has Had the Training." *St. Louis Post-Dispatch,* September 16, 2003.

Bell, Kim. "Bill Would Put Weapons Issue Before Voters." *St. Louis Post-Dispatch,* April 24, 1998.

————. "Concealed Guns Protect Public, Ex-Officer Says. Senate Panel Backs April Vote on Issue." *St. Louis Post-Dispatch,* May 5, 1998.

————. "Heston Urges OK of 'Sane, Sensible' Concealed-Gun Law." *St. Louis Post-Dispatch,* March 24, 1999.

————. "House OKs Vote on Weapons if Senate Approves, Referendum in '98." *St. Louis Post-Dispatch,* May 14, 1997.

————. "More Guns Equal Less Crime, Prof Says." *St. Louis Post-Dispatch,* March 20, 1999.

————. "New Ad Uses Wrong Weapon to Urge Opposition to Concealed-Gun Measure." *St. Louis Post-Dispatch,* March 27, 1999.

————. "Opponents of Proposition B Replace Misleading Ad." *St. Louis Post-Dispatch,* March 30, 1999.

————. "Post-Dispatch Ad Check. (1 of 2 articles)." *St. Louis Post-Dispatch,* March 27, 1999.

————. "Post-Dispatch Ad Check. (2 of 2 articles)." March 27, 1999.

Berger, Jerry. "Talent's Campaign Uses 9–11 Observance to Drum Up Support for Senate Hopeful." *St. Louis Post-Dispatch,* September 13, 2002.

Bertelson, Christen. "Win, Lose or Draw—It's Over." *St. Louis Post-Dispatch,* April 11, 1999.

Best, Kathleen. "Crime Bill Leaps Hurdle: 6 in GOP Join Democrats." *St. Louis Post-Dispatch,* August 26, 1994.

Birnbaum, Jeffrey H. "In Swing States, Kerry Reaches for the Gun Votes." *Washington Post,* August 9, 2004.

"Black Thursday." *St. Louis Post-Dispatch,* September 13, 2003.

"Blunt: Federal Concealed Weapons Law Is Long Overdue." *Jefferson City News Tribune,* July 17, 2004.

Bradley, Donald. "Warning of Guns' Danger. Brady Joins Concealed-Weapons Vote Fight." *Kansas City Star,* March 16, 1999.

Brady, Sarah. Press Release. www.bradycampaign.org/about/press/release.asp ?Record=314. 2001.

Branch-Brioso, Karen. "Justice Department Footnote Marks Policy Reversal." *St. Louis Post-Dispatch,* May 12, 2002.

————. "Soft Money Did the Hard Work in Elections, Study Says." *St. Louis Post-Dispatch,* February 7, 2001.

Broder, David. *Democracy Derailed.* New York: Harcourt, 2000.

Brown, Peter, and David Abel. *Outgunned: Up Against the NRA—The First Complete Insider Account of the Battle over Gun Control.* New York: Free Press, 2003.

Bryant, Tim. "Clergy, Elected Officials Gather Here to Denounce Concealed Weapons Proposal as Dangerous." *St. Louis Post-Dispatch,* March 27, 1999.

———. "Gun Law Is Contrary to State Constitution, Judge Says." *St. Louis Post-Dispatch,* October 11, 2003.

———. "Judge Permanently Blocks Missouri's Concealed Guns Law." *St. Louis Post-Dispatch,* November 8, 2003.

———. "Lawsuits against Gun Makers Are Misuse of System, Spokesman Says." *St. Louis Post-Dispatch,* October 29, 2003.

———, and Bill Lambrecht. "Justice Looks into Dowd's Campaign against Prop B." *St. Louis Post-Dispatch,* April 2, 1999.

"Buying New Laws." *St. Louis Post-Dispatch,* April 2, 1999.

Campbell, Matt. "Events Include Speech by Interior Secretary Gale Norton." *Kansas City Star,* May 18, 2001.

———. "Heston, NRA Set for KC Meeting." *Kansas City Star,* May 10, 2001.

"Capitol Briefs." *St. Louis Post-Dispatch,* March 24, 1999.

Charton, Scott. "Carnahan Explains Why He'll Veto Abortion Bill. Proposal to Create Crime of Infanticide Goes Too Far, He Says. 8th Override in History Is Possible." *St. Louis Post-Dispatch,* May 23, 1999.

———. "Concealed Guns Not Banned from Fairgrounds." *Jefferson City News Tribune,* August 18, 2004.

———. "Missouri Keeps Ban on Concealed Weapons." *Jefferson City News-Tribune,* April 7, 1999.

———. "Missouri to Vote on Concealed Guns." *Jefferson City News-Tribune,* March 28, 1999.

"Conceal-Carry Boosters Point to New Mexico Court Ruling." *Columbia Daily Tribune,* January 13, 2004.

"Concealed Gun Cases Allowed to Proceed." *Jefferson City News-Tribune,* June 11, 2004.

"Concealed-Gun Costs Are Called Hard to Predict. Spending Could Be More in Later Years, McCaskill Says." *St. Louis Post-Dispatch,* January 26, 1999.

Connolly, CeCi, and Terry Neal. "Bush Denies He'd Toe the NRA Line." *Washington Post,* May 5, 2000.

Cox, Chris. Press Release. www.nraila.org. September 12, 2003.

Culp, Karen. "Bill to Carry Concealed Guns Stalls in Senate." *Springfield News-Leader,* May 15, 2002.

Dahl, Dick. "NRA Sees Room to Grow as Faithful Adjunct to the GOP." *Nation,* October 4, 2002.

Dao, James. "In Hunters' Havens, Gun Control Is Risk for Gore." *New York Times,* May 13, 2000.

———. "NRA Leaders Cast Gore as Archenemy." *New York Times,* May 21, 2000.

———. "The 2000 Campaign: The Ad Campaign; Portraying Bush as a Pawn of the N.R.A." *New York Times,* May 9, 2000.

"Debate Excerpts." *St. Louis Post-Dispatch*, October 22, 2002.

Deslatte, Aaron. "Holden Vetoes Concealed-Gun Bill." *Springfield News-Leader*, July 4, 2003.

———. "Override Effort Fails on Foster Care Veto." *Springfield News-Leader*, September 11, 2003.

———. "Senate Overrides Gun, Abortion Vetoes." *Springfield News-Leader*, September 13, 2003.

———. "Vetoes Leave Holden in an Odd Spot." *Springfield News-Leader*, September 13, 2003.

Dialing, Paul. "MidwayUSA Business Plan Hits Bull's Eye." *Columbia Daily Tribune*, July 27, 2002.

Dine, Philip. "Army Will Investigate Senator's Leave for Vote. Missouri Legislator Left Cuba for Vote on Gun Bill." *St. Louis Post-Dispatch*, September 26, 2003.

———. "Labor Upbeat Despite Losses. Business, Other Special Interests Gleeful about Perceived Gains." *St. Louis Post-Dispatch*, November 8, 1996.

Diuguid, Lewis. "Concealed-Weapons Law Wouldn't Make Everyone Feel Safer." *Kansas City Star*, March 8, 1995.

Downs, Anthony. *An Economic Theory of Democracy*. New York: Harper, 1957.

Drew, Elizabeth. *Whatever It Takes: The Real Struggle for Political Power in America*. New York: Penguin Books, 1998.

Eardley, Laura. "Most in Survey Want No Change in Gun Law." *St. Louis Post-Dispatch*, October 15, 1992.

Ellis, Richard J. *Democratic Delusions: The Initiative Process in America*. Lawrence: University of Kansas Press, 2002.

"Excerpts from the Forum." *St. Louis Post-Dispatch*, October 25, 2002.

Fitzmaurice, Leo. "Brady Calls for 'Burial' of Concealed Weapons Plan." *St. Louis Post-Dispatch*, April 20, 1995.

Flory, Josh. "Gun Issue Unresolved." *Columbia Daily Tribune*, February 27, 2004.

———. "Permits on Hold in Boone." *Columbia Daily Tribune*, March 2, 2004.

Franck, Matthew. "Social Issues Such as Gay Marriage Separate Blunt, McCaskill." *St. Louis Post-Dispatch*, October 28, 2004.

Freeman, Gregory. "Gun-Lock Bill Could Prevent Tragic Deaths." *St. Louis Post-Dispatch*, March 8, 1992.

———. "Handguns Kill Their Owners." *St. Louis Post-Dispatch*, February 12, 1993.

———. "U.S. Attorney Takes Dead Aim against Concealed Weapons." *St. Louis Post-Dispatch*, March 21, 1999.

"Fun with Guns and Beer." *St. Louis Post-Dispatch*, March 14, 1999.

Ganey, Terry. "Brady Lobbies against Concealed Weapons, Will Greet Pontiff." *St. Louis Post-Dispatch*, January 25, 1999.

———. "Carnahan, NRA Square Off After Gun Vote Fails. Governor Hopes Other States Will Hear Voters' Message. Opponents Object to Carnahan's Role." *St. Louis Post-Dispatch*, April 8, 1999.

———. "Concealed-Carry Backers Outspend Foes by 3–1. Most of Money Touting Plan Comes from Outside Missouri, Records Show." *St. Louis Post-Dispatch,* April 8, 1999.

———. "Concealed-Gun Backers Say Foes Are Using Fear Tactics." *St. Louis Post-Dispatch,* March 12, 1999.

———. "Concealed Guns Measure Has Substantial Backing Statewide, Poll Indicates Support Is Strong among Men, Current Owners of Weapons, Undecided Voters Are Called Key." *St. Louis Post-Dispatch,* March 29, 1999.

———. "Concealed Weapon Law Faces New Lawsuit." *St. Louis Post-Dispatch,* March 13, 2004.

———. "Concealed Weapons Bill Approved by House. Measure Faces More Opposition in Senate." *St. Louis Post-Dispatch,* March 29, 2002.

———. "Concealed Weapons Foes Get Change in Wording on Ballot." *St. Louis Post-Dispatch,* January 22, 1999.

———. "Concealed Weapons Opponents Seek to Delay Appeal before State High Court. Nixon Wants Hearing on Dec. 3, But Challengers Say They Need More Time." *St. Louis Post-Dispatch,* November 12, 2003.

———. "County Resident Sues to Carry Concealed Gun. No Formal Application So He Brought His Own." *St. Louis Post-Dispatch,* March 16, 2004.

———. "Court Upholds Wording of Weapons Measure." *St. Louis Post-Dispatch,* March 6, 1999.

———. "Former Highway Patrol Chief Sues Auditor over Wording of Concealed Weapons Measure." *St. Louis Post-Dispatch,* February 6, 1999.

———. "Gun Advocates Swarm Capitol to Back Bills. One Measure Would Allow Carrying of Concealed Weapons." *St. Louis Post-Dispatch,* March 1, 2001.

———. "Gun Bill Proposal Could Mean New Vote Here. Missouri House Debates Concealed-Weapons Options." *St. Louis Post-Dispatch,* April 19, 2002.

———. "Holden's Lawyer Meets with Backers of Concealed Arms." *St. Louis Post-Dispatch,* March 6, 2001.

———. "Holden Says He Supports a Public Vote on Concealed Weapons. A Compromise Is Being Discussed in Legislature." *St. Louis Post-Dispatch,* March 16, 2001.

———. "House Overrides Gun, Abortion Vetoes. Senate Gets Measures Today." *St. Louis Post-Dispatch,* September 11, 2003.

———. "House Panel OKs Concealed Weapons Bill. Legislator Says Bill Differs from One Rejected by Voters in Missouri." *St. Louis Post-Dispatch,* April 6, 2001.

———. "Just a Good Ol' Boy from Ozarks, Danny Staples Is a Force in the Senate." *St. Louis Post-Dispatch,* April 7, 1996.

———. "KMOV Rejects Anti-Bush Ad from Group Promoting Gun Control." *St. Louis Post-Dispatch,* September 7, 2000.

———. "KMOV Won't Show Ad That Criticizes Sen. Ashcroft." *St. Louis Post-Dispatch,* October 13, 2000.

————. "Law's Sponsor Gets Permit. Crawford Wanted to Test Process, Look for Problems." *St. Louis Post-Dispatch,* March 2, 2004.

————. "Lawmakers May Delay Changes in New Concealed Weapons Law." *St. Louis Post-Dispatch,* March 21, 2004.

————. "Majority in Poll Are Opposed to Concealed Guns. Result Reflects Result against Weapons Proposal of Three Years Ago." *St. Louis Post-Dispatch,* April 30, 2002.

————. "Measure to Bar Cities from Suing Gun Makers Advances." *St. Louis Post-Dispatch,* May 14, 1999.

————. "Measure Outlawing Suits by Cities against Gun Industry Dies." *St. Louis Post-Dispatch,* May 15, 1999.

————. "NRA gives $75,000 to Support Gun Bill in Missouri." *St. Louis Post-Dispatch,* March 28, 1999.

————. "NRA-Led Supporters of Concealed Weapons Are Fast and Flexible. Their Weapons Range from 'Fax Alerts' to Mass Mailings." *St. Louis Post-Dispatch,* January 18, 1999.

————. "Officials Are Sued over Concealed Weapons Ballot Measure." *St. Louis Post-Dispatch,* February 4, 1999.

————. "Override of Gun Bill Veto Seems Destined for Defeat. Legislature Will Convene This Week to Consider a Number of Holden Vetoes." *St. Louis Post-Dispatch,* September 8, 2003.

————. "Panel Is Expected to OK Concealed Weapons Bill but Time Is Running Short for State House Proposal to Reach Final Vote." *St. Louis Post-Dispatch,* April 4, 2001.

————. "Post-Dispatch Ad Check." March 2, 1999.

————. "Post-Dispatch Ad Check (Proposition B)." *St. Louis Post-Dispatch,* February 27, 1999.

————. "Proponents Paid Out $3.8 million for Prop B." *St. Louis Post-Dispatch,* March 17, 1999.

————. "Public Vote Acceptable to Sponsor of Gun Bill. Concealed Weapons Proposal Is Up for Debate This Week." *St. Louis Post-Dispatch,* March 24, 1996.

————. "RCGA Unit's Stance on Gun Bill Is Misstated by Backers of Ballot Measure." *St. Louis Post-Dispatch,* March 11, 1999.

————. "Rape Victim Makes Ad in Favor of Gun Measure." *St. Louis Post-Dispatch,* March 17, 1999.

————. "Second Rape Victim Speaks—Against Concealed Weapons." *St. Louis Post-Dispatch,* March 19, 1999.

————. "Senate Vote Keeps Gun Permit Files Confidential. Concealed Carry Records Are Not Open to Public." *St. Louis Post-Dispatch,* March 10, 2004.

————. "Senate Votes to Prohibit Suits against Gun Makers. Missouri Legislators Want to Bar State, Cities from Seeking Damages." *St. Louis Post-Dispatch,* March 9, 2001.

———. "Supporters of Concealed Guns Begin Ad Campaign." *St. Louis Post-Dispatch,* February 27, 1999.

———. "Two in House Ask Lobbyists to Disclose Clients' Positions on Weapons Issue. Opponents Say It Is Attempt to Intimidate." *St. Louis Post-Dispatch,* March 10, 1999.

———, and Kim Bell. "Concealed Carry Will Make Missouri Safer or It Will Make the State a Scarier Place to Live. Voters Will Decide the Issue Tuesday." *St. Louis Post-Dispatch,* April 4, 1999.

———. "Concealed Guns Is a Dead Heat, Poll Shows; Undecided Voters Are Key Factor." *St. Louis Post-Dispatch,* April 3, 1999.

———. "NRA Boosts Weapons Measure Effort by $650,000." *St. Louis Post-Dispatch.* April 6, 1999.

———. "Urban Voters Defeat Prop B; Voter Turnout Hits a Record. Rural Support for Gun Measure Wasn't Enough." *St. Louis Post-Dispatch,* April 7, 1999.

———, and Bill Bryan. "Some in Police Group Oppose Weapons Plan. They Say Billboards Touting Concealed-Carry Plan Mislead. Board Voted 12–1 to Back Measure." *St. Louis Post-Dispatch,* March 14, 1999.

———, and Virginia Young. "Concealed Gun Bill Reappears. State Senator's Plan Jeopardizes Crime Bill." *St. Louis Post-Dispatch,* March 4, 1994.

"Getting Tough on Crime." *Kansas City Star,* November 29, 2000.

Gibbons, Mike. "Remarks on the Floor of the Missouri Senate on the Occasion of the Veto Override Attempt (HB 349)." September 11, 2003.

Goldstein, David. "Blue Dogs Gain Force." *Kansas City Star,* December 8, 1996.

Goldwater, Barry. "Acceptance Address at the Republican National Convention," 1964.

Gugliotta, Guy. "Blue Dog Democrats May Have Their Day in a Kinder, Gentler Congress." *Washington Post,* November 24, 1996.

"Gun Case Remains on Track." *Columbia Daily Tribune,* December 19, 2003.

"Gun Foes File Lawsuit over Funding Issue." *Columbia Daily Tribune,* March 13, 2004.

"Gun Groups Take Stand against Lawsuits. Makers, NRA Ask States to Stop Cities' Litigation." *Kansas City Star,* February 5, 1999.

"Gun Law Deserves Full Court Debate." *Springfield News-Leader,* October 22, 2003.

"Gun Law Foes, Supporters Get Day before High Court." *Columbia Daily Tribune,* January 23, 2004.

"Gun Rights Backers Eager for Decision. Courts Won't Rush Ruling, Official Says." *Columbia Daily Tribune,* February 26, 2004.

"Gun Ruling Raises More Mandate Issues." *Columbia Daily Tribune,* February 29, 2004.

"Gunmakers Can't Be Sued over Crimes, Court Rules. Decision in California Denies Trial for Survivors of Massacre in 1993." *St. Louis Post-Dispatch,* August 7, 2001.

"Guns." *St. Louis Post-Dispatch,* August 12, 1999.

Guzy, M. W. "When Money Talks, Politicians Listen." *St. Louis Post-Dispatch,* July 5, 2000.

Haley, Jean. "Concealed Weapons Checked." *Kansas City Star,* March 14, 1994.

———. "Gun Safety Postponed." *Kansas City Star,* May 10, 1994.

"Hancock Doubts Law's Viability." *Columbia Daily Tribune,* January 27, 2004.

Harlow, Summer. "Candidates Speak on Concealed Weapons." *St. Louis Post-Dispatch,* July 10, 2002.

Hartsfield, Wallace, Robert Lee Hill, Patrick J. Rush, and Michael Zedek. "Faith Leaders Oppose Prop B." *Kansas City Star,* March 31, 1999.

Henley, Danny. "Sheriffs in No-Win Situation." *Hannibal Courier-Post,* April 12, 2004.

Hernon, Peter. "Tired of Vulnerability, Say Gun Law's Backers." *St. Louis Post-Dispatch,* March 25, 1992.

"Heston Predicts at NRA Convention That He Will Be Re-Elected President." *St. Louis Post-Dispatch,* May 20, 2001.

"Hidden Guns Add to Risks." *Springfield News-Leader,* March 31, 1999.

Hirschfeld, Julie. "Ross Puts $50,000 of His Own into 2nd District Campaign." *St. Louis Post-Dispatch,* August 2, 1996.

Holden, Bob. "Conceal-and-Carry Veto." www.gov.state.mo.us/legis03/HB349vl.htm, 2003.

———. "SB 13 Veto Letter." www.gov.state.mo.us/legis03/SB13vl.htm, 2003.

Holleman, Joe. "Most Oppose Law to Allow Concealed Handguns." *St. Louis Post-Dispatch,* August 14, 1995.

Hood, Rich. "The Gun Lobby's Misleading Promises. A Look at the Results of Concealed Carry in Texas Should Give Pause to Those Inclined to Vote 'Yes' on Proposition B." *Kansas City Star,* April 4, 1999.

Horrigan, Kevin. "Who Will Have the Courage to Face Up to the Gun Lobby?" *St. Louis Post-Dispatch,* March 11, 2001.

Hoover, Tim. "Concealed-Carry Bill Clears Senate." *Kansas City Star,* May 3, 2003.

———. "Concealed Guns Bill Advances to Holden. Fight Looms in Fall over Promised Veto." *Kansas City Star,* May 6, 2003.

———. Fixes for Gun Law Languishing. Inaction Would Leave Sheriffs in Tight Spot." *Kansas City Star,* May 7, 2004.

———. "Guns Banned in Public Buildings. Holden, KC-Area Counties Act before Law Takes Effect." *Kansas City Star,* October 7, 2003.

———. "House Races Generate Extraordinary Interest." *Kansas City Star,* August 5, 2001.

———. "Judge Delays Ruling on Gun Law. Temporary Injunction Still in Place." *Kansas City Star,* October, 24, 2003.

———. "Lawsuit Pulls Sheriff into Concealed Weapons Saga." *Kansas City Star,* March 13, 2004.

————. "Lobbying Intensifies as Gun Vote Nears. Missouri Senate Focus of Veto Battle." *Kansas City Star,* August 22, 2003.

————. "More Battles over Guns Expected This Year." *Kansas City Star,* March 2, 2004.

————. "Sheriff Halts Weapons Permits." *Kansas City Star,* March 8, 2004.

————. "Sheriffs Prepare to Issue Gun Permits." *Kansas City Star,* September 20, 2003.

"House Committee Kills Concealed-Guns Measure." *Kansas City Star,* April 17, 1996.

"House Races Include Some Libertarians, Taxpayers. Many Candidates Raise Issues of Taxes, Schools. Terms Are for Two Years." *St. Louis Post-Dispatch,* October 31, 1998.

Hunter, Kathleen. "Warrior-Legislators Face Dilemma: Give Up One Job?" *Stateline.org,* August 31, 2004.

"Issue's Defeat Cause for Pride." *Springfield News-Leader,* April 7, 1999.

Jackson, Derrick Z. "Missouri Smites 'Moses.'" *Boston Globe,* April 9, 1999.

Jeffrey, Greg. Schmid Lawsuit. www.wmsa.org, 2004.

"Judge Delays Weapons Law." *Jefferson City News Tribune,* October 11, 2003.

"Judge Throws out Cincinnati's Lawsuit against Gun Industry, Calling Claims Vague." *St. Louis Post-Dispatch,* October 8, 1999.

"Judicial Review of Laws Warranted." *Springfield News-Leader,* October 12, 2003.

Kale, Clayton. "Organization That Advocates Gun Control Targets Ashcroft, Says He Has Worst Record in Congress. Senator Is No. 1 on Group's 'Dangerous Dozen' List." *St. Louis Post-Dispatch,* September 20, 2000.

Kavanaugh, Lee Hill. "Show Business Role in Firearms Issue. Charlton Heston Seeks Proposition B Votes." *Kansas City Star,* March 24, 1999.

————. "Texas Legislator Speaks in Favor of Proposition B." *Kansas City Star,* April 3, 1999.

Keller, Rudi. "Governor, NRA Up Ante on Prop B." *Columbia Daily Tribune,* April 1, 1999.

————. "Prop B Backers Seek Retribution for Prop B Loss. Website to List Opponents' Contributors." April 8, 1999.

————. "Urban Voters Send Gun Measure Packing." *Columbia Daily Tribune,* April 7, 1999.

Koehler, Greg. "Officials Say Proposition B Helped Boost Turnout in Several Counties." *Springfield News-Leader,* April 8, 1999.

Koenig, Robert. "Anti-Handgun Group Is Scoring Victories. Organization's Resources Are Dwarfed by Those of the NRA." *St. Louis Post-Dispatch,* May 10, 1992.

————. "Folksy Style Helps Volkmer Survive." *St. Louis Post-Dispatch,* October 28, 1992.

————. "Harold L. Volkmer." *St. Louis Post-Dispatch,* October 16, 1994.

Kohler, Jeremy. "Conceal-Carry Bullet Landed in Nearby Condo. Neighbors Say Incident Raises Questions about Consequences of Law." *St. Louis Post-Dispatch,* March 21, 2004.

Kraske, Steve. "Carnahan Blasts Talent for GOP Ad on Homeland Security." *Kansas City Star,* October 23, 2002.

———. "Gun Battle Key in Fight for Governor." *Kansas City Star,* October 23, 2003.

———. "Rothman-Serot Leaves the Fray. Disillusionment with Politics Intensifies Her Calls for Finance Reform." *St. Louis Post-Dispatch,* May 29, 1994.

Kropf, Martha, Anthony Simones, E. Terrence Jones, Dale Neuman, Allison Hayes, and Maureen Gilbride Mears. "The 2000 Missouri Senate Race." In *Soft Money and Issue Advocacy in the 2000 Elections,* edited by David B. Magleby. Report of a Grant Funded by the Pew Charitable Trusts, Center for the Study of Elections and Democracy, Brigham Young University, 2001.

Kuhnhenn, James. "Ashcroft and Wheat Trade Jabs. Crime Bill Isn't Tough Enough, Republican Says. But GOP's Danforth Backed It, Democrat Notes." *St. Louis Post-Dispatch,* August 28, 1994.

———. "Issues Narrow Opponents' Contrast." *St. Louis Post-Dispatch,* November 5, 1994.

Lambe, Joe. "Battle Rages on Concealed Guns. Foes Call Idea 'Idiocy.' Backers Contend It Would Cut Crime." *Kansas City Star,* March 17, 1994.

———. "County Toughens Gun Stance. Repeat Offenders Face Five Years under New Plan." *Kansas City Star,* November 28, 2000.

Lambrecht, Bill. "Republican 'Blue Dogs' Organize." *St. Louis Post-Dispatch,* November 30, 1995.

"Lawmaker Receives Gun Permit." *Columbia Daily Tribune,* March 2, 2004.

"Lawmakers Attempt to Hide Concealed Guns." *Kansas City Star,* May 6, 2001.

Leger, Robert. "Rights to Guns Not Absolute." *Springfield News-Leader,* April 4, 1999.

"Lessons from Courthouse Rampage." *St. Louis Post-Dispatch,* May 7, 1992.

Lhotka, William C. "Gunman Struck While Panel Was Discussing Security." *St. Louis Post-Dispatch,* May 6, 1992.

———, Kim Bell, and Virgil Tipton. "Man Kills Wife in Court. 5 Wounded as Rampage Erupts in Divorce Case." *St. Louis Post-Dispatch,* May 6, 1992.

Lieb, David. "Anheuser-Busch Dumps Holden, Backs McCaskill." *Jefferson City News-Tribune,* October 8, 2003.

———. "Crawford Allowed to Intervene in Concealed Guns Lawsuit." *Jefferson City News-Tribune,* April 6, 2004.

———. "Gaming Commission Relaxes Rule on Concealed Guns in Casinos." *Kansas City Star,* August 25, 2004.

———. "Military Says Dolan Didn't Knowingly Engage in Wrong Doing." *Jefferson City News-Tribune,* January 7, 2004.

————. "Nixon Voices Personal Concerns about Concealed-Carry Gun Law." *Jefferson City News-Tribune,* January 7, 2004.

————. "Opponents to File Lawsuit against Concealed-Guns Law." *Jefferson City News Tribune,* October 8, 2003.

————. "Osage County Begins Issuing Concealed Gun Permits." *Jefferson City News Tribune,* October 1, 2004.

Limbaugh, Stephen N., Jr. *Alvin Brooks, et al. v. State of Missouri.* SC85674, February 24, 2004.

Lindecke, Fred W. "Concealed-Guns Debate Rages." *St. Louis Post-Dispatch,* April 22, 1994.

————. "Hopefuls Wade into Gun Mire." *St. Louis Post-Dispatch,* June 8, 1992.

————. "Horn Counts on Mood Swing by Voters in 2nd District." *St. Louis Post-Dispatch,* June 8, 1996.

————. "Horn Objects to Rival's Appeal for GOP Voters." *St. Louis Post-Dispatch,* June 8, 1996.

————. "House Passes Weapons Bill. Concealed Gun Amendment Attached to Anti-Crime Bill." *St. Louis Post-Dispatch,* April 13, 1994.

————. "Police Chiefs Oppose Gun Bill." *St. Louis Post-Dispatch,* March 31, 1992.

————. "Political Circuit." *St. Louis Post-Dispatch,* March 31, 1996.

————. "State Senate Panel Rejects Concealed-Weapons Bill." *St. Louis Post-Dispatch,* April 30, 1992.

Little, Joan, and Terry Ganey. "Victim Rips Concealed Arms Bill." *St. Louis Post-Dispatch,* May 6, 1992.

Loeb, Isidor, and Floyd C. Shoemaker, eds. *Debates of the Missouri Constitutional Convention of 1875.* 12 vols. Columbia: State Historical Society of Missouri, 1944.

Loftus, Tom. *The Art of Legislative Politics.* Washington, D.C.: National Council of State Legislatures, 1998.

Lokeman, Rhonda. "Why Do Gun Backers Hide behind Women? Empowerment Doesn't Involve Packing a Piece." *Kansas City Star,* April 4, 1999.

Lott, John. "False Alarms Are Being Sounded on the Conceal-Carry Issue." *Kansas City Star,* April 3, 1999.

Madison, James. Federalist Paper no. 10. *The Federalist Papers,* edited by Gary Wills. New York: Bantam, 1982.

Mann, Linda. "Concealed Weapons: How Do They Stand?" *Kansas City Star,* July 13, 2002.

Mannies, Jo. "A-B Drops Support of Holden over Guns. Concealed-Weapon Veto Was Key, Sources Say." *St. Louis Post-Dispatch,* October 2, 2003.

————. "Anti-Gun Lobby Fires Broadside at Volkmer." *St. Louis Post-Dispatch,* October 25, 1992.

————. "Attention Turns to Political Fight after Holden's Expected Veto." *St. Louis Post-Dispatch,* May 11, 2003.

———. "Carnahan Attacks Ashcroft on Gun Control Record, His Donations from NRA." *St. Louis Post-Dispatch*, May 10, 2000.

———. "Carnahan 'Bounces Back' in Latest Poll." *St. Louis Post-Dispatch*, September 22, 2002.

———. "Carnahan Holds on to Her Influence in Democratic Party." *St. Louis Post-Dispatch*, May 11, 2003.

———. "Carnahan's Skeet Shoot Points Up Guns' Role in Senate Race." *St. Louis Post-Dispatch*, May 11, 2002.

———. "Debate over Social Issues Heats Up as Election Nears." *St. Louis Post-Dispatch*, October 15, 2000.

———. "Democrats Assail GOP as Pawns of the NRA. Carnahan, Party Leaders Hold Jefferson Days Here." *St. Louis Post-Dispatch*, June 20, 1999.

———. "Democrats Make Pitch at Labor Conference, AFL-CIO President Praises Carnahan." *St. Louis Post-Dispatch*, September 17, 2002.

———. "Events on Same Day Illustrate Carnahan's, Talent's Strategies." *St. Louis Post-Dispatch*, November 25, 2001.

———. "Fight against Prop B Pushed Robin Carnahan into Spotlight." *St. Louis Post-Dispatch*, April 11, 1999.

———. "GOP Picked Up Two Seats by Pushing Key Issues, Observers Say." *St. Louis Post-Dispatch*, January 28, 2001.

———. "Governor Says He Would Back Bid to Reverse Concealed Guns Law. Opponents Are Expected to File Lawsuit Today." *St. Louis Post-Dispatch*, October 8, 2003.

———. "Group Petitions for Concealed Weapons." *St. Louis Post-Dispatch*, February 11, 2000.

———. "Gun Enthusiasts Here Plan to Flock to Convention in KC. Politics Will Be Prominent Topic at NRA Gathering." *St. Louis Post-Dispatch*, May 18, 2000.

———. "In Countdown to Election, Parties Shun Undecideds, Concentrate on Loyalists." *St. Louis Post-Dispatch*, September 29, 2002.

———. "It's No Fish Story, Missouri Democrats Insist: Talent Doesn't Have a Permit." *St. Louis Post-Dispatch*, September 26, 2002.

———. "Jim, Sarah Brady Back Wheat, Laud His Gun-Control Stance." *St. Louis Post-Dispatch*, October 25, 1994.

———. "A Little Governor Bashing Gets Results for Democratic Candidates." *St. Louis Post-Dispatch*, August 12, 2001.

———. "NRA Boosts Talent at Workshop, Gun Rights Group Offers Election Aid to Activists." *St. Louis Post-Dispatch*, September 25, 2002.

———. "Parents, Women Are Credited with Defeat of Prop B." *St. Louis Post-Dispatch*, April 13, 1999.

———. "Senate Hopefuls Debate Crime, Health. Democrats Criticize Rep. Alan Wheat's Absence from Forum." *St. Louis Post-Dispatch*, April 25, 1994.

———. "Talent Says He Would Not Sign Gun Measure as Governor." *St. Louis Post-Dispatch*, April 8, 1999.

Menner, Laura Bauer. 1999. "Police Split on Concealed Guns." *Springfield News-Leader,* April 4, 1999.

———. "Voters Veto Concealed Guns." *Springfield News-Leader,* April 7, 1999.

———. "Weapons Measure Flawed, Leaders Say." *Springfield News-Leader,* March 3, 1999.

Menner, Laura Bauer, Jennifer Portman, and Bob Linder. "Conceal-and-Carry: The People Speak. How Would It Work?" *Springfield News-Leader,* March 29, 1999.

"Metropolitan Area Digest." *St. Louis Post-Dispatch,* May 18, 2004.

"Metropolitan Area Digest." *St. Louis Post-Dispatch,* January 21, 2005.

"Metrowatch." *St. Louis Post-Dispatch,* February 24, 2000.

Miller, Andrew. "NRA Ads Attacked Candidates. More Than $100,000 Spent in Regional Races." *Kansas City Star,* November 8, 1992.

Mintz, John. "In Bush NRA Sees White House Access." *Washington Post,* May 4, 2000.

"Missouri Capitol Briefs." *St. Louis Post-Dispatch,* April 30, 1998.

"Missouri Offices." *St. Louis Post-Dispatch,* October 18, 2004.

Missouri Revised Statutes. Title III, Chapter 21, Section 21.750.

Montgomery, Rick. "Concealed-Carry Proposal Divides Congress, Gun Groups." *Kansas City Star,* November 13, 2002.

———. "Gun Forces Shift Focus from Bills to Ballots." *Kansas City Star,* May 4, 2002.

———. "New Government Stance on Gun Rights Stirs Cheers, Fears." *Kansas City Star,* May 12, 2002.

"More Guns Not the Answer." *Springfield News-Leader,* April 1, 1999.

Mosley, Jim. "Armed: Concealed-Weapons Law Leaves Many Doors Ajar." *St. Louis Post-Dispatch,* May 18, 1992.

Murphy, Kevin. "Battle Heats Up over Vote on Concealed Guns. Missouri Would Be First State to Let Its Citizens Decide Issue if House Follows Senate's Lead." *Kansas City Star,* March 9, 1995.

———. "Gun-Control Issue Not Dead, Carnahan Says. Governor Wants to Let K.C., St. Louis Impose Tougher Regulation." *Kansas City Star,* February 24, 1994.

———. "Hidden-Weapons Bill Falls. '95 General Assembly Ends without Vote on Issue." *Kansas City Star,* May 13, 1995.

———. "Measure Would Allow Concealed Guns for Some Missouri Prosecutors, Plus Retired Judges and Officers, Would Be Covered." *Kansas City Star,* April 16, 1997.

———. "Senate Says No to KC Gun Rules." *Kansas City Star,* March 24, 1994.

National Opinion Research Center. 1999 National Gun Policy Survey. www.norc.uchicago.edu/new/gunrpt.htm. 1999.

National Rifle Association. "Firearms Preemption Laws." www.nraila.org//Issues/FactSheets/Read.aspx?ID=48. 2004.

————. "Key Talking Points on S.659/S.1805." www.nraila.org/CurrentLegislation/Read.aspx?ID=770. 2004.

————. "National Organizations with Anti-Gun Policies." www.nraila.org/Issues/FactSheets/Read.aspx?ID=15, 2004.

————. "Political Victory Fund." www.nraila.org/issues/factsheets/read.aspx?ID=48. 2002.

————. "Protecting the American Firearms Industry from Junk Lawsuits." www.nraila.org/images/lsprem.jpg. 2004.

————. "Range Protection Laws." www.nraila.org/Issues/FactSheets/Read.aspx?ID=49. 2004.

"No Support from NRA on Concealed Weapons." *St. Louis Post-Dispatch,* April 10, 1996.

Noguchi, Yuki. "Anheuser-Busch Support of Gun Measure Is Called 'Irresponsible.' Sarah Brady Assails What Brewer Says Was Only Its Opinion Given to Group." *St. Louis Post-Dispatch,* March 23, 1999.

————. "City's Suit Includes Arguments Used in Cases by Other States, Cities." *St. Louis Post-Dispatch,* May 1, 1999.

————. "St. Louis Plans to File Suit against Gun Manufacturers. City Would Be 6th Seeking to Recoup Costs of Crimes." *St. Louis Post-Dispatch,* March 4, 1999.

Oakley, Jeannie. "Jeannie Oakley." *St. Louis Post-Dispatch,* August 29, 2002.

"Officials Breathe Easier over Failure of Hidden Guns, but Issue Isn't Dead." *Kansas City Star,* May 28, 2001.

Oliver, Tim. "MO LTC Map." www.learntocarry.com/news/data/ MO_LTC_Map.shtml. 2004.

O'Neil, Tim. "Missouri Proposition B: Concealed Weapon: Two Area Chiefs Object to Ad, Say It Overstates Police Power." *St. Louis Post-Dispatch,* April 2, 1999.

————. "NRA Is Trying to Buy Victory on Proposition B, Opponents Say." *St. Louis Post-Dispatch,* April 1, 1999.

Pierce, Rick. "School Officials Denounce Proposition B, but Columbia News Conference Is Canceled." *St. Louis Post-Dispatch,* April 3, 1999.

Piott, Steven L. *Giving Voters a Voice.* Columbia: University of Missouri Press, 2003.

Portman, Jennifer. "Loopholes Not Real, Author Says." *Springfield News-Leader,* March 29, 1999.

Potterfield, Larry. "NRA Support." www.midwayusa.com/midwayusa/applications/nrapage.exe/gettotal. 2004.

Powers, Marc. "Lawmakers Urge Action on Fix for Concealed Weapons Law." *Southeast Missourian,* April 20, 2004.

————. "Missouri Senate Breaks Tradition to End Filibuster." *Southeast Missourian,* May 4, 2003.

"Progress Amid the Rhetoric." *St. Louis Post-Dispatch,* March 20, 2000.

"Project Ceasefire Gains in Missouri." *Jefferson City News Tribune,* December 26, 2003.

"Protect the Police." *St. Louis Post-Dispatch,* March 12, 2004.

Quilici v. Village of Morton Grove. 695 F.2d 261. 7th Cir. 1982.

Ratcliffe, Heather. "St. Louis County Wins in Court." *St. Louis Post-Dispatch,* October 12, 2004.

Rice, Mike. "Danner, Graves Square Off in Closely Watched Race." *Kansas City Star,* November 1, 2000.

———. "6th Race Attracts National Spotlight. Danner Withdrawal Brings a Big Field." *Kansas City Star,* July 24, 2000.

Riley, Claudette. "Rep. Jim Kreider, D–Nixa, Held Forum to Answer Questions and Get Feedback." *Springfield News-Leader,* April 2, 1999.

"The Road to Hell." *St. Louis Post-Dispatch,* November 12, 2003.

Rock, Steve. "Concealed-Carry Investigation Sought." *Kansas City Star,* March 11, 2004.

———. "Gun Ruling Stymies Counties. Funding Issue Is Unresolved." *Kansas City Star,* March 8, 2004.

Ross, John. "Missouri Gun Laws Help Criminals." *St. Louis Post-Dispatch,* March 31, 1992.

"Ruling Sets Up Appeal on Gun Law." *Columbia Daily Tribune,* November 8, 2003.

Runkel, David, ed. *Campaign for President: The Managers Look at '88.* Dover, Mass.: Auburn House, 1989.

St. Louis County Police Department. "St. Louis County Police not accepting applications to obtain concealed carry endorsement." March 11, 2004.

Schlect, Eric. "Trial Lawyers Want to Profit from Anti-Gun Sentiments." *St. Louis Post-Dispatch,* December 14, 1999.

Schlinkmann, Mark. "Federer Will Challenge Gephardt, Ross Will Face Talent in November." *St. Louis Post-Dispatch,* August 5, 1998.

———. "Gun Permit Applicants May Face Line." *St. Louis Post-Dispatch,* March 19, 2004.

———. "Harmon Will Challenge State Restriction on City Gun Rules." *St. Louis Post-Dispatch,* August 5, 1999.

———. "St. Louis Files Lawsuit against 27 Defendants in Gun Industry." *St. Louis Post-Dispatch,* May 1, 1999.

———. "Smith and Wesson Reaps Reward for Gun Safety. 29 Cities, Counties Will Give Preference to Company, Others Following Its Lead." *St. Louis Post-Dispatch,* May 1, 2000.

———. "State's Defeat of 2 Congressmen Last Occurred in '52." *St. Louis Post-Dispatch,* November 5, 1992.

Schmid, Dale. "Crime Prevention and Public Safety Committee Testimony." www.sacmo.org/testimony.htm. 2003.

———. "Messages from the President." www.sacmo.org.

Schmitz, Matt. "Thousands Still Need Revenue Department's Endorsement for Conceal-Carry." *Jefferson City News Tribune,* July 16, 2004.

Scott, Laura. "Ashcroft's Risky Bet on Guns." *Kansas City Star,* April 15, 1999.

———. "Kinnamon for Democrats." *Kansas City Star,* August 1, 1996.

"Senate Backs Gun Owners' Privacy." *Columbia Daily Tribune,* March 10, 2004.

Sentell, Will. "Concealed Guns Measure Declared Dead in Missouri." *Kansas City Star,* April 2, 1996.

———. "Missouri House Challenges Governor over Gun Measure." *Kansas City Star,* April 2, 1999.

———. "True Costs Still Anyone's Guess." *Kansas City Star,* March 7, 1999.

———. "Weapons Supporters Don't Want Referendum. Missouri House Bill Would Legalize Concealed Guns." *Kansas City Star,* March 26, 1998.

"Sheriffs' Request Spurs Turmoil over Weapons." *Columbia Daily Tribune,* March 10, 2004.

"Sheriffs Should Wait on Gun Permits." *Springfield News-Leader,* February 29, 2004.

Shesgreen, Deirdre. "Gun Control Advocates Turn Efforts from National to Local Government." *St. Louis Post-Dispatch,* March 30, 2001.

———. "Judge White Agrees to Testify at Hearing, Panel Aide Says." *St. Louis Post-Dispatch,* January 10, 2001.

———. "Measure's Defeat Could Aid Gun Control." *St. Louis Post-Dispatch,* April 8, 1999.

———. "Republican Jim Talent's Campaign Is Upbeat after Debate with Carnahan." *St. Louis Post-Dispatch,* October 23, 2002.

———. "Smith and Wesson Will Redesign Guns, Marketing; 30 Cities, Counties Agree to Drop Their Lawsuits." *St. Louis Post-Dispatch,* March 18, 2000.

Shinkle, Peter. "19th Century Lawyer Is a Big Gun in Concealed Carry Battle." *St. Louis Post-Dispatch,* October 26, 2003.

———. "NRA Brief Supports Concealed Gun Law. St. Louis Judge Who Blocked Measure Will Hold a Hearing This Week." *St. Louis Post-Dispatch,* October 22, 2003.

Shirk, Martha. "Fresh Fight on Guns. Child-Safety Measures, Zones Around Schools Face Stiff Opposition." *St. Louis Post-Dispatch,* March 29, 1992.

Shurley, Traci. "Sides Make Points on Gun Issue." *Springfield News-Leader,* April 4, 1999.

Sigman, Robert. "More Threats from the Gun Fringe." *Kansas City Star,* May 21, 1995.

———. "Opinion: Why Many Business Groups Fear Prop B. Executives Worry about On-Premise Shootings and Legal Liability if Concealed Carry Passes in Missouri." *Kansas City Star,* March 21, 1999.

Sloca, Paul. "Guns, Abortion Likely to Top Veto Session." *Springfield News-Leader,* September 8, 2003.

———. "Old Law Enforcement Guns Often Are Sold to Pay for Upgrades. Highway Patrol Once Owned Gun Used in Jefferson City Shooting." *Jefferson City News-Tribune,* July 13, 2003.

State ex rel. N.M. Voices for Children, Inc. and Dr. Victor LaCerva v. Denko. 2004.

Stern, Eric. "Gun-Control Advocates Gather at Pistol Range to Protest Talent's Support of Concealed Handguns." *St. Louis Post-Dispatch,* October 6, 2000.

————. "Holden May Be a Handicap for Rural Democrats. Two Candidates in Special Elections Have Declined to Campaign with Governor." *St. Louis Post-Dispatch,* August 2, 2001.

————. "Post-Dispatch Ad Check." *St. Louis Post Dispatch,* October 27, 2000.

————. "Senate Race in Northeast Missouri Focuses on Guns, Abortion." *St. Louis Post-Dispatch,* January 19, 2001.

————. "Senate Tentatively OKs New Statewide Vote on Guns." *St. Louis Post-Dispatch,* May 15, 2002.

Suhr, Jim. "Appeals Court Rejects St. Louis City's Lawsuit against Gun Makers." *Jefferson City News-Tribune,* July 28, 2004.

Sullinger, Jim. "Sebelius Vows Veto of Concealed Carry." *Kansas City Star,* April 3, 2004.

"Texas Rejects Missouri Concealed-Gun Permits." *Kansas City Star,* July 30, 2004.

Theimer, Sharon. "Special Interests Spend Millions to Influence Vote. Groups Are Focusing on 'Moving Real People to the Polling Booth.'" *St. Louis Post-Dispatch,* October 27, 2002.

Thompson, Jake. "Danner Undecided on Whether She'll Back Brady Bill. Gun Lobby Supports Her House Campaign and Rates Her Highly." *Kansas City Star,* March 21, 1993.

Trefethen, James, and James Serven. *Americans and Their Guns: The National Rifle Association's Story through Nearly a Century of Service to the Nation.* Harrisburg, Pa.: Stackpole Books, 1967.

U.S. vs. Miller. 307 US 174, 1937.

Wade, Susan, and Dean Curtis. "Training an Emotional Issue." *Springfield News-Leader,* April 4, 1999.

Wade, Susan, and Christina Dicken. "Conceal and Carry: The People Speak." *Springfield News-Leader,* March 29, 1999.

Wagar, Kit. "Battle over Guns: Amid Heated Rhetoric, Missourians Face Vote on Concealed Firearms." *Kansas City Star,* March 7, 1999.

————. "Concealed-Gun Bill Advances. House Gives Initial OK to Missouri Drivers." *Kansas City Star,* March 14, 2002.

————. "Concealed-Guns Bill Passes House. Senate Gets Weapons-in-Vehicles Measure." *Kansas City Star,* March 14, 2002.

————. "Concealed-Weapons Proposal to Be Rewritten in Missouri." *Kansas City Star,* January 22, 1999.

————. "Firearms Proposition Failing in Partial Vote. Support Strong in Rural Areas." *Kansas City Star,* April 7, 1999.

————. "Gun Bills Back in Missouri Politics." *Kansas City Star,* March 14, 2001.

————. "Gun Proposal Lacks Support in City. Poll Shows 60% in KC Oppose Measure That Would Legalize Carrying a Firearm." *Kansas City Star,* February 28, 1999.

————. "Holden, McCaskill Trade Criticism." *Kansas City Star,* July 20, 2004.

————. "House Overrides Gun and Abortion Vetoes. Missouri Senate to Vote on Both Today." *Kansas City Star,* September 12, 2003.

————. "Judge Blocks State's Gun Law. Concealed-Carry Ruling Is Appealed." *Kansas City Star,* November 8, 2003.

————. "Merits of Concealed Weapons Debated. Forum Draws Both Sides on Issue." *Kansas City Star,* August 4, 2003.

————. "Missouri Overrides Holden Vetoes. Way Cleared for Concealed Guns." *Kansas City Star,* September 12, 2003.

————. "Money and Messages Flow as Gun Campaigns Near End." *Kansas City Star,* April 6, 1999.

————. "New Gun Law's Details Perplex Some. Opponents Say Disclosure Needed." *Kansas City Star,* September 23, 2003.

————. "NRA Boosts Yes-on-B Campaign. Gun Rights Group Gave $2.2 Million." *Kansas City Star,* March 31, 1999.

————. "Pro-Gun Attitude Retains Strength. Littleton, Colorado Has Little Effect on Missouri View." *Kansas City Star,* April 24, 1999.

————. "Pro-Gun Forces Get More NRA Funds." *Kansas City Star,* April 1, 1999.

————. "Prop B Roused Intense Drive. But Will Voters' Zeal Match Campaign's?" *Kansas City Star,* April 4, 1999.

————. "Rural Support Wasn't Enough for Gun Forces. Each Side Seeks Validation after Voters Sound Off." *Kansas City Star,* April 8, 1999.

————. "Senate Skirmish Getting Expensive. Control of Chamber at Stake for Parties." *Kansas City Star,* January 17, 2001.

————. "Stakes High in Gun Debate. Missouri Campaign Is Expected to Be Costly, Emotional." *Kansas City Star,* January 24, 1999.

————. "Voters Split on Concealed-Gun Issue. Statewide Poll Shows Proposition Is a Toss-Up." *Kansas City Star,* January 24, 1999.

————. "Weapon Bills Likely to Get a Major Push. Concealed-Carry Plans Offered in Missouri." *Kansas City Star,* March 25, 2002.

————, and Steve Kraske. "Analysis: Holden Faces More Obstacles. Veto Overrides Hurt Governor, Critics Say." *Kansas City Star,* September 14, 2003.

Walters, Steven. "Threats, Switches Mark Wisconsin Gunfight." *Stateline.org,* February 5, 2004.

Watson, Bob. "Sheriffs Seek Help to Fix Concealed Weapons Law." *Jefferson City News Tribune,* April 8, 2004.

West, Darrell M. *Air Wars: Television Advertising in Election Campaigns, 1952–2000.* Washington, D.C.: CQ Press, 2001.

White, Ronnie. *Alvin Brooks, et al. v. State of Missouri.* SC85674, February 24, 2004.

Wiese, Kelly. "Missouri Lawmakers Pass Ban on Obesity Lawsuits." *Jefferson City News Tribune,* May 12, 2004.

Young, Virginia. "Concealed-Gun Bill Loses Round One in Missouri Senate." *St. Louis Post-Dispatch,* March 11, 1994.

———. "Concealed-Weapons Supporters Vow They'll Try Again." *St. Louis Post-Dispatch,* May 14, 1995.

———. "Danner Looks for Opening to Press His Challenge." *St. Louis Post-Dispatch,* October 26, 2004.

———. "500 Rally at Missouri Capitol to Support Teaching of Firearm Safety to Youngsters. Afterward, Children from St. Louis Area Protest Gun Violence." *St. Louis Post-Dispatch,* March 16, 2000.

———. "House Approves Concealed Guns. Critics Lament 'License to Kill.'" *St. Louis Post-Dispatch,* March 24, 1992.

———. "Jet Banks Says His Gun Stance Provoked Death Threat." *St. Louis Post-Dispatch,* May 12, 1995.

———. "NRA Doesn't Want Vote on Gun Bill." *St. Louis Post-Dispatch,* March 16, 1995.

———. "NRA Led Blitz on Concealed Weapons. Legislators Cite Calls from Constituents." *St. Louis Post-Dispatch,* March 25, 1992.

———. "Sen. Banks Takes On Concealed Weapons. Senate Majority Leader Launches a Filibuster." *St. Louis Post-Dispatch,* May 11, 1995.

Index